The
Starseed
Signals

Link Between Worlds

A RAW Perspective
on Timothy Leary, PhD

The
Starseed
Signals

Link Between Worlds

A RAW Perspective on Timothy Leary, PhD

Robert Anton Wilson

Introduction by
John Higgs

HILARITAS
PRESS

International Standard Book Number: 978-1-952746-07-9
2020, Hilaritas Press

Cover Design by amoeba
eBook Design by Pelorian Digital

Robert Anton Wilson photo by Roger Ressmeyer
Timothy Leary photo: unknown photographer
Timothy Leary and Joanna Harcourt-Smith photo: Getty Images

Thanks to Raquel Scherr of the Berkeley Barb Archives
for permission to republish the interview,
"Leary Trades Drugs For Space Colonies"

Hilaritas Press, LLC.
P.O. Box 1153
Grand Junction, Colorado 81502
www.hilaritaspress.com

We can never be sure that the opinion we are attempting to stifle is a false opinion; and if we were sure, stifling it would be an evil still.

– John Stuart Mill, On Liberty

Make the most of the Indian Hemp, and plant it everywhere.

– George Washington, Vol 33, p 270 of Collected Works

Man is a creature that must be surpassed.

– Friedrich Nietzsche, *Thus Spake Zarathustra*

Our Lady of Outer Space

Reach down for the sun, reach down
for the stars, reach deeper for the secret
places of the body of her the stars adorn.
You are lost and found in her embrace.
There is nowhere else for you to fall and
no escaping from her love for she is
black and pulsating source,
her million twinkling nipples
nurse all life,
her jeweled ardent body
twines around you always
and there is no place
to go but
home
to
her

– Arlen Riley Wilson

Table of Contents

A note from the publisher

In 1974, Robert Anton Wilson wrote a book about the ideas and tribulations of his friend, Dr. Timothy Leary. At the time, RAW was living in Berkeley, California with his wife Arlen and their two younger children, Graham, age 14, and Luna, 13, their youngest daughter. It would be a couple of years before RAW's own family trials would figure into this story, but in 1974, RAW's focus was on the compelling events surrounding his friend's incarceration one hundred miles north of Berkeley, at Folsom State Prison. Intriguingly, this book would not be published until some 46 years later, having been put aside and then lost for decades.

In January of 1975, we know that RAW enlisted the aid of his friend, Discordian founder Greg Hill, to photocopy the manuscript, and we get a clue about RAW's optimism, despite the circumstances, when he wrote to Hill, "I grow more convinced that Tim is managing it all, whatever it is, and using the government while they think they are using him, It has the earmarks of Sixth Circuit all over it I think." We also know the manuscript was sent to at least one publisher, and possibly more, without finding interest, but the exact reasons for RAW's abandonment of the project remain unclear.

The devastating murder of his daughter Luna at the age of 15 in 1976 rocked the foundations of the world for RAW and his family. Struggling to make sense of things, RAW's next book would be the autobiographical *Cosmic Trigger: Final Secret of the Illuminati*, which was first published in 1977. The unpublished manuscript of *The Starseed Signals* was left to languish; perhaps Leary's release from prison in 1976 made the project less pressing, or RAW's personal family trauma caused him to be disinclined to follow through. Perhaps RAW's many mentions of Leary's theories in later books made *The Starseed Signals* less of a priority. We just don't know for sure.

In 1986, RAW wrote *The New Inquisition* which had as a partial focus the persecution of Timothy Leary and Wilhelm Reich. In some respects, *The Starseed Signals* seems like an earlier attempt to address that same kind of injustice, as the book was written while Leary was experiencing an inquisition, a victim of the Nixon administration and the general punitive zeitgeist.

RAW was notoriously disinterested in keeping track of his own papers as the family moved from place to place, and his copy of the manuscript disappeared from his possession. Fortunately, Greg Hill kept a copy, but even that was almost lost to history, and would be slowly dissolving in a trash dump somewhere if not for a sustained interest in Discordianism.

It turns out that Dr. Bob Newport, a friend of Discordian founders Kerry Thornley and Greg Hill, as well as a good friend of RAW's, rescued Hill's archives from "death-by-dumpster," as Discordian historian Adam Gorightly poetically describes it. Some years later, Dr. Bob passed the archive on to Adam. Within those boxes of papers, Adam found the manuscript for *The Starseed*

Signals. Adam approached a European publisher about the book, and the publisher contacted RAW's daughter, Christina, trustee of the RAW Trust, who agreed to work with that publisher. That was in 2009, and we suspect Eris had a hand in the publisher essentially dropping the ball for the next seven years or so. After the creation of Hilaritas Press, Christina finally got her first glimpse at this unpublished RAW title. After taking a good look at what the publisher had created, and in comparing it to RAW's original typewritten manuscript, we together decided that Hilaritas Press could, and should, do a much better job at preparing the book for publication. It then took some years, and a fair amount of money paid to lawyers, for the RAW Trust to get out of that original contract with the publisher. Hilaritas Press reconstructed the book from the original manuscript, and actually uncovered some segments that the first publisher had oddly left out, presumably because they were too hard to decipher. Most of Bob's hastily hand-drawn charts and diagrams were simply pasted into the first publisher's document, but we assumed that RAW would have wanted his drawings to be redone, as was the case in all of his other books, in order to present a more professional and legible rendering. The only exception to that is the "Kether" chart, which we mostly left as RAW drew it simply because it was legible enough, and we liked to see a bit of RAW's "hand" kept in the manuscript.

While there are a few passages that RAW later adapted and used in *Cosmic Trigger*, *The Starseed Signals* stands as its own unique title in the Robert Anton Wilson canon, and offers a revealing look at the tumultuous early years of the 1970's. Turn to the back of this edition to see a number of letters between RAW and Greg Hill written at the time this book was composed.

We want to offer our ever-grateful appreciation to Adam Gorightly, aka, The Wrong Reverend Houdini Kundalini of the Church of Unwavering Indifference, as he was far from indifferent and wonderfully helpful in getting this Hilaritas Press edition to the public. Many thanks, Adam!

– Richard Rasa
Publisher, Hilaritas Press

Robert Anton Wilson

Timothy Leary, PhD

FOREWORD:
THE TIMOTHY LEARY YOU DESERVE

By John Higgs

"You get the Timothy Leary you deserve."

That was a phrase used by Leary when he wanted to shrug off criticism. Reality is a Rorschach test, he argued, and what you see reveals as much about you as what you are looking at.

When I was writing a biography of him back in 2004, I came to appreciate how insightful this phrase was. It was possible to write a factually accurate, well researched account of his life that portrayed him as a hero. It was also possible to write an equally accurate and factual account that painted him as a villain. In the same way, valid accounts of his life could make him out as a clown, or a pioneer, or a charlatan, or a genius. It boiled down to what you chose to leave out, as much as what you chose to include.

It's disturbing, but regardless of what you want Leary to be, you can find ample evidence that this was exactly how he was. You are forced to ask, to what extent is my perspective on Timothy Leary an image of him, or an image of me? When Leary's many enemies portray him in the most extreme negative light, are they showing us how he was, or are they showing us their fears, prejudices and their limited view of the world? And likewise, with Leary's defenders and admirers – and I include myself in that small but merry bunch – are we highlighting something of value in the man, or just our blind optimism and gullibility?

The difficulty in nailing Leary down is the main reason why, for all the drama and extraordinary adventure of his life, we have yet to see a proper telling of his story on film or television. I have lost count of the amount of Leary projects that have been attempted over the last couple of decades, but they usually fail due to an inability to define their leading man at the script stage. Some try and portray him as a wise sage, and others see him as a brave and foolhardy adventurer, but none seem able or willing to capture his neurological relativity or his mercurial, shifting character. They try to paint him as either Odin or Thor, in other words, when he should really be Loki.

To form opinions about Leary that have value, we need to look at something less subjective and more objective than our views about his character. The obvious place to look, you might think, is his work, ideas and theories. In this book, Robert Anton Wilson mentions an anti-Leary book by Charles Slack, which had just been published. He notes that Slack not only doesn't engage with Leary's theories and work, he doesn't even mention them. This has since become a common motif of anti-Leary literature.

Much can be said about his contributions to the field of psychotherapy. Leary's 1957 publication of *Interpersonal Diagnosis of Personality* was praised in the 1958 *Annual Review of Psychology* as, "perhaps the most important clinical book to appear this year . . . Rarely has psychology found a way of placing so many different data into the same schematic system, and the implications of this are potentially breathtaking." Stephen Strack, of the U.S. Department of Veterans Affairs noted that by the middle of the 1960's, "more than a dozen major research lines could be traced to his work, and hundreds of additional publications have credited Leary as a primary resource . . . it is difficult to find a more influential single source than *Interpersonal Diagnosis of Personality.*"

Thanks to anti-Leary books such as Robert Greenfield's *Timothy Leary: A Biography* (2006), psychedelic research currently follows a 'blame Leary' narrative. The negative public perception of psychedelics and psychedelic researchers, this argument goes, is solely down to the terrible irresponsible behaviour of this one man. If it wasn't for Leary, psychedelics would be a respected form of academic study and the drugs would be legally used in therapeutic situations. When Leary's ideas are utilised, such as his crucial theory of set and setting, he is typically not credited. The positive cultural aspects of the 1960s psychedelic explosion are ignored, and so is the issue of how many of these psychedelic researchers would have even heard of these drugs had it not been for Leary's evangelical crusade.

Having met a number of psychedelic researchers, I'm not entirely convinced that the legal and cultural status of psychedelics wouldn't still be problematic in a world without Leary. Nevertheless, the 'blame Leary' narrative has become a useful one. A scapegoat is clearly needed, and his mercurial character can play that role better than anyone. If doing so successfully convinces governments to allow more psychedelic research, then why not blame Leary, in the name of the greater good? One problem with this scenario, though, is that it means his actual ideas continue to be ignored. This is a great shame, because Leary's advocacy of psychedelics was only part of a much larger intellectual project.

What's remarkable about this previously lost and unpublished-until-now manuscript from Robert Anton Wilson is not only that he puts forward the case for Leary's ideas, but he does so at the time when Leary's reputation was at its lowest. The sixties were over, and the paranoia of the 70s had begun. Leary was yesterday's man, lost somewhere deep within the American prison system, denounced by former friends and rumoured to be snitching on the entire counterculture. It was said that his mind was gone, fried on acid. This wasn't a good moment, all things considered, for Leary to claim that he was going to build a fleet of interstellar spaceships and leave earth by the year 2000 in order to seek out space angels. You can understand why Wilson was unable to find a publisher for a pro-Leary book at that particular point in time.

I confess, I don't believe that Leary was right when he argued that we were going to become immortal beings and leave earth to spend Eternity out among the stars. I do not agree with his metaphor that Earth is a womb. I would be delighted to be wrong about this, of course, but that is how things look from my perspective, at this particular point in time, in a culture with a greater understanding of biology, systems theory and the interconnected nature of the biosphere. Leary, in contrast, was living in a culture that was still thrilled by the moon landings and the TV series *Star Trek*.

From the perspective of the twenty-first century, we can't help but see many of his claims – such as the idea that people will live to be 400 years old by the year 2000 or that he will still be alive in five and a half billion years – as extremely funny. It is never wise to predict a time frame for solving a problem before you know how that problem can be solved.

It is interesting, though, to look back at Leary's ideas in the era of Elon Musk. There are aspects of Leary's thoughts which Musk is making a reality, not least the idea that a route away from Earth will come from private sector individuals rather than governments. It would be interesting to know if Musk had ever read Leary's book *Terra II*. Other ideas mentioned here, such as the notion that politicians should have the same legal responsibility to act on scientific fact as doctors and engineers, also seem like their time may one day come. Leary always argued that being a futurist was like going to bat for a baseball team. A futurist should not be expected to get everything right, but they could be judged on their batting average.

When I look back at Leary's prison-era claims, it seems to me that his mind had found a way to protect itself from his situation. He needed to reconcile his self-image as a brilliant, pioneering psychologist who had freed himself from robotic behaviour and who was in no way a victim, with the fact that he was denounced, ridiculed, considered insane and locked in solitary confinement in Folsom Prison. In a situation like this, most people would break under the cognitive dissonance. The ideas you're about to read about kept him from suffering during this period, so they have value for that reason.

This was not Leary's finest hour, and neither was it Robert Anton Wilson's. The trappings of scepticism which are so important to Wilson's philosophy are all present in this book. He starts by requesting that the reader does not accept anything included as dogma, asks them "What do you think?" at the end of Chapter Seven and in Chapter Fourteen requests that the reader "Do the experiments and find your own explanation." Yet it must be said that in this book Wilson shows a lot less scepticism than usual about data which supports Leary's ideas, be that data relating to plant telepathy, life extension or the theories of Wilhelm Reich. We are not yet seeing the Wilson who wrote *Cosmic Trigger* in 1977, who remained stubbornly agnostic about whether he was being contacted by aliens from Sirius. It was his committed focus on multiple-model agnosticism that made Wilson such an important writer, both in his own time and in the twenty-first century. From the evidence of this book, however, it appears that there was one thing which he was not sceptical of. That was the necessity of defending a friend.

Given this, it would be easy to dismiss this book as a historic curio were it not for the fact that it engages with the core of Leary's ideas at a time when they were, as now, being routinely ignored. In particular, he traces the evolution of Leary's eight circuit theory. This is one of the rare psychological models which includes both normal and non-normal states of consciousness. It is the only one I know of that was developed from a scientific and a mystical perspective simultaneously. Although I remain sceptical of the teleological nature that Leary claimed for the model during the mid 70s, and the idea that our mental evolution was 'pre-programmed', the model still stands up well with that framing removed. In all the madness of the mid-70s, Wilson recognised that there was something important here, and he stood his ground to defend it.

Leary's eight circuit theory is fascinating and extraordinarily ambitious, and it offers great insight into many different aspects of the human mind. Even without this theory, we would still value Wilson and Leary for their neurological relativity and their concept of reality tunnels. But the larger question remains, which is how accurate is Leary's eight circuit model? This theory was his life's work. It is the reason why he claimed that drugs were ultimately just tools for him. The model still has some loyal supporters, but generally speaking it remains largely ignored and undebated. That it takes a long-lost book from nearly half a century ago to raise the issue is entirely in keeping with our culture and its current 'blame Leary' narrative.

If that 'blame Leary' narrative does provide an adequate scapegoat to allow for further psychedelic research, we will hopefully gain new insights into the stranger states of consciousness. We will then need new models to describe what is found, and we will see how this new data compares with the eight circuit model. In that scenario, it might just be that Leary's current role of scapegoat leads to a reassessment of what he considered to be his life's work. Perhaps we will eventually conclude that the eight circuit model is the most useful model for the entirety of human consciousness, both normal and expanded, that we have. Or perhaps it will act as a stepping stone on the way to a bigger and better theory of consciousness. Leary would have loved that outcome more than anything.

You get the Timothy Leary you deserve, as we know. But perhaps we also deserve the Timothy Leary that Robert Anton Wilson got.

John Higgs
Brighton, England
23 June 2020

Chapter One

The Antipodes of the Mind

What will be the next step in biological and social evolution? Here are two clues. (1) You are more likely to find the evolutionary agents closer to jail than to the professor's chair. (2) Look to that social freedom most abused, most magically, irrationally feared by society. Exactly that freedom which you, the intellectual, the liberal, would deny to others. Good. Now you are getting close.

Timothy Leary, Harvard Review, 1963

This is a journey inward and outward, an exploration of what the late Aldous Huxley called "the antipodes of the mind"— those deeply buried and carefully locked portions of human consciousness where we possess knowledge and powers not normally accessible to the sociable Ego. We are venturing into what the Swiss psychologist, Carl Jung, called the "collective unconscious," which Timothy Leary also calls the "neurogenetic archives."

Dr. John Lilly concludes his own report on visits to these Deep Inward yet Far Out regions (*The Center of the Cyclone*, Lilly, 1972) with the warning, "My own skepticism is intact—please keep yours. Skepticism is a necessary instrument in the exploration of the unknown." We will be discussing theories that are decidedly unconventional, some of our data is bizarre, outré, witchy, spooky, or downright incredible. We will present evidence that makes a plausible case that certain extremely far out theories are more likely to be correct explanations of the data than are any of the more conventional theories currently accepted. But we do not ask the reader to accept anything here as dogma.

If this book encourages further investigation and original thinking, it will have served its purpose; if it leads only to blind faith in the hypotheses it puts forth, it will have failed entirely.

This is a book about Timothy Leary, who may safely be called the most controversial scientist alive today; but it is also about independent investigations by myself and others which tend to either confirm, enlarge or significantly alter the conclusions Dr. Leary has formulated from his own research. We are concerned with drugs and sex, ESP and magic, flying saucers and beings who appear (by human standards) godly.

The data will be presented in such a way that the reader will share in both the excitement and the frequent confusion and bafflement of the investigators. In places we will get a bit technical about our scientific details, but we are quite frankly writing for the general public and every possible device has been utilized to make the story easy to follow. Some years ago, the English biologist and mathematician J.B.S. Haldane took up the study of yoga, inspired by certain provocative writings of the skeptical and witty modern mystic Aleister Crowley. I have not found any account of Dr. Haldane's actual experiments and experiences with the yogic arts, but he did summarize his conclusions in a sentence that is very worthy of deep reflection.

"The universe," said Dr. Haldane, "may be, not only stranger than we think, but stranger than we *can* think."

My own recent experiences led me to formulate this thought in an even more startling way. "The universe," I told Timothy Leary in one of our meetings at Vacaville prison, "may be, not only more intelligent than we think, but more intelligent than we *can* think."

Dr. Leary evidently quoted this to his wife, Joanna, because she later wrote, in a letter to members of the Starseed group—San Francisco Bay Area students of Dr. Leary's work — "The universe may be, not only more erotic than we think, but more erotic than we can think." Enough. Too much. The reader has been adequately warned. We are heading into some unearthly territory and those who get through life by the two easiest paths—that is, by believing everything they are told, or by believing nothing they are told—will find it a rocky road ahead. I don't want you to believe or disbelieve any of this at first sight. I want you to think, judge, evaluate.

(And *do try* to forget that the local branch of the Holy Inquisition is looking over both our shoulders as we proceed . . .)

On July 23, 1973, in an experience to be described fully later in this book, I had what appeared to be a telepathic communication with an intelligence existing on, within or near the star Sirius.

Whether this experience was what it appeared to be or was something else ("hallucination" is a convenient label for the "something else") is examined when the experience is discussed at length. This question is, for the time being, immaterial. The experience was the curtain-raiser for the Starseed Drama.

I was performing morning and evening yoga that summer and, to my consternation, the rest of July and August was marked by a repeated phenomenon that was unlike any previous yogic experience in my life. Repeatedly, especially on Sunday evenings, I had the visual impression of Dr. Timothy Leary flying over the walls of Folsom prison, where he was then confined. If I tried to banish this image and return to my meditation, it would recur, with more urgency. Dr. Leary's face also appeared, in close-up, with an expression of meditative serenity.

Toward the end of August I wrote an article on Tantric yoga for the Chicago *Seed*, an underground newspaper. The article appeared in two parts, in the September and October issues, under the title "Serpent Power, "(my notion of a way to tie Tantric concepts onto the tail of the popular *flower power* slogan of the 1960s.) In this article, I wrote explicitly (and somewhat adventurously, since my Sunday night flashes of Leary had not been confirmed by any psychics I knew): "Tim may still be experimenting with telepathy. The vibes seem strongest on Sunday evenings, around 8 California time (which would be 10 Chicago time.) Try tuning in." If any *Seed* readers did succeed in tuning in, they never wrote to tell me about it. I mention this *Seed* article only as documentation for skeptics, showing that I am not inventing this story out of whole cloth.

In January 1974, Dr. Leary published *Terra II*, in which he reported his experiments during July-August 1973, attempting to achieve telepathic communication with higher Intelligences elsewhere in the galaxy. Dr. Leary "received" 19 transmissions — the so-called Starseed

Transmissions — which he cheerfully admits may be hallucinations. He presents evidence and arguments that they may also be not-hallucinations.

As soon as I read *Terra II*, it was obvious to me that I had somehow, during my yoga sessions, tuned in on Dr. Leary's brain-waves. My July 23 communication from Sirius was either part of the Transmissions from the higher minds of the galaxy or was part of Dr. Leary's hallucination, telepathically shared with me.

Dr. Leary, however, did not mention Sirius as the site of the transmissions. I thereupon began a communication with him, to be reported in this book, during which I kept Sirius as a hole card, never mentioning it to him. It seemed to me that if, in future transmissions, he recognized Sirius as the origin of the signals, this would be one additional block in the tentative structure of possible proof that the Starseed signals are not-hallucinations.

In the following months, writing letters back and forth and occasionally visiting Dr. Leary in his new cage at Vacaville Prison, we began collaborating on a book to be titled *Periodic Table of Energy*, containing a new theory of evolution suggested by the Starseed Transmissions.

At one point in April 1974, I received what seemed to be another Transmission, concerning the Tarot/amino acid correspondences Dr. Leary was developing. When I transmitted this to Dr. Leary, he reported back that the same data had been received simultaneously by English poet Brian Barritt, in Switzerland, and was reported in a letter that arrived at Vacaville a few days after mine.

Although naturally cautious and skeptical in temperament, I began to really feel the emotional excitement of the possibility that the Starseed signals were not-hallucinations.

As of this writing, communication between Dr. Leary and myself has been cut off for 3 1/2 months. Indeed, communication between Dr. Leary and all his friends has been severed for that period; he has been held incommunicado by federal police, while "leaks" in the press report that he is informing against old friends about drug activities in the 1960s. Meanwhile, rumors circulate among Leary's friends and associates that he has been victimized by psycho-surgery, brainwashing, and/or every paranoid fantasy out of *1984*; that he is already dead; that he is alive and lying his head off to create a witch-hunt similar to the Moscow Purge Trials of 1936–37 or the Joe McCarthy epoch here; that he is mad or imbecilic; etc.

I think it is time for me to put on record everything I know about Dr. Leary, about metaprogramming the human nervous system with LSD and yoga, and about the Starseed messages and their implications for religion and occult sciences.

Conversation, Vacaville Prison. May 23, 1974:

WILSON: Giordano Bruno, the first philosopher in history to suggest that there were higher Intelligences in this galaxy, was a Tantric adept.

TIMOTHY LEARY: Yeah, I know.

WILSON: Oh, you've read Francis Yates' *Giordano Bruno and the Hermetic Tradition*?

LEARY: No. It was obvious from his writings. Tantra is always the first of the Secrets.

At our last meeting, Timothy was exuberant and, for

him, strangely secretive. "I'll be out soon," he said. "It's all falling into place."

The following week he was moved from Vacaville to Terminal Island, near Los Angeles. Joanna told all of us who were his friends in the Bay Area that letters to him were pointless, since he would be moved again shortly.

The Great Silence began. Weeks passed.

Mike Horowitz, archivist for Leary, came to me one night with a strange story. Joanna Leary had appeared at his house with three men whom she claimed were from a photocopying company. She had a letter in Timothy's unmistakable hand-writing, instructing Mike to turn over the archives for photocopying and permanent storage.

"They were cops," Mike told me. "I could smell it."

"What the hell . . ."

"I don't know," Mike said. "I just don't know . . ."

We booted it around for hours. If Timothy was making a deal with the Feds, what sort of deal? Paranoia drifted in and out of the room as we discussed, theorized, reconsidered.

I did a Tarot divination, at Mike's insistence. (I distrust my own readings, when personal emotion is involved.) I forget my interpretations but I remember that the card showing "resultant of the affair" was The Star. According to Kenneth Grant's *Magical Revival*, this card represents Sirius.

I performed another divination on Timothy, for another baffled friend, a week or so later. The Star came up as "the resultant" again.

Coincidence?

In September, the paranoia descended in full force.

Leaks began to appear in the Hearst press, obviously planted by the federal cops, that Timothy was ready to testify against any and all of his former friends to get himself out of jail.

Damnably, those of us who had watched the metamorphoses of Leary from scientist to Guru, from Guru to Marxist revolutionary, from revolutionary back to scientist, knew that he was capable of virtually any further transformation, however unlikely it would appear in ordinary psychology. Leary the Fink *was* a possibility.

The Berkeley *Barb* printed an undocumented story that Joanna, Tim's wife, had been busted for cocaine. "Aha," voices said, "that's how the Feds got Timothy to crack . . ." But the story wasn't checkable. "It's all a scam," other voices claimed, "the Feds are trying to panic us . . ."

Then the second wave of rumors began.

The Fiendish Psychologists at Vacaville had tampered with Tim's head. He was a zombie, like McMurphy at the end of *One Flew over the Cuckoo's Nest*; Kesey, like the true shaman he was, had knowingly predicted Leary's fate ten years before it happened.

Watergate was still erupting; even the most resolute anti-paranoids and skeptics about Conspiracy theories were pushed, more and more, into admitting that the Government was capable Of *Anything* . . .

And none of us were able to get a message in to Timothy or an answer out. He was totally incommunicado with the Feds.

I look into the past more and more, trying to understand the roots of the madness and the possible transcendence that grips the American public. Is Leary just Charlie Parker all over, dope-possessed genius and shaman? Is Nixon really John Wayne or is he Conrad Veldt ("Vee in the Gestapo haff waysss of making people talk . . .")?

Lao-Tse says, in Leary's translation:

What is above is below
What is without is within
What is to come is in the past

Or is Tom Paine more apropos with his terse and urgent prose; "The trade of governing has always been monopolized by the most ignorant and the most rascally individuals of mankind"?

It was 1961 and I had dropped out of engineering to become a writer; but the necessities of supporting four small children soon made me a writer in name only. I was creating "advertising copy," which is to prose what Rock is to music or Nick Kenny to poetry. "Greens that are bright and bold," I would type in a kind of masochistic trance, "greens that are soft and subdued. Greens that blend gently and greens that contrast dramatically. They're all here in this fine mosaic-look jacquard spread from famous Cannon Mills . . ."

Everybody else in the organization was an apprentice alcoholic, and I soon began to join them in their three-martinis-for-lunch ritual. I was getting my real writings published, yes—in underground papers that paid $15 or less, and in literary quarterlies that paid $0.00 and two free copies of the issue containing my piece. There was no youth Revolution yet, no Peace Movement, no sign of anything on the horizon but endless miles of plastic and Coke bottles.

If the liberals were having a honeymoon with John Kennedy, I personally found him even more deplorable than the egregious Eisenhower. The Bay of Pigs offended everything basic to my social conscience; it was brutal for the U.S. to attack such a small nation as Cuba (I thought of an adult beating up a child); it was sneaky, treacherous and dishonest; it was imperialistic in the classic sense; it was vile. The world in general seemed to hail JFK as a new messiah; I decided the world was mad, and retreated as far from the world as I could without taking my wife and kids to live in Mammoth Cave.

I had my first trip on December 28, 1962, in an old slave-cabin in the woods outside Yellow Springs, Ohio. We had rented the cabin from Antioch College for $30 per month and had an acre of cleared land to grow food on, thirty acres of woods to seek Mystery in. I was working as Assistant Sales Manager at the Antioch Bookplate Company in Yellow Springs, and we had found (we thought) how to drop out of the urban society without starving to death.

Several friends, in the previous two or three years, had told me about peyote, and eventually I was ready to try it. The press hadn't discovered psychedelic drugs yet, there were no scare stories about "bad trips"; I expected, quite simply, a mind-blowing religious experience and I got a mind-blowing religious experience. Psychedelics are, as Dr. John Lilly says, "meta-programming substances," and you generally get out of them what you program yourself to expect from them. I suffered the usual delusion of the first trip; I thought I was reborn.

When, in the following weeks, it became obvious

that I was not *entirely* reborn, and that many neurotic, depressive and egotistic programs still remained in my central computer, I was disillusioned. But the trip had been so interesting and ecstatic . . . I tried again. And again. And again and again and again. By mid-1963, I had logged 40 trips and it was obvious to me that peyote was, indeed, a magical chemical, as the Indians claim, but that one had to be a true magician to know how to use it profitably.

I don't intend to recount my 40 peyote trips in any detail here. In Leary's terminology, each trip involved a transmutation of consciousness from the symbolic level (Third Circuit) to sensory and somatic levels (Fifth Circuit). I learned to experience rapture, bliss, transcendence. Each time, the Body was Resurrected, Osiris rose from his tomb, I was godly and eternal for awhile. Each time, the yo-yo effect (as Dr. Richard Alpert calls it) came into play immediately afterwards: I came down again. The next trip brought me back up, of course, but then, once more, I came down again; up-and-down, up-and-down, the yo-yo effect. It was alternately inspiring and exasperating.

But a change in my mind (my "neurological functioning," Leary would say) was, slowly and subtly, beginning to happen.

I frequently had the "hallucination" of telepathic communication with plants, both when I was up on peyote and when I wasn't. "Hallucination" was the judgment of my engineering-trained ego; it sure *seemed* real, each time it happened. But I knew too much to take it seriously . . . and I continued to know too much until late in the 60s, when Cleve Backster's research with polygraphs established beyond all doubt that human-plant telepathy is occurring all the time, usually outside the conscious attention of the human participant.

Increasingly, I was on the edge of a great Revelation; but it was always lost. My mind wasn't ready for it — after all, I was neither a trained psychologist nor a shaman.

Let me emphasize here that my 40 peyote trips did not, in my mind, constitute "drug abuse." The federal authorities, in their hysteria over this subject, seem to have invented a strange semantics in which any "drug *use*" is "drug *abuse*;" although this is palpably absurd, the public has been propagandized into forgetting that there is a real distinction between using and abusing medications.

The hysteria is revealed for the illogical thing it is by the simple fact that peyote is forbidden only to white and black Americans; Indians may use it quite legally, and 500,000 of them—members of the Native American church—use it in their monthly sacraments. The Supreme Court has ruled that any interference with this church violates the first amendment ("religious freedom"), but attempts by whites and blacks to form similar peyote churches have, paradoxically, been ruled illegal. This is transparently racist, but it will probably take a generation for the prejudice to clear and the obvious legal issue to be recognized. The present legal decisions — deciding religious freedom questions on a racial basis — are based on the historical accident that the Native American church already existed as a widespread religion in the U.S. and Canada *before* the anti-psychedelic hysteria swept through government. In ordinary logic, if Indians have a right to practice a certain religion, then whites and blacks and Orientals and Chicanos also have the right to practice that religion.

I regarded my peyote experiments as scientific research, not as religion; but I did recognize religious implications. Meanwhile I remained sane, held my job as

Assistant Sales Manager, and remained a good husband and father, according to the judgment of my wife and children. If this is "drug abuse," then Donald Duck is Jerry Ford's speech writer.

Several times I "contacted" an Energy or an Intelligence that seemed to deserve the description "superhuman." It was obvious to me that I could easily, with a different cast of mind, describe these encounters as meetings with actual gods or angels. (Quanah Parker, the great Cheyenne war-chief who was converted to pacifism by peyote and founded the Native American Church, used to say "The white man goes into his church and talks *to* Jesus. The Indian goes into his tipi, takes peyote, and talks *with* Jesus.") I choose, instead, to regard these experiences as X's—unknowns—and to seek, in each experiment and in my reflections between experiments, to find a psychological, neurological or even parapsychological explanation.

My attitude was not irreligious, but trans-religious. I was quite willing to pray during a peyote trip (to Jesus, or to Peyote Woman, or to any of the Native American spirit-guides) but I regarded the prayers as part of the necessary mental preparation for proper mind-expansion. In other words, I took a Jungian attitude—the phenomena were not to be dismissed as "mere hallucinations," but they were not accepted as not-hallucination until confirmed by other data. My telepathy with plants, therefore, was not fully accepted as "real" until after Backster and several other scientists confirmed plant-ESP by polygraph readings.

Some of the students at Antioch College took to hanging around our farm and rapping with us about back-to-nature and anarchism, the two obsessions in my life at the time. I was much influenced by Ralph Borsodi and Mildred Loomis of the School of Living, and shared their absurdly impractical vision of millions of people dropping out of the urban rat-race, returning to a homestead economy, and gradually forming libertarian communities of quasi-Jeffersonian quasi-anarchist bias. (The propaganda I wrote for the School of Living in those days might have had some effect; several hundred thousand — not the millions yet — have made some effort toward such a new rural drop-out culture.)

The students also turned me on to various other drugs more or less like peyote. Antioch is always two-to-ten years ahead of fads elsewhere and the New Idea in 1962 was crashing through Huxley's "Doors of Perception" with a chemical skeleton. The more I investigated and experimented, the more I became convinced that it wasn't quite that simple; one needed, not just the appropriate neurochemicals, but an intelligent methodology. I didn't know where the methodology was to be found. Some of the results obtained by some of the students, without an adequate scientific understanding of the drugs, were almost as unpleasant as the celebrated "bad trips" of later years, although lacking newspaper hysteria at that time, nobody knew a bad trip was supposed to drive you crazy and they all recovered in a few hours.

The strangest adventure I had in those twenty-odd months of psychedelic explorations occurred *one day after* a peyote trip, when I was supposedly back in "normal" space-time again. I was weeding in the garden and a movement in the adjoining corn-field caught my eye. I looked over that way and saw a man with green skin and pointy ears dancing. I watched for nearly a minute, entranced, and then he faded away, just a hallucination.

Or was he? Who can *prove*, beyond all doubt, that he

14

was not a being of an order of energy usually invisible to us, suddenly and temporarily rendered visible by the new sensitivity of my nervous system? Similar beings have been described by psychics of many races, since the dawn of time—the fairy-folk, dryads, satyrs, the "allies" of Don Juan, the elementals of Paracelsus, the retinue of Pan, the gnomes and sylphs.

"My skepticism is intact." Yes: and it is larger than ever. Nowadays I am skeptical about anyone claiming to be able to say with certainty that such beings exist, or that they don't.

Marcel Vogel (whose corporation, Vogel-Luminescence, has developed the red color used in TV, fluorescent crayons, and the psychedelic colors popular in 1960s poster art) has been studying plant consciousness and vegetative telepathy for ten years now. In one experiment, Vogel and a group of psychologists tried concentrating on sexual imagery while a plant was wired up with a polygraph to reveal its "emotional" (electro-chemical?) responses to their thoughts.

'To their mutual surprise, the plant came to life, the pen recorder oscillating wildly on the chart. This led to the speculation that talking of sex could stir up in the atmosphere some sort of sexual energy such as the "Orgone" discovered and described by Dr. Wilhelm Reich, and that the ancient fertility rites in which humans had sexual intercourse in freshly seeded fields might indeed have stimulated plants to grow.'

(Secret Life of Plants, Tompkins and Bird)

The bureaucrats who burned Dr. Reich's books in 1957 were quite convinced he was a quack and a crank. The bureaucrats who imprison Dr. Leary today are no less

righteous and dogmatic. It is still obscure to some of us
exactly how the resort to cops, clubs, courts and cages can
possibly resolve controversial scientific questions . . .

Also: if the primitive shamans did not have the
polygraph instruments of Backster and Vogel, how *did*
they learn that plants are sentient and telepathic? What
instrument did they use? The answer seems to be the
human nervous system; but not in its natural state. As Dr.
Weston La Barre, anthropologist, documents at length in
his exhaustive study, *Ghost Dance: Origins of Religion*,
the chief device of shamanism is neuro-chemistry, and our
ancestors acquired their strange (and prophetic) doctrines of
spirits-in-the-vegetation from "astral trips" carried on with
the aid of at least 2250 different neurochemicals. Among
them, most prominent in the new world was *peyote*.

I am not trying to persuade the reader, with this
loose argument, that "fairies" or "elves" really exist. Not
at all. I am merely trying to illustrate both the promise
and the extreme complexity of research with these
metaprogramming substances. Plant-human ESP is real:
hundreds of researchers by now have confirmed Cleve
Backster's pioneering investigations in that field. Peyote,
and similar chemicals, stimulates this plant-human
telepathy. The same chemicals, historically, have led
shamans to believe in entities like the elves, gnomes,
angels, gods, etc. We are being very careless if we assume
either that we should ignore this monotonously-repeated
neurological finding (human nervous system + these
chemicals = visions of supernatural beings) or if we assume
that the enigmatic entities in question exist in exactly
the way the shamans and mystics, untrained in science,
imagine them to exist.

It is the purpose of this book to present the evidence

for a possible explanation of such encounters between humans and Higher Intelligences.

Chapter Two

The Madness of the Sixties

Warning: fear causes chromosome damage.
—graffito, St. Marie's place, 1967

Students of the human mind in general, and of the political mind in particular, may eventually solve all their mysteries if they concentrate on one datum that symbolizes the normal working of normal human mentalities: during the 1960s, the United States government insisted on placing people in cages, to discourage them from possibly harming themselves with marijuana. There was admittedly no evidence that marijuana really was harmful and, indeed, all the evidence scientifically known (as summarized in the English Hemp Commission Report of 1892, the U.S. Army Canal Zone study of 1926, the Laguardia Report of the 1943, the Zinberg-Weil study of 1968, etc.) indicated that marijuana was probably totally harmless.

Nonetheless, the guardians of the public shrewdly pointed out that *future* evidence *might* uncover hidden dangers not found in these studies. Since this argument is unanswerable (except by those who can prove they are time-travelers), one must admit that, yes, in 2009 somebody might prove grass leads to hangnail. (For that matter, in 2109, it might be discovered that potatoes lead to hernia . . .) Always vigilant to save us from possible threats, the government then must assume that some such danger might possibly exist, and therefore if we dare to take such a risk and actually smoke a joint of the weed, we must be brought back to our senses by being placed in a cage for a while, like a mad dog.

The effects of this are debatable. Most of the young people thrown into jail during the sixties for smoking grass were non-criminal types and not always karate experts. They were, however, young and therefore more sexually attractive than the old. The prevalence of homosexual rape in our prisons is much higher than the naive realize; when I was Associate Editor at *Playboy* we printed many letters from ex-cons testifying to the universality of the practice of raping youngish males in these human dog-pounds. (One case we uncovered involved a boy who had been homosexually raped 40 times.) While this may or may not be permanently harmful to the victim—many of them do commit suicide, as Leary reports in his *Jail Notes* — the general violence-level is certainly not conducive to their emerging from the cages as high, holy, saintly beings.

Michael Aldrich, Ph.D. has studied the persecution of drug-cults throughout history — the destruction of peyotism by the Mexican inquisition, the extermination of hemp-using witches in medieval Europe, etc. — and calls this "psychedelic genocide." The term may sound extreme, but the U.S. Government itself talks of making "war" on drugs; since drugs cannot be punished really, this is actually a "war" on people, like other wars.

Thomas Szasz, M.D. provides us with some

perspective on governmental semantics:

> The Nazis spoke of having a Jewish problem. We now speak of having a drug-abuse problem. Actually, "Jewish problem" was the name the Germans gave to the persecution of the Jews; "drug-abuse problem" is the name we give to the persecution of people who use certain drugs.

This is worth keeping in mind. Rightly or wrongly, Timothy Leary has become the symbol of *everybody* who is interested in experimenting on neuro-chemical re-programming — the philosophical Aldous Huxleys and Colin Wilsons, the theological Dr. Walter Huston Clarks and Alan Wattses, the clinical-experimental Dr. Abrahamsons and Dr. Osmonds, the jet-setters and hippies and bored housewives and freaks and crazy teenagers and Hells Angels and fools and dealers — the users and the abusers. Timothy Leary has been punished for all their sins—for intellectual curiosity, for violation of taboo, for creativity and for recklessness, for stupidity, for freakiness. He is being punished for all the radical political ideas he endorsed and for dozens of radical ideas he never endorsed. He is more a Symbol than a man. In this chapter I want to describe my first meetings with Dr. Leary and give some picture of the man behind the Symbol — what he really said and did, what he really believed, what he was trying to accomplish.

I met him *after* I had experimented with peyote and given up the experimentation as too advanced for my capacities at the time. I went to see him as a clinician who knew more about such chemicals than I did.

By mid-1964 the Acid Scandal had been in every publication from Bangor to Walla-Walla and Timothy Leary had replaced Aldous Huxley as the prophet of the Drug Revolution. Meanwhile, I had seen and/ or read about several bad trips with acid or peyote or the "magic mushroom" (psilocybae mexicana) and had cooled considerably on the project of indefinite self-experimentation with these potent potions. I had also moved back to New York—something I had often vowed I would never do—and was an Associate Editor at Ralph Ginzburg's FACT magazine, which was later crunched up by the courts after Ralph was convicted of libeling Barry Goldwater.

I wanted to interview the controversial Dr. Leary for FACT, but Ralph, with that strange prescience which marks his career, said that the psychedelic drug excitement was all over (1964) and nobody was interested anymore (1964) and Timothy Leary would soon be forgotten (1964). Still, I wanted to meet Dr. Leary. I finally finagled a freelance assignment from Paul Krassner of *The Realist* and made the journey (soon to be repeated by countless psychologists, clergymen, rock stars, oriental gurus and young seekers-after-wonder) up the Hudson to the Millbrook Ashram.

This was still early on in the history of what Charles Slack later called "the Madness of the Sixties." Timothy Leary, although already an arch-heretic fired from Harvard for unauthorized research and poor usage of the first amendment, was not yet into his Oriental trip; he was studying the *Tibetan Book of the Dead* that summer (and was later to adapt it, with Dr. Richard Alpert and Dr. Ralph Metzner, into his LSD-programming manual, *The Psychedelic Experience*), but he was otherwise still heavy into Scientific Clinical Psychology. Not once during the day I spent with him did he say "when I used to be a psychologist," as he was much given to saying later on in the frantic sixties. So many accounts have been written of the Millbrook Ashram that I won't go into details. There was a black guy standing on the roof of the main building, playing beautiful jazz trumpet all by himself, as I drove up, and the famous psychedelic collages were hanging on walls in virtually every room, but by and large it was much like any place where scholars held learned seminars. If G. Gordon Liddy was already hiding in the bushes, peeking through his binoculars for Sex Orgies and other crimes, he must have been very bored that particular day. There was also a Jesuit priest there, and he and I and Dr. Ralph Metzner got into a very complicated discussion of B.F. Skinner's theories. It later developed that the Jesuit, himself a clinical psychologist, thought I was another psychologist and believed "the visiting reporter" was in another room with Leary.

Later he asked me if I had majored in psychology, and was surprised to find most of my college years had been in the physical sciences. My knowledge of psychology comes entirely from omnivorous reading and several friendships with people in the field, but it may partially explain why Timothy Leary and I had a different sort of relationship than Tim usually has with writers and journalists.

Tim struck me, on first meeting, as a typical middle-aged academic type, although more athletic than most. I mention this because he looked much younger in later years, like the song by Dylan says:

> I was so much older then,
> I'm younger than that now

When we discuss metaprogramming theory later, and Paul Segal's investigations of amino acids related to psychedelics and aging, we will find some evidence that Dr. Leary's youthful image may have a bio-chemical explanation.

Besides being an athletic young-middle-aged man, Tim was singularly free of the space-time compulsions of normal Americans. He stands as close as a Mexican when he talks to you, and he is apt to look straight at you without the usual American eye-shifting. If this makes you nervous, he backs off and allows you to relax; but, basically, he is most comfortable himself within the *intimate* relationship. And, of course, the famous Leary grin was already part of him.

He also used "fuck" quite normally and without emphasis, as a transitive verb. Around then, intellectuals and academics were beginning, at least among friends, to use casual sex-slang in place of those horrible clinical terms like "copulation" or "coitus," but Tim was the first one I ever heard say "fuck" in a descriptive manner, not as a swear-word in anger.

"The best results come when you fuck somebody you really love, during the acid trip," he said. "That's when the nervous system is most open, most unconditioned, and ready to take a completely new imprint."

Dr. Leary was exuberant and enthusiastic about his research, of course, but he had not adapted a messianic *persona* yet. That only came later, after he had been thoroughly irritated and disgusted by governmental repression of himself and other LSD researchers, and I have always privately suspected that a great deal of the LSD-Guru image was a deliberate game on his part, an attempt to get around the taboos erected by the Washington bureaucrats and confront them with a genuinely religious mass-movement which they couldn't forbid without mangling the first amendment.

This strategy has proven to be wrong. Dr. Leary had too much faith in the first amendment and in the courts. We now know that religious freedom is no more secure than any other freedom, if enough people in Washington are really frightened and really hostile about the new mysticism.

That day in Millbrook Timothy was about as pious as an engineer explaining his new bridge.

He was delighted that I understood enough psychology to understand terms like "zero-sum game," "reinforcement," "transaction," etc. and he was especially pleased that, unlike any other interviewer he had met, I was familiar with his book, *Interpersonal Diagnosis of Personality*, and wanted to question him about how the space-time transformations of the psychedelic voyage correlate with his space-time definitions of personality types in that work.

"LSD takes you out of the normal space-time ego," he said vehemently. "I always go through a process in which the space game comes to an end, the time game comes to an end, and then the Timothy Leary game comes to an end. This is the peak, and at this point the new imprint can be made, because all the old imprints are suspended for a while then."

I asked about the impression, encountered by myself on peyote and by others on LSD, that one is actually out of the body at that crucial moment.

"Until I can design an experiment to really test that one out," Timothy said, "I just don't know. It's merely subjective at this point." Indeed, my most persistent impression throughout the day was that Timothy Leary was a man who hated, loathed and despised anyone who would commit the epistemological sin of "speculating beyond the data." Every question I asked him was answered either with a summary of experimental results or with a promise that he hoped to find a way to check it experimentally as the work proceeded. Leary emphasized to me, as he did to all reporters, that the psychedelic drug experience is a synergetic product of three nonadditive factors: (1) the dosage of the chemical used; (2) the set— the subject's expectations, space-time-emotion games, personality profile, etc.; and (3) the setting—the actual space-time location. I understood him perfectly and quoted him accurately; I have often wondered why other reporters understood him so poorly and misquoted him so outrageously. The synergetic theory of "dosage, set and setting" may be Dr. Leary's outstanding contribution to the science of psycho-pharmacology (we will talk later about his contributions to other sciences) but journalists in general understood him about as well as one who might write that Einstein discovered e = something-or-other.

Mostly, we talked about game-theory that day. Timothy had, indeed, been playing baseball on the Millbrook lawn when I arrived, and baseball thereupon haunted our conversation on the metaphoric level. He had thrown out the concept of "psychologist" and "patient" back in '57, replacing it with "research team," because he was convinced that the hierarchy implied in "psychologist" (top dog) and "patient" (bottom dog) predetermined certain conclusions, but now he wanted to examine everything in terms of the von Neumann-Morgenstern game model. "What are the players actually doing in space-time?" he would ask me rhetorically. "Who's at bat? Who's pitching? What are the rules of' the game? How many strikes before you're out? Who makes the rules? Who can change the rules? These are the important questions. Anybody around here caught talking about 'sickness' or 'neuroses' or 'ego' or 'instinct' or 'maturity' or any of that jabberwocky gets thrown the hell out. We've got a contract among ourselves that we're going to talk sense, and that means talking about what we actually see when we look where the bodies are in space-time and what movements they're making."

This was, indeed, the basic methodological position Leary had taken in *Interpersonal Diagnosis of Personality*, back in the fifties, but had been intensified by his growing disgust for the high failure rate of the psychological professions and his admitted desire to be even more hard-science in orientation than his arch-rival at Harvard, behaviorist B.F. Skinner. So many people were bemused or bewildered by Leary the Guru in the next few years that this background of his work was never fully understood.

During the prisoner rehabilitation project of 1961-62, for which he was commended by the Massachusetts Department of Corrections, Dr. Leary refused to let any co-workers speculate on whether the cons were getting "sicker" or "better." "Where are their bodies in space-time? What are they doing?" he would ask. He had developed his 7-dimensional game model by then and insisted on analyzing all behavior in terms of the 1. Roles being played 2. Rules tacitly accepted by all players 3. Strategies for winning (or for masochistic winning-by-losing) 4. Goals of the game, purposes served 5. Language of the game, and its semantic world-view implied 6. Characteristic space-time locations and 7. Characteristic movements in space-time. "If you can't describe those seven dimensions of a group's behavior, you don't understand their game," he told me. "Most so-called 'neurosis' is just somebody programmed to play football wandering around a baseball field with the result that he and everybody else know something is odd somewhere. If they can all find the meta-language to explain to each other the difference between baseball and football there is no 'neurosis' at all." And so on. The *Tibetan Book of the Dead* was merely "the rules of one type of consciousness-alteration game." It was useful for LSD-programming because LSD seemed to be able to "suspend imprinted neurological games" and "allow re-imprinting of new games."

This libertarian variation on Skinner's authoritarian behavior model was profoundly exciting and stimulating to me—as a former engineering aide, mathematics major, science-fiction fan and "science groupie" — I was thrilled as a musician hearing first notes of what sounds like possibly the greatest symphony since Ludwig's *Ninth*. I was bowled over and fell in love with Timothy Leary's head. (Ten years later, when worried that the psycho-surgeons at Vacaville might tamper with that brain, I tried to persuade the California ACLU to sue to have Dr. Leary's head declared a national treasure. But that is jumping too far ahead.)

"I was always sorry that I never met Einstein," I told my wife, driving back to New York City that night. "Now maybe I'll be a hero to my grand-children because I met Timothy Leary."

In January 1960 I accepted an invitation to come to Harvard University to initiate new programs in what was then called Behavior Change. I was convinced that mental illness could be cured; that drastic limitations on human intellectual and emotional function were caused by inflexible states of mind, static imprinted and conditioned neural circuits which created and preserved artificial and malfunctional states of perceived reality.

I believed the nervous system to be a bio-chemical-electrical network capable of receiving and creating a changing series of adaptive realities if and when the chemical key for altering consciousness was found and employed in the context of an adequate theory. In the then Zeitgeist of Salk, Fleming, Pauling, I believed that the right chemical used correctly was the cure. The 'career ailment' I had selected as curable was human nature.

To oversimplify, I believed that man did not know how to use his head, that the static, repetitive conditioned circuit known as the normal mind was itself the source of 'dis-ease' and that the task of the psychologist-neurologist was to discover the neurochemical for changing mind, i.e. to allow for new imprints of new realities and new conditioned sequences. Our initial experiments at Harvard suggested that LSD might be such a drug."

— Timothy Leary, letter to *Current History*, May 1974

The Vietnam War began to heat up by 1965 and the U.S.A. began to disintegrate. The Establishment, looking around for a "cause" to explain the disintegration, decided to blame it all on drugs. Somehow, Timothy Leary got elected as the cause of the cause, the Demon who was responsible for the drugs. One year after Ralph Ginzburg declared Tim Leary not newsworthy enough for FACT magazine, Tim was a hundred times more famous, and infamous, than Lyndon Johnson.

Meanwhile, I was going up in the world, and going down, and going up-and-down. I left FACT and edited four girlie magazines simultaneously for a Schlockfactory, where I also wrote an astrology column for the tabloid newspaper produced there and occasionally helped invent the "news" they printed (e.g. MAD HUNCHBACK SELLS HUNCH TO BUTCHER: WOMAN POISONED BY HUNCHBURGER.) I was a reporter for *Home Furnishings Daily* for a while, and then toiled on another schlock tabloid. I became an Associate Editor at *Playboy* and helped put out a radical neighborhood newspaper in my spare time.

One day in 1966, Tim Leary popped into the *Playboy* office and he and I had lunch together. I remember telling him that I had recently found quite a few references to "Leary" and "LSD" in *Finnegans Wake*, and asked what he thought of that. He said Leary was a common Irish name and LSD in Ireland means "pounds, shillings, pence." Then we got into serious rapping and he told me that the inorganic chemicals were more intelligent than the organic chemicals. This was the only explanation, he said, for some of the "psi" phenomena encountered on LSD trips; besides, he added, the inorganic is older than the organic and therefore *must be* smarter. I must have looked as if I suspected that he was putting me on, because he gave out a bark of the famous Leary Laugh, tapped his temple knowingly, and said in a mock-diagnostic tone, "Pretty far gone, eh?"

We veered away from that one — I now realize he was groping toward his later theory of the seven levels of consciousness inside the human body—and we talked about LSD in cancer research. He was very excited and hopeful about various successful applications of LSD in treating terminal cancer patients.

I mentioned a TV show about the Spring Grove

research on LSD and alcoholism. "Did you notice Dr. Unger *hugging* that one tripper?" Tim asked. "That's the sign that he's been to Millbrook. Any therapist who *hugs* an LSD tripper has studied with us." He seemed to regard this as at least as important as any of his theoretical-methodological contributions to psycho-pharmacology. Actually, the taboo against touching the lowly "patient" was breaking down in psychotherapy generally throughout the 60s; but Timothy, typically, was more enthusiastic and exuberant about it than anyone else.

A few nights later, I ran into Tim again, at Hefner's mansion. He was boozing it up and had his eye on a Bunny he obviously intended to prong as soon as possible, so we had no lengthy conversation.

In the introduction to *Beezebub's Tales to His Grandson*, the great mystic Gurdjieff tells a story that is meaningful in many dimensions. As a boy, Gurdjieff lived in a small Turko-Russian town where everybody was awakened at 6 a.m. by a factory whistle. One day, being up early, Gurdjieff went out to the factory and watched the man who blew the whistle. To the boy's surprise, the man first faced the town and shouted every obscene and profane expression in the vivid Turkish language. Then he blew the whistle.

Years later, as a man, Gurdjieff went out again early in the morning and watched. Sure enough, before blowing the whistle, the man turned to the town and shouted a stream of vile and profane insults. Gurdjieff then approached and demanded an explanation of this odd behavior.

Said the man, "What do you think they say about me when they hear the whistle? Nobody wants to be awakened from sleep, you know . . ."

In the 1960s, Timothy Leary blew a whistle in the darkness. Some awoke just far enough to recognize him as a menace; and he is still suffering their vengeance.

It is, in fact, rather peculiar to look back, in 1974, at a book like David Solomon's anthology, *LSD*, published by Putnam in 1964. Here we find scientists such as Dr. Humphry Osmond, Dr. James Terrill, Dr. Charles Savage, Dr. Donald Jackson, Dr. Sanford Unger (whose willingness to hug patients is mentioned above), Dr. Jonathan Cole, Dr. Martin Katz, Dr. Eric Kast, etc. reporting beneficial and interesting changes in consciousness (and behavior) induced by LSD in a proper set and setting. Here we find philosophers like Aldous Huxley and Dr. Alan Watts contemplating the potentials of these chemicals with optimism and hope. We also find Dr. Leary writing the introduction to the volume and treated as a much-respected colleague by most of the scientific contributors. In short, the whole volume seems to have fallen out of a time-warp from another universe. Was all this really published only ten years ago? Weren't all the contributors thrown in jail at once? What kind of world was it back then, when this subject could be discussed scientifically, objectively, rationally? We find it hard to remember that innocent age, before the Hysteria descended on this country—before the midnight raids and no-knock laws, before all such research was stopped by government ukase, before Dr. Leary was recreated by the press in the image of a Mad Scientist . . . And yet it was only ten years ago.

It would be extremely bad taste, of course, to hint that *all* the scientists who once believed in the potential of LSD research have not been converted to the counter-belief that such investigations are Devilish and Evil. It would be especially tasteless to report that many are willing to say, in private, that they still believe what they believed before the hysteria, but are unwilling to be quoted in public. This implies massive professional cowardice, does it not? And yet I know more than a dozen who have made this statement to me, and who do not fully grasp the extent to which I despise them even while keeping my promise not to print their names. It is a delight to mention that Dr. John Lilly is still willing to say the same things he said before the Hysteria, and even goes further lately. (He told a *PENTHOUSE* interviewer in 1973 that, under current FDA rules, Fleming's penicillin research would have been illegal, and that bureaucratic rationalizations for these rules are "horse-shit." Thank you, Dr. Lilly.)

As Dr. Leary writes in *The Curse of the Oval Room* (1974):

> Very few Americans, even in these post-Watergate days, understand how Nixon set up his very own Special Secret elite police. Under the guise of "drug control" this Orwellian coup was accomplished with the approval of middle-aged liberals. It was so simple. The Narc budget jumped from 22 million to 140 million . . . Constitutional rights were suspended and martial law (no-knock, stop-and-frisk, curfew etc.) was imposed selectively on one easily identifiable segment of the population . . . fear descended upon the land. The spokesmen for the counter-culture were arrested, harassed, silenced. The press cooperated completely . . .

In the course of the Terroristic campaign described by Leary, he himself was repeatedly arrested, convicted of owning two joints of marijuana (he claimed it was a frame-up, but liberals weren't interested in *his* claims, since the cops are the new gods of corporate liberaldom), sentenced to *30* years, had the highest bail in U.S. history ($5,000,000), was kidnapped in Afghanistan in violation of 148 court-rulings holding such body-snatchings illegal where extradition treaties are not enforced, was kept in chains for a while and then kept in solitary confinement in the next cell to a madman (Charles Manson), and has now been held incommunicado for several months with none of his old friends allowed to send messages to him or receive messages from him.

All this has happened in broad daylight, with the liberals and the ACLU unable to recognize that the constitution is being mauled and mangled even worse than the freedom of scientists to publish and discuss their findings.

It is both amusing and pathetic to read the rhetoric of the 60s today. Dave Solomon's introduction to *LSD: The Consciousness Expanding Drug*, for instance, ends up:

> No social authority can successfully arrogate to itself the right to dictate and fix the levels of consciousness to which men may aspire, whether these states are induced pharmacologically or otherwise. Die Gedanken sind frei.

Mr. Solomon evidently suffered from the illusion that we are living in a sane, free and scientific world. We now know otherwise. *Die Gedanken sind nicht frei.*

It is even more ironic to read the calm and judicious words of Dr. Humphry Osmond, after summarizing all the clinical evidence in 1964: "I believe that these agents have a part to play in our survival as a species . . . The psychedelics help us to explore and fathom our own nature." You will look in vain for scientific evidence, published after 1964, that disproves this verdict. There is no such scientific evidence, since all research has been stopped by government. Dr. Leary is a caged creature today to warn other scientists that they, too, can be punished as he is being punished, if their curiosity strays outside the limits that bureaucrats consider permissible.

Voltaire announced the Age of Reason a few centuries too soon.

Chapter Three

Top Dog and Bottom Dog

> We are sheep kept to provide wool for our masters
> who lead us and keep us as slaves of illusion . . . We
> have a chance of escape, but we like being sheep. It is
> comfortable.
>
> G.I. Gurdjieff, quoted by Kenneth Walker,
> *A Study of Gurdjieff's Teachings*

I spent five years as an Associate Editor at *Playboy*,
or somebody did. The "I" who went to the office 8 or 10
hours a day, 5 or 6 days a week, was a certain Robert Anton
Wilson who lived in those years, 1966-1971, in certain
space-time dimensions; he is emphatically not the "I" who
writes the present book.

You all want to know, of course, does Hef really fuck
all the Playmates, and is he really homosexual?

I have no real inside information — Hef does
not socialize all that much with the editors — but my
impression is that he has made love to a lot of the
Playmates, by no means all of them, and that he is not
homosexual.

Sorry.

My job was editing the letters in the *Playboy Forum*, not to be confused with *Dear Playboy* or the *Playboy Advisor* (please!). *Playboy* may be the only magazine with three letters columns, and I was assigned to the *Forum* because I had a natural affinity for that work, which also involved writing the italicized replies in which the *Playboy* position was stated. This was straight old-fashioned plumb-line libertarianism, and (since that is my philosophy as well as Hefner's) I enjoyed myself immensely. Never before, and never again, have I earned so much money for writing exactly what I really think.

One of the writers in the promotion department was taking a trip every weekend, on something his dealer told him was LSD. He heard me reading my poetry at a coffee house one night, decided I wasn't plastic, and began to cultivate a friendship. Since our wives also dug each other, it was okay.

One day, Cary (never mind his full name) told me that he had received telepathic messages from outer space on several of his recent trips. I did not perfectly hide my instant skepticism, and he clammed up immediately. I never heard another word from him on that subject. Later he quit *Playboy* and went off to try to crack Hollywood.

I wish I hadn't lost contact with Cary. Now I'm ready to listen to his outer space stories without prejudice.

By the time of the Democratic Convention Horrors of 1968, I was smoking pot fairly regularly — like everybody else in *Playboy*'s editorial department, and at every other magazine I knew, and throughout the communications industry. (I was still steering clear of LSD. The peyote trips of 1962-63 had convinced me that one needed advanced training in either shamanism or psychology to handle the psychedelics properly.)

One night while I was happily stoned on the weed and alone at home — the kids were asleep, Arlen was out at a Women's Lib meeting — I made a discovery. Leary's *Psychedelic Experience* was all about this fact, but he was talking about super-potent LSD there, and I hadn't thought the same rule applied to earthy, down-home grass. The discovery is that most of the phenomena of self-hypnosis are quite easily replicable on grass, without the tedious training involved in ordinary hypnosis. That is, I could re-program any sense organ at will. Instead of pot being an unplanned voyage into unexpected sensory thrills, it became a deliberate program of sensory enrichment. I could turn music into colors, into caresses, into *tastes*; I could grow to gigantic size, or shrink down inside my own cells and molecules; I could *tune* my nervous system like a combination microscope-TV set. I had discovered Leary's Fifth Circuit.

Several extraordinary months of experiment soon revealed that I could do much of this without pot (although it remained easier *with* pot, of course) and I began at long last to understand what Freud meant by *projection* and Buddha by *maya*. It became quite clear to me, that whatever "reality" means ultimately, our everyday experience is almost entirely self-programmed.

Since 99 pot-heads out of a hundred still haven't discovered this neurological art, it occurs to me that my previous experiences had helped to make it possible for me. I have in mind particularly a bout of Reichian bio-psychological therapy in the mid-1950s, which broke up some of my muscular inhibitions and freed part of the inborn energies; several years of enthusiastic involvement with General Semantics, which largely delivered me from the tyranny of ideas and opened me to the otherwise unthinkable (although not enough, as we have seen, for me to take the possibility of interstellar telepathy seriously when first presented to me); and, of course, my 40 trips on the sacred cactus, *peyotl*.

I soon discovered that pot could be a tool by which I might "adjust" my nervous system as casually as one adjusts the picture on a TV set. I lived then, not in one static and unchanging "reality," but in a variety of Gestalts each one recognized as a collaboration between myself and the non-verbal energy continuum of this incredible universe. I had achieved what Korzybski calls "consciousness of abstracting," awareness of the usually-unconscious mechanism by which each of us makes the world over in his/her own image.

I now took up yoga, quite unmystically and with hardly a grain of piety. I understood that yogic training — whatever else it might comprise — is a method of freeing the nervous system from *conditioned perception*. The aim is to learn to *see* (as Don Juan keeps telling Castaneda in those four marvelous books of occult wisdom) because most of us, most of the time, do not *see* but only dream and hallucinate, according to the program fed into our perception-system by our parents' arid society. Between pot and yoga, I quickly demonstrated to myself by direct experience that the nervous system can be freed from virtually every perception and reflex that makes up our ordinary spectrum of possibility.

Alan Watts, the skeptical theologian and experimental mystic, was doing similar research in those years, and coming to similar conclusions. During one of his visits to Chicago, he said to another *Playboy* editor, "But, my dear man, reality is only a Rorschach ink-blot, you know."

Alas, to those who haven't done the research personally on a neurological level, this is hardly comprehensible; the editor remained skeptical. (Later Paul Krassner of *The Realist* put the same thought more colorfully: "Reality is silly-putty." And, with an attempt to bait the Establishment, Randolfe Wicker of Underground Uplift Unlimited put out a button saying "Reality is a crutch." Those without the experience to understand were not really enlightened by such aphorisms and concluded that a certain segment of the intelligentsia was going mad . . .)

Actually, no student of science (or especially of optics and neurology) can deny that:

a) most seeing is conventional and conditioned; we see what we're trained to see;

b) it is quite possible to learn to see differently; Anything called "hallucination," "mania," "psychosis" or even "blind prejudice" comes under classification (b). Consider then the next step:

c) it is possible for those with enough skepticism and intelligence to learn to see not only differently but *more* and *better*.

This can only be judged by experience and experiment, in a free scientific community. The lack of such scientific freedom — the government threat to cage any scientist who follows Dr. Leary in exploring such matters — does not close the question but only leaves it perpetually open. There is no *a priori* grounds to justify the assumption that normal modes of nervous-system functioning in our society are the highest and most accurate that humanity can ever attain. Indeed, such an assumption is transparently self-regarding and self-serving. The ban on further scientific research, and the terror that inspires that prohibition, allow the suspicions that this glaringly obvious relapse to the mentality of the Holy Inquisition is inspired entirely by blind fear and intolerance. It is always the case: those who are really sure of themselves do not fear further research; those who do fear such research are not at all sure but just hysterical.

Along about this point in my career as an unlicensed yogi Tim Leary came to Chicago with his "Death of the Mind" road-show and I did not find him nearly as impressive as earlier. He came on stage barefoot, burned incense, did a lecture on Buddha illustrated with psychedelic slides and weird lighting effects, and more or less seemed like an oriental Billy Graham. It seemed to me that a brilliant scientist had turned himself into a second-rate messiah, and I found it corny. Little did either of us realize that Dr. Richard Alpert was soon to do the whole Asia Trip over and *for real*.

A day or so later I met Tim on the street outside the *Playboy* building and we had lunch together again. He was more turned-on, vibrant, joyous and grandiose than ever, but he also had even more sense of humor than previously and kept poking fun at his own Guru act. I don't think either of us said it aloud, but we seemed to share the secret that much of his current "act" was just agitprop for the one cause he really believed in: the possibility that LSD, *wisely used*, could re-program enough nervous systems to basically change "human nature" before we laid ourselves and our planet to waste. He was Fleming, and LSD was his penicillin for what Nietzsche dubbed the "sickness called man."

Somehow, we got talking about Dr. Wilhelm Reich, and I compared Tim's growing legal problems to Reich's. Tim was even more bitter about the psychological-psychiatric professions than the avowed Reichians I knew;

he insisted that the professionals had not only stood aside while the government destroyed Reich but had actively encouraged the persecution. But the parallel did not worry him.

"I'm in great health in all respects," he told me, with the wise and genuine Leary grin. "I fully expect to live past the hysteria and persecution, till everything I've claimed is confirmed and accepted, till it's used every day in every clinic in the world, till it becomes dull truism." Then he grinned ever more broadly. "But then I'll be espousing some new heresy, I hope, and be in hot water again."

The parallel between Dr. Leary and Dr. Reich seems more and more striking, more and more ominous, as I ponder it. Jung's term, "synchronicity" — meaningful coincidence: occult *pattern* — seems to fit the case, which has almost the repetitious quality of crude poetry or a sea chanty. Thus:

Dr. Reich was recognized as brilliant in early youth, throughout his profession; Dr. Leary was recognized as brilliant in early youth, throughout his profession.

As Reich's theories became more socially "dangerous" rumors insisted that he was mad; as Leary's theories became more socially "dangerous" rumors insisted that he was mad.

Both men used free sexual energies in ways socially forbidden.

Both men were the targets of smear campaigns by professional associates (the inaccurate rumor that Dr. Reich had been in a mental hospital in Europe; the vile hatchet-job on Leary in Charles Slack's *Timothy Leary, The Madness of the Sixties, and Me.*)

Both men pleaded for independent researchers to check out their work and either prove or refute it; both were ignored by the majority of their profession, which admittedly condemned them without such investigation.

Both men were persecuted by government; both fled several times from several countries.

Both were temporarily attracted to Marxism, but ultimately rejected it vehemently.

Both asserted a definite conspiracy to destroy them; both had some evidence that such a conspiracy existed.

In each case the persecution involved "odd" or "weird" elements suggesting either incredible stupidity by the government or some still-hidden Mystery which has not been revealed.

Both claimed extra-terrestrial intelligences had contacted them.

Both attempted to investigate scientifically the subjects which are usually left to mystics or occultists.

Both were married several times and had numerous affairs; both were obviously the subject of acute sexual jealousy ("emotional plague," in Dr. Reich's terminology) by some of their persecutors.

Both were accused, like Socrates, of corrupting the youth.

Both felt a strong parallel with Giordano Bruno, magician, alchemist, pioneer of modern astronomy, political conspirator, arch-heretic, first man to assert the existence of Higher Intelligences in this galaxy. Bruno was burnt at the stake; Reich and Leary imprisoned.

In both cases, many people seemed curiously willing to believe the most disgraceful charges without any confirmation or supporting evidence; there seemed a definite *will to believe* the worst in each case. Both were pronounced sane by government psychiatrists while the charge of "insanity" was still widely used to explain away their observations and clinical experiments as "hallucination."

Both were called messiahs or cranks (Reich was a "Greenwich Village Swami," according to the FDA; Leary a "drug cultist" according to the same FDA) both actually retained ordinary scientific method, but admittedly supplemented it with methods traditionally called spiritual (Reich called these disciplines "bio-energetic," Leary calls them "higher circuits of the nervous system".)

Both threatened the mechanism of authority-and-obedience.

My work on the *Playboy Forum* was alternately exhilarating and depressing — exhilarating when we kept somebody out of jail (through publicity and/or the legal activities of the Playboy Foundation); depressing, when we failed. I read more and more letters from people in jails — men and women caged because they had violated some taboo or another. (*Playboy* only defended "victimless criminals," those who had not committed force or fraud against their neighbors, but were punished for consensual behavior between adults.) I had always been a libertarian and an individualist; I had always disapproved of these crimeless crime laws that enforced Judeo-Christian religious prejudice on the entire community; I had always shared the standard Jeffersonian-Millian objection to such priestly tyranny in a secular nation. Now, I began to *feel* as well as understand the problem. The issue was not abstract; the people were real people, locked in real cages, and subject to very real brutality, including a great deal of homosexual rape. Those who urged total abolition of the cage-system — such as psychiatrist Karl Menninger and journalist John Barlow Martin—seemed to me to have the only sane attitude. You cannot "reform" a cage. You cannot "humanize" *punishment*, which is always the kind of torture acceptable to the society in which it occurs.

Eventually, the *Playboy* position, progressive as it was, failed to satisfy my growing empathy with the caged, my accelerating anger and disgust that a so-called civilized nation could practice the barbarity of locking men and women in cages.

In 1969, I helped to organize, along with the Industrial Workers of the World (Chicago branch) and a group of young, hippie-oriented I.W.W. hangers-on who called themselves the Nameless Anarchist Horde, a demonstration outside Cook County jail, demanding not reform of prisons but total abolition. We got remarkably little publicity in the media, and I doubt that we had any effect at all; but it was the first time anyone since Eugene V. Debs, for the socialists, and Emma Goldman, for the anarchists, had explicitly demanded *ending all prisons*, over fifty years earlier.

Joffre Stewart, the black anarcho-pacifist poet who is one of the few ornaments of beautiful soul in the hellhole of Chicago culture, is typical of the kind of people tormented and tortured by the cage-system. On a questionnaire from a sociologist examining life-styles among pacifists, Joffre answered the question "How many times have you been arrested? Why?" as follows:

The Starseed Signals

9 times for anti-war activities;
8 times for anti-tax activities;
17 times for walking on Chicago streets while
being black.

It is literally true that the major crimes are all legal —
i.e. the theft of the land, the natural resources, etc. by gangs
of bandits known as banks and corporations is legitimized
by government, and protected by government force. The
second-level crimes, by Mafia groups, are also "protected"
by the well-known inter-group cooperation between the
Mafia and the two major political parties. A few low-level
criminals are caught occasionally, and sent to jail, and
that is supposed to justify the whole cage-system. In fact,
these persons are a minority in the prisons, and are made
worse by the cage-experience, whereby society is further
endangered and not helped at all by prisons.

The real function of the cages is to control the decent,
honorable, humane members of society. Without the
cages, few of us would serve in unjust wars, pay taxes to
support those wars, or cooperate otherwise with the bullies
and tyrants who govern us. As Emmett Grogan, the great
Catholic anarchist, used to say, *"A society with jails is
itself a jail."* The purpose of the cages is to terrorize us into
animalistic, dog-like submission; to prevent our behaving
as responsible adult humans.

I remember the great scene in *My Little Chickadee*
where W.C. Fields is about to be hanged. As the noose is
slipped about his neck, he is asked if he has any last words.

"Um, yes," he replies thoughtfully. "This will certainly
teach me a lesson."

The comment is brilliant, not just on capital
punishment, but on punishment per se, which never teaches
any lesson except desire for revenge.

As the 1960s progressed, and the "war on drugs" escalated, our jails filled with more and more young people convicted of *desire to experiment on alterations of consciousness*. I became convinced that *Mad* magazine was right in claiming "the missing link between ape and civilized humanity is *us*."

Back in present time again, 1974 and "the center will not hold, mere anarchy is loosed upon the world."

Timothy is still incommunicado: the latest rumor has it that he has testified against the Weather Underground, to a Grand Jury in Chicago. Nobody I know likes the Weatherpeople at all, but this report fills us with sadness and disgust: the weather folks, after all, put their head on the block when they helped Timothy escape from San Luis Obispo Jail in 1970. It is not exactly noble for him to turn around and help the Feds chop off those heads now. Even the most right-wing people I know do not regard this kind of personal disloyalty as a sign of rededication to the American Principles . . .

"If Tim does get out this way," said one mutual friend, "he'll have to drive around in a tank and live in a castle. Otherwise he is one dead dodo."

The real tragedy, to me, is that nobody now seems to remember the very real possibility that Tim's scientific heresies may someday be confirmed; that he may emerge as the outstanding, scientific pioneer of our century.

Leary's career is, after all, classical. Similar rites of degradation and expulsion from the tribe were visited upon most of the great scientists, philosophers and artists of the past; but we never like to think that we might be as narrow-minded, bigoted and short-sighted as our ancestors. The people they persecuted may have been heroes of enlightenment, yes; but the people *we* persecute, by God, are as guilty as hell. Semmelweiss was right about puerperal fever, says the average M.D., but the guy *we* kick out of *our* medical society is a dangerous quack. Dreyfus may have been innocent, but Alger Hiss was not. Those who believed that they had absolute truth on all subjects in 1910 or 1810 or 1740 or 300 B.C. were obviously deluded, but we know enough today to condemn anybody whose ideas are unconventional.

The notion that we might, just possibly, have jailed another Jesus, another Galileo, is not pleasant to contemplate. Therefore, in keeping with Freud's pleasure principle, we refuse to contemplate it.

In a Psychology 2 class at New York University, 1957, I had a very heated argument with the instructor, a PhD, about Dr. Wilhelm Reich, who then occupied the position now held by Dr. Leary — Number One on the Shit List of the A.M.A. and the American Psychiatric Association. Whether Dr. Reich was right or wrong, I said, burning his books in an incinerator was unconstitutional. (The burning had only occurred a few months earlier.)

"That's a legal issue," said the good professor, "and law isn't my field. As a psychologist, I know that Reich was paranoid and unsound. His theories are worthless, and if the books circulate, people will be misled into quackery when they need real psychiatric treatment." Since then Dr. Reich's muscular-energetic therapy has been adapted and used by several schools of modern therapy: some Gestalters, the Rolfers, the Bio-Energetics people, Janov's "Primal Scream" therapists, etc. Dr. Reich's claim that there are psychosomatic factors in many cancers is confirmed by several studies, summarized in Dr. Klopfer's *Psychological Variables in Human Cancer*. Dr. Reich's sexual heresies are accepted by the majority of younger psychologists and the *avant* third of the general population. Dr. Reich's "orgone energy field" around the human body has been photographed by Kyrlian photography. Free schools, based on roughly Reichian principles of self-regulation, are thriving everywhere. Even if a dozen of Reich's other ideas turn out to be wrong or useless, the fact is clear: his basic methodology was correct and can be usefully adopted and/ or adapted by therapists of many schools.

Nonetheless, ignorant bureaucrats in government literally killed Reich; his personality, Dionysian and exuberant as he was, could not survive the torture of the cage, and he died of a heart attack after eight months in prison. The academic community looked on and offered not one single brave gesture in support of scientific freedom. Not one.

I used to lose my temper repeatedly in those days: "This is no way to settle scientific questions—throwing the researcher into jail, burning his books, forbidding further research in that area. This is the Holy Inquisition all over again." Older, wiser, academic gentlemen would seek to calm me: "But, you see, young man, Reich *is* a quack. The whole scientific community agrees that his work is unsound . . ." "The whole scientific community," I would almost scream, "agreed that Semmelweiss was unsound . . ."

"Ah, but that was in the monarchist and tyrannic Austro-Hungarian empire, and the medical societies were afraid of government spies and Roman catholic pressures. Today we have a *free* scientific community and all ideas are tested objectively . . ."

(The "free" scientific community was forbidden, by FDA decree, to experiment with Reich's orgone accumulators. The young heretics who *were* interested in Reich — I knew several of them — could not obtain his books without great difficulty, due to the burning of most of them. Dog-eared copies of *Cancer Biopathy*, for instance, passed from one young heretic to another, like the scrolls of the middle ages. Those who repeated Reich's experiments and obtained positive results were not allowed by academic committees to make these experiments part of their PhD dissertations . . . Ah, freedom! Ah, democracy! Ah, bullshit!)

Of course, it is inevitable that a great innovator shall be misunderstood; but it is *not* inevitable that he should be persecuted. The misunderstanding arises naturally out of the fact that an innovator is, by definition, thinking about the previously unthinkable — it takes a while for others to catch up. This is a fact of neurological evolution. Those who do not understand have a perfect right to demand, "I wish he would explain," or even, after he attempted to comply, "I wish he would explain his explanation" (as Byron said of Wordsworth.)

But persecution of the innovator is not so inevitable; recall, again, Christ, Socrates, Bruno, Galileo, Semmelweiss, Mesmer, Reich. The irrationality and hysteria against such men is just a sudden eruption of that latent neophobic anxiety which always co-exists with neophilliac curiosity in the higher mammals.* A mammalian reflex of pure neophobic panic, without reasoned reflection, is a misuse of the potential richness of the human nervous system—as Leary realizes, and Korzybski and Gurdjieff knew before him.

~•~

* I am assuming here that both neophobia (fear of the new and different) and neophilia (delight and curiosity about the new and different) are necessarily for survival. Pure neophobia leads to stagnation. Pure neophilia leads to reckless adventurism and

contra-survival. Finding the rational balance between these
extremes is the role of the objective intelligence.

~•~

Korzybski, founder of General Semantics, described
such glandular behavior as *"copying animals in our
nervous reactions."* To say that the Timothy Leary we fear
(or love) exists only in our own nervous systems is quite
literally true. Mathematician Eric Temple Bell's warning
that "the map is not the territory" is always pertinent, even
when the "map" is a theory as oft-confirmed as Einstein's
relativity. When the "map" is a newspaper story, the
tendency to identify it with the "territory" is even more
pernicious. The popular images of Timothy Leary, formed
largely of adrenalin-traces and other glandular fear-rage
secretions, relate to the real Leary no more closely than
Mickey Mouse relates to a real rodent or the *yellow*-colored
lemon abstracted by our optic nerve relates to the real fruit
— which is, of course, *blue* (even though we never see it
that way.)

There might be much truth in Korzybski's insistence
that the difference between humans and other terrestrial
animals lies in our ability to become *conscious* of
abstracting — to learn, slowly, after millennia of
neurological evolution, that the yellow lemon we see
is a creation of our optic nerves, that the man we hate
is a projection of some hidden aspect of ourselves, that
the universe we describe scientifically has the structure
of our own logical processes. If this "consciousness of
abstracting" is not *the* difference, between us and our dogs,
it is certainly an important difference.

As long as we continue to *copy the dogs and cats in
our neural behavior* — forming quick abstractions from
our senses, responding with the glandular mechanism

triggered by such an identification—the behaviorists will have no trouble with their thesis that we are no different from dogs and cats. *Only when we use the higher neural centers does a difference emerge and strict behaviorism becomes less convincing.*

Dr. Leary's scientific work, his philosophical and religious speculations, his basic importance in the history of thought, begins from this recognition of neurological hierarchy. His first major contribution to scientific psychology, *The Interpersonal Diagnosis of Personality* (1957) is a study in comparative realities, the power politics of perception and emotion. Its thesis, in colloquial terms, is that "ego" is a social conspiracy for which one person at a time gets blamed.

The grid on the following page shows the basic *gambits* or *transactions* used in interpersonal relating, the complex process by which A and B define themselves to each other.

Look first at the inner circle; all gambits here are rational; they make sense in *some* situations. If we were all rational beings, we would use each of these at various times, depending on the circumstances. This is seldom the way we actually function. Most of us have favored gambits — out near the perimeter — conditioned emotional reactions learned early and established as habits. The ominous fact is that each such habit tends to "draw" an opposite response and thus set in motion a stereotyped interpersonal transaction in which each party tends to form a rather caricatured view of the other.

Behaviors out toward the perimeter of AP (managerial-autocratic) seek responses near the perimeter of HI (self effacing-masochistic), and *vice versa*. This basic up-down (top dog-bottom dog) polarity is based on traditional mammalian dominance-submission rituals and can be observed *equally in a baboon herd or a meeting of corporation executives.*

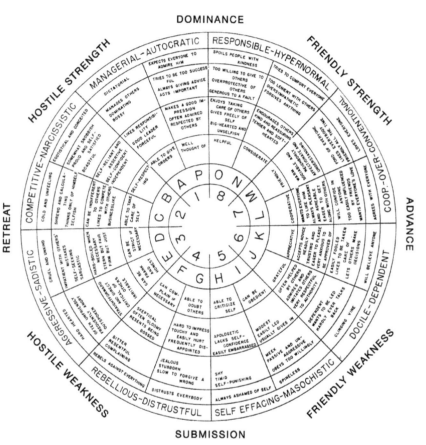

LEARY'S INTERPERSONAL GRID

That is, in either the baboon herd or the meeting of the Board of Directors, one will easily find the *alpha males*, who are dominant, and the others, who are submissive. Among the executives, the gambits will start (and usually remain) in the "reasonable" area near the center of the grid—the number one *alpha* will be "able to give orders," "well thought of," "good leader," "forceful," etc. and the submissive members will be "obedient," "modest," "easily led," etc. Under real conditions of conflict, however—or if the *alpha* is particularly addicted to his games—the primate emotional-glandular circuits soon go into operation. Behavior then moves outward toward the perimeter of the grid. The alphas become "dictatorial," "bossy," "act important," "dominating," etc., while the others correspondingly become "shy," "timid," "spineless," etc. In extreme cases, the mammalian signals appear physically, as the dominant person or group literally swell up, bluster and growl, while the others shrink, cringe and come as close as a tail-less species can to "crawling away with their tails between their legs." In terms of Dr. Leary's current reformulation of these observations in neurogenetic language, all this is "Second Circuit" behavior, using the genetic codes that go back to the first appearance of hierarchy and territoriality among the amphibians and reptiles 500,000,000 years ago.

Similarly, the forward-back polarity (based on the ventral-dorsal asymmetry of the organism) is represented on the grid by the "pushy" aggressive-sadistic DE section, which tends to draw replies from the reciprocal FG section, rebellious-distrustful. (See grid for details.) Again, normal behavior stays near the center of the grid ("frank," "honest," "strict where necessary," "stern but fair" on the one hand and "complain if necessary," "able to doubt others," and "skeptical" on the other); but, under real stress, or with persons addicted to the chemical charges released by the glands in playing these roles, behavior will again move outward on the grid toward the extremes of "cruel and unkind," "sarcastic," "angry," etc. and the reciprocal "rebels against everything," "distrusts everybody," "resentful" etc.

It is fascinating to observe how the *signals* defining the roles are expressed without any conscious thought by the participants.

For instance, consider the following dialogue between Joseph Smith, vice-president, and John Jones, worker.

> JONES: Joe, I think it's time I got another raise.
>
> SMITH: Well, we'd like to give you a raise, Mr. Jones, but . . .

What's wrong? Obviously, the *signals* have been reversed. Jones, the bottom dog, should not say "Joe," but "Mr. Smith;" and Smith, the top dog, should not say "Mr. Jones," but "John." It is by this continuous reinforcement of roles, mostly pre-conscious, that we continue the games of authoritarian society.

Most of the signals are non-verbal and have been studied by the sciences of *kinesics* (body-movement) and *proxemics* (use of body-aura space), two fields especially concerned with Dr. Leary's questions, "Where are the bodies in space-time? What movement events are they making?" To continue the above example, it is "right," "proper," "normal," etc. for Smith, the boss, to *put his arm around Jones's shoulder* as he leads him to the door after the interview. The normal (homosexual-phobic) taboo against males touching each other is suspended here, because this touch signifies mastery via patronage.

It would seem "strange," "eccentric," "bizarre," etc. if Jones initiated the touch and put his arm around Smith's shoulder. (Similarly, a Martian would recognize the "male chauvinism" of our society by noting that men may initiate the touching of women, but women normally may not initiate the touching of men.)

Dr. Leary offers two further illustrations that are worth quoting. First, "HOW A POIGNANT WOMAN PROVOKES A HELPFUL ATTITUDE."

> A patient comes to a psychiatrist for an evaluation interview. She reports a long list of symptoms — insomnia, worry, depression — and a list of unfortunate events—divorce, unsympathetic employer, etc. She cries. Whether her expressions are scored separately and summarized (on the grid) or judged on the overall, we derive a clear picture of a JK approach — "I am weak, unhappy, unlucky, in need of help."

The psychiatrist is virtually forced into the ON program in dealing with this patient, as Dr. Leary goes on. (In fact, many become psychiatrists because they "enjoy" the ON game, it feels "natural" to them, it is their basic program imprinted in infancy-childhood.) This, of course, is no real help at all; the patient will become less miserable but no less "weak"; it is emphatically not a cure. Moving from the center of the grid outward toward the perimeter, the transactions (gambits) between the patient and the therapist are likely to take the form of a double crescendo:

Patient	Psychiatrist

ROUND I
  Grateful-apprecitative   Helpful-considerate

ROUND II

Often helped by others;	Enjoys taking care of patient;
admires and imitates psychiatrist;	gives freely of self;
very respectful to authority;	big-hearted and unselfish;
accepts advise readily;	encourage her;
trusting and eager to please;	kind and reassuring;
very anxious to be approved of	tender and soft-hearted

ROUND III

Dependent; wants to be led;	Too willing to give to patient;
hardy ever talks back;	overprotective of patient;
easily fooled;	generous to a fault;
likes to be taken care of;	too lenient with patient;
lets doctor make decisions	over sympathetic; forgives anything

ROUND IV

| Clinging vine; | Spoils patient with kindness; |
| will believe anything | tries to comfort all the time |

Both are enjoying themselves immensely; each is
playing his/her favorite emotional game. That the patient
is steadily growing even more incompetent to deal with
the outside world is easily forgotten. This two-person
Victim-Rescuer game (widely discussed in works of
Transactional Analysts) has such enduring charm, in fact,
that even therapists most aware of its dangers and its
counter-therapeutic results can hardly avoid being drawn
into it part of the time, with some patients. (Indeed, part of
the time it is necessary, as a stage *preliminary* to therapy.)
This emotional up-down relationship is discussed further
in the present book, under the headings of the Sly Priestess
and the Hierophant.

Dr. Leary's second illustration is "HOW THE PENITENTIARY TRAINS THE PRISONER FOR CRIMINAL AGGRESSION."

> In prison psychiatry . . . it is virtually impossible for the doctor as well as for the patient to shake off the institution's implicit punitive contempt for the inmate. The penitentiary administration tells the prisoner, by the prison architecture, the structure of the guard-inmate relationship, and by every nonverbal cue possible that he is a dangerous, evil, untrustworthy outcast. The prisoner often responds to this interpersonal pressure by accepting the role he is being trained for. That is, BCD pulls EFG . . . Thus . . . the recidivist criminal is least anxious when he is in passive rebellion against a strong punitive authority which feeds him and beats him.

This is the epitome of the authority-and-submission game (sadomasochism) which underlies patriarchal civilization. It is, in fact, the most monotonous of the "static imprinted and conditioned neural circuits" which make up what we call the normal mind. In Eric Berne's terminology, it is the critical Parent-Adapted Child game.

A third illustrative example worth mentioning is buried in so much mathematical field-theory that I simplify, and paraphrase: Child A is playing with a wagon. Child B enters the playground, seizes the wagon, throws dirt on Child A, and runs off. Child A cries. At this point, Child C, who has watched from a distance, approaches the victimized Child A and hugs him consolingly. *Child A pushes Child C away and cries louder.* (Remember?) Child C now throws more dirt on Child A and runs off to play with Child B. BCD "pulls" EFG and EPG, reiterated, "pulls" more BCD. In other words, Child B is learning to play the born-to-lose game and training others to play it with him.

Dr. Leary now regards all these conditioned-imprinted circuits as "larval." Webster provides us with the definition: "LARVA, the immature, wingless, and often vermiform feeding form that hatches from the egg of many insects, alters chiefly in size while passing through several molts and is finally transformed into a pupa or chrysalis from which the adult emerges and flies away. 2. The early form of any animal that at birth or hatching is fundamentally unlike its parent and must metamorphose before assuming the adult characteristics."

Earth-society and earth-neurology is larval, Dr. Leary believes; we are at the embryonic stage of development. The first four circuits of neurological signal-reception and Gestalt-formation which have evolved here in the 3 1/5 billion years since DNA was seeded onto earth are merely our womb-life. When we are "born" — ejected from the earth-womb into the galaxy — we will begin operating on four higher circuits, which have thus far only appeared in chance mutants, trained yogins and shamans, drug trippers or exceptionally advanced scientists and philosophers. It is the larval, embryonic nature of earth-life that explains the crudity and primitive nature of the first four circuits and the monotonous, mechanical games analyzed on the interpersonal Grid.

"The spirit is willing," says the Bible, "but the flesh is weak." In Leary's terminology, "spirit" is represented by the occasional *futique* visions of higher-circuit functioning which appear to all of us occasionally—the perpetual archetype of Heaven and Utopia glimpsed by all men and women, at least in fantasy; the "flesh" is the conditioned and imprinted games of our daily robot-life. The mechanistic nature of these games, furthermore, is such that *the most irrational party dominates most often.*

Alfred Adler, of course, had anticipated Leary in noting how many subtle ways the allegedly weak dominate the allegedly strong, but Leary's perspective is wider and more ominous. This can best be grasped by centering in on the inner circle of the grid. It will readily be seen that *all* gambits here are appropriate in some circumstances — the ideally sane man or woman should be flexible enough to give orders *and* obey orders, take care of himself *and* cooperate with others, doubt others *and* doubt himself, etc., depending on rational feedback from the environment, i.e. what is objectively happening. Few of us retain this flexibility for long after birth. Family gambits and favored rituals soon train us to restrict our gambits to one segment and move out toward the "extreme" perimeter position, instead of being able to give orders under appropriate circumstances we become compulsively addicted to giving orders in all places and at all times. Or we lose the capacity to give orders entirely, and become the meek, passive, spineless person who can't act at all unless someone else is present to tell us what to do. Or we can get equally enmeshed in some other inflexible gambit out near the perimeter of the grid, such as the compulsively cruel, unkind, sarcastic game or the unrelentingly suspicious, distrustful, complaining game. In any of these cases, we have lost our rational capacity to adjust to the situation and have correspondingly become more "neurotic," i.e., more irrational. But this makes us more powerful, not less powerful. (Those who retain flexibility and rationality try one gambit after another in dealing with such a compulsive, and eventually find the one gambit that is reciprocal to his game — submission to the authoritarian, counter-suspicion and hostility to the paranoia, masochism to the sadist, etc. Thus the less reasonable party eventually dominates, if the situation lasts long enough. (Fortunately, we can often walk away and avoid getting conned into such games. When the compulsive game-player is a boss, a spouse, or a parent, however, quite often *we*, instead of they, will land in psychiatric care.)

It can readily be seen that Dr. Leary had a bright and successful future ahead of him after completing the systematic exposition of the interpersonal grid in 1957. A method of scoring a person's transactions on four levels — thereby finding an average interpersonal profile after all four are placed on the grid — provides for one of the most general-purpose diagnostic tools in the history of psychotherapy; and the therapeutic applications are clearly spelled out in the text. If Dr. Leary had stopped his intellectual development at this point, and spent the next 17 years popularizing his work, he would be today the well-esteemed founder of another "school" of psychology, like Dr. Berne's Transactional Analysis, Dr. Janov's Primal Therapy, etc. This is not the path of the innovator. Dr. Leary (and in this he is much like Dr. Wilhelm Reich, who eventually landed in prison for much the same reasons) has seldom stopped to work out all the implications of his discoveries, popularize them, consolidate his position, etc. Instead, he rushes on to new discoveries and formulations, leaving it to dedicated students to follow along on his trail, trying to explain each new creative leap to a confused and increasingly skeptical scientific community and a growingly alarmed general public.

Thus, having given a memorably precise, operational, specific analysis of the neurological traps in which humanity currently imprisons itself, Dr. Leary plunged onward to seek methods of escape. His next period of research dealt with the chemical foundation of the compulsive patterns observed in the *Interpersonal Diagnosis of Personality.*

Meanwhile, the Leary Interpersonal Diagnostic Test — known as "the Leary" for short — gradually came into wider and wider use as the sixties passed. It is ironic to note that, while the decade slipped by (and more and more politicians captured the hearts and votes of the ignorant masses by denouncing the Mad Doctor Leary) the diagnostic system bearing his name crept into more and more clinics, testing bureaus, university admission exams, hospitals, etc. (Simultaneously, his "team" model for therapy was more frequently copied, and the old psychologist-patient dichotomy more often softened . . .) By 1970, when Dr. Leary was sentenced to 30 years in the cages of the California Archipelago—the world's third largest prison system; only Russia and China have more human beings in this form of sensory-sexual-deprivation torture — the final irony appeared. The Leary was used by the California penal authorities in classifying convicts; Dr. Leary had the unique distinction of being given his own test. He carefully answered so as to appear a docile personality and was shipped to a minimum security prison, where escape was comparatively easy . . .

But that is jumping ahead again. By the time I met Timothy in 1964 he had spent 4 years researching the possibility "that organic neuro-chemicals could be used as instruments for studying the nervous system, for freeing brain from the limits of mind, for training human beings to develop new neural circuits for reception and transmission." His conclusions are summarized in "How To Change Behavior" (1963), in which ordinary consciousness is defined as *strategic*, manipulating games on the Interpersonal Grid. Using Eric Berne's "Alcoholism" game as illustration, we can summarize Leary's 7-dimensional game model thus:

1 - *Roles*. (In the alcoholism game, these consist of alcoholic Victim, moralistic Persecutor, and tolerant Rescuer.)*

2 - *Rules*. (These are always tacit, but nonetheless clear-cut. The Rescuer may drop out of the game if they are violated. E.g. the Victim must repeatedly confess "guilt.")

3 - *Strategies*. (E.g. if the habitual Persecutor and Rescuer are not available, the Victim will draft two substitute players.)

4 - *Goals*. (Chiefly, escape from the other games of authoritarian society, with built-in masochistic punishment for each escape.)

5 - *Language and values*. (The metaphysical theory implied in the language used, i.e. the pretense that the Victim is "ill." Dr. Thomas Szasz's *Myth of Mental illness* contains a detailed analysis of how the myth of "illness" in modern psychiatry allows and encourages these compulsive game-players to continue their imprinted-conditioned larval behavior and avoid growing up.)

6 - *Characteristic space-time locations*. (The alcoholic knows where to assemble with other victims and program the binge.)

7 - *Characteristic space-time movements*.

~•~

* The terms used here—Victim, Persecutor, Rescuer—are from Dr. Berne's *Games People Play* (1963.) The basic structural analysis goes back to Dr. Leary's *Interpersonal Diagnosis of Personality* (1957), in which the alcoholism game of a corporation executive was analyzed as part of a three person transaction involving the alcoholic executive (Victim), the Comptroller of the corporation who wanted to fire him (Persecutor) and another executive who kept trying to "reform" him. (Rescuer.)

Leary's analysis of how such games involve varying rewards for each "player" is echoed most clearly in Berne's works, but has been picked up also by increasing numbers of psychologists of all schools.

~•~

It is both amusing and depressing to become conscious of the extent to which most human behavior is structured by this seven-dimensional game grid. There only seem to be four groups who ever transcend the game-level of behavior; and all four are, quite naturally, regarded with either horror or reverence (or both horror *and* reverence.) They are:

1 - Epileptics. (Dostoyevsky, Julius Caesar, St. Paul, Mohammed, etc. have given eloquent testimony to the trans-game consciousness at the onset of the epileptic spasm.)

2 - Shamans and yogis; technicians of the occult.

3 - Some (not all) so-called schizophrenics.

4 - Adepts (as distinguished from mere users or abusers) of the drugs Dr. John Lilly calls metaprogramming substances. These drugs, in turn, are either regarded as sacred or diabolical or both, e.g. peyote (used by the 500,000 American Indians of the Native American Church), the magic mushroom of Mexico (psilocybae mexicana), the magic mushroom of Asia (amanita muscaria), Indian Hemp or marijuana (used by tantric yogis, voodooists, Brazilian magick societies, etc.) and LSD.

Since epilepsy and schizophrenia have definite drawbacks, it should be obvious why Dr. Leary centered his research into nongame consciousness on, first the "sacred" chemicals and then on yoga and shamanism.

It must be reiterated that almost all humans are imprinted and conditioned to monotonous-mechanical repetition of only a few simple games out near the perimeter of the Interpersonal Grid. As Eric Berne points out, we generally know our favorite game well enough to begin playing it within a half-hour of arriving in a new city. A Los Angeles man landing in New York with a desire to have homosexual intercourse and then get beaten unconscious and robbed by his partner will find the characteristic space-time locations and set the game in operation much quicker than an outsider would think possible. The same is true if the game calls for heterosexual intercourse and subsequent robbery. It is also true, but seems less paradoxical, if the game calls for intercourse, hetero or homo, without subsequent punishment.

The Interpersonal Grid was based entirely on empirical observations, by Leary and his co-workers at the Kaiser Foundation Hospital in San Francisco in the mid-50s, on what interpersonal transactions were actually performed by the bodies of neurotic patients in space-time. It completely ignores and transcends the pseudo-diagnostic language popular in psychiatry and among those psychologists who naively imitate the "illness" model which psychiatrists have illegitimately transferred from the medical sciences to the behavioral sciences.

It is amusing to note that all the perimeter positions on the grid are recognized in folk-wisdom and have vernacular labels. Working clock-wise around the circle, we find that AP is known as "the Big Wheel," "the Big Shot" or, more sarcastically, "the Big Shit." ON is "Mr. Nice Guy" or "Mom." LM is "the Mark" or "the Savage" to confidence-trickers, the "nebbish" in Yiddish. JK is "the Fuck-up," "the Dumb Dora," "the cry-baby." HI is the "injustice collector," the "Mama's boy." FG is "born to lose," "Born to raise hell" (some of these types tattoo such mottoes on their arms) or "the trouble-maker." ED is "the son-of-a-bitch on wheels," "the operator," "the exploiter." CB, finally, is the "mean motherfucker," "the dirty louse," the executive whose employees have the highest illness and absentee record in the corporation.

Most humans are, quite simply, addicted to the chemical kicks involved in the glandular processes that set one of these games in motion. Few, however, play the same game at all times. Rather, the average person has two, three or four favorite games and switches around between them as the environment provides opportunities. (Many an HI submissive-masochist at the office can become a CB great dictator with his wife or children — as illustrated in James Joyce's unforgettable short story, "Counterparts.")

When you meet somebody who is not playing a role on the Interpersonal Grid, you have met what Leary calls a "post-larval human." These are still comparatively rare and are seldom to be found in pyramidal structures such as corporations, bureaucracies or armies; they are usually professionals, free-lancers or drop-outs. The organized matrix of society is dominated by compulsive repetition of the robot-games of the Interpersonal Grid which is why all progress is slow, painful and often violent. This is why the innovator is so often hated with a passion that borders on insanity.

Charles Slack, in his *Timothy Leary, the Madness of the Sixties and Me*, is a perfect example of such blind hatred. The book, dedicated to destroying Dr. Leary's reputation forever, might be expected to contain some remarks on the Interpersonal Grid, explaining that it is not really as important or as novel as it looks. Such polemic is normal, if somewhat dishonest, practice in attacking controversial scientists such as Dr. Leary. Slack, however, goes further. *He doesn't mention the Interpersonal Grid at all.* Nor does he mention Leary's seven-dimensional game model, his pioneering 1940s work on race relations, his definition of the three conditioned and four unconditioned modes of consciousness, *or any of his scientific work.* Like a commissar in *1984*, Slack disposes of Leary's scientific credentials in the most direct way: he sends the records down the "memory chute" to the incinerator.

Slack actually writes, *apropos* of Leary's background: "Leary *spent the war in a Pennsylvania hospital* and by 1950 had *acquired his professional meal-tickets* for American psychology: a Master of Science degree from Washington State University and a Doctorate in Philosophy from the University of California at Berkeley." (Italics added.) Sure *sounds* like Leary was doing something underhanded, doesn't it? Without the slanting and Slack's peculiar hate-obsession, what the sentences say is that Dr. Leary worked in a hospital and then earned an M.S. and a PhD.

But we cannot understand the hate that seeks to destroy Dr. Leary until we understand the full, extraterrestrial meaning of his research and his theorizing.

Chapter Four

Beyond the Conditioned Reflex

When a blind man who has never touched water
suddenly falls into a pool, he knows that something
has happened to him.
— Jalāl ad-Dīn Muhammad Rūmī, 13th Century Sufi

Buddha says that we are all sleepwalkers. Gurdjieff
says we're wandering around in a kind of hypnoidal trance.
Thomas Vaughan, the witty 17th Century alchemist, says
that nobody has ever *seen* the earth, i.e. we only see our
own projected hallucinations. Jesus says, in the apocryphal
Gospel of Thomas, that human beings seem to be drunk
and incoherent. All mystics, whatever their language,
agree that we need to *wake up*. In the initial stage of this
awakening, however, we find ourselves, like the blind man
in Rumi's metaphor, aware only of one fact: something new
is happening.

In Leary's terminology, what is happening is that we
are *turning on* and *tuning in*: turning on new circuits in our
nervous system, tuning in to the new signals now available.

The Gestalts (patterns) integrated from previous signals are breaking down; we are forming new Gestalts, new patterns of signal-reception, creating a new "map" of the universe.

Dr. Leary's current writings define 24 possible modes of neurological functioning: 24 ways of integrating signals and constructing Gestalts (maps) out of these signals.

The early, larval modes are all controlled entirely by the reward-punishment matrix of authoritarian society. Behavior on these levels is as robotic as the most hard-nosed behaviorist of the Pavlov-Skinner philosophy claims. There is no "free will," no "human dignity," no real "individualism" anywhere on these primitive levels. As the witty Sufis and their great Occidental spokesman, Gurdjieff have insisted (long before the behaviorists imagined they made this discovery) "normal" human functioning historically has been characterized by the *delusion of freedom* and the reality of total enslavement.

Bergson's claim that all humor is based on sudden "revelation" of the hidden robotism in human behavior may be a bit exaggerated, but *most* humor does contain this element. Sexual humor, in particular, revolves around the chemical-mechanical facts usually hidden by our conditioned social hypocrisy. ("Is that a gun in your pocket," Mae West asks, "or are you just glad to see me?") Bernard Shaw is a great comic artist, and not just another socialist-propagandist, because his wit exposes the mechanisms of all his characters, including his own spokesmen—as when professor Higgins's stumbling pratfall in *Pygmalion* abruptly exposes the emotional-sexual involvement he has been hiding under a cloak of intellectual-scientific detachment.

I once knew a young lady who actually had five abortions during the 1960s — when contraception was easily available to persons of her educational-economic level, and abortion was still illegal and extremely dangerous. Any suggestion that she was a robot would, of course, be rejected by her with great indignation. Eric Berne would say she was playing the Red Riding Hood game; on the Interpersonal Grid she was compulsively addicted to the perimeter positions of HIJ.

Everybody knows why Dagwood Bumstead is always late for work; the partial revelation of ordinary humor allows us to laugh at his desperate last-minute dash for the bus he always misses. A full revelation of his robotic plight—that of the ordinary adjusted citizen—would turn the comic strip into tragedy. The "inevitability" of tragedy, like that of comedy, is only acceptable in an artistic ("imaginary") context. When yogins, Sufis or behaviorists tell us the same inevitability inflicts itself on our real life, we abandon them and go elsewhere for more comforting teachers.

William S. Burroughs often says his novels are studies in "the algebra of need." I once asked him to define that algebra.

"Very simple," he said. "Give a junkie a key to the backdoor of a pharmacy, and you can predict with 100% scientific accuracy what will happen next." The same accuracy is possible with those who are addicted to money, status, power, being victims, sarcasm, rebellion, or any of the perimeter positions on the Interpersonal Grid. The neuron, Dr. Leary says in one of his most memorable aphorisms, "is a junkie sultan." It demands exactly the glandular release of these psycho-chemicals which give it the "kicks" it has been imprinted and conditioned to need.

Paul Reps' *Zen Flesh, Zen Bones* tells the story of a 19th Century Zen monk who lived as a hermit in a small hut outside Hiroshima. A young girl in the town, being pregnant, was pressured by her parents to name the seducer and said it was the monk. After the birth, the indignant parents of the girl took the child out to the hut, handed it to the monk and said, "This is yours. *You* raise it."

"Is that so?" said he.

Six years later — after the monk had patiently fathered and mothered the child for that period, with all the hassles of changing diapers at night, having it cry during his meditations, caring for it in illnesses, etc.—the girl, being remorseful, confessed that the real father was a young fisherman. The parents, full of guilt, went out to the monk's hut, confessed their error, and took the child to raise as their own.

"Is that so?" said the monk, as they left.

The "inscrutability" and strange humor of this (and many other zen stories) rests upon *absence* of the usual *robot reflexes*. The monk did not indignantly deny fatherhood, did not complain "I can't raise a child; I have my meditations to do," etc. in the first instance. Again, in the climax, he did not weep and holler, "you can't take it! I raised it, I love it, it's mine!" etc. He was operating on a different set of neural circuits, above the usual conditioned reflexes.

Dr. Leary's scientific studies of LSD, psilocybin and similar metaprogramming drugs are all concerned with the transition from conditioned-reflex behavior to unconditioned higher-circuit behavior. His basic experimental claim that such neuro-chemicals *do* open the nervous system to unconditioned "free" states was, in fact, anticipated by the Czech psychiatrist, Dr. Jiri Roubichek, who had concluded (*Artificial Psychoses*, 1957) that "LSD inhibits conditioned reflexes." During this period of inhibition of the usual robot-mechanisms, Leary and several other investigators found (before this research was stopped by law), it is possible to *turn on* and *tune in* the nervous system to later, evolutionarily-more-advanced, less animalistic circuits.

The most important of Leary's drug studies was undertaken in cooperation with the Massachusetts Department of Corrections and used psilocybin to metaprogram the compulsive games of various convicts soon due for parole. This study showed that convicts who had been in Dr. Leary's metaprogramming sessions were *twice as likely* to remain free after release as were the control group. That is, one year later, 80 per cent of Leary's group were still outside, not convicted of any new crimes, whereas the control group, like the national average for released convicts, showed only 40 per cent still outside. This was remarkable in a field where attempts to change behavior have been traditionally bootless. The bodies of Leary's cons, in space-time, were mostly *outside* prison; the bodies of others released at the same time, were mostly back *inside*.

Here, of course, the first misunderstanding arises. Opponents of metaprogramming drugs (psychedelics) and exponents of such drugs have *both* written as if Aristotle's either/or logic were still the standard scientific methodology. The opponents insist that Dr. Leary's personal skills as therapist made all the difference to the convicts, and the chemical neural-programmer was irrelevant. The enthusiasts write as if the chemical is magical all by itself. The actual process of metaprogramming (forming new neural circuits, new minds) seems to be something like this:

$$B_n = B_0 + P_n + MS$$

where B_n is the new behavior elicited, B_o is the old behavior extinguished, P_n is the new program applied during the sessions (Leary's own existentialist-transactional therapy, in this case; but P_n can equally be other kinds of psychotherapy, instruction, hypno-tapes, artistic experience, "submersion" learning programs, mystic suggestion, etc.) and MS is the metaprogramming substance (psilocybin, in this case; LSD, hashish, DMT and various others have also been researched.) The "correct theory" of which Dr. Leary spoke above is the knowledge of which P_n is appropriate for which behavior changes.

Dr. Leary expressed the equation this way in the early 60s: the result of such "unpredictable" drugs can be predicted from the formula, result = dosage + set + setting. Dosage is our MS, setting the new program, P_n and set of the subject is chiefly his old behavior, B_o.

Dr. Leary's method with the convicts had used psilocybin as the MS (metaprogramming substance) and existential-transactional therapy as the P_n (new program.) Psilocybin is the active alkaloid in the magic mushroom scientifically called *psilocybae mexicana*, which Mexican Indians have called *tecnactl* (God's flesh) for over 3000 years. Existential-transaction therapy is Dr. Leary's own creation, a blend of Rollo May's existentialist version of Freudian-Jungian analysis with Leary's own transactional schemata of games (where are the bodies in space-time? What are they actually doing?). Leary generally defined himself as the "coach," and the convicts as men at bat; his role was to feedback information to them about what behaviors seemed to prevent them from batting home runs (happy, loving relations) and what behaviors led to strikes or fouls (bitterness or violence). But everybody took turns at being coach, as well as batter, and the

The Starseed Signals

convicts were encouraged to coach Leary on what mistakes he made while at bat. This terminology was not mere cuteness; "Baseball has a language," Leary told me emphatically in 1964, "which describes behavior exactly and rates it mathematically. It is the perfect model for behavior-analysis. As physicists would say, every term is operationally defined: you know what movements in space-time you are talking about. The language of psychology at this point is, by comparison, metaphysical and pre-scientific.

"Besides," he added, "baseball language is mathematical and therefore free of good-evil dualisms. A good batter is not defined as perfect — we don't expect him to bat 1.000, and if he even reaches .400, he's regarded as a superman and goes into the Hall of Fame. Most people expect to bat 1.000 in the father game, the mother game, the worker game, and all other games, and feel like total failures and 'sinners' if they drop as low as, say, .700. The baseball language helps bring them out of that metaphysical framework and back to reality."

As theologian Walter Huston Clark mentions in his book *Chemical Ecstasy* (which contains an excellent summary of Dr. Leary's convict-rehabilitation work, including many interesting "religious" experiences of the caged men), one of the cons produced a most amusing (and prophetic) poster when the program was stopped due to hysterical anti-Leary publicity in the press. The poster showed Leary grinning and said

WARNING
THIS MAN IS ARMED WITH COMPASSION
AND IS A DANGER TO THE STATE

The Commonwealth of Massachusetts
Department of Correction
Massachusetts Correctional Institution, Concord

West Concord, Mass.

February 16, 1962

Mr. Edward Flynn
Community Service Branch
M.I.M.H.
Bethesda, Maryland

Dear Sir:

  We are most pleased to endorse the Program here at the Institution sponsored by Doctor Timothy Leary of the Harvard Faculty.

  We are naturally interested in any rehabilitative effort, but are impressed with this approach, bringing as it does, a fresh outlook and a new technique to a Program, which to date, presages, at least in some instances, most beneficial results. Wisely, no claims that this endeavor will revolutionize the treatment techniques of social failures or misfits, but rather a quiet professional approach embodying personality and character evaluations and re-evaluations coupled with controls, has been the choice of approach and the results hopefully will establish solidly any claims to follow.

  It is the desire of this Administration to cooperate with Doctor Leary to the fullest and it is our hope that his experiment may continue and eventually make a major contribution to the behavioral sciences.

        Very truly yours

        Superintendent

ESG/ma

Letter commending Dr. Leary's work in convict rehabilitation using the psychedelic drug, psilocybin and transactional-existential therapy.

As mentioned above, the synergetic (non-addictive) combination between the P_n of transactional-existentialist therapy and the MS (psilocybin) has not been widely understood. The most widespread misunderstanding—for which Dr. Leary has been blamed by the press, ironically, even though he has always sought to correct this error—has been to ignore P_n entirely. A few million enthusiastic self-experimenters, many of them not really young or hippie-oriented, ingested psychedelics during the 1960s, without a new program, and hedonistically tripped through inner space with an accidental P_n arbitrarily "chosen" by the environment, i.e. by sheer chance.

It can be safely said that the results of accidental P_n were subjectively very diverse, varying from ecstatic or occult new mentations to terrors and anxieties, but the new behavior was not uniformly impressive. Others who observed this failure of new behavior to appear (or who were culturally hostile to such new behavior as did manifest itself) thereupon proclaimed that psychedelics were just another kind of intoxicant and did not change behavior at all (or changed it for the worse).

If one had a dime for every time Dr. Leary spoke of "dosage, set and setting" during those years, one would be rich now, but the message did not get across to many, either among his admirers or his critics. Both groups are still arguing about the drug substance itself, with little reference to the set and setting parameters.

Meanwhile, another perplexity had arisen — another excellent chance for misunderstanding. It so happens that the metaprogramming drugs open the nervous system to various potentialities not previously recognized by orthodox Western science. These include kinds of consciousness or awareness long recognized by yogis,

Tantrists, Sufis, shamans, witches, magicians, etc. and usually described pejoratively as "hallucinations" by those committed to what they imagine is a materialistic orientation. (Actually, this is a dogmatic allegiance to one theory about matter.) When Dr. Leary began to speak of these alternative levels of consciousness as positive, or possessing positive values, it seemed to many that he had lost his scientific skepticism and could no longer distinguish "reality" from "hallucination."

Of course, Dr. Carl Jung (among others) had made the same claim earlier; but Jungian psychology has never been popular in American academia. The assumption that statistically normal consciousness is the only valid consciousness is deeply ingrained here, and held with a fanaticism that would be obviously absurd were it fully conscious; in fact, only the tacit and unconscious nature of this normal=average=OK equation prevents it from being recognized as the highly intolerant dogma it is.

For perspective, let us look back at the definition of the seven components of a game, and employ an anthropological rather than a "psychological" example this time. The normal way of settling disputes among the anarchistic (Stateless) Eskimos is the *dromesang*. In this social game, the two disputants have the role of satirical singers. The *rules* are that they take turns singing against each other, each waits politely until the other finishes singing his own verses, etc. The *rituals* involve smoking, blowing smoke angrily, etc. The *goal* is to win the verdict of the community. The *language* is restricted to verse and humor. The *characteristic space-time location* is the camp-fire. The *characteristic movements* are specified: each contestant crouches, rather than sitting or standing, etc. To the Eskimo this is the "normal" "natural" way to settle a dispute. We have an equally complicated and arbitrary game in our culture; it is known as *trial by jury*.

That kind of consciousness which is restricted to playing the local games for whatever rewards the local society offers is "normal" or "natural" consciousness in that place and time. *Since it is not "normal" or "natural" elsewhere, the first conclusion of every traveler is that "foreigners are all crazy," i.e. not "normal" and "natural."* This web of culture, as anthropologists call it, is described as "game consciousness" or "symbolic consciousness" by Dr. Leary. It is consciousness defined and limited by the local roles, rules, rituals, goals, language, characteristic space-time locations, and characteristic space-time movements. It makes an American feel ashamed if he is dispossessed from his apartment for inability to pay the rent; a Japanese samurai of classic times ashamed if his "Lord" performs a dishonorable act (18 Samurai once committed suicide over such a non-personal disgrace); a Hindu proud if he was born into a certain caste; an Englishman proud if he rises into a caste that he was *not* born into, and so forth. How well we play the local games, and which games we particularly enjoy playing, defines our position on the interpersonal transaction grid.

The kinds of consciousness that do not relate to game-playing are, then, outside the area of Freud's *Realprinzip* (reality-principle). The either-or logic of Freudian psychology then is forced to place them under the rubric of the *Lustprinzip* (pleasure-principle.) This either-or underlies the uncritical inference that these altered states of awareness must be "hallucinatory," or at least unimportant.

It has been the ninety-year labor of parapsychology to prove that these altered states of consciousness are *not* hallucinatory; that they lead to what the mystics call *siddhis* (powers) such as ESP, PK, clairvoyance, etc. As Arthur Koestler notes sardonically in *The Roots of Coincidence*, to reject the data of parapsychology at this point is to assert a conspiracy of deception by thousands of researchers, on all five inhabited continents, over nearly a hundred years. To all but the most dogmatic, it is easier to accept the data.

Similarly, research on metaprogramming substances by Dr. Leary and others, seems to force us to accept the second claim of the mystics, namely that these altered states of consciousness lead to wisdom, or deeper perception, or Enlightenment, or illumination, or something fit to be categorized by such enthusiastic labels. Again, the explanation of "hallucination" does not seem to fit the data. Playing the local games is not the only function of the human nervous system. *It seems to have a larger function, transcending this tribe and this time, relating to evolution on a cosmic scale.*

But what *are* these altered states of consciousness, outside the usual social games? Dr. Leary's first attempt to categorize them is in a long paper called "The Seven Tongues of God" (1968; earlier drafts 1964, 1965.) Here the hypothesis is that there are six such levels, in addition to "normal" socially-conditioned game-consciousness. While this model is not perfect by any means—and was extensively revised later—it is necessary to look at it briefly. We will have some orientation, then, about where we are going in this exploration of the nervous system. In fact, we are imperceptibly sliding *from the this-worldly to the other-worldly, from the terrestrial to the extraterrestrial.*

Remember: the first job of the DNA after seeding on a wombplanet, according to Leary, is *survival*. The robot-reflexes we have been studying are all quite adequate on some levels, quite inadequate and misery-producing on other levels, but they are all part of the primary survival-program.

The freeze-reflex of the rabbit, for instance, is quite adequate in most situations in the forests where the rabbit normally lives. Once frozen into immobility, the rabbit is fairly invisible to most predators; the freeze is thus an evolutionary "relative-success." It only becomes regressive and anti-survival when humans appear, lay down asphalt highways, and run automobiles. The rabbit who freezes in the path of a speeding car dies. The larval reflexes are no longer adequate.

The higher circuits come into play, Dr. Leary thinks, when a species has evolved far enough to develop a nervous system capable of multi-channel tuning. The alternate channels of alternate consciousness-states are given in the table:

See the next page

TABLE 1: The seven levels of energy consciousness, the drugs which induce them and the sciences and religions which study each level.

Level of Energy Conscious- ness	Drect- ing Intelli- gence Com- muni- cations Center	Com- muni- cations Struc- ture	Science	Drug to produce this level	Religio- on cen- tering on this level	Reli- gious meta- phor	Art using this level of energy	Sacramen- tal method
1. Atomic	Nucleus of atom	Electron	Physics Astro - physics	LSD* STP	Bud- dhism	White Light	Psyche- delic light, electron- ic music	Until psy- chedelics, sponta- neous
2. Cellular	DNA	RNA	Biology, Bio- chemis- try	Peyote, Psilo- cybin, Yage	Hindu- ism	Reincar- nation	Hindu art	Prolonged fasting
3. Somatic	Auto- nomic nerve plexes	Organs of body	Physiol- ogy	MDA Hashish	Tantra	Chkras Kund- alini	Bosch	Sensory depriva- tion
4. Sensory	Brain	Sense organs	Neurol- ogy	Mari- juana	Zen, Sufism, warly Chris- tianity, Hasidic	Satori	Sensory art	Incense Dance Music Chanting, etc.
5. Mental - Social	Mind imprint plus condi- tioning	Social behav- ior	Psychol- ogy	Pep pills	Judaism Protes- tantism	Christ Messiah	Repro- ductive art	Sermons
6. Emotion- al stupor	Endo- crine centers	Emo- tional behav- ior	Psychia- try	Alcohol	Cathol- icism Funda- mental- ism	Devil	Propa- ganda	Super- stitious ritual
7. Void			Anes- thesiol- ogy	Nar- cotics Poisons	Death cults	Black Void		Suicide Ritual murder

*While many drugs induce awareness at more than one level (for example hashish turns on at levels 4 & 5), only LSD can move consciousness to all seven levels (often at the same instant).

Level 7, coma or the void, is characteristic of traumatic accident, sleep, or heavy use of such narcotics as opium and heroin. Most of the nervous system is turned off or inactive; the person is *totally* "unconscious" or "semi-conscious." We need to go back down to this level at least once a day, in sleep; under acute shock or stress, we go there at once, as in fainting.

Level 6, emotional stupor, is characteristic of rage-fear tantrums, emotionalized religious revivals, heavy alcohol use, etc. The higher nervous system is mostly turned off, but the glandular circuits are ready to release any and all of the mammalian territorial or hierarchical (pecking-order) signals. (It is amusing to consider the revival meeting from this perspective. The preacher possessed by his "god" is the alpha male doing a baboon domination-ritual; everybody else is cowed into a crawling, or kneeling, submission-ritual.)

Level 5 is normal emotionalized-conditioned game consciousness, which takes thousands of different forms in the thousands of tribes studied by anthropology, but is everywhere mis-defined as "reality."

Level 4 is sensory awareness. Here the end-organs are particularly excited and attention flows from the usual cortical game-strategy computer into sheer sensual joy in being aware and alive. Zen and Sufi training are chiefly concerned with turning on this level of neural awareness; it can also be accomplished quite easily (but temporarily) by smoking marijuana or hashish. The proper sort of re-imprinting during the hashish-high can make the sensory awareness increasingly permanent; this is an old secret of the Tantric Hindus and the famous Ismaeli sect of Sufism. (See my *Sex and Drugs; A Journey Beyond Limits*, for details about this "sex-magick," as it is called.)

An example of sensory consciousness can be found in jazz musician Mezz Mezzrow's *Really the Blues*, in which he tells of a fire in a building where he and some friends were smoking the weed. While everybody else fled, the pot-heads calmly discussed the beauty of the spectacle, the humorous rush of the non-stoned people, and the details of when they should make their own exit. (They did get out alive . . .)

Level 3, somatic awareness, moves attention into the autonomic nervous system and their feedback loops in the organism-as-a-whole. Many forms of Hindu and Sufi exercise, involving the movement of the "kundalini" (sex-energy) out of the genitals into other organs (so-called "chakras") key off this level; MDA and hashish are also likely to perform this "resurrection of the body," especially if combined with the yogic kundalini programs.

(Many of the "mysteries" and "enigmas" of mysticism become clear when one opens this circuit of awareness. In one famous Zen story, the monk is meditating when the *roshi* — teacher — enters the room. The *roshi* demands, as a test, "What is, is what?" The monk raised his fist silently. "Boat won't move in shallow water," says the *roshi* contemptuously and leaves. The next day, he enters the room again during the monk's meditation and repeats, "What is, is what?" The monk raises the same fist, again in silence. "I apologize," says the roshi, "I see I was wrong yesterday." This only *appears inscrutable* if we try to compute it on the level 5 game-strategy circuit. On level 3 body-consciousness—awareness of one's own bio-energy and that of others—the communication-failure and subsequent communication-success are quite clear.)

Level 2, cellular consciousness, moves our attention to the DNA itself. This extraordinary claim — which may be Dr. Leary's most important hallucination or discovery — is discussed *passim* throughout the rest of this book. Let us note here that such a neural-molecular circuit, if it exists, *explains the kind of memory used to prove "reincarnation," Jung's "racial or collective unconscious," the Hindu "Atman" or world-soul, the "Holy Guardian Angel" of Sufic and Cabalistic magic,* etc. It seems that only the most masochistic schools of yoga (prolonged fasting or self-torture), the most sensual schools of Tantra (sexual yoga) or the powerful drugs peyote and psilocybin, can move consciousness this far from the usual game-awareness.

Level 1, atomic consciousness, finally, moves awareness down the chemical ladder to the "inorganic" (so-called) and creates those enthusiastic verbalizations about "the White Light," "the stage beyond life and death," etc. characteristic of mystics who have followed a particular path for many years and achieved total mastery of all the other levels of awareness. LSD, notoriously, places one on the atomic level without such previous discipline, although briefly.

This theory rests on Dr. Leary's assumption-definition, *"Consciousness is energy received and decoded by a structure."* Western science has traditionally assumed that consciousness is limited only to those structures that Western scientists have been able to communicate with historically, and Leary's theory is therefore somewhat startling. It might help us to look at it objectively if we remember that Oriental yogis, primitive shamans, deviant Western scientists (such as Bruno of Nola, Paracelsus, Goethe, Mesmer, Wilhelm Reich, Fechner, Burbank, Carver) and pantheistic philosophers have all held to the Leary position, and that the traditional Western-science viewpoint is based on nothing more than the historical accident that Thomist Christianity separated "spirit" and "matter" so thoroughly that science was left, after rejecting Christian "spirit" with a peculiarly inert ("dead") matter as their hypothetical monad. Poets and lovers, as well as primitives, have always known that this "dead" matter was just a map which scientists have absent-mindedly confused with the territory.

To the best of my knowledge, there is no physical-science data yet which tends to confirm Dr. Leary's assumption of an atomic consciousness or *neuro-electronic circuit* which therefore rests on interpretations of data collected by his own and others' neurological research. Molecular consciousness or a neural-molecular circuit of information, however, is supported by several independent lines of research, within science and elsewhere. For instance (1) Prof. McConell of Indiana University has shown repeatedly, in experiments begun in 1957 and still continuing, that cannibal worms somehow acquire the learned maze-solving knowledge of the worms they have eaten. Molecular transmission of information is the only theory thus far that can explain this. (2) Dr. Ruth Sager of Columbia has had similar results with paramecia. (3) RNA fed to the senile has resulted in restored memory; discontinuing the RNA caused a fading of memory and relapse into senility. (4) Some form of "reincarnation" theory pops up in every religion based ecstatic experience; it is lacking only in those religions based on dogma without such personal experience. (5) Jung's work on the "race memory" has not yet been refuted by all his critics; some Jungian patients definitely remember things they haven't learned since birth.

In this connection, it is interesting to note that Sufic

and European occultism, concentrating on communicating with the "Guardian Angel," has often used methods (sex and drugs) similar to those of Tantrists seeking to "find the true self" and "remember past incarnations." The Guardian Angel is like the "true self ", a label for the non-verbal event of remembering past history, which can be past molecular history. Moses Miamonides, who was trained in Sufi magick, has a paragraph that is interesting in this connection:

> "Angel" means messenger . . . Say to a person who believed to belong to the wise men of Israel that the Almighty sends his angel to enter the womb of a woman and to form there a fetus, he will be satisfied with the account, he will believe it. But tell him that God gives the seed a formative power . . . and that this power is called an "angel" . . . and he will turn away.

It can hardly be denied that Maimonides is describing what we now call the DNA, with its associated RNA "messenger molecules" and the whole "molecular memory" suggested by McConnell's worms and similar genetic research. This is now called Circuit 7, the Neurogenetic Circuit.

If, then, consciousness is *energy received and decoded by a structure*," molecular consciousness, atomic consciousness, cellular consciousness, somatic consciousness, and sensory consciousness are modes of knowing that precisely fit the mystic's claim of im-personal or trans-personal *gnosis* that does not pass through the usual symbolic game-play of the socially-defined ego-awareness. Dr. Leary has succeeded in giving us a scientific map that actually fits the territory explored by the mystic.

It will readily be seen that these alternate levels

of consciousness take us entirely off the Inter-Personal Transaction (game-playing) grid; this is partly why they have been traditionally ignored or dismissed as pathological by extraverted Western science. Of course, yoga, which is also a science, has recorded each of them (under a more complex Hindu name) but this is easily ignored by those who define science as the discoveries *made by white people in the last 300 years.* (The racial and cultural chauvinism of this outlook is not noted by those dogmatically committed thereto.)

Two of Dr. Leary's most important books, *The Psychedelic Experience* (with Dr. Richard Alpert and Dr. Ralph Metzner) and *Psychedelic Prayers from the Tao Te Ching*, are meta-programming manuals, to be used with LSD, in shifting consciousness to the alternate levels. *Psychedelic Experience*, based on the *Tibetan Book of the Dead*, leads directly to atomic consciousness ("the White Light") and *Psychedelic Prayers*, from Lao-Tse's *Tao Te Ching*, is a full meta-program moving through sensory, somatic, molecular and atomic levels. To restate our behaviorist equation in consciousness terms:

$$C_n = C_0 + P_n + MS$$

where C_0 is the old (game) consciousness. C_n is the new consciousness, and P_n is the meta-program, Tibetan or Chinese as the case may be. It will readily be seen that differences appear, depending on which program is used, and that those who merely take the metaprogramming substance (MS) without a new program cannot really expect a *permanent* new consciousness. (Or, more gravely, the P_n will be accidental, dependent on the chance or hazard of the environment: hence, the notorious "bad trip," so sensationalized by the press.)

The value of this approach in psychotherapy is not yet fully known (due to the government suppression of such research.) An indication of what we may hope for is given by a case reported by Dr. Leary's old associate, Dr. Richard Alpert, as quoted in my book, *Sex and Drugs: A Journey Beyond Limits*. The patient had been totally homosexual for ten years (after a few unsuccessful heterosexual attempts in adolescence) and was highly desirous of changing his orientation. Dr. Alpert used behavior therapy, in the Wolpean form of "progressive desensitization," as his P_n; this consists of taking the patient, step-by-step, into previously frightening programs and relaxing his muscles each time anxiety appears. (This is based on the Reich-Janov-Lowen assumption that emotional anxiety is keyed off by repressed muscular spasm — the Reichian "muscular armor.") The meta-programming substance was LSD. There were only three therapy sessions.

In the first session, Dr. Alpert and the patient merely discussed what they were trying to accomplish and the methodology they would use. In the second session, the meta-programming substance (LSD) was given, and the patient examined hard-core erotica of a heterosexual nature; every time anxiety appeared, the progressive desensitization was used. He was able to "respond" in a heterosexual way, i.e. he masturbated. In the third session, the metaprogramming substance was given again, and a "surrogate wife" (a female friend of the patient) was present. Progressive desensitization was again used as P_n each time anxiety appeared. Eventually, the patient was able to perform heterosexual intercourse, for the first time in ten years.

A follow-up six months later revealed that the P_n of heterosexuality was now firmly established.

Comparison with other forms of psychotherapy (especially Freudian, but even including behavior therapy without the metaprogramming substance) indicates that such rapid behavior change is extremely rare. We must consider possible, then, Dr. Roubichek's claim that "LSD inhibits conditioned reflexes," Dr. Lilly's definition of LSD as a "meta-programming substance," and Dr. Leary's highly controversial claims that this drug, properly used, is the most important psychological discovery of our time. Public hysteria preventing further research is indeed shortsighted. (Hundreds of similarly dramatic case histories can be found in the records of Leary, Osmond, Grof, Hoffer, *et al.)*

Gay Liberationists who are grinding their teeth and muttering about "brain-washing" should recall that (1) the patient requested the change in this case and (2) the change is equally easy the other way (B_o = heterosexuality, B_n = homosexuality.) This is not an insignificant point; much social policy hinges upon whether these metaprogramming substances (and newer techniques) are to be employed in a libertarian way or in an authoritarian way. Dr. Leary's "Two Commandments of the Neurological Age" may be one of his most important contributions to thought, even though they still (1974) are hardly understood:

1. Thou shalt not alter the consciousness of thy neighbor without his consent.

2. Thou shalt not prevent thy neighbor from altering his or her own consciousness.

The first of these commandments is violated daily by the forcible administration of various drugs to mental patients, practices like involuntary psycho-surgery, electro-shock, the coercive Ritalin program for "hyperactive" school children, etc. The second commandment is violated by repression of LSD research, our hysterical anti-drug laws, victimless crime laws preventing people from experimenting in harmless alternative lifestyles, etc. All of this creeping totalitarianism is opposed by civil libertarians, of course, but few aside from Dr. Leary realize that this issue will become the most important social debate of all as we progress further into "the neurological age." Briefly, control of consciousness and behavior is advancing from *craft* (empiricism, the medieval "guild" approach of orthodox AMA or APA psychiatry, hit-or-miss therapy, etc.) and becoming a true theoretical-practical logico-empirical integral *science*, comparable to physics or chemistry. This is the definition of *the neurological age*. The most vital issue before us is: shall this knowledge be controlled by an elite (as present practice already anticipates) or shall the individual decide the destiny of his or her own nervous system (as Leary's commandments suggest)? Only those aware of the speed with which new techniques are appearing can appreciate the seriousness of this question.

In one of the most famous Zen stories, a monk asks the Teacher, "What is Buddha?"

The answer: "The poplar tree in the courtyard!"

There are a million-and-one sublime and symbolic interpretations of this, but those with the most background in actual Zen meditation (meta-programming the nervous system for higher fidelity of signal-reception) always insist that it means just what it says: "The poplar tree in the courtyard!"

As Korzybski notes in *Science and Sanity*:

One of the most baffling problems has been the peculiar periodicity or rhythmicity which we find in life. Lately, Lillie and others have shown that this rhythmicity could not be explained by purely physical nor purely chemical means but that it is satisfactorily explained when treated as a *physico-electro-chemical structural occurrence.* The famous experiment of Lillie, who used an iron wire immersed in nitric acid and reproduced, experimentally, a beautiful periodicity resembling closely some of the activities of *protoplasm and the nervous system* show conclusively that both the living and the non-living systems depend for their rhythmic behavior on the chemically alterable film, which divides the electrically conducting phases . . . in both systems, the electromotive characteristics of the surfaces are determined by the character of the film . . .

In his seminars, Korzybski stressed again and again that, if we are going to talk sense about human behavior, we must give up words like "mind" and "soul," which were borrowed from philosophers (who, being bankrupt, are in no position to loan anything); we must talk scientifically of the actual nervous system and its actual chemical, electrical and structural properties. This is what Leary attempts to do in his seven-level model of kinds of awareness depending on what level of structure the nervous system is "tuned in" to.

In this connection, consider the long-neglected researches of Sir J.C. Bose, who demonstrated around the turn of the century that *reaction curves* in metals and living systems are often *mathematically identical.* "Further work began to convince Bose that the boundary line between so-called 'nonliving' metals and 'living' organisms was tenuous indeed . . . To his awe and surprise, the curves produced by slightly warmed magnetic oxide of iron

showed striking resemblance to those of muscles . . .
When he chloroformed plants, Bose discovered that they
were as successfully anestheticized as animals; and that
when the narcotic vapor was blown away by fresh air like
animals they revived . . . Bose (also) . . . got similar curves
of muscles and metals responding to the effects of fatigue
or of stimulating, depressing and poisoning drugs." —
Tompkins and Bird, *Secret Life of Plants*.

Sir Robert Austen, leading authority of metallurgy,
also believed metals are alive and hinted at this before the
Royal Society, but was rebuffed. He later defended Bose's
researches vigorously.

Said Dr. Bose himself; "It was when I came upon
the mute witness of these self-made records"—of metal,
plant and animal response-patterns — "that I understood
for the first time a little of that message proclaimed by my
ancestors on the banks of the Ganges thirty centuries ago:
'They who see but one, in all the changes of the universe,
unto them belongs Eternal Truth—unto none else, unto
none else!'"

This atomic consciousness, like the molecular
"memory", is the beginning of an explanation of the data of
the mystics and the shamans. A label like "hallucination"
explains nothing and merely evades the question.

If Dr. Leary is right, then, in his assumption-definition,
"Consciousness is energy received and decoded by a
structure," we do not possess one "mind," as we normally
think. The "one mind" is merely a delusion caused by
the conditioning (reward-punishment) which directs our
attention in socially-demanded directions. Along with,
above, below or aside from that normal ego, we are
also thinking bodies, thinking cells, thinking molecules
3½ billion years old, and thinking atoms as old as the
cosmos . . .

And this is the scientific translation of the mystics' age-old claim that each of us is, deep inside, identical with "God." "God" is only a shorthand term for the various kinds of conscious intelligence (atomic, molecular, cellular, organic) within us. As Leary liked to phrase it in his "Death of the Mind" road-show appearances as Guru, "Your body is as old as the universe." Unlocking this structural knowledge within the nervous system, with or without drugs, is always a mind-blowing experience, for the synergetic product of all these coherent (although usually non-verbal) consciousnesses does indeed have all the cosmic dimensions of the theologians' "God."

Chapter Five

New Maps of the Mind

Man is not the body but the mind, and mind is a
star entire.

—Paracelsus

Acid-trippers, admittedly, report the damndest things.

A friend of mine, on an acid voyage with his wife,
nude in the woods, saw bright sparkling rays coming
out of the nipples of her breasts. Hallucination? Kyrlian
photography shows similar patterns . . . Dr. Alan Watts,
author of *The Way of Zen* and *Beyond Theology* and other
mystical works, saw strange rays in the sky, over the
hill beyond his house, while on LSD. Investigating the
next day, he climbed the hill and found there was a radar
station there. Hallucination, the night before — or a new
sensitivity to signals by his nervous system?

Dr. Stanley Krippner, on a psilocybin trip in 1962, saw
John F. Kennedy shot in the head. Kennedy's assassination
occurred over a year later, in 1963. Coincidence?

At the beginning of the twentieth century, a gifted
Viennese biologist with the Gallic name of Raoul Francé
put forth the idea . . . that plants move their bodies as freely,
easily, and gracefully as the most skilled animal or human,
and that the only reason we don't appreciate the fact is that
plants do so at a much slower pace than humans . . .

No plant, says Francé, is without movement; all growth
is a series of movements; plants are constantly preoccupied
with bending, turning and quivering . . .

The whole vegetable world, says Francé, lives
responsive to the movement of the earth and its satellite
moon, to the movements of the other planets of our solar
system, and . . . the stars and other cosmic bodies in the
universe . . .

Francé . . . believed plants to be possessed of all the
attributes of living creatures including 'the most violent
reaction against abuse and the most ardent gratitude for
favors . . . but what he had already put into print was either
ignored by the establishment or considered heretically
shocking. What shocked them most was his suggestion that
the awareness of plants might originate in a super-material
world of cosmic beings to which, long before the birth
of Christ, Hindu sages referred to as 'devas' and which,
as fairies, elves, gnomes, sylphs and a host of other
creatures, were a matter of direct vision and experience to
clairvoyants among the Celts and other sensitives . . .

It has taken the startling discoveries of the 1960s . . .
(to prove that) plants may at last be the bridesmaids at a
marriage of physics and metaphysics . . .

In Cleve Backster's research, "once attuned to a

particular person, plants appeared to be able to maintain a link with that person, no matter where he went, even among thousands of people. On New Year's Eve in New York City, Backster went out into the bedlam of Times Square armed with a notebook and stopwatch . . . Back at the lab, he found that each of three plants, monitored independently (by polygraph), showed similar reactions to his slight emotional adventures . . .

Backster experimented with a female friend to establish whether her plants remained attuned to her on a seven-hundred-mile plane ride across the United States. From synchronized clocks they found a definite reaction from the plants to the friend's emotional stress each time the plane touched down for its landing . . .

Backster's medical consultant, the New Jersey cytologist Dr. Howard Miller, concluded that some sort of 'cellular consciousness' must be common to all life . . .

"*Sentience*," says Backster, "does not seem to stop at the cellular level. It may go down to the molecular, the atomic and even the sub-atomic." – *The Secret Life of Plants*, by Peter Tompkins and Christopher Bird. (Avon, 1974.)

The first pot-smoker I ever knew was a black jazz musician who was my friend in the late 1950s. Although unwilling to experiment with "drugs" at that point, I was curious enough to ask about the experience. One of his illustrations has always stuck in my mind. "Take a quarter out of your pocket," he said. "Look at it. *You don't really see it.* A little kid handling a quarter for the first time *really*

sees it. Now, if you smoke a reefer and then look at the quarter, you'll *really see* it again, for the first time since childhood."

This is what Leary called level 4, sensory consciousness. (It is renamed circuit 5, the neurosomatic or rapture circuit, in his current writings.) It is the first sign of approaching success in all schools of yogic or occult training. Pot puts you there *instantly* (although only for a short period of time.)

"Directly afterward," wrote Dr. R.M. Bucke in *Cosmic Consciousness*, "there came upon me a sense of exultation, of immense joyousness accompanied or immediately followed by an intellectual illumination impossible to describe. Among other things, I did not merely come to believe, but I saw that the universe is not composed of dead matter, but is, on the contrary a living presence; I became conscious in myself of eternal life." This is level 1, atomic consciousness—called circuit 6, the ecstasy or neurophysical circuit, in Leary's current writings. Similarly, the majority of acid-trippers or yogi adepts eventually "remember past lives." This is cellular consciousness or circuit 7, the neurogenetic circuit.

Describing these experiences as "hallucinations" is a quick easy verdict but not necessarily accurate.

When Dr. Wilhelm Reich began reporting that he was able to see a bio-energetic field around his patients, with a special instrument he designed called an orgonoscope, orthodox AMA medicine and orthodox APA psychiatry, refusing to look through the orgonoscope just as Inquisitors three centuries earlier refused to look through Galileo's telescope, pronounced that Dr. Reich was "hallucinating." Reich died in prison in 1957. In the mid-1960s Kyrlian photography made these bio-energetic fields visible to all.

Nevertheless, so great is the weight of established opinion on all of us that I, myself, seeing these fields every time I used peyote in the early 1960s, could never quite make up my mind if they were real or just auto-suggestion provoked by reading Reich's books. Part of my skepticism was justified—it is always wrong to jump to conclusions hastily; it's always wise to question and question again — but part of it was an unconscious decision not to be an eccentric even in the privacy of my mind.

Virtually every user of pot and LSD knows that these drugs are sexually stimulating, as I discussed at length in my *Sex and Drugs: A Journey Beyond Limits*. This knowledge, again, is repressed; the official verdict is that the sexual effects of these chemicals is still unknown. One is tempted to ask, "Unknown to whom?" As Professor William McGlothlin remarked, in an area where scientists are forbidden to do research, only outlaws possess real knowledge. Such a situation is hardly what the Renaissance and the Age of Reason philosophers had in mind when struggling to free curiosity from the cage of Tradition.

By the mid-1960s, several millions in Europe and America had sampled the new metaprogramming substances, with results that can safely be called controversial. Dr. Leary, as the most unfrightened and objective observer on the scene, quickly became the scapegoat who was metaphysically "to blame" for any new behavior which the conservative, the timid, the prudish found disconcerting. As he himself has written in *Neurologic* (1973):

During the 1960s millions of Americans and West Europeans changed their mode of thinking by the self-administration of psychedelic drugs in the intellectual atmosphere generated by such models as

Bob Dylan, the Beatles, the Rolling Stones, oriental gurus and PSY PHI prophets. The effects of this neurological revolution have been to set up such a controversial social confusion that it will take a new generation of psychologists and sociologists to assess the Effects . . . American psychology and psychiatry, indeed, the new American culture has discovered the Rapture Circuit. Sexual liberation, sensual training, hedonic dress and grooming, massage, the eroticization of all forms of art (all related to the use of rapturic drugs, e.g., cannabis, by the avant third of the population) define the cultural revolution of the sixties . . .

(This) hedonic revolution . . . was the culmination of "the childhood of time," the joyous, infantile discovery by an entire generation of the body as plaything, the delights of direct sensuality. The history of other spatially successful civilizations teaches us that play and display, the worship of Eros and beauty is a vulnerably indulgent phase, essentially incapable of protecting itself, existing as an irresponsible elitist froth on the Circuit Four grim, serious social structure.

Darwin, Woodstock and the French Revolution taught the lesson. Evolve or perish.

The Rapture Circuit, as Dr. Leary increasingly emphasizes, is a necessary but insufficient stage in our evolution as a species. The fact that it *is* necessary needs some emphasis, since every social institution has a vested interest in preventing such raw pleasure, and the nervous system as a whole is conditioned to recoil from it in terror. (This terrified "recoil" is known in Reichian bio-psychology as "pleasure anxiety" or, in more specific form, as "orgasm anxiety." Erich Fromm, in a different context, has described it as the "robotization" of civilized humanity, and our consequent "fear of freedom." The reader can discover his own share of it by simply asking which things he would like to do and is afraid of attempting. If these things harm nobody, his block against them is probably an irrational imprint.) In *Principles of Hedonic Psychology* (1970) Dr. Leary examined the taboo against pleasure and the transcendence of this taboo.

Truly pleasurable behavior, he asserts, *is unconditioned behavior*. The misleading, misnamed and mischievous Freudian categories of "reality principle" and "pleasure principle" limit the notion of "reality" to socially conditioned behavior controlled (from above) by punishment and reward. This terminology "implies that only the artificial, conditioned ontology of the current social order is real; that natural pleasure is somehow not real but rather a hallucination, or even a psychotic outburst." Behaviorism, even more than psychoanalysis, limits its attention to socially-coerced patterns of reward and punishment, and implicitly or sometimes explicitly declares that spontaneous, naturally pleasurable, unconditioned behavior doesn't exist. "The entire range of pleasurable experiences, of natural, unconditioned encounters, has gone unstudied, unlabeled, undefined."

Dr. Leary's observation of, and experimental participation in, many aspects of the Hedonic Revolution of the 1960s provides him with a broader perspective than Freudianism or Behaviorism. There are, he proposes, three levels of conditioned experiences based on reward-punishment and well-studied in modern psychology:

I - Unconsciousness, where our normally repressed desires are expressed, via dream, in symbolic form. The province of Freudians, Jungians and their imitators.

II - Conditioned Emotional Excitement, consisting of glandular responses to conditioned stimuli in the external world: objects of terror, awe, lust, rage, etc. Studied by most schools of psychology, especially Behaviorists.

III - Conditioned social consciousness, comprising all the game playing and strategic maneuvering analyzed previously on the Interpersonal Grid. The special arena of social psychologists and group-dynamics (Lewinite) therapists.

These correspond, in general, to what Dr. Leary has previously called the levels of coma, emotional stupor and symbolic consciousness. In this book, the first is ignored; the latter two become the Emotional Power circuit and the Symbolic Circuit.

There are also four *unconditioned* levels of experience mostly ignored by modern psychology or dismissed as "sick," "psychotic," "hallucinatory," etc. ("To implement the goals of the state it serves through control of the apparatus of conditioning," Dr. Leary notes, "psychology has become more and more a science of social control." As such, it *must* define unconditioned behavior as perverse.)

I - *Unconditioned sensory delight*. This is characteristic of successfully-trained yogis or shamans and of dope-adepts. It is operationally identified by (1) conspicuous absence of the "normally" expected (socially-conditioned) emotional robotism. The yogi or pot-head will *not* get angry just because he is in a situation to which we have all been conditioned to respond with adrenalin-rushes and explosive rage. (See our Zen story in the previous chapter) (2) Movements and postures focused on *sensory* input rather than *emotional* or *intellectual* input.

II - *Somatic rapture*, characteristic of very advanced yogis and LSD trippers. This is operationally identified by (1) again, absence of conditioned responses and (2) movements that focus on the autonomic nervous system, especially the sexual or eliminative centers. Such behavior is under special taboo if pleasurable, but excused if painful — which is why there is so much sadism in "acceptable" entertainment, while pleasurable spasm is restricted to "smut" and "pornography," two labels that tell us just what society thinks of ecstatic joy.

It is legal and permissible everywhere in the U.S. to show a film of a human writhing in spasmodic and convulsive somatic states (autonomic system, sub-ego behavior) *if and only if* pain is the trigger. Since such purely somatic behavior is an occasional necessity we become an increasingly sadomasochistic society. The Rapture Circuit, in which these convulsions are produced by pleasure, remains taboo. Linda Lovelace is a figure of fun to the sophisticate, an object of hatred to the prude, but a napalm manufacturer is respected and might be invited to sit on a presidential Commission on Violence. Only the domination of brain by conditioned-repetitious circuits (reward-punishment) explains such glaring contradictions and irrationalities, the butt of every satirist from Mencken to Lenny Bruce.

Dr. Reich came to the conclusion that the somatic rapture function, or orgasm-reflex, was largely atrophied in modern humanity, although a quasi-orgasm remains in the majority. (The success of books on how to achieve sexual climax, from Van Der Velde to Masters and Johnson, is mute testimony that the minority which doesn't even achieve this diluted quasi-orgasm is quite sizeable enough to make a book into a best-seller overnight.) In Dr. Leary's terminology, the reward-punishment conditioning of society keeps most people operating on the conditioned circuits and unable to leap the Anxiety Barrier to unconditioned somatic spasm. As poet Kenneth Rexroth once said, this is really what all the revolutions are about.

III - *Unconditioned genetic behavior.* Dr. Leary has some trouble defining what he means here; later writings make clear that he was trying to describe the manifestation of the primordial genetic type free of the entire apparatus of socially-conditioned games that usually mask it. This happens regularly in so-called "schizophrenic breakdowns," and, indeed, however it happens the person and his associates are likely to identify what is occurring as pathological. *It is not.* It is shocking only because unconditioned natural behavior is so rare among conditioned humanity.

IV - *Neuro-electrical ecstasy,* experienced during epileptic seizures, electro-convulsive shock, electrical brain stimulation and heavy doses of LSD. This is the "White Light" of the yogis, "stopping the world" in Don Juan's shamanism, Satori in Zen Buddhism. Atomic consciousness. The Sixth Circuit in the present book.

The fact that what Wilhelm Reich called "pleasure anxiety" provokes what Erich Fromm called "flight from freedom" illustrates Dr. Leary's thesis that pleasure *is* freedom. The danger of scientific investigation of this area, as Reich and Leary have found out on their way to jail, is that the psychologist here touches, and threatens to de-activate, *the very mechanism of social control.* The judge who sentenced Dr. Leary to ten years imprisonment denounced him as an "irresponsible hedonist" and a "menace to society." *National Review,* the leading Permian Era "bite-'em-before-they-bite-us" Warrior Conservative magazine, listed Timothy as one of "the three most dangerous men alive," the other two being Norman O. Brown and Marshall McLuhan, whose work also concerns unleashing sensory awareness from social conditioning. While Dr. Leary is well aware of the limitations of the Hedonic culture of the 60s (see the quote below) he is also brutally explicit in describing the extent to which conditioned emotional games deprive us of primordial somatic joy. In *The Politics of Ecstasy* (1968), he wrote with humorous but terrible truth:

> At one time, when we were trustingly slumbering, a selfish, insane, power-hungry combine of exploitive conspirators suddenly moved in and systematically censored and manipulated what was to hit our eyes, ears, nose, mouth, skin. A well-organized conspiracy to enslave our consciousness. A science fiction horror movie in which our captors decided exactly which energies and sensory stimuli we could encounter . . . Using Pavlovian conditioning of reward and punishment, our grim rulers lead us unsuspectingly to do exactly what they wish . . .
>
> We have taken leave of our senses. We have been robbed blind. Sensory conditioning has forced us to accept a "reality" which is a comic-tragic farce illusion.

In *Neurologic* (1973), Dr. Leary points out the terror of moving from the conditioned robot-consciousness of society to unconditioned ecstatic freedom:

> Consciousness seems to be invading all the forbidden and dangerous areas: the "below," the "behind," the "wrong," and the "cross-sexual." (The nervous system warns) "Danger! Red alert! . . . Watch out! You are helpless! . . . Unknown! Beware! . . . Evil! Irresponsible! Violation of sex role."
>
> The instinctive terrors mastered by sky divers, scuba divers, and the various death-defying, circus performers

are as nothing compared to the panic momentarily experienced by the nervous system which transcends its four life-long and life-preserving larval circuits. We can understand the taboo, the awe, the alienation that is felt—the interpretation of danger, stupor, madness, and diabolical possession.

Dr. Joel Fort, former advisor on drug problems to the World Health Organization, puts the matter more simply. "Marijuana," he says, "is a drug well-known to cause paranoid and hysterical behavior in legislators who haven't tried it."

How the penitentiary degrades the prisoner . . . "Obscene touching" is not allowed between convicts and their wives or girlfriends, in California prisons. What constitutes "obscene touching" between lovers is at the discretion of the guards, of course.

This is literally having a man by the balls, as Paul Goodman once noted.

"Torture" is what they do in other countries, or in other ages. What we do here and now is not "torture" but "punishment."

Please explain the difference between "torture" and "punishment" in 25 words or less, concentrating on where the bodies are in space-time and what movements they are making.

It might be objected to the Reich-Leary thesis that it is inconceivable that the majority of human beings are really trapped in the same conditioned-reflex robotism as domesticated and well-trained poodle-dogs. If this were so, it can be argued, then there would be very little real intelligence in our social institutions or our private lives. Most people would be cowed, confused, miserable wretches, constantly seeking for some "miracle cure" to their obvious neurosis, constantly at odds with one another and guilty-fearful-uncertain in most situations but the most routine and programmed, constantly subject to fits of hysterical rage and terror when any of these routines or programs are challenged. Society as a whole would be a vast madhouse, in which starvation exists next to palaces of splendor, insane cruelties are practiced on all sides and ignored by the calloused and terrorized masses, and we would be constantly drifting toward self-destruction.

Well? That is a fairly good description of the actual state of this planet today, isn't it?

The Hedonic Revolution of the 1960s was surprisingly benign in most of its manifestations. Recall girls putting flowers in the M.P.'s rifles at the Pentagon demonstration, the mass-mind anarchist harmony of Woodstock, the generosity behind the Civil Rights and peace movements. The reaction of the authorities was one of such violent hatred and persecution that what is left of the counter-culture exists in a kind of embittered shell-shock today. The very mechanism of authoritarian society — the restriction of consciousness to the reward-punishment circuits — was threatened, we can now see, and it almost appears that Dr. Leary's persecutors, like Dr. Reich's, will not be satisfied until the heretic is not only caged but killed.

It occurs to me that I would still defend Timothy

Leary if I believed all his scientific claims are invalid. This is a basic philosophical-political posture which seems obligatory to me.

Dr. Leary has been bold (maybe too bold), questioning, pioneering, innovative, daring, above all creative. The government, as usual, has been timid, unquestioning, regressive, conservative, cowardly, above all stagnant. He represents growth, or the possibility of growth. They represent stasis. (Is not *State*, in fact, etymologically related to *stasis*?) He acts on the imperatives of creative mind; they, on the rigidities of dogmatic power.

It is the classic, and hideous, pattern: Leary calls for further research; admits he may be wrong; cares to laugh at himself; can be proven (as far as anything in psychology can be proven) to possess high intelligence; is competent in the field of which he speaks. The bureaucrats who persecute him attempt to prevent further research; will never admit that they might be wrong; have no humor; can be proven to be mediocrities and worse; are incompetent at everything except holding their jobs.

Leary's arguments are fact, statistical evidence, clinical studies, and his own flair for humor, poetry, propaganda; their arguments are cages and clubs and guns, informers, spies, snooping, no-knock laws, tyranny.

If Leary is wrong in all his theorizing, he is still right in asking for scientific judgment; if his persecutors are right in their fears, they are still wrong in relying on force to settle an intellectual debate.

It is precisely that simple and basic.

As the war against (wise and unwise) psychedelic experimentation has escalated, most of the traditional civil liberties once treasured in this country have been trampled in the dust. As novelist William S. Burroughs pointed out in a Drug Revolution panel I edited for *Playboy*:

> Drug control is a thin pretext, and getting thinner, to increase police powers and to brand dissent as criminal. The pretense of looking for narcotics gives the authorities the right to search any person or premises at any time, and the police are continually lobbying for more anti-narcotics laws and stiffer penalties . . .
>
> The standard practices of forcing young people to become informants under the threat of prison if they don't cooperate, or of undercover agents encouraging narcotics violations in order to run up a score of arrests, pose a threat to any American way of life in which one could reasonably take pride.

To which Baba Ram Dass (formerly Dr. Richard Alpert) replied feelingly:

> I also think such practices are ill-advised because they just increase the paranoia of human beings toward one another. The lack of respect for the privacy and dignity of the individual in this society is a sign of the sickness of the times.
>
> In fact, Dr. Leary is imprisoned, and hundreds of thousands of others are imprisoned, because the government is trying to settle a scientific-philosophical debate by the tactics of terrorism. We all know how well that worked for the Holy Inquisition in its battle against Protestantism, Copernican astronomy and liberalism . . .

Korzybski writes:
Mental illnesses (infantilism included) appear as semantic arrested development or a regression to lower levels, to those of the primitive man, the infant, the

animal . . . The animal is *not* conscious of abstracting; man can become so . . .

The verbal division of 'body' and 'mind' remains verbal, and also involves a language whose structure does not correspond to the structure and functioning of the organism. We have already emphasized over and over that the organism works as-a-whole, and that, therefore, any elementalistic splittings cannot lead to satisfactory results . . .

The main symptoms of physical and 'mental' illnesses are few and simple . . . The colloidal structure of protoplasm accounts for this peculiar simplicity and for the small number of fundamental symptoms . . . Our present commercial 'civilization' can be characterized as of an infantile type, governed mostly by structurally primitive mythologies and language often involving primitive semantic reactions. One need but read the speeches of different merchants, presidents and kings to be thoroughly convinced of this . . .

We should remember that the nervous system of the human child is not finished at birth . . .

In dementia praecox the nervous system appears in a state of colloidal over-dispersion . . . in infants the colloids appear more dispersed than in adults The colloidal behavior of the nervous system can be altered by special chemical treatment with drugs . . .

On national grounds, the adult infants standardize all they can . . . Not wanting to 'think,' or to bother about differences, they fancy they can regulate life by legislation and they keep busy manufacturing laws which are very often impractical and self-contradictory. When they pass several thousand laws a year, these become a maze and a joke . . .

This pathological tendency probably accounts for our so-called 'civilization' being at an infantile level, based, as it is, on selfishness, 'sense' gratification, might, brutal competition, acquisitiveness, etc. . . . As Burrow well said, the problems of war are more the problems of psychiatry than of diplomacy . . .

The human brain has vast areas which, at present, have no definitely known functions. Perhaps, with the older lack of consciousness of abstracting, the flow of nervous energy was misdirected or absorbed by the older ways of 'feeling' and 'thinking' in the lower centers. Thus, the available energy was not sufficient to utilize the higher centers to the full extent.

—Alfred Korzybski, Science and Sanity

Poet Allen Ginsberg said it more simply. In *Howl* (1957), he described this planet as "an Armed Madhouse."

Chapter Six

The Neurogenetic Code

We have certain preconceived notions about location in space which have come down to us from our ape-like ancestors.

—Sir Arthur Eddington,
Space, Time and Gravitation

Spy novels and spy movies are more popular than ever. This seems to be the archetypal art form of our century, as the revenge-tragedy was to the Elizabethans, or the seduced-and-abandoned theme was to the Victorians. Every age gets the parables it deserves, and needs. Wilhelm Reich became aware of this, toward the end, and just before they hauled him off to die in prison he wrote an essay, "On Spying and Hiding," in which he pointed out that snooping and concealment are both pathological behaviors based on infantile sexual trauma.

Reich is obviously right, and there is more than social conflict involved in the current obsessions with spying for the government and hiding from the government. Watergate is the comic-tragic epic of a society mad with voyeurism . . .

Dr. Leary points out, in *The Curse of the Oval Room,* that G. Gordon Liddy during his raids on the Millbrook Ashram* was obsessed with the possibility that Leary had "naked women" somewhere on the premises. Timothy comments:

> As with most other guilt-ridden "sexual deviates," the voyeur is invariably a political conservative — shocked, moralistic, and censorious about behaviors which he compulsively and secretly seeks to discover. We think of the priest in the confessional or of the vice squads or of J. Edgar Hoover, forbidding extramarital expressions to his agents at the pain of discharge, and who, himself unmarried, presumptive virgin, voyeur extraordinaire, guarded files containing reports, tapes, and photos of the sexual peccadilloes of American politicians.

~•~

* These raids never resulted in a single successful prosecution, but Liddy used them to get into the White House as a "drug expert" and then to create the Watergate psychosis.

~•~

Watergate was, indeed, the climax of a decade of ever-increasing spying and snooping by government. The idea of officials being public servants has been completely forgotten; they regard themselves, and are accepted as, terrible policemen of a treacherous, undependable and childish public. Berthold Brecht, encountering the same attitudes in socialist East Germany, commented that "if the government doesn't trust the people, it should dissolve them and elect a new people." Such irony has been missing over here and most people are quite frankly terrified of a government originally intended to be their servant. We are very naive about totalitarianism . . .

I never believe it when a person tells me "I've had
twenty (or a hundred, or five hundred) acid trips," unless
the speaker was actually involved in legal LSD research
before the hysteria banned that research in 1966. Almost
always, in other cases, the correct formulation is "I've had
twenty (or a hundred, or five hundred) trips on *something*
somebody told me was LSD."

In late 1970, I finally had a trip on *something*
somebody told me was LSD. I had been reading my poetry
at the University of Wisconsin, Madison, and a student
slipped me a tab of the famous Clear Light afterwards, to
express his appreciation.

Why did I take it? I had written a great deal about
the perils of black market acid; about the neurological
Russian Roulette involved in trusting the product of
illicit entrepreneur's bathtub acid factories; about the
well-documented fact that at least half the "LSD" on the
black market in the late 60s was actually the dangerous
PCP once sold legally as a tranquilizer and then removed
from the market because of bad side-effects; about the
studies which had shown that even the real LSD on the
market was cut with speed, strychnine or real garbage.
Why did I take it? I was in an adventurous and possibly
desperate mood. Five years as Associate Editor at *Playboy*
at 20 thou per annum had given me all the status and
security one could hope to find in the mad 1960s but left
me fundamentality empty and unhappy. I wanted something
else out of life, but I didn't know what it was I wanted.

The trip was a bummer. A monstro-bummer. A disaster.
I will never stop being *grateful* for it. Yes, that is the

paradox of these metaprogramming sessions: the bad trips can be potentially much more beneficial than the good trips. I wept for five hours, clock time, but I seemed to endure the three and a half billion years of evolution on planet earth, all of it pointless and cruel and wasted. I resigned from the human race. I understood Buddha's First Noble Truth, "All living is suffering." I died the death of five thousand cuts. I cried my eyes out.

By dawn's early light, Arlen and I had a very serious discussion. Fifteen years earlier I had given up engineering, with 20 credits to go toward a degree in math and electrical engineering and 5 years experience as technical assistant in a research lab, because I wanted to be a writer. In that fifteen years, the necessity of supporting a family of four children had led me to produce enough prose to fill an encyclopedia, 97% of it sheer journalism or other crap. At the age of 38, I could not continue on that path. I had to write what I needed to write; I needed to write what I had to write. "If the worst comes to the worst, we'll go on welfare," Arlen said; the worst didn't come to the worst until three years later . . .

Meanwhile, Timothy had been going up in the world, and going down, and going up-and-down. His initial marijuana bust in Texas was overturned by the Supreme Court, but the government found some new charges and started a second round of the Let's-Put-Leary-in-a-Cage game. In 1969, while running for Governor of California, he had urged doubling the salary of all police. (They had arrested him twice in the previous week, and he called that "a little better than average.") The next week he was busted again, while living in a tipi as part of an experiment in learning American Indian culture-values, and issued the following rather trippy press release:

God's plan continues to work perfectly. Yesterday's Cavalry raid on our Indian tipis is designed to show to the American public the ghoulish length to which Mr. Reagan's police will go in their war against youth.

Our government has destroyed 50,000 of our bravest youth in Asia and they have imprisoned 50,000 of our holiest youth in this country for spiritual-psychedelic crimes.

Now, I am told, I am to be arrested for "contributing to the delinquency of a minor." Well, since this is a religious struggle we are engaged in, I proudly confess to having contributed to the delinquency of over 50 million young people, who are, in fact, rapidly becoming a majority.

But why not mention some of my other crimes? I lead the charge against Custer at Little Big Horn. I helped lose the war in Vietnam. I advocated the heresy that the world is round. Me and forty-eight other long-hairs brought down the Roman Empire two thousand years ago. And we are bringing down your plastic-metal empire, President Nixon.

President Nixon, Governor Reagan, you cannot stop the future with guns and jails. Wake up and look around. We, whom you seek to imprison, are the happiest, healthiest, handsomest, most humorous folk around. And we intend to show in the gubernatorial election of 1970 that we, the peace-loving, fun-loving, are an overwhelming majority.

We have the numbers and we have the vision for the future. In this week's issue of the Los Angeles *Free Press* we have published our program to make the State of California a serene and healthy place to live. We have spelled out harmonious solutions to every one of the problems that now plague our citizens.

Governor Reagan, if you have a better program for youth, a better program for the Blacks, a better solution to oppressive taxation, then put away your state police tactics and debate with us openly in the public forum.

Governor Reagan, President Nixon, let's end the generation war. Let's smoke the peace pipe. Let's come together. If you continue to spurn our offers of reconciliation, I solemnly promise that you will never be elected to public office again and you will go down in history as enemies of the young, which means, enemies of the peaceful future which we are creating.

Reagan and Nixon were unmoved. Dr. Leary was finally placed in a cage on January 27, 1970. Nine months later — a few weeks before his fiftieth birthday, and already a grandfather — Timothy justified his "youth-culture" image by an athletic climb across a fifty-foot cable over the prison wall to freedom. He left behind a note to the officials:

In the name of the Father and Mother and the Holy Ghost — Oh, Guards — I leave now for freedom. I pray that you will free yourselves. To hold men captive is a crime against humanity and a sin against God. Oh, guards, you are criminals and sinners. Cut it loose. Be free. Amen.

Within a few months, Timothy was again imprisoned, by the Black Panther Party in Algiers. A second escape brought him to Switzerland, and a new imprisonment. The search for freedom was beginning to look barren. But then, under a propaganda campaign by American intellectuals led by playwright Arthur Miller and poet Allen Ginsberg, the Swiss government released Timothy, allowed him to remain in their territory, and refused to extradite him back to his cage in the California Archipelago. He was the first scientist-political-offender since Peter Kropotkin to make such a heroic escape from tyranny and remain at large.

We were in Mexico at the time, and I was writing two books under contract to Playboy Press and Dell. My whole family celebrated, in spite of Nixon and Kent State and Cambodia and everything, Timothy Leary was free and there seemed to be some hope for the world.

July 15, 1971

Mr. Ludwig von Moos
Federal Councillor
Head of the Federal Dept. of Justice & Police
Bern, Switzerland

The American P.E.N. Center representing over 1100 writers urges the Swiss Government to grant Dr. Timothy Leary asylum as an act of compassion. No good purpose will be served by returning this writer/scientist to an American prison. American writers are disturbed by the way that Dr. Leary's writings were cited as evidence in his trial, particularly in the imposing of the extraordinary sentence of more than 20 years in jail for possession of a small amount of marijuana. It would seem that Dr. Leary has been sentenced, if not convicted, for his views on drug use; he, therefore, qualifies as an intellectual refugee and we ask the Swiss Government to grant him asylum as it has hundreds of other writers, artists, and political figures who have sought refuge in Switzerland after having been forced to flee from other countries.

Thomas Fleming
President

Arthur Miller
International Vice President

David Dempsey
Chairman,
Writers in Prison Committee

On January 18, 1973, Dr. Leary was kidnapped by American agents in Afghanistan and returned to his cage.

The current rumor is that Joanna has been a government agent all along, assigned to "break" Timothy Leary and destroy his influence on youth, by leading him to become an informer.

This is sheer bullshit, according to Wavy Gravy of the Hog Farm. "I toured with Joanna for the Timothy Leary Defense Fund," says Wavy simply, "and I never saw a woman so totally in love with her man."

Dr. Wesley Hiler, former psychologist at Vacaville Prison and now my neighbor in Berkeley agrees. "Joanna quite simply *adores* Timothy," he told me. "She would never hurt him in any way.

"But," Dr. Hiler added thoughtfully, "Joanna would cheerfully cut anybody else's throat, to get Timothy out of jail."

I want to write about *Neurologic* now. I think it's Dr. Leary's most important book, and I'm going to be getting technical in here for a while.

Don't forget the gut-level importance of the subject-matter. *Neurologic* was written in 1973, *after* Timothy had been imprisoned in this country; escaped jail; joined Cleaver's gang of political refugees in Algiers; got re-imprisoned by *them*; escaped again; fled to Switzerland;

was re-imprisoned a third time; got released and received political asylum; got forced out of there by an inaccurate U.S. government accusation that he was the "criminal mastermind" behind an international hashish-smuggling ring (charges later dropped for lack of evidence, and probably made without good faith by the Watergate Mafia); moved on to Afghanistan; and was there blatantly kidnapped in broad daylight by U.S. agents. When asked in Switzerland, "When did you first start thinking of escape?" (a question referring to his prison-break), he deliberately misunderstood and answered whimsically, "At the age of 12." It was clear to him that his scientific work was a vast escape-plan for every man and every woman on earth: escape from the compulsive reflexes that imprint each nervous system into more-or-less total conformity with the local tribal games. He realized fully that authorities in many places regarded him as more dangerous than any merely political revolutionary. He was kept in chains after his recapture, and he wrote *Neurologic* on the floor of a solitary confinement cell.

The subject of *Neurologic* is Dr. Leary's concept of *serial imprinting*. (By coincidence, Dr. Konrad Lorenz won the Noble Prize for his c.1940 discovery of *imprinting* itself the same year, 1973, that Leary wrote *Neurologic*.) Imprinting can be popularly categorized as the peculiar kind of conditioning which is almost entirely irreversible. According to Lorenz, it only occurs in the early stages of life, immediately after birth. For instance, a European snow-goose, by nesting with its mother, imprints a female image which determines its future sexual behavior. When Dr. Lorentz, through over-zealous care of his experimental birds, accidentally imprinted himself on one of them, as the mothering image, that bird subsequently continued the imprint in adulthood, ignoring female geese and pursuing Dr. Lorenz sexually around the yard. While ordinary conditioning can generally be removed by counter-conditioning, imprinting cannot. It is rather like the distinction, in chemistry, between thermoplastic casts, which can be melted down and recast in a new form, and thermosetting casts, which cannot be changed until the object is destroyed chemically.

Dr. Leary proposes that in human beings the imprints are not all received immediately after birth, but come in series throughout the life experience. Normally, only four such imprints are taken, he says, but there are three others that can be accomplished under special circumstances. Each imprint takes the form of a new neurological circuit, as follows:

1 - The Bio-Survival Circuit, mediating forward-back movement or aggression-retreat. The imprint here follows dynamic gradients even older than the nervous system itself, going back to the amoeboid level and the dawn of life circa 3.5 billion years BCE. The forward imprint determines an aggressive, curious, neophilliac personality structure—basically, the DE position on the Interpersonal Grid. The backward imprint determines a sociable, incurious, neophobic personality, similar to LM on the Interpersonal Grid. Once again, watching where the bodies are in space-time and what movements they are making provides our description of what sort of imprint has been taken on this circuit.

(My wife asked me to haul the garbage from the kitchen to the backyard, after writing the above. In the yard I encountered a tomcat sitting on top of the garbage bin. His first-circuit imprint was immediate backward vector—flight—followed by slow, cautious forward vector—return—as he observed that I was non-hostile. For survival purposes, this imprint should have that kind of self-correcting or "feedback" effect, changing as the signals from the other indicate. All too often such a feedback is missing and the imprint is totally backward. This is called "autism" or "childhood schizophrenia." The infant, strongly imprinted by an unloving or over-strict parental figure, withdraws totally.)

The Bio-Survival imprint, then, is basically a forward-back program in space-time—forward to that which has been associated with the safe, cuddly, good, nurturing, motherly, sociable etc.; backward away from that which has been associated with the dangerous, bad, noxious, cruel, destructive etc. It is the right-left axis of the Interpersonal Grid:

LM ◄─────────► DE
Circuit One

2 - The Emotion-Locomotion circuit, mediating up-down or domination-submission. The imprint here follows neuro-glandular reflexes that began with the first amphibians 500 million years ago, when territoriality and hierarchy appeared. This imprint determines whether personality games shall be basically swelling-up, blustering, dominant or shrinking-in, cringing, submissive. Dogs, turtles, rodents, baboons and The President of your local Bank all use the same body-signals on this circuit. Look closely and see. This is the up-down axis of the Interpersonal Grid:

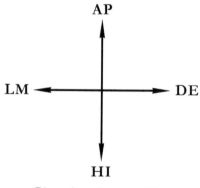

Circuits One & Two

Let us look again at the Interpersonal Grid (see figure in Chapter Three). The reader will profit vastly by taking the time to darken those segments which fit his or her most common interpersonal games. (If in doubt, cross-hatch a doubtful segment; but darken the ones you are ready to admit apply most of the time.) The figure that emerges from this—when obtained by four different methods, i.e. self-evaluation, evaluation by other members of a therapy group, evaluation by the Leary questionnaire, and evaluation by professional therapists— gives the four parameters of the personality in the Leary Diagnostic System, which can then be averaged onto a single Grid. The reader in this case is getting a cruder and simplified version based only on self-knowledge, which often contains self-deception. Nonetheless, such a graph gives some specificity to our generalizations here.

The shape of your graphs is basically the shape of the early imprints on Circuit I and Circuit II. This is the neurological cage in which you live, and the strength of it can be easily determined by deliberately trying to reverse polarity and adopt the opposite programs. *The anxiety experienced in that attempt is the strength of the reward-punishment imprint that formed your 7-dimensional game strategy.* This anxiety (known technically as "resistance") is encountered in every type of behavior change technology ("psychotherapy.") The enthusiasm for metaprogramming chemicals results from experience, convincing successful experimenters that the imprint and its associated anxiety can be suspended by these chemicals long enough to allow a new, self-chosen imprint of more rational, adult programs.

LEARY'S INTERPERSONAL GRID

The first imprint is programmed when the infant begins to crawl. He/she literally lives for a while in a flat-earth forward-back world, between the vectors of "safe" and "dangerous." Since *ontology recapitulates phylogeny* — the oldest, safest generalization in biology — the infant is literally operating on the forward-back circuits of the first unicellular organisms.

The pre-programmed metamorphosis to the second circuit is triggered by *standing erect*. The child becomes a "toddler" and enters the up-down vectors of family politics—the emotional-power games of father, mother, siblings, visitors. The territorial and hierarchal games of this circuit are, again, totally animalistic and mechanistic.

Listen: "A jackdaw sits feeding at the communal dish; a second bird approaches ponderously in an attitude of self-display with the head proudly erected, whereupon the first visitor moves slightly to one side, but otherwise does not allow himself to be disturbed. Now comes a third bird, in a much more modest attitude which, surprisingly enough, puts the first bird to flight; the second, on the other hand, assumes a threatening pose, with back feathers ruffled, attacks the latest comer and drives him from the spot." The signals seem to be mixed? Not at all: "The explanation: the latest comer stood in order of rank midway between the two others, high enough above the first to frighten him and just so far beneath the second as to be capable of arousing his anger. Very high caste jackdaws are most condescending to those of the lowest degree and consider them merely as dust beneath their feet; the self-display actions of the former are here a pure formality and only in the event of too close approximation does the dominant bird adopt a threatening attitude, but he very rarely attacks." – *On Aggression*, classic study of imprinting by Nobel-Prize winner, Dr. Konrad Lorenz. (Like Leary, Dr. Lorenz has made himself unpopular in Certain Quarters for noting out loud the same imprints in human social groups.)

These "larval imprints," as Leary calls them, all have definite survival purpose. The flock, herd, tribe, nation *needs* a variety of role-playing robots, since each role might at certain times be the one needed. The DNA has not produced these mechanisms just to make philosophers embarrassed and reformers disgusted; animals and so-called "primitive" humans often take special care of those with extremely weird imprints, knowing (on the cellular level?) that they might prove useful in special situations. Our society, consigning all deviant imprints to cages, is too rationalistic to heed its cellular archives.

This relativistic-evolutionary point having been made, it must be added that, if Dr. Leary is right, it is now time in our 3½ billion year career on this planet to *graduate* from the larval circuits and imprint the higher circuits. Is it an accident that the most grossly animalistic imprints are beginning to appear increasingly ridiculous and/or "pathological" to the *avant* portion of humanity?

Two paradigms of the second circuit are worth mentioning. The first is in Chaplin's comic masterpiece, *The Great Dictator*, in which Chaplin, as Hitler, and Jack Oakie, as Mussolini, go to a barber-shop together. Each keeps jacking up his own barber chair, to have the Top Dog position; the other then jacks up his own chair; and so on, until they both bang their heads on the ceiling.

Caricature? Many executives, understanding these mechanisms, have built their desks and chairs at a higher level (a few inches) than the visitors' chair. Talking to them is always a Bottom Dog game on the animal-signal level.

The second paradigm was found by Dr. Leary in *Newsweek*, April 22, 1974, and pasted into the first draft of the unpublished manuscript, *Periodic Table of Energy*, on which he and I were collaborating when the federal forces withdrew him into isolation. It reads:

> Perhaps because of their similarities, they can let down their hair with each other in a way they seldom can with outsiders. One White House staffer, for example, described a game of King of the Pool that Rebozo and Mr. Nixon once were spotted playing in the President's Key Biscayne swimming pool. It was late at night, after several drinks. First, Mr. Nixon mounted a rubber raft in the pool and fought against being dumped by the swimming Rebozo; then they changed places, and Mr. Nixon tried to overturn Bebe.

3 - The Mental-Manipulative Circuit, at right angles to the Interpersonal Grid, i.e. coming out of the page at you mediates right-left cortical choices and open-close reflexes. The toddler activates this circuit and is imprinted when he/she learns to open-close the hand, thereby seizing, examining, utilizing the environment. This muscular coordination *acts in conjunction* with (causality is obscure here) the similar open-close muscular control of the larynx leading to speech and questioning. (The open-close or "digital" type computer circle, not surprisingly, imitates this kind of human mentality.) There soon follows the capacity for thinking, which Leary, following the Behaviorists, regards as *sub-vocal speech*, subtle open-close vibrations of the larynx.

Imprinting, conditioning and programming this circuit can be a lifelong process. Once the child learns that the universe has been labeled and packaged, semantic neophilia overwhelms him/her. "What is this? What is that called?

How does this work?" Such neophilliac curiosity can last a lifetime, as parents are exhausted and replaced by teachers, instructors, professors, graduate schools, learned societies, original research etc.

One of the tragedies of humanity at present (i.e. circa 4000 BCE-2000 AD — a mere instant of cosmic time, actually) is that Circuit Three types, who acquire all the real knowledge and expertise (higher programming), have little skill at, or knowledge of, the "power politics" of the second emotional-domination circuit. Ever since Plato, various detached observers (third circuit types themselves) have noticed this periodically, and suggested that the traditional primate pattern of rule by the second Circuit *Alpha Males* should be replaced by the rule of Third Circuit philosophers. The primate imprints remain strong enough that most of humanity vehemently rejects this proposal, and, indeed, the rumor that a political candidate might be a Third Circuit "thinker" rather than a Second Circuit "bully" is enough to defeat any candidate. (Most recently, Nixon, although widely recognized as shifty and crooked, was chosen as "the lesser evil" in 1972—the favorite verbalization of those voting for him, I found in experimental interviews. This was because McGovern, rightly or wrongly, had acquired a Third Circuit scholar-teacher image.)

See image on next page

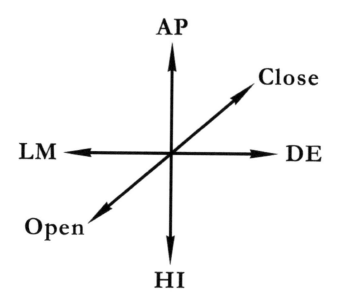

Circuits I, II, III integrated
"Three-Dimensional Ego-Space"

Primate cellular wisdom may be right, in the long run. The Top Dog position is so sacred and surrounded by mystification that a Third Circuit person, however brilliant, might find himself/herself, when cast in that role, totally unable to cope with it. *It does not compute on the third circuit*; it is "irrational," "sub-rational." Third circuit intelligence only functions properly in a (more-or-less) "free" or libertarian, quasi-anarchistic, community-of-equals, which is what most learned societies start out to be.

The third circuit, incidentally, seems to imprint chiefly the left lobe of the brain, which is in many ways a digital computer. There is some statistical evidence that this left-lobe imprint is genetically connected with right-handedness and links with *both* meanings of the word "dexterity." Left-handed persons, quite often, do not imprint the third circuit adequately and remain "open" or mentally unimprinted, "sinister" in certain ways; they are more likely to later imprint the fifth circuit, which seems to employ chiefly the right lobe of the brain, often thought to be an analog computer. Mystics are right-lobe types and their "analogic" or "magical" thinking often seems crazy or bizarre to third circuit scientists.

(These three circuits, and associated imprints, formed between birth and the achievement of articulate speech, form the basic "ego" or self-image, which is a standpoint, or point-of-view, relating to the three dimensions of Euclidean space: forward-back, up-down, right-left. Insights from outside this framework, whether called ESP or intuition, are always felt as uncanny, spooky, weird. Every technician of the occult — guru, magician, shaman — concentrates on encouraging such out-of-body insights in his pupils, to weaken the thermosetting nature of the 3-dimensional ego imprint.)

4 - The Socio-Sexual Circuit mediates strutting, display, courtship, mating, nest-building, care of the egg, etc. This is imprinted at puberty and narrows the polymorphous sexuality of the mammal, humankind, into the specific sex-role defined by the local tribe. As usual, the imprinting techniques are imperfectly understood by society, and — just as the normal male imprinting for "aggression" often misfires and creates a chronically "withdrawn" imprint on the first circuit, or the normal imprinting for submission in women sometimes doesn't take and a Feminist is created instead, etc. — the normal (in this society) sex-role is often reversed. Such persons are usually cruelly persecuted, although Konrad Lorenz's homosexual goose was tolerated by his flock without such "human" prejudice intervening.

When the first four circuits are imprinted, the basic self-definition usually does not change again until the catastrophe and ecstasy of death. In other words, most 40-year-olds or 60-year-olds or even 80-year-olds are still playing the games imprinted on them between birth and puberty. This is why most people have the same basically conservative, mildly paranoid cast of mind, reflecting the basically conservative, mildly paranoid parameters of the feudal-peasant societies of most human history.

5 - The Rapture or Neurosomatic Circuit opens when sensory and somatic consciousness – is achieved – perhaps via drugs in the cannabis family or nitrous oxide, perhaps through disease as epilepsy or schizophrenia, perhaps through traumatic accident (near-death, shock), perhaps through a deliberate training in the empirical methods discovered by shamans and yogis throughout history. This can happen at any age; but the new imprint reshapes the ego, and even the body, just as dramatically as the crawling that opens the first imprint, the standing erect that opens the second imprint, the dexterity-insight that opens the third imprint, or the biological eruptions of puberty that open the fourth imprint. The rapturous individual does not have "problems" the same way that those operating the interpersonal games of the first four circuits have "problems"; the rapturous person is not on the interpersonal grid at all.

The symbolic or strategic calculations of the game-playing ego (first four circuits) depend entirely on the values imprinted upon the dualities of forward-back, up-down, right-left, dexterous-clumsy, domination-submission, good-evil, etc. Life is experienced through the grid of these dualities and appears as a problem, as chess or monopoly or any other game of strategy is a problem, but more urgent than other games because defined socially as "reality." The rapturous person is merely here, now, sensing, rejoicing, participating; awareness is usually in the end-organs, not in the strategic computer center of the forebrain (except when real danger occurs).

It is Dr. Leary's conclusion that most of the tension, depression, chronic tiredness, persistent anxiety etc. of "normal" game-playing consciousness is due to the continuous overuse of the second, Emotion-Locomotion Circuit. That is, the emotional person is "a lurching lunatic," he says, because the emotional-glandular circuits are turned on almost all the time, the person enters each situation with reflexes evolution formed only for emergency (real danger), such as when being bitten by a bear.

It is part of the tragedy of contemporary humanity that (in addition to the general lack of knowledge about the techniques of imprinting and using the higher circuits) the Second Circuit is actually glorified and worshipped by many. Poets and spokesmen for the "Romantic" movement, for instance, continually praise the emotional-tantrum orientation as "deep" and "profound." We have all heard so much of this philosophy of anti-philosophy, it seems so "natural" to us, that we are apt to be surprised when it is denounced by a Korzybski or a Gurdjieff; and we can hardly imagine why it seems so comical to a non-Westerner such as the Sufi businessman-mystic Idries Shah, whose books frankly express the attitude that Occidentals are over-emotional children in adults' bodies.

In the wake of Fanon's writings, alas, many "radicals"

or "leftists" have climbed onto the Second Circuit bandwagon, regarding chronic emotional turmoil as the only "correct" attitude and encouraging childishness as a political stance. The fear-rage glandular kick — addiction to adrenalin, adrenolutin and similar stress-induced chemicals — is so romanticized by these persons that we are apt to overlook the fact that they are attempting to live life hour-by-hour on the reflexes that were created only for special emergency situations.

Dr. Leary adds that the lower circuits are highly contagious:

> When children are exposed to restricting rage, violence, or fear during the critical imprint period, subsequent conditioning associates the emerging reaction — rage, withdrawal, flight, anxiety — with the stimuli . . . An ominous aspect of the emerging emotional reaction is that it invariably triggers off a mutual fear response in others present, attracts attention, gives status . . .

> Unhappily, fear and restricting violence can become addictive kicks, reinforced by schizophrenic policy-makers and an economic system which depends upon restricting freedom, and upon the production of fear and the inciting of violent behavior.

Indeed, the absence of the "expected" emotional imprint in young (unimprinted) infants is often disturbing to parents, who will fancy that they have birthed a monster. More often, the lack is remedied at once, and the child is *coached* (as in Leary's baseball model) on how to develop the appropriate emotional-glandular response. "Don't just stand there—hit him back!" is usually programmed into male children very early, although not into females; the infant's spontaneous reaction, like that of the family dog, is most often to skulk away, submissively, from superior power, except when the unconditioned rage reaction is keyed off by intense fear. As Lorenz documents in *On Aggression*, the unconditioned attack reflex always contains a *mixture* of fear and rage; either fear or rage alone will not do it. Here we see concretely the truth of Leary's observation that unconditioned emotional programs are emergency devices. The rage-fear attack reflex has frightened off many a bully in 3½ billion years of evolutionary learning.

The conditioned emotional reactions, created by parental and societal reward-punishment imprinting, are not restricted to evolutionary emergencies. In fact, in most people they run busily along all day, every day; a fact that notoriously makes philosophers weep and reformers despair. Understanding that these inappropriate imprints ("neuroses") have the same glandular mechanism as real emergencies should provide more sympathy for the sufferers (and those not afraid to be eccentric may share the hope of Dr. Leary, Dr. Lilly and other less publicized researchers who believe that re-imprinting is *easy* with the proper metaprogramming drug and the right program).

This parallels the analysis of Perls, Hefferline and Goodman (in *Gestalt Therapy*) which explains that most people function on a level of "chronic low-grade emergency"; but Dr. Leary gives an evolutionary neurogenetic interpretation of why we misuse our nervous systems that way. Too much emotion by the parents or parent surrogates, when imprinting the second circuit, leads to chronic, daily, hour-by-hour emotionalism (consistent Circuit Two behavior) in the offspring, for the rest of their lives. This starts when the child stands up, and the later dexterity-analysis or engineering-logic facilities of Circuit Three are not imprinted until the child begins asking questions constantly and manipulating tools. Thus, in most people, reason remains — as all cynics have noted — the slave of emotion, and is generally used only to justify the reflexes (passions, compulsions) of the glandular system. Circuit Two checkmates Circuit Three.

When Circuit Five, rapture, is imprinted, the emotional circuits finally become relatively dormant; and then objective reason becomes possible, as Gurdjieff predicted. Circuit Five plus Circuit Three can checkmate Circuit Two.

6 - The Neurophysical or Ecstasy Circuit is imprinted when the nervous system becomes aware of itself — free of the body and the earlier imprints — as a conscious entity which can take virtually any form imaginable. Dr. John Lilly defines this state subjectively as follows: "In the province of the mind, what is believed true is true or becomes true, within limits to be learned experientially and experimentally. These limits are further beliefs to be transcended. In the province of the mind there are no limits." This is the discovery of "the God within" in the traditional language of mystics. Experientially, it is the awareness that I am not male, American, white, middle-aged, or any other category; I am not the previous space-time imprints; I am not my opinion of myself; I am unknown and unknowable. The nervous system discovering the nervous system is totally plastic; this is both the "no-mind" or "no-form" of Zen Buddhism and the "omniform" of Platonic idealism. The nervous system sees no color, feels no pain, wants nothing, loses nothing. Buzz, flash, joy are about the only words describing this in English; the Orient speaks of Samadhi (Union) or Satori (Awakening) or similar mystic concepts. The point of transition from the rapture imprint to the ecstasy imprint is all in direction of attention: the rapture imprint converts all external impressions into joyful energy-transformations, the ecstasy imprint converts the nervous system itself into joyful energy-transformations.

The yogis, Buddhists, Christian saints, etc. who smiled in bliss while being burned alive or otherwise tortured were functioning on the Sixth Circuit. Nietzsche envisioned this invulnerability to environmental accident or malice and imagined that he who could function this way was a Superman. Dr. Leary's sunny smile and intense compassionate involvement with others, all through the years of his persecution and imprisonment, are contemporary examples of functioning on the Sixth Circuit.

The joy of the rapturous Fifth Circuit, then, is totally arbitrary – as in the worry, pain, anxiety, depression etc. of the first four circuits. The nervous system intrinsically feels nothing. Feelings are a function of which circuitry we are using and how that circuit has been imprinted. The mystics have been right all along in saying that "nothing is but thinking makes it so"; Dr. Leary has finally put their insight into scientific neurogenetic language.

7 - The Neurogenetic Circuit is located *within* the individual neurons, unlike the previous circuits which mediate processes *between* neurons. This imprint is formed by the shut-off of space-time imprints and outlying sensory and somatic receiving centers. Body-time is disconnected; the neuron tunes in to its own rhythms, hundreds of millions of signals per second. Euclidean-Newtonian-Aristotelian mechanism cease to apply; the awareness is in Einsteinium dimensions. According to Dr. Leary, this is literally true and is *not* a metaphor: signals-per-second within the neuron corresponds to miles-per-second outside the body and time is transformed by the neurogenetic imprint just as it is by speed-of-light. We enter Eternity.

Reviewing, we can now see that metaprogramming (in Dr. Lilly's sense) extends far beyond the "psychotherapeutic" level of re-imprinting heterosexuality on homosexuality, or reasonable aggression on chronic timidity, or ability to reason on compulsive emotionalism, etc. Metaprogramming can re-imprint the total nervous system, *and thus change all our inherited ideas about location in space, existence in time, the reality of pain. etc.;* in short, the "reality" known by ordinary programming of the first four circuits is only one "reality" and many others can be created, all equally "real." The intelligent schizophrenic or introspective epileptic (cf. Dostoyevsky) is quite right in speaking of such alternative realities; only their lack of control over these circuits prevented them from making their case convincing to skeptics. The Neurogenetic Age allows every man and woman to tune their nervous systems to whatever level of functioning they wish. This technology already exists (since the mid-60s); only hysteria and prejudice prevent it from being used.

Of course, the Neurogenetic Age has other implications also, since any program can be imprinted with the right techniques. Government monopoly on these techniques raises possibilities which make current abuses (psycho-surgery, aversion therapy etc.) mere jokes by comparison with what can be done. A society of drones, or zombies, as in Huxley's *Brave New World*, is remarkably close to being practical at the very moment you read these words. *The import of Dr. Leary's "Two Commandments" cannot be grasped until this point is fully understood.* Charlie Manson, a freelance operator without government funding, has already demonstrated how to program a transformation of values that Hitler would have envied; and Manson did not have control of the press, radio, technology, police, etc. as Hitler did. He merely knew how to combine P_n (a program based on traditional Cabalistic magic, Scientology and racism) with MS (metaprogramming substances varied, in this case, from LSD to belladonna) and created B_n which included totally emotionless murder.

Chapter Seven

The Caged Panther

> But in the caged panther's eyes, "Nothing, nothing
> that you can do," green pool, under green of the
> jungle, caged, "Nothing, nothing that you can do."
> —Ezra Pound, The Pisan Cantos

On the sixth circuit — neurophysical consciousness
— we seem to be in direct communication with atomic
and subatomic energies, initial experiences almost always
have a quality of light—the "white light of the void," the
Sun-God archetype, the experience of decentralized cosmic
energy-intelligence.

During this "oceanic experience" (Freud) or "peak
experience" (Maslow) all the ordinary imprints are totally
suspended. One is no longer "in" socially-defined space,
socially-defined time, or "in" the socially-defined ego.

One becomes "Nemo" (no-man) in the traditional
language of alchemical-Rosicrucian occultism. This is the
"Nothing more precious than all things" in the riddling
language of Thomas Vaughan. The next imprint is crucial,
because it will *set* just like the first imprints of infancy

and remain as a new habit, a new function, a new neural network.

Leary's own career illustrates the possibilities of metaprogramming the "self" after the sixth circuit is opened or activated. The Leary I met in 1964 was the very model of a Harvard scientist, tightly hooked into precise measurement, operationally-defined terminology, the whole logical-positivist/Wittgenstein trip, in which theory is always related directly to experience by language tailored to the experience and all undefined or traditional terms were avoided scrupulously to escape the semantic contagion they might contain. The Leary of the late 60s, re-imprinted by taking LSD in an Oriental Guru set-and-setting, was "no longer interested in the science-game," as he often said. He lived and broadcast the ecstatic Tantric path, colloquialized by himself in the peculiarly American mantra, "Turn on, Tune in, Drop out." After this first bout of prison and a series of disillusioning experiences with the appeals system and the higher courts, Leary abolished the Guru as thoroughly as he had abolished the Scientist and became the Revolutionary.

"We still feel there is a place for the urban guerilla," he told an interviewer from WMCA while in Algiers. "They should escalate the violence. They should start hijacking planes, they should kidnap prominent sports figures and television and Hollywood people in order to free Bobbie Seale," he raved on enthusiastically. This was most certainly not Guru Leary or Scientist Leary; this was a whole new imprint.

After Eldridge Cleaver placed Timothy under "revolutionary arrest" for characteristically Learyan heresy, Tim began to lose interest in the Revolutionary imprint. He had always leaned toward a kind of pacifistic individualism, in all his ego-roles, and he nowadays often compares his imprisonment by Cleaver to the persecution of Solzhenitsyn in Russia. "The grim socialisms of Russia, China and America" are described in *Neurologic* as entirely comparable in all respects, equally stagnant and anti-evolutionary.

In the Switzerland interlude, Timothy experimented with telepathy and Crowley's magick; perhaps he was starting to re-imprint the Guru image again. An extraordinary mystic experience in Bou Saada, North Africa, while fleeing the Black Panthers, had convinced him that there were "higher" or more complex neurological circuits than any he had yet reached, and he was eager to explore them. The fact that Crowley had achieved one of his most successful contacts with supposed "angelic beings" or secret chiefs at Bou Saada seemed significant, Timothy told me later. Crowley had used the John Dee "Enochian" system of magick in his 1909 Bou Saada experience, and Tim might well have gone on to program himself into an Enochian magician at this point. Instead, new scientific theories about all these "occult" phenomena began to dawn on him, and he has been quite busily reprogramming himself into the Leary-the-Scientist trip ever since, despite the distractions provided by government agents who keep seizing his body and moving it from one cage to another.

It is this mercurial quality of the neurological adept that makes such people invulnerable to the usual social pressures that exact total (or grudging partial) conformity from most of us.

Crowley explains, in his *Confessions*, why he became Count Vladimir Svaroff for a while in 1896:

I wanted to increase my knowledge of mankind.

I knew how people treated a young man from Cambridge . . . Now I wanted to see how people would behave to a Russian nobleman. I must say that I have repeatedly used this method of disguise — it has been amazingly useful in multiplying my points of view about humanity.

Again, explaining his authorship of *Hail Mary*, a pious volume of verses that bespeaks orthodox Roman Catholic belief, Crowley says:

I simply wanted to see the world through the eyes of a devout Catholic, very much as I had done with the decadent poet of *White Stains*, the Persian mystic of the *Bagh-i-Muattar*, and so on . . . I did not see why I should be confined to one life. How can one hope to understand the world if one persists in regarding it from the conning tower of one's own personality?

The one-personality game, indeed, is the "delusion of egotism" that all schools of mysticism attempt to cure as the first step toward illumination. Just so, Don Juan Matus, Yaqui Indian shaman, explains this aspect of the mystic path to anthropologist Carlos Castaneda in *Journey to Ixtlan*:

"That is the little secret I am going to give you today," he said in a low voice. "Nobody knows who I am or what I do. Not even I . . . How can I know who I am, when I am all of this?" he said, sweeping the surroundings with a gesture of his head.

The sixth circuit neuro-programmer has no "personality" in the normal way that men and women have personality. (The first time I succeeded in a sixth circuit operation, I said to my wife, "I am no longer human." I had no Nietschean grandiosity at all, however; rather, I was strangely humble and totally awed. I had abruptly realized that everything I regarded as *human* was merely a game humans have tacitly agreed to play with each other, We are all metaprogrammers, whether we know it or not—or, to cite the infamous Nietzsche accurately for once, "We are all better artists than we realize." Most of the misery of mankind results from confusing our art-works with reality – mistaking the map for the territory, to repeat mathematician Eric Temple Bell's great metaphor.)

Crowley and Gurdjieff, the great adepts of modern Europe, left behind thousands of confusing legends, all mutually contradictory. The mystery of these men is solved when one realizes that they no longer possessed a "self" in the way ordinary people possess — and are possessed by — self. Charles Slack is probably not consciously lying when he portrays Timothy Leary as a vicious criminal psychopath; and Jane Kramer, in their review of Slack's book in *NY Times Book Review*, is not lying either when she claims Timothy is not a criminal but a "mixture of innocence and arrogance . . . very nice, very charming man of no great intellect" (!); nor am I lying, nor is Dr. Wesley Hiler lying, in reporting that Leary's IQ seems *above* the genius level. "You can be anyone you want to be this time around" is one of Tim's favorite metaprogramming metaphors; as he explained during the escape trial: "When I drive a Cadillac, I *am* a Cadillac; when I drive a Pontiac, I *am* a Pontiac."

To summarize and review briefly:

On Circuit One, the crawling infant knows only the dimensions of *forward* (to pleasure) and *back* (from danger.) On Circuit Two (first opened by the amphibians and most visible in territorial rituals), the *up* (dominate) and *down* (submit) axis crosses the forward-back axis;

this imprint forms when the infant begins to toddle. The first circuit imprint is then re-imprinted on a higher, more complex level; circuits one-and-two together form the parameters of swelling-blustering-aggression-rage or shrinking-cringing-retreating-fear exhibited in territorial, "ideological", emotional and other quarreling behavior.

Circuit Three imprinting begins when the child starts to *handle* and *question*; the nature of the imprint determines, firstly, the re-imprinting of circuits one and two in this new context; secondly, the choice of *left* cortical dominance (dexterity, fluency, *active* orientation) or *right* cortical dominance (intuition, art, *passive* orientation); and thirdly, within the active or left cortical domination type, which handlings shall be dexterous and which taboo (cf. masturbation prohibition, discouragement of manual skills in ruling classes, etc.) and which verbalism shall be free and rational (logical) and which shall be blocked, inarticulate, "thoughtcrime" or otherwise verboten.

Circuit Four, imprinted at adolescence, again re-imprints all the previous circuits in a sexual context, creating either sexually-aggressive or sexually-timid, sexually-dominant or sexually-submissive, sexually-responsible or sexually-irresponsible, "good" or "evil" (tribally defined), etc. This is usually the final imprint and all four circuits then have adapted the polymorphous and undefined infant into a fairly good mirror of the local *games*. Behavior then generally remains thus fixated until death. The Interpersonal Grid shows which games are favored by each individual and locates the ego in these Euclidean dimensions and dualisms.

The later circuits, more recent in evolutionary time and hence more complex and precise than the earlier, move consciousness out of the Euclidean-Newtonian-Aristotelian context of a flat earth in linear space and absolute time etc. into a non-Euclidean, non-Newtonian, non-Aristotelian context of a round earth in curved space and relative time. They represent a true mutation of consciousness, which has been appearing randomly for thousands of years and which could not be explained in ordinary language by those who achieved it (the mystics). *In modern scientific terms, Dr. Leary suggests, this new orientation can now be understood and used. It is the neurology of extraterrestrial humanity.*

Circuit Five, imprinted by rapture, re-imprints the symbolic consciousness of the first four circuits. Dualisms collapse, as all mystics have testified. This is appropriate for men and women living in zero-gravity, where the up-down and forward-back and left-right dualities cease to have their flat earth "reality." Circuit Six, imprinted by ecstatic self-discovery of the nervous system by itself, allows the transcendence of all previous circuits ("In the province of the mind what is believed true is true or becomes true . . ." — Dr. Lilly.) and makes the mind poly-form or no-form rather than uni-form. This is appropriate for relating to the non-human intelligences we will be meeting in deep space. (It seems that space-travel is only possible and desirable when the local chauvinisms are *thoroughly*, not partially, outgrown. What person, who is only male, only white, only American, etc. — or only "human" as historically defined — can relate adequately to a native of Sirius?) Circuit Seven, imprinted by DNA memory itself within the neuron, transcends the mammalian, the animal, the earthian and creates the true cosmic consciousness necessary for joining with inhuman beings in harmony, in an Einsteinian space-time sense above the polarized "space" and "time" of individualized point-of-view.[*]

~•~

* Point-of-view or individuality remains intact, a function of the nervous system's physical parameters, even after the normal imprinted ego has been transcended. DNA consciousness on the Seventh Circuit is beyond even point-of-view. It is life itself thinking.

~•~

It is significant that the language of mystics seems to fall into two categories: (1) statements of the logically impossible, i.e. self-contradictory and (2) statements of the "palpably untrue" (H.L. Mencken's verdict). The first class of mystic utterances, we can now see, relate to the non-dualistic functioning of the later neurological circuits; these statements are illogical because either/or logic is a code relating to the dichotomies of the first four circuits. When this is grasped, it is obvious that the mystics are neither fools nor lunatics. How then may we account for the statements in the second class, the "palpably untrue?"

Dr. Leary argues in *Terra II* (1974) that statements were untrue only because undated; that they were, in fact, prophecies. The DNA blueprint — the vectors of evolution, terrestrial and extraterrestrial—can be read (although with some local distortion) by anyone who imprints the Seventh Circuit. Mysticism is neurogenetics expressed in pre-scientific symbols (the "archetypes" of Jung's "collective unconscious"?). Thus, the statement that we are the children of the gods means that DNA came to earth from outer space—as Francis Crick, co-discoverer of DNA, now believes is proven by the chemical evidence. The statement that we will go back to heaven, to our home in the stars, to rejoin the gods, etc. means that we will achieve interstellar flight and discover the Higher Intelligences who seeded the DNA throughout this galaxy (and perhaps throughout other galaxies). The doctrine of immortality, usually expressed as something *to be achieved* by "spiritual work" (Christianity with its innately immortal "soul" is an exception to the majority of mystical revelations), means that life-extension to an indefinite point is possible.

The last point, being one of Dr. Leary's most startling projections, is worthy of some further analysis. When *Terra II* was published (January 1974), Dr. Leary based his prediction on his own seeming success in telepathic communication with interstellar intelligence and on directions already evident in biochemical research; but the next month, February, he was startlingly confirmed. Dr. Leary specifically predicted that life extension to around 400 years would be achieved by 2000 AD. The confirmation, from Michigan State University, was that research is already under way on a drug that might extend life to 200 years. Segerberg's *The Immortality Factor*, published since then, provides more evidence of similar research going forth in various quarters, and suggests that life extension into many centuries is achievable somewhere between the 1980s and 1990s.

If we retain an earthside perspective, this does not suggest "immortality" in the near future, but Dr. Leary's extraterrestrial perspective brings in a surprise factor. If a starship leaves earth circa 2000 AD with a crew possessing the biochemical life-expectancy of 300-500 years, a tour around the galaxy occupying, say, 400 years ship-time will, by the Einstein formulae, return to earth circa 4,000,000,000 AD. Even if the galaxy is not the home of the starseeders (who transmitted DNA about in space); even if the crew do not contact higher races with more advanced technology; even so, on returning to earth, they will contact a science four billion years ahead of ours. *Space travel is time travel*. The first starship crew need never die, then, and since some of this crew are alive today, some readers of this sentence, quite likely, are immortals. This is the decoding of the mystics' "palpably untrue" statement that we can rise to the heavens and live forever.

The reader may be staggered at this point, but *Terra II* is merely a reasonable, scientific, logical exploration of the consequences of Dr. Leary's assumption that the later neurological circuits have a function in addition to the sheer hedonistic pleasure of "turning on, tuning in, and dropping out." In fact, *each* circuit, he now believes, has 3 stages: (A) *hedonistic input*, in which the new energy released by the DNA is receptively enjoyed—the toddler's joy in gamboling about, the adolescent's "phallic narcissism" when the sex circuit is first activated, etc.; (B) *the new imprint or integrating program* itself, in which the new energy is intelligently used — walking to the next room to get what you want, mating with a neurological counterpart, etc.; and (3) *evolutionary output* — the "mate" or goal of the program. The pothead who has learned to turn on the rapture circuit and just groove on everything hedonistically, and also the yogi in such bliss that he drops out of society and slowly starves, are seen as identifiable types by Dr. Leary: persons fixated on the narcissistic input level (A) Just as maturity means (B-C) walking toward sane goals, rising to dominate our own emotions and not other people, handling dexterously rather than brutally, speaking truthfully and not deceptively, mating lovingly and not exploitatively, so, too, on the higher circuits. The purpose of the rapture (Circuit 5) is to transcend the local imprints and grow wiser; ecstasy (Circuit 6) is to increase insight and objective intelligence; the neurogenetic (Circuit 7) is to transcend humanity itself. Only then can we talk as equals to "those gods who made the heavens," the star-seeders.

In essence, then, the Terra II project is the greatest jailbreak in history; the only precedent is the migration of European drop-outs to America at the dawn of the clipper ship era. Such time-space transformations (until wireless, America was separated from Europe by time as well as space) are seemingly necessary when the evolution of neurological mutants demands separation from the parent-organism. One can say in 1974 of Earth exactly what a rational observer could have said of Europe in 1674 or 1774: the old culture will neither adjust to the new, nor will it learn to tolerate and stop persecuting. The new culture must find its own place in the universe.

Ezra Pound, perhaps the greatest poet since Shakespeare, surveyed the debris of World War II from his death-cell at Pisa and spoke in the language of a caged panther: "Nothing. Nothing that you can do." The intervening three decades have confirmed that view for the neurologically sensitive and turned-on: Earth civilization has come to an impasse. As Dr. Leary writes in *Terra II*, "It will he possible, indeed, it will be necessary, for Terra II to initiate new ways of living, experiments in sociology, psychology, ethics, and neurology, which cannot be performed in Terra I societies. It is impossible, for example, to evolve new social forms on this planet. This was the lesson of the 1960s. Experimental mutants cannot occupy the same space as species dominants. Any visible changes in lifestyle, sexual social pattern, mode of consciousness, will be ruthlessly suppressed. The Catholic Pope opposes birth control and every police chief in the world itches to barber the long-hairs. Etc." Humanity must mutate to survive. Such mutation will be crushed if attempted on Terra I. Terra II, then, is the logical, practical, biologically and historically programmed, inevitable alternative.

(There are those who refuse to face these facts, who believe that the larval imprints of the first four circuits can be re-imprinted in large enough numbers to make survival on this planet possible. *Terra II* does not cast a pall of negativism over such hopes. Rather, Dr. Leary insists that the research and development spin-offs of the Terra II project should be given free to the peoples of Earth; he even indicates reasons why the socio-cultural shock of Terra II itself might induce many Terra I "rulers" to accept this new knowledge and apply it. But the attempt to save Terra I without leaving ourselves the escape hatch of Terra II is territorial nostalgia and neurological conservatism carried to the evolutionary *kamikaze* point.)

Terra II is conceived by Dr. Leary as a non-governmental, free-enterprise, cosmopolitan project involving all races and ethnic groups of Terra I. To ask how it will be financed is like asking the first émigrés from Europe how they expected to finance the voyage to America; those who want to go, will find a way. (For the beginnings, Dr. Leary suggests donations from millionaires who would like to live forever in galactic space and will buy into the voyage; research contracts and patents owned by scientists working on the starship, the immortality pill, and similar spin-offs; sale and lease of media rights.) The crew should consist of 5000 human beings, equally divided among men and women, representing all ethnic groups, picked for neurological traits such as high intelligence; proven capacity to function in scientific, executive or artistic innovation, creativity, etc. These are the people who can see alternatives and possibilities beyond the larval imprints of the early circuits and who live today in frustration because these possibilities are forbidden on

Terra I.

In *The Murder of Christ*, Dr. Wilhelm Reich (writing as the prejudice of the old Terra I culture was closing in on him, about to railroad him to jail and burn his scientific books in an incinerator) gives an interesting parable about some prisoners in a huge jail cell. Some dream always of escape; others sink into despair ("Nothing. Nothing that you can do"); still others attempt to "reform" the cell, make it more humane and decent, etc.; another group preaches that we belong in the cell because of "sins" in past lives; a few have detailed escape plans, involving "necessary" violence and "military" discipline (the path to another cell). The odd thing Reich says, is that *the door is wide open all the time, but nobody dares to move toward it.*

Dr. Reich meant this as a metaphor about the "muscular armor" which, according to his theory, anchors our early infantile imprints and causes us to repeat at 40 or 60 or 80 the same few games we learned in our first years. From Dr. Leary's point of view, the muscular armor is only a secondary reaction to our addiction to those glandular chemicals which keep the early imprints of the first circuits perpetually programming the same stereotyped responses. The mystics and the shamans have understood this for at least three or four millenniums; but they have had no positive proposal except the original imprint program of the higher circuits. *Terra II* offers a program and an evolutionary output for those higher circuits and their energies. It is the first practical, scientific, rational, pragmatic, totally sane alternative ever offered to the neurological elite who usually drop out of human society and merely watch quizzically from the sidelines.

In evaluating the prophecies of *Terra II*, we must remember that the basic claims offered therein are (if humanity survives) quite inevitable. Life-extension to the immortality point, journeys to the stars, and contact with Higher Intelligence are the metaprograms earth-life has been following since the beginning. The only question that remains open is: shall this happen in the libertarian and sane way Dr. Leary envisions and urges, or will it all fall under the auspices of governments, Second Circuit territoriality and imperialism, the glandular programs that are no longer evolutionarily appropriate?

According to Dr. Leary, the answer is cheerful and inescapable. Those operating on the lower circuits can neither understand nor envy the Terra II vision. (NASA with its clown-shows of WASPS playing golf on the moon etc. indicates about as far as the Circuit Two-Three mind can go.) The interstellar field is entirely open to those who have the higher circuit imprints necessary to share the vision and activate it. The message has been transmitted by the publication of *Terra II*; each human will react as determined by his or her degree of neurological evolution. Those who are staying in the old jail cell of earth, are staying; those who are going, are going.

As Dr. Leary's wife, the beautiful Joanna, has written: "Become very intelligent. That's our method of propulsion."

Friends in the Bay Area, who met Joanna Leary, Tim's new wife, and his attorneys, informed me that Tim had literally been kept in chains for a while after his return to San Luis Obispo's Men's Colony (prison). I was furious; and I was bitter in particular at the lack of protest from the academic community. It seemed absolutely undeniable to me that, *whatever Timothy's ideological or other offenses*, the first amendment had been trampled horribly in the government's persecution of him, along with academic freedom and separation of church and state (he *is*, since 1967, an ordained Hindu priest and the two marijuana cigarettes which ostensibly justify his 30-year prison sentences *are* part of the standard meditation technique of Shivite Hindus). The independence of science from government, the right to publish unpopular opinions, and the whole tradition of Anglo-Saxon civil liberties were also involved. After all, the judge did cite Timothy's *published writings* in setting an impossible bail, and this alone makes Dr. Leary's imprisonment a constitutional issue of burning significance.

I was between royalty statements from my publishers, and unable yet to sell a third book, so we had to go on Welfare for a while. Nevertheless, I took $15 out of our meager larder and had 1000 copies of the following one-page protest printed:

WHY IS DR. TIMOTHY LEARY IN PRISON?

Dr. Leary is in prison because his bail has been set so high that he cannot pay it and get out while his case is under appeal.

Nobody accused of the same "crime" as Dr. Leary (possession of less than one ounce of marijuana) has had such a high bail in living memory.

Why was Dr. Leary's bail set so high? Because (in the words of the judge who set the bail and refused to reduce it) Dr. Leary's scientific and religious ideas are "dangerous."

THIS IS A VIOLATION OF THE U.S. CONSTITUTION. The Constitution states flatly that men and women in this country may not be punished for their scientific or religious ideas — not by jail, not by high bail, not by any legal action at all. In fact, excessively high bails are explicitly forbidden in the Constitution.

So: there is no doubt that Dr. Leary's constitutional rights have been violated, and that he is being punished beyond the law for having ideas that the judge did not like.

Does this concern you?

Yes, very definitely. As columnist Mike Royko once noted, "There is a democratic principle about injustice: If enough people support it, they'll ALL get it."

A survivor of the Nazi concentration camp at Buchenwald told reporters, "When they came for the Jews, I didn't protest because I'm not Jewish. When they came for the Jehovah's Witnesses, I didn't protest because I'm not a Jehovah's Witness. When they came for the trade unionists, I didn't protest because I'm not a trade unionist. *Then they came for me.*"

In 1956, the U.S. government jailed Dr. Wilhelm Reich *and burned his books in an incinerator in New York City.* Only 18 scientists in the whole country protested, because Dr. Reich had been offensive and arrogant in presenting his theories.

Throughout the 1960s, the government warred against all doctors who believed in the krebiozen cancer treatment. Many of these doctors were harassed, a few were put through the expense and agony of long court trials. Again, few scientists and teachers protested: Dr. Ivy, chief exponent of krebiozen, had offended the establishment by speaking too frankly and angrily about his critics.

Today, health food and vitamin therapists are under attack.

Every scientist, every doctor, every teacher, every writer and scholar, every man or woman with an unpopular idea is a potential victim of government orthodoxy, if we do not defend the Constitution and demand *that punishment of researchers be stopped,* however radical their theories may be.

The fight for Timothy Leary's rights is the fight for

mind itself, for our right to think, to publish our thought, to speak out.

The civil liberties you save may be your own. In the wake of Watergate, how sure are you that they're not already bugging your phone or watching you?

ROBERT ANTON WILSON
PO BOX 693, GUERNEVILLE, CALIF. 95446

I sent this out to every psychology department (and some of the sociology departments) in every university in California, and to all the newspapers.

Some of the papers printed it in their letters column.

I never received a single reply from the halls of Academe.

Meanwhile, I had become embroiled in another of Timothy's grandiose schemes. Together with a bright long-term con named Charles Newsome — a self-educated jailhouse lawyer who regularly wrote his own legal appeals and those of many other cons — Timothy had cooked up a plot to end the system of keeping men in cages forever. Under the name P.R.O.B.E. (Public Reform Organization for Better Education), Leary and Newsome, and an outside attorney named Walter Culpepper, were suing the state of California for committing fraud against the taxpayers in maintaining prisons as we know them.

The logic of the suit was certainly novel. Statistics were quoted that California prisons produce a graduate crop of new criminals each year at a higher percentage than Harvard produces scholars, the Air Force Academy produces officers, etc. In other words, one could scientifically predict that sending a man to a California prison was more likely to make him a life-long criminal than sending him to Harvard was likely to make him a scholar. This statistical argument was based largely on the Kilgore Report, a study of the failure of California's prisons written by a scholarly committee of experts in 1971, under commission from the governor.

The Kilgore Report, indeed, suggested that continuing the prisons was continuing the crime problem, and that a new solution was badly needed.

The P.R.O.B.E. suit charged that, by ignoring this scientific recommendation, Ronald Reagan and other state officials committed negligent fraud equivalent to that of an engineer who builds a faulty bridge when standard texts reveal his error, or a doctor whose mistakes fall below the permissible failure level and indicate incompetence. *Politicians have the same responsibility to know, and act upon, scientific fact as do doctors, engineers, or other professional people.* Politicians, the suit claims, are not merely public entertainers and have legal responsibility to act intelligently. When they default, this is criminal negligence.

This is remarkable reasoning, like most Leary productions. Certainly, we have never heard anything like it before; when Nixon rejected the scientific findings of the marijuana and pornography commissions, many criticized him for demagogy, but nobody thought he might be committing criminal negligence. Yet, why not? Are politicians mere clowns and actors? Is that our concept of administration? Or are they supposed to be at least as objective and responsible to their clients (the public-at-large) as doctors and engineers? Face the issue directly, says P.R.O.B.E.: do we want responsible government, or are we willing to settle for admitted irresponsibility?

Obviously, if the P.R.O.B.E. argument is ever accepted the world will be much different, politicians will have to pass intelligence tests and general information tests, and show at least as much real knowledge of sociology-social psychology-economics-penology as, say, a civil engineer has of physics-mathematics-thermodynamics-architecture. If his actions reveal ignorance of neglect of such knowledge, the politico can be removed for deceiving and abusing his clients, the citizenry.

I met with Walter Culpepper, the P.R.O.B.E. attorney at his modernistic Berkeley home. Walter regarded Leary as a genius, and refused to admit P.R.O.B.E. was an attempt to force Circuit Three logical-empiricism into the emotional-robotic Circuit Two ape-world. He insisted that he expected to win, and he had glorious plans to help get similar suits started in other states — "At minimum, forty-nine of them," he said with a Learyan hope-spring-eternal grin.

Walter showed me the P.R.O.B.E. legal papers, and I found that Timothy, true to form, had an alternative for the State once they closed down the prisons. In fact, he had three alternatives:

1 - Crimes-without-victims should be abolished. It is unJeffersonian, unAmerican and thoroughly medieval to punish people for behavior that harms nobody; such puritan emotionalism wastes taxpayers' money, distracts cops from real crimes, and sends people to cages where they might easily go berserk and emerge as psychopaths or real criminals.

2 - Crimes-against-property should be a matter of

restitution, not *punishment.* The criminal must pay back the victim a sum equal to the property stolen or damaged. If the criminal cannot pay, due to poverty, Leary proposes that the state pay the victim in his place. The criminal then really has a literal "debt to society," and Leary proposes that he pay it off by working at some socially-useful State labor, such as hospital orderly or forest ranger. This would cut the State budget for salaries for such jobs and benefit the taxpayer directly. Keeping these thieves or vandals out of jail would benefit the taxpayer indirectly by lowering the penology budget. Finally, this reform benefits all victims of such crimes, since they'll really get back what they lost.

3 - For crimes of violence, Leary recommends colonies — not *cages* — in which the violent offender could be accompanied by wife or girlfriend or family-unit and where there would be no sensory-sexual deprivation torture similar to our dog-pound cage system in today's prisons. Neurological retraining and reprogramming, Leary says, should be available to these violent persons, if they want it, but they should never be compelled to accept such invasions of neural integrity. Release back into the major society would be contingent upon proven capacity to function non-violently in emotional space-time games. During this colony-exile, the offender would never be punished, only segregated from non-violent society.

When I read this plan, I thought it was the sanest approach to penology I'd ever seen. Not everybody agrees with me, however; a letter in the October 1974 *Playboy*, commenting on the P.R.O.B.E. suit says that these proposals prove Dr. Leary has "a pitifully drug-rattled mind."

What do you think?

Chapter Eight

One Star in Sight

That shall end never that began.
　　All things endure because they are.
Do what thou wilt, for every man
　　And every woman is a star.
Pan is not dead; he liveth, Pan!
　　Break down the bar!

To man I come, the number of
　　A man my number, Lion of Light;
I am The Beast whose law is love.
　　Love under will, his royal right —
Behold within, and not above,
　　　　One star in sight!
　　　　— Aleister Crowley, *One Star In Sight,* pamphlet for
　　　　　　neophytes entering the Argentura Astrum

Dr. Andrija Puharich, a neurologist of some
professional reputation, asserts that Uri Geller, Israeli
psychic, is in communication with extraterrestrials.
The learned community says Dr. Puharich has flipped
out. Dr. John Lilly hints that he has also received such

communications. Academia, relieved that Dr. Lilly is only hinting and not saying it outright, happily ignores the potential breakthrough. Dr. Leary *insists* he has received extraterrestrial transmissions; he is obviously nuts, says the Establishment.

Let me record my own extraterrestrial contacts, from the beginning. The reader can form his own judgment of my sanity.

One day in 1970, shortly before I resigned from *Playboy*, I had lunch with Alan Watts and his lovely wife, Mary-Jane. I had known Alan off and on since 1957 and his charming expositions of Zen Buddhism, Taoism and Vedanta had led me to occasional bursts of involvement with those disciplines, including several months of training in Za-Zen (sitting Zen meditation) with Yasutani Roshi, the Zen Master who lives in Hawaii but occasionally gives Zen seminars on the mainland. Eventually, I found the Zen discipline wasn't my bag and switched to hatha yoga, which may be equally tedious but at least tones up the body (and produces amusing ESP flashes as a side-effect, in many cases), whereas Zen is nothing but intolerable boredom until the point when it eventually works.

Alan, like me, was an enthusiastic admirer of Timothy Leary and during the luncheon we spoke principally of the idea of Alan's writing a defense of Leary for *Playboy*; it was then (1970) obvious that legal maneuverings to get Tim out of his cage would take a long time and none of us had any clue that Tim was meanwhile conspiring to break out and flee the country. Alas, *Playboy*'s older and wiser editors decided that Timothy Leary was old news (1970) and would soon be forgotten (1970) and all the rest of it— the same prescience shown by Ralph Ginzburg in 1964.

Toward the end of the lunch, Alan asked me about

my current writing projects, and I told him a little about
the 3-volume novel, *Illuminatus! or Laughing Phallus
Productions presents or Swift-Kick Inc. or Telemachus
Sneezed or The Untidy Ape: A Head Test.* I described the
great Bavarian Illuminati conspiracy (believed in by many
right-wingers) which was the basis of that fantasy, and I
happened to mention the Eye in the Triangle, which is said
to be the symbol of the Illuminati.

"That reminds me," Alan said. "The best book I've
read in years is called *The Eye in the Triangle.* It's about
Aleister Crowley." He went on to recommend the book
highly.

All I knew about Aleister Crowley was vague
and unfavorable. He was said to be a Satanist, a Black
Magician, a sadist, a nut, a narcotics addict and a sexual
degenerate of monstrous proportions. I had somehow or
other also heard that he had climbed higher on Chogo Ri
than any other mountaineer in history and had set several
other climbing records, and that intrigued me. Few junkies
have the stamina for such exertions, and I wondered a bit if
some of Aleister's infamous reputation were exaggerated.

I bought *The Eye in the Triangle*, which was by Dr.
Israel Regardie, Crowley's secretary in the 1920s and now
a Reichian psychologist in Los Angeles. Dr. Regardie
emphasized the link between Crowley's Tantric magick[*]
and Reich's bio-energetic psychology. As a former Reichian
patient, I understood easily that the "astral" energies used
in Crowleyean magick were the same phenomenon as the
"orgone energy" used in Reichian therapy.

~•~

[*] Crowley's spelling. The *k* is to establish a distinction from
ordinary stage magic or conjuring.

~•~

I'd soon plowed my way through all of Crowley's books still in print and began correspondence with Dr. Regardie.

Since I was educated as an engineer and still regard myself as possessing a scientific and skeptical mind, it might seem strange that I was able to take something calling itself magick with any degree of seriousness. Actually, it was fairly easy. There were two steps in my argument with myself.

1 - The so-called magick "powers" actually exist; parapsychology calls them by such names ESP (extra-sensory perception), precognition, clairvoyance, clairaudience, PK (psychokinesis), etc. It is absurd to reject the data of parapsychology at this date, after confirmation by several thousand academic investigators, in a hundred universities on four continents, over a period of nearly a century. It is more reasonable to accept the data.

2 - If such powers exist, it is *possible* and by n*o means implausible* that some of the secret societies of magick adepts in which Crowley was initiated (The Hermetic Order of the Golden Dawn, the Ordo Templi Orientis, the Argentum Astrum, the Sufi Order, etc.) really did possess what they claimed; training methods that unleashed these powers in any student willing to work hard at the appropriate exercises.

It astonishes me that so many scientists, now willing to accept proposition #1 above, have not moved on to proposition #2, which is at least *possible* and worthy of investigation. Instead, the parapsychologists, here and in Russia, are still repeating one another's hit-or-miss methods, hauling people without ESP or PK into laboratories to see if these powers occur at random in the general population, or testing those who admittedly stumbled into ESP, PK etc. by accident, not knowing how they do it or what they are doing, e.g. the Danish psychic, Peter Hurkos, who developed a high degree of ESP after banging his head in a fall and admittedly has less idea than the scientists *what the hell he is doing.*

I began experimenting with the methods of magick training given in Crowley's books. Many of these exercises were frankly borrowed from hatha yoga, in which I already had some experience; many were similar to the methods of tribal shamans, such as Don Juan Matus, whose training of the anthropologist, Carlos Castaneda, is full of Crowleyean techniques; many came from Tibetan and Indian tantra, the art of turning sexual ecstasy into mystic mind expansion. (In Leary's terms, tantric sex is a method of opening the Fifth Circuit and then forming a bridge to the Sixth Circuit.)

In 1971, while in Mexico, I read an interview with Timothy Leary, then in Switzerland, printed in the Los Angeles *Free Press.* To my surprise and delight, Tim was also investigating Crowleyean methods and the interview was full of quotes from Crowley; Tim was engaged also in telepathic research with the English poet, Brian Barritt.

My eventual judgments on Aleister Crowley, the man, are contained in *Lion of Light*, a biography of him, which may be in print before or after this present book. Crowley, the teacher, I unhesitatingly regard as the greatest practical mystic of the 20th century — perhaps of all time.

The Crowleyean system, very briefly, is a synthesis of three elements:

1 - Traditional western occultism, or "magick." A
secret teaching, out of 19th Century Rosicrucianism,
possibly going back through Renaissance magick societies,
medieval witchcraft, the Knights Templar, European
Sufis, etc. to Gnosticism, and thence back possibly to the
Eleusinian Mysteries and Egyptian cults. Basically, this
is, as Crowley says, "physiological experiments"—using
ritual, sometimes drugs, sometimes sex, to jolt the nervous
system into "higher" (fifth circuit, sixth circuit, seventh
circuit) functioning and reception of signals usually not
received on the first four (survival) circuits.

2 - Traditional Eastern yoga, including hatha yoga
(meditation plus physical exercises to make meditation
easier and more natural) and tantric (sexual) yoga.

3 - Modern scientific method. Crowley taught
total skepticism about all results contained, the
keeping of careful records of each "experiment," and
logical-philosophical analysis at each stage of increased
awareness. To one student, he wrote vigorously:

"God within us" means precisely nothing at all . . .

I know I'm a disheartening kind of bloke, and it does
seem so unfriendly to jump down a fellow's throat every
minute or so when he tries to put it ever so nicely, and it
is too easy—isn't it— to play the game of sanctimonious
grandiloquence, and surely what was said was perfectly
harmless, and . . .

No, N.O., no: not harmless at all. My whole object
is to train you to silence every kind of hypothetical
speculation, and formulae both resonant and satisfying. I
want you to abhor them, abominate them, despise them,
detest them, eschew them, hate them, loathe them . . .
and to get on with your *practice.**

~•~

* *Magick Without Tears*, by Aleister Crowley, edited by Israel
Regardie, Llewellyn, 1973.

~•~

Sounds rather like Dr. Leary's "Where are the bodies in space-time? What are they actually doing?," doesn't it?

It is this synthesis of Eastern and Western traditions, with modern scientific analysis and semantic clarity that was Aleister Crowley's major achievement. His philosophy erected on top of this methodology — a blend of Nieitzschean Supermanism, anti-Christian bias, and a kind of anarcho-fascist Darwinianism in politics — is to be accepted or rejected on the same grounds as any other philosophy. Crowley's method of research in higher consciousness is quite independent of that philosophy.

After one year of experimental neuro-programming by Crowleyean methods, I seemed to have changed my basic personality in a variety of ways. My wife and children agreed that I was objectively, in space-time-emotional vectors, less introverted, more extraverted; less worried, more optimistic; less emotional, more rapturous; less selfish, more involved with everybody; etc. — in general, less *dead*, more *turned-on*.

The first non-subjective, clear-cut "occult" effect occurred in the summer of 1972, during a visit to Yellow Springs, Ohio, where we had lived for three years in the early 1960s. I was doing a Tarot "divination" for my oldest daughter, Karuna. All Tarot readings to this date, however pleasing to my subjects, had been inconclusive to me; every "hit" could be explained as intuition, reading their body language subliminally, lucky guessing, etc. This time, I told Karuna—somewhat surprised at my own audacity—that her previous boyfriend, Roy, would suddenly contact her. (She hadn't seen him in a year.) The next morning, the phone rang, and I said at once, again surprised at my self-confidence, "That's Roy." It was.

Lucky guessing? My magick diary (Crowley insists on keeping such a record of all experiments) soon contained similar direct hits, on a weekly basis. I also developed what all occultists call "inner certainty;" that is, I *knew* when this sixth circuit faculty was operating and could be trusted. This is hard to verbalize, but it is exactly as specific as the inner sense that you are about to become ill and vomit, or that a head cold is coming on, or that you are reaching sexual climax and will ejaculate soon. It cannot be mistaken.

I have now developed a system, based on Crowley combined with Dr. Leary and Dr. John Lilly, in which any ordinary person can be trained to obtain similar results within six weeks, at least on a sporadic and occasional basis. Further development of the sixth circuit, of course, requires further training.

My most outstanding experience to date occurred on April 26, 1974. I was working with a group of Bay Area witches, who call themselves the New Reformed Orthodox Order of the Golden Dawn. During the part of the ritual in which the group "raises the Cone of Power" (molds the Kyrlian field/orgone field into a cone which can be directed at will by the members), I had a vision of my son, Graham, who was then in Arizona with some friends. Graham was lying on the ground and cops were walking toward him. I could see no more: but I hastily placed a smaller "cone of power" around him as a protective device and left a telepathic message that he should phone me in the morning. I was somewhat scared, imagining that he might have been in an auto accident.

The next morning when the phone rang, I said at once "That's Graham." (I often announce phone calls before answering them, these days.) It was, and he told us of his adventure with "the pigs" as young people call our gallant law-enforcement officers. He and his friends had been sleeping in the woods, when some cops drove into the clearing, and discovered their car. The kids expected, at minimum, to be chased out of the woods and sent on their way; more likely, by previous experience, they feared being jailed over night, until parents of each and every one of them were contacted and it was proven conclusively that none of them were runaways. (Nobody under 21 has *any* civil liberties in the U.S.A.)

The cops walked toward the spot where the kids were sleeping. Those who had awakened, including Graham, watched them come. Then, abruptly, the cops turned around, walked back to their car, and drove away.

We checked the times. The incident occurred a few minutes before midnight. So did my astral vision. Whether or not my "cone of protection" drove the police away is an experimental question to be determined fully only when enough rigorous scientific work in this area has been accomplished. I am satisfied, at minimum, that there is more to Crowley's magick than *mere* self-hypnosis.

January 18, 1973, was my 41st birthday. Karuna, our oldest daughter, informed me in the morning that, in addition to the sun being in Capricorn (my sign), the moon was in cancer (my wife's sign.) Although I am extremely skeptical about astrology, I decided to keep careful records of anything significant that might occur that day. A few hours after awaking, I heard on the radio that Timothy Leary had been kidnapped by American agents in Afghanistan. I was plunged into depression, and realized for the very first time how much I cared for that brilliant but incautious man, whom I had actually met less than a dozen times in the decade. A few hours later, my youngest daughter, had her first menstrual period: dawn of the fourth circuit, as Leary would say. I wondered what Carl Jung, who coined the word *synchronicity* for apparently meaningful coincidences, would make of this bundle of syn-chrons . . .

In the afternoon, profoundly depressed about Leary's bad luck, Arlen and I were waiting in the woods behind our farm. (We were living in Mendocino County.) Suddenly, I had a flash of Timothy grinning. "They'll put him in maximum security, now," Arlen was saying. "He'll probably commit suicide within a year." Tim grinned more impudently.

"No," I said quite happily. "The very first photo we'll see he'll have the old Leary grin flashing again." I was totally convinced, certainly, that Dr. Leary's neurological researches had brought him to the point where he had control over emotional programs and could transcend suffering of all sorts.

A few hours later, we drove into a pizza parlor in Mendocino to celebrate my birthday. On the way, we bought an evening newspaper. There, on page one, was the Leary Grin.

Timothy Leary, Ph.D, with Joanna Harcourt Smith
being kidnapped in Afghanistan, January 18ᵗʰ, 1973
(Photo from Getty Images)

On June 6, 1973, I took a programmed trip on something I was told was LSD. The program was in two parts, basically; I remained in a dark room, eyes closed, lying on a bed during most of it. Part one was the playing back, on a tape recorder, of Dr. John Lilly's "Beliefs Unlimited" hypnosis tape; this was repeated several times during the first 3 hours of the experiment. During the 3-5 hours, I played a tape of myself reading Aleister Crowley's invocation of the Holy Guardian Angel.

Dr. Lilly's tape runs as follows:

In the province of the mind, what one believes to be true is true or becomes true within certain limits, to be found experientially and experimentally. These limits are beliefs to be transcended.

Hidden from one's self is a covert set of beliefs that control one's thinking, one's actions, and one's feelings.

This covert set of hidden beliefs is the limiting set of beliefs to be transcended.

To transcend one's limiting set, one establishes an open-ended set of beliefs about the unknown . . .

By allowing, there are no limits; no limits to thinking, no limits to feeling, no limits to movement. By allowing, there are no limits. There are no limits to thinking, no limits to feeling, no limits to movement.

That which is not allowed is forbidden. That which is allowed, exists. In allowing no limits, there are no limits. That which is not allowed is forbidden. That which is forbidden is not allowed. That which exists is allowed. To allow no limits, there are no limits. No limits allowed, no limits exist.

In the province of the mind, what one believes to be true either is true or becomes true. In the province of the mind there are no limits. In the province of the mind, what one believes to be true is true or becomes true. There are no limits.

This is deliberately encouraging "gullibility," of course; but it is quite easy to re-establish scientific skepticism about results obtained, *after* the experiment is over. Skepticism *during* the experiment prevents such results.

The Crowley invocation, frankly, looks like pretentious rubbish in print. Aloud, it vibrates, moans and sings with eerie power, as it directs one to alternately envision the "Holy Guardian Angel" as a solar-phallic lion of terrible energy, next as an erotic sex-goddess, then as the Great Wild Beast Pan, then as a green and earthy mother-spirit, and finally as a Total Void at the heart of everything.

I achieved a rush of Jungian archetypes, strongly influenced by the imagery of Crowley's invocation, but nonetheless having that peculiar quality of external reality and *alien intelligence* emphasized by Jung in his discussion of the archetypes. I also "lived" through several "past lives"—including additional details about one "past life" previously unearthed under hypnosis by New York hypnotist, Jack Rowan, and also Sufi saint lives, medieval witch lives, a life as a Grandmaster in the Bavarian Illuminati (which may, or may not, explain why I was moved to write a 3-volume novel about the Illuminati), and, finally, an uprush of "memories" of animal existence, as an ape-creature, a rodent, a slug, a bug, a fish, and then a series of deaths and rebirths as animal, void, human, void, human, void, animal, void, Star!, void, molecular intelligence vibrating through time, and, at the peak, as union of Shiva and Kali, twin gods linked in eternal orgasm according to Bengali Hinduism. I saw and understood quite distinctly that Shiva was also Brahma and Jehovah and Pan, etc., while Kali was also Venus and Aphrodite and Virgin Mary, etc. and that the universe actually is the *living* embodiment

of this Divine Couple and not at all a dead machine.
In short, I opened the genetic archives at the memory
bank in Dr. Leary's Seventh Circuit, the neurogenetic
consciousness.

I entered Samadhi and understood, at last, that the bliss
of the mystic is truly beyond the floating rapture of the fifth
circuit, being based on *understanding of* and *participation
in* that planet-wide Consciousness which is in all of us and
in that pre-organic atomic structure that we mistakenly call
"dead matter."

I understood Gandhi's insistence, "God is in the rock,
too — *in the rock!*"

I appreciated Eckhart's paradox, "Split a stick of wood,
and the Christ is in there, too!"

I laughed merrily at Crowley's joking seriousness in
telling one disciple, Frank Bennett, that the Holy Guardian
Angel is merely "our own unconscious" and meanwhile
telling another disciple, Jane Wolf, that the Holy Guardian
Angel is "a separate being of superhuman intelligence."
I even more appreciated his boffo one-liner in *Magick in
Theory and Practice*, where he speaks of sexual yoga in
code as a form of sacrifice and says that he thus sacrificed
"a male child of perfect innocence and high intelligence"
150 times a year since 1912. The sacrifice in sexual yoga is
the semen, which is, indeed, a male child and does indeed
contain, within the DNA code, a very high intelligence, the
genetic blueprint of planet earth.

I staggered in bliss to my desk and typed out "Few
of our ancestors were perfect ladies and gentlemen. The
majority of them weren't even mammals and looked like
alligators or Gila Monsters." The normal paranoia in our
culture (fear of animals) has not bothered me since then;
I took a pro-life imprint and I am now as cuddly with

snakes as with dogs or cats. (I'm especially fond of the boa-constrictor and python kept as familiars by my friends, the St. Louis witches, Morning Glory and Tim Zell.)

I lost all fear of death, knowing it to be literally impossible. I understood the wit of Yeats' fine line, "Man has created death."

I was whacked out of my skull.

The next day, and in the following weeks, my yoga meditations were vastly enriched, and I occasionally went for days on end conscious of the two minds thinking, my mind and the System Mind, or as Suzuki Roshi used to say, Little Mind and Big Mind. I had no further doubts about Cleve Backster's polygraph research, seemingly demonstrating telepathy in plants and yoghurt, because I shared frequently in the Big Mind where all this occurs.

On July 22, 1973 — six weeks after the trip — I was ready to try again, without the supposed LSD. (Which might have been mescaline, or STP, or PCP, or fly-paper for all I know.) (Stay away from black market drugs, my friend; don't let these experiments lead you astray. Agitate for resumption of legal, scientific LSD experimentation.)

This time, I used the Lilly tape and the Crowley invocation again, without drugs, but with certain rituals of Tantric sex-trance involving the cooperation of the Most Beautiful Woman in California.

I remember thinking, during the six weeks between major experiments, that whatever I had tuned into was *not* Cosmic Consciousness but a kind of planetary consciousness; I wondered who coined the term, "cosmic consciousness," and what it contained . . .

This time I moved in space-time fan-wise, unlike the backward-in-time movement of the supposed-LSD trip. I became almost conscious of a kind of galactic star-network, an intelligence that seemed to me not fully-formed but *evolving*. Somehow, this linked in my mind with the Sufi teaching that Allah is constantly recreating himself every second. The trip was full of light and joy, the White Light of the Void jazz you've all heard, but dim, not fully achieved. I went off into sleep not-quite-satisfied.

The next morning, July 23, I awoke with an urgent message from Dreamland and scribbled quickly in my magical diary, "Sirius is very important." There was more, almost at the tip of my tongue, but I couldn't remember it.

During the a.m. I looked through my occult books, seeking references to the Dog Star, Sirius; although skeptical about astrology, I assumed that the Dream-message was some hint that the Sirius cycle should be part of my magick experiments in the future. Astrology seems like nonsense to me, but I was willing to give it a try, in the open-ended manner of Dr. Lilly's "Beliefs Unlimited" exercise.

In *The Magical Revival* by Kenneth Grant, current Outer Head of the Ordo Templi Orientis, I found:

> *Phoenix* was Crowley's secret name in the Ordo Templi Orientis . . . The Phoenix was also an ancient constellation in which Sothis, or Sirius, was the chief star . . . According to Pliny the life of the Phoenix had a direct connection with the great year of cyclic renovation . . . The constellation once known by that name was an image of the Sohiac or Siriadic year (26,000 normal years) . . . the Great Year of the Egyptians . . .

> Crowley identified the heart of (his magical) current with one particular Star. In Occult Tradition, this is "the Sun behind the Sun," the Hidden God, the vast star Sirius, or Sothis . . .

This was interesting, no doubt, but, since I had already

skimmed parts of Grant's book, it didn't *prove* anything.

Nonetheless, it was definitely intriguing. I went to town and browsed in the public library. Imagine my state of mind when I discovered that this very day, July 23, when I had received the message "Sirius is very important," is the day when, according to Egyptian tradition, the "occult link" (through hyperspace?) is most powerful between Earth and Sirius. Celebrations of the Dog Star, Sirius, on July 23 are the origin of the expression "dog days," meaning late July and early August days.

News of astronaut Ed Mitchell's successful telepathic transmissions from the moon to Earth were in the newspapers later that year. Sirius is nine light years away, and I began to wonder if telepathy can jump that far . . .

Meanwhile, throughout the rest of July and August I began to receive the telepathic impressions of Timothy Leary described at the beginning of this book.

I wrote to the warden of Folsom and asked for permission to correspond with Dr. Leary. Bureaucratic red-tape being what it is, this permission was delayed several weeks.

Meanwhile, I did some more browsing in Grant's *Magical Revival* and found this:

> The candidate in the New Aeon, however, identifies himself with the *other Horus*, the Sun behind the sun, represented by the Star of Set, Sirius, which shines perpetually in the darkness of Nuit, and which in actual fact is visible from all inhabited parts of the earth. This is the one Star in Sight which forms the title of Crowley's Manifesto of the *Argentum Astrum*.

Argentum Astrum, the most secret of Crowley's magick organizations, means Silver Star.

Was it possible that the dream-truncated message "Sirius is very important" actually came to me, across space, from Higher Intelligences dwelling within or near that vast Star? I was not quite ready to take that thought seriously — although I wondered quite a bit about Cary, my old friend at *Playboy* whose "outer space" experiences I had once been so quick to doubt. I also remembered that Dr. John Lilly hints rather strongly in *The Center of the Cyclone* that he and various unnamed investigators connected with the Arica Institute have received interstellar guidance at times. That astronomical distances are human programming symbols was not yet clear to me, however, and I was still, in General Semantics jargon, confusing the map with the territory. That Earth and Sirius are virtually nudging each other, from the perspective of non-human dimensions, was not yet a thinkable thought . . .

I was more intrigued, for a while, by the date: July 23. I had never known that Sirius and Earth had a link on that day, but I had long been involved in a complicated joke involving deluding amateur occultists into thinking 23 was a very mystical number. Co-conspirators in this joke had helped me fill occult journals with inconspicuous 23s which would become very conspicuous to anybody who heard our 23 myth and started looking. Now, it seemed that I had become the victim of my own joke, in typical Sorcerer's Apprentice fashion. The universe was trying to tell me that 23 was really occult, after all. This was so absurd that it eventually seemed more meaningful than any rational theory about this odd experience.

Then Timothy Leary crossed my path again.

Shortly after my telepathic flashes of Leary

(July-August 1973) ended, Walter Culpepper, the attorney for P.R.O.B.E. — the suit to end the cages of the California Archipelago — had a benefit for the Leary Defense Fund and P.R.O.B.E. Two rock groups played and then we were shown "At Folsom Prison With Timothy Leary, PhD," produced by Joanna Leary.

The film blew my mind. Timothy came on screen and immediately flashed the famous Love-Peace-Bless grin at the camera — as if he were greeting visitors to his home. I never saw a man look less like a suffering martyr. He took a chair and answered the interviewer's questions in a serious and thoughtful manner, explaining that he wasn't interested in drugs anymore since they had only been "microscopes" to him: tools to reveal the focus and refocus possibilities of the nervous system. He wanted to talk about something more exciting now: Outer Space. The interviewer kept leading him back to drugs, and Leary kept maneuvering back to cosmic dimensions.

I began to notice an odd thing: Timothy looked younger than he had in the 1960s.

The interviewer asked Leary about his feelings concerning imprisonment. Tim said that he had been framed—the two marijuana cigarettes had been planted by the arresting officer, he insisted—but then he grinned beatifically again and said that, nonetheless, prison was a valuable experience. "No other psychologist," he said with a twinkle, "can see our society from this perspective. The black and the poor," he added, "know so much that an ordinary scientist never learns . . . !" He went on cheerfully in that vein insisting that, together with being imprisoned by Communist Eldridge Cleaver, being imprisoned by Republican Ronald Reagan was one of the two most educational experiences of his life. He was kidding and not kidding, and he added, quite blissfully and without menace, "I'll never see our society the same way again, now that I know how it looks from the bottom up."

He finally led the interviewer to ask about the strange design on his prison uniform. "This is Starseed," Tim said, proud as a new father. The emblem was that strange miniature infinity-sign, the nucleotide template formed as DNA imprints messenger-RNA to start a new growth program.

Starseed, however, was not just *any* nucleotide template. It was the one recently found on the meteor which landed in Orgeuil, France, in the 19th century, when scientists re-examined that rock. It is the first scientific proof that the mechanism of chemical "intelligence"—the building of life-programs (RNA) out of information codes (DNA) — exists elsewhere in the universe.

Starseed, Leary enthusiastically told the interviewer, proves that cellular intelligence is not exclusively Earthly. It therefore increases the probable grounds to believe many forms of life and intelligence exist in space-time.

Other cons in Folsom, after Leary left, picked up the Starseed symbol, carved it on belts, painted it on sketch pads, sewed it on clothing, and formed bull sessions to rap with Hal Olsen (life-termer, illustrator of Leary's *Terra II*) and Lynn Benner ("the Tuxedo Bandit" and one unit in Leary's four-person telepathy team) about the implications of Higher Intelligence and the transcendental implications of modern science.

Olsen, who has taken up the study of physics, believes that meeting Timothy Leary was the most important incident in his life. He writes to me frequently, and hopes for eventual parole, intending to use his cartoonist's skills to publicize and raise money for the flight of Terra II.

When I saw Culpepper next he told me that Leary was currently obsessed with Black Holes and trying to obtain every book in print about that astronomical anomaly. The Black Hole seems to have more gravity than any other cosmic entity and nothing that falls into a Black Hole can ever escape. It seemed like a metaphor on Folsom Prison itself; but Culpepper said Leary was developing a whole new cosmology based on evolution *toward* Black Holes and beyond space-time as we know it.

Down on earth, however, Culpepper was concerned with moving the P.R.O.B.E. suit along, since he still insisted that it had a chance of winning in the courts. Like myself, Culpepper is convinced that keeping people in cages is barbaric behavior, and he will try some other way to end this cruelty if P.R.O.B.E. fails.

I wrote a few articles publicizing P.R.O.B.E. and meanwhile went on researching Sirius. I was quite moved, as you will readily understand, when I found the following in O.T.O. Grandmaster Kenneth Grant's new book, *Aleister Crowley and the Hidden God:*

> Crowley was aware of the possibility of opening the spatial gateways and of admitting an extraterrestrial current into the human life-wave . . .

> It is an occult tradition — and Lovecraft gave it persistent utterance in his writings — that some transfinite and superhuman power is marshalling its forces with intent to invade and take possession of this planet . . . This is reminiscent of Charles Fort's dark hints about a secret society on earth already in contact with cosmic beings and, perhaps, preparing the way for their advent.[*]

~•~

* Grant here quotes, in a footnote, from Fort's *The Book of the Damned*, ". . . some other world is not attempting but has been, for centuries, in communication with a sect, perhaps, or a secret society, or certain esoteric ones of this earth's inhabitants."

~•~

. . . Crowley dispels the aura of evil with which these authors invest the fact; he prefers to interpret it Thelemically, not as an attack upon human consciousness by an extraterrestrial and alien entity but as an expansion of consciousness from within, to embrace other stars and to absorb their energies into a system that is thereby enriched and rendered truly cosmic by the process . . .

Explaining again the name of the A.A. (Argentum Astrum), the inner initiates of the O.T.O., Grant adds:

The order of the Silver Star is thus the Order of the Eye of Set, "the Son behind the Sun," represented astronomically by the Star of Isis, which is Sothis (Sirius.) . . . The Silver Star (A.A.) is Sirius. Horus is the "son" of this God, and Sun (or Father) of our solar system . . .

Chapter Nine

Out of the Black Hole

This signal is being transmitted from the Black Hole of American society. A Black Hole is a dense space with a heavy gravitational pull. Matter which falls into a Black Hole fades from view and disintegrates in the stress of gravity. Given a sufficient time, its radiation becomes too feeble to be detected from without. Although the matter of the Black Hole cannot re-escape as matter, some of it may manage to escape in the form of feeble red radiation. Some cosmologists suggest that Black Holes are the link to another realization of matter. They may be passages to another universe. Just as the manholes of Paris lead to another world beneath the street. Well, the Black Hole is a fine place from which to scan the universe. It's beyond pure, undiluted bad. As good as good can be.

Out here, beyond good and evil, one sees the human race in pain, injured nervous systems propelling robot-bodies in repetitious, aimless motion along paths labeled right and wrong.

—Timothy Leary, *Terra II*

After seeing "At Folsom Prison with Timothy Leary, PhD," I again renewed my campaign to obtain permission to correspond with him. Some of the delays were due to bureaucratic red tape. Others were deliberately created by Joanna, who has consistently acted in ways that leave all of Leary's friends confused and somewhat paranoid about her motivations. Many old Learyans dropped out of the Leary circle when Joanna appointed Dennis Martino, a self-confessed narcotics informer, in a key position. Joanna explained that Dennis was no longer an informer; Joanna, it now appears, lied . . .

In October 1973, I finally received permission to begin corresponding with Dr. Leary at Folsom Prison. It started out with a letter about the general philosophical implications of tuning the nervous system to higher fidelity of signal-reception and very carefully did *not* mention my July 23 experience with Sirius. (I was fairly sure that my July-August impressions that Timothy was doing telepathic experiments had been accurate, but I had no idea yet that he was attempting *interstellar* telepathy.) His answer was full of characteristic humor and—typically—picked up (see the last paragraph) that I was holding something back:

> Timothy Leary
> B 26358
> Represa, Ca. 95671
> Oct 13, 1973

Dear Bob,

The administration here talked to me about two weeks ago . . . about your letter. The delay in responding is my own. I get so busy here etc. The prison administration is perfect. They act as a Van Allen belt protecting my privacy, screening out distractions and possibly dangerous intrusions.

I think that they realize that some new message, some new hope can come from my present meditation and research. (They wouldn't express it this way, but they are very interested in what my mind produces, concerned that it help and not hurt their aspirations etc.) Think of me as an improved-model Einstein—at the Princeton Center for Advanced Psychology — think of the warden as the Dean of the Institute, protecting his genius from secular interruptions etc. The prison administration is incredibly intuitive. The people they refuse visiting privileges are exactly those people who come to exploit me or whose love for me is flawed. They tend to sense who really understands and with them there is never any problem about mail-visit etc. This is a fascinating process.

Well, it all is.

And, with this introduction, let me say that when they told me that you had written and asked if I wanted to correspond with you . . . and when I said, with enthusiasm, "Yes" I want to correspond with him . . . then the authorities have cooperated most civilly. So you are now on my correspondence list. The channels are open . . . and let us exchange signals.

(My gratitude towards the prison warden must not be misunderstood. They are too possessive and jealous — terrible states to be in. Their love and dependence on me are too restricting. They are terrorized that I might leave them . . . in the lurch, so to say. This is unhealthy for them . . . I bring them some excitement, light, humor, spark of personal interest, something to talk about at home or at the club etc. And I cause not the slightest negative moment . . . ah, this may not be exactly true . . . some guards may be jealous of the fact that I am closer to prisoners than to guards?)

I haven't written you because I knew that you were in touch with Joanna. Or could be. Joanna and I are beautifully mated. She acts for me with perfection and vice versus. Most contact with the "outside" (or whatever we call the prison of America) is done through Her. Keep in close touch with Her—if you can. She moves with swift precision.

I spend most of my time pondering on the evolutionary situation. Trying to figure out what is happening etc.

The results of this research are very pleasing to me, to Joanna, and to those who receive our transmissions.

At the moment the metaphor is this: This planet is a womb . . . for the pre-natal protection of Life which was seeded on Earth 3 billion years ago. We have not been born yet. We are in a larval, inter-uterine condition etc. The writhings and political convulsions may be birth-pains.

We are about to be born. Being born means to leave the womb. Leave the planet Earth. Astrobstetrics. Astro-obstetrics.

Joanna has the recent tapes and will share them with you.

I sense you as a loving, devoted-to-truth person. Perhaps one of the few who understand a fragment of what I have been doing. If my megalomaniac ambitions and plans have any validity . . . then it is sadly true that there are very few living beings who can understand my plans. You have a certain perspective. There is certain heaviness about your transmissions. Perhaps that is because you are shy, afraid of being condemned as an "eccentric"??

Why don't you read some of the scripts that Joanna is transmitting and then signal me.

We are in communication . . . across the parsecs . . . good. Shine on.

(signed) Timothy Leary

P.S. Maybe you could write a "good book." It would take an all-out effort.

I wrote back, but remained mum about Sirius. Instead, just for the hell of it – and to convince him I was not afraid of being considered "eccentric" – I used my official Discordian Society letterhead.

(The Discordian Society is a religious organization devoted to the worship of Eris, Greek goddess of confusion and chaos. We "prove" her existence by reversing the Thomist arguments for the existence of Jehovah: "Just look around you, buddy. If there's no Eris, *where did all this chaos come from?*" The stationary bears the imprint of the Joshua Norton Cabal, this being a cabal of the Discordian Society located in the Bay Area — other Cabals including the Tactile Temple of Eris Erotic in Los Angeles, the Colorado Encrustation in Denver, the John Dillinger Died For You Society in Chicago, etc.; Timothy, however, seems to have thought Joshua Norton Cabal was a person's name. Actually, Joshua Norton—or Norton I, as he preferred — was a San Franciscan of the last century who elected himself Emperor of the United States and Protector of Mexico. Bay Area historians still argue whether Norton was a psychotic or a clever con man; in any event, he was "humored" by the citizenry of the time and, in effect, lived like an Emperor. As Greg Hill, co-founder of Discordianism, has written, "Everybody understands Mickey Mouse. Few understand Hermann Hesse. Hardly anybody understands Einstein. And nobody understands Emperor Norton." The Discordian Society, I may add, is not a complicated joke disguised as a new religion but a new religion disguised as a complicated joke. Post-Heisenberg Zen, actually.)

Timothy replied:

Timothy Leary
B 26358
Represa, Ca. 95671
Nov 1, 1973

Dear Bob,

Quick response . . . to indicate that transmission is working well from this galaxy to yours.

Your stationary amazed me . . . could you explain any of it? Like ODD3140Aftllbii? And who is Joshua Norton Cabal?

Earth as womb is not metaphor. Look at diagrams of the earth with the Van Allen belt around it as fluffy protective cushion. Delicate egg earth. Nature works with perverse (obverse?) humor. We are embryonic within our Mother's womb. As individuals. Ontology recapitulates Phylogeny. The generic species Life on this planet is embryonic. When we get in the Time-ship, i.e. Sperm ship, Terra II and leave the solar system we shall as a species be born. Galaxy is nursery school. All this is explained in Terra II, a book just finished and which Joanna can show you. Everything gets to me through Joanna.

You can send in clippings. I look forward to the Lilly interview.

Actually the Warden here is very protective of me. He is like a gruff Zen abbot. He doesn't want me to be bothered with visits or correspondence which would bring me down, slow up my scientific work etc. As long as I sit in my cell and write science fiction books . . . everyone is happy.

Yes, G.I. Gurdjieff is my direct successor. I have never doubted that his baraka was transferred to me . . . perhaps by some intermediary. I love Him and I resonate to his wisdom more than anyone else's.

Crowley . . . the coincidences-synchonicities between

my life and His are embarrassing. Brian Barritt and I had a visionary experience Easter Sat-Sun in Bou Saada, the Algerian town where C. had His. etc.

Your diagram made perfect sense.

I enjoyed your article on Neopuritanism. Although the topic is a bit low level. It was full of sparkling ideas and funny things.

Have you met Joanna? 433-0252. 110 Alta St, San Francisco, Ca.

I look forward to your next emission. Shine on.

(Signed) Timothy Leary

(The diagram that "made perfect sense" to Dr. Leary was a crude attempt to describe evolution as a step-by-step progression from atomic consciousness through molecular and cellular states to ego-consciousness ; and so-called "mystic awakening" as the reverse process of shifting consciousness backward from ego to cell and molecule downward to atom. It was, of course, based on his concept that *"Consciousness is energy received and decoded by a structure."*) *

~•~

* This idea should be getting a little bit clearer each time we revert to it, as further data give its context.

~•~

I wrote back discussing the odd links between Leary's work and that of Crowley and Gurdjieff, and mentioning the evidence that they were *both* taught certain advanced techniques of consciousness-expansion by the Sufi lodges of the Near East. I also mentioned that Rasputin might have had the same sort of Sufi training during his wanderings.

Leary's reply blew my mind:

Timothy Leary
B 26358, Represa,
Ca. 95671
Nov 15, 1973

Dear Bob,

Loved your letter . . .

Is Laughing Buddha Jesus Norton Vonnegut the highest form of wisdom you've contacted? The Grateful Dead have a Hypnocracy game going . . . along same lines. Alan Watts is groping towards this position.

Are you in touch with teachings, methods, teachers etc. that transmit Higher Intelligence. That you are totally hooked into?

If so, would you tell me.

I don't believe in secrets. I am forced to accept elites — which are genetic, neurological, personal — not race, class etc. Or maybe?

I believe that Higher Intelligence can be contacted and have described how to do it and what They transmit etc. Have you contacted Joanna. 433-0252? Ask Her to send you a copy of *Terra II.*

You mention that Crowley, G. and Rasputin may have had contact with the same Sufi lodge. Do you think this "lodge" actually exists in the human sense of Masters in the Middle East who send G and C and R out as emissaries? This is the most exciting idea I've puzzled over for ten years.

I have seen what can be transmitted through one unit. The one that I belonged to. Where are the others?

I await your reaction to *Terra II.* Maybe you have reacted already. Anyway, it all looks perfect.

Shine on,

(signed) Timothy Leary

I'm amazed that you haven't contacted Michael Horowitz.

When I got in touch with Mike Horowitz, I heard, for the first time, about the Starseed Transmissions.

Meanwhile, Dr. Leary was shifted from Folsom to Vacaville and my communication with him temporarily shorted out. Once again, I had to apply for permission to correspond, fill out the right forms when they were finally mailed to me, and then wait for the new warden's decision. I felt increasingly like one of the scholars of the Middle Ages, trying to keep up communication with a fellow investigator while the Inquisition created as much static as possible.

(The Inquisition never ended, you know. All that has happened — the "progress" we boast of so naively — is that capital punishment has been abolished as punishment for heresy, but the heretics are still punished. Our cages are full of them; Dr. Leary is merely, at the present time, the most conspicuous example.)

It should be remembered, in evaluating the Starseed signals, that a few months before this experience, three government psychiatrists testified (at the escape trial) that Dr. Leary was perfectly sane and possessed a high IQ; and that Dr. Wesley Hiler, who saw Dr. Leary every day after the transfer to Vacaville, emphatically agrees with that verdict.

As recounted in *Terra II*, during July - August 1973, Tim Leary had formed a four-person telepathy team in an attempt to use Tantric (sexually sublimated) energy as a cone to achieve contact with Higher Intelligences elsewhere in the galaxy. The experiment was aided, and in a sense made necessary, by the rules of torture in California Archipelago prisons, which do not allow the men to consummate sexual union with their wives and sweethearts. The persons involved were: Dr. Leary and his wife, Joanna;

another convict, Wayne Benner, and his girlfriend, a journalist who prefers to be known only as Guanine.

The repressed sexuality of the four experimenters was regarded as an energy bank and was directed, by traditional magick theory, outward into the galaxy, seeking a communicating Mind to answer it. Anger, rage, depression and similar Second Circuit emotions otherwise exacerbated by the prison situation were similarly directed into the energy bank, transmuted into pure yearning and aimed outward as Cosmic Questing.

The Starseed Transmissions — "Hallucinations" or whatever — were received in 19 bursts, seldom in recognizable English sentences, requiring considerable meditation and discussion between the four receivers before they could be summarized, eventually, into the following message:

It is time for life on Earth to leave the planetary womb and learn to walk through the stars.

Life was seeded on your planet billions of years ago by nucleotide templates which contained the blueprint for gradual evolution through a sequence of biomechanical stages.

The goal of evolution is to produce nervous systems capable of communicating with and returning to the Galactic Network where we, your interstellar parents, await you.

Life on planet Earth has now reached the halfway point, established itself, and evolved through larval mutations and metamorphoses to the seven brain stage.

At this time the voyage home is possible.

Assemble the most intelligent, advanced, and courageous of your species, divided equally between men and women. Let every race, nationality, and religion be represented.

You are about to discover the key to immortality in the chemical structure of the genetic code, within which you will find the scripture of life. The time has come for you to accept the responsibility of immortality. It is not necessary for you to die.

You will discover the key to enhanced intelligence within the chemistry of the nervous system. Certain chemicals, used wisely, will enable your nervous system to decipher the genetic code.

All life on your planet is a unity. All life must come home.

Total freedom, responsibility and interspecies harmony will make the voyage possible. You must transcend larval identities of race, culture and nationality. Your only allegiance is to life. The only way you will survive is to make the voyage home.

The Japanese people are the most advanced race on your planet and will give protection to the company.

We are sending a comet to your solar system as a sign that the time has come to look to the stars.

When you arrive back home you will be given new instructions and powers. Your sperm ship is the flower of terrestrial life. As soon as the company is formed and the voyage begun, war, poverty, hatred, fear will disappear from your planet and the most ancient prophecies and celestial visions will be realized.

Mutate!

Come home in glory.

The concept of immortality was the most mind-boggling part of this communication to me. I thereupon spent several months investigating the question: Is it possible for human beings to achieve immortality in this generation?

My investigations are summarized in the next chapter. Briefly, it is now at least arguable that the Immortality

Formula — certainly the most significant part of the Starseed Transmissions — is quite likely to be chemically discovered in the next few years.

Meanwhile, Comet Kahoutek, as predicted in the Transmissions, arrived in the solar system and speeded inward toward the sun, while astronomers announced an unprecedented spectacle and Leary's disciples chortled at the confirmation.

Then the comet fizzled, leaving us wondering.

In 1904, in one of the most extraordinary magickal experiments of his life, Aleister Crowley contacted a Higher Intelligence named Aiwass, who dictated to him *The Book of the Law*. Crowley's admirers and disciples around the world today have a hundred-and-one interpretations of this cryptic and haunting text. What follows is my own reactions upon re-reading *The Book of the Law* shortly after studying the Starseed Transmissions for the first time.

> Had! The manifestation of Nuit.
> The unveiling of the company of Heaven.
> Every man and every woman is a star.
> Every number is infinite; there is no difference.

Nuit, *the Egyptian divinity of the stars*, seems to tell us, in these four opening verses, that we are Her children. She goes on to declare that the life-spirit (DNA code?) is the same everywhere in the galaxy:

> Come forth, o children, under the stars, & take your fill of love.

> I am *above* you and *in* you. My ecstasy is in yours.

The Starseed Signals

My joy is to see your joy. (Italics added.)

The union of mankind with the stars is precisely forecast:

They shall gather my children into their fold; they shall bring the glory of the stars into the hearts of men.

I am Infinite Space and the Infinite Stars thereof . . .

(The acrostic on I.S.I.S. in here may or may not be meaningful.) And the sign shall be my ecstasy, the consciousness of the continuity of existence, the omnipresence of my body . . .

O Nuit, continuous one of Heaven, let it be ever thus; that men speak of Thee not as One but as None; and let them speak not of thee at all, since thou art continuous!

None, breathed the light, faint & faery, of the stars, and two.

For I am divided for love's sake, for the chance of union.

This seems to me a vividly poetic pre-statement of Leary's theory that the Higher Intelligence is "divided", by sending out DNA seed to fertilize every womb-planet in the galaxy, "for the chance of union," the return of these "children" after they have evolved past the larval circuits into higher modes of consciousness.

Invoke me under my stars . . .

I love you! I yearn to you! . . . Put on the wings, and arouse the coiled splendor within you: come unto me!

The Star-Mother, Nuit, is definitely calling us home. The "coiled splendor" may even suggest the DNA helix within which, Leary and other investigators now think, is the secret of immortality.

"Come unto me" is a foolish word; for it is I that go . . .

The life-code of the DNA is the same in our starry parents and in ourselves; we are One Mind, basically. But shortly comes a more interesting text:

Is a God to live in a dog?

A reference to the great Dog star, Sirius? Instructions on contacting this Intelligence are quite specific:

To worship me take wine and strange drugs whereof I will tell my prophet & be drunk thereof!

The Immortality Pill is directly mentioned:

Think not, O King, upon that lie: That Thou Must Die: verily thou shalt not die, but live.

The predictions about the 20th century (this was dictated in 1904, remember) were profoundly disturbing to Crowley but are, by now, largely realized:

Now let it be understood first that I am a god of war and of Vengeance. I shall deal hardly with them . . . I am the warrior Lord of the Forties; the Eighties cower before me & are abased.

It seems rather clear that the Starseed Transmissions acquired a heavy Timothy Leary flavor in passing through the Leary nervous system, just as *The Book of the Law* took on a distinctly Crowleyean aroma in passing through Crowley's brain and hand; but the underlying message nonetheless is surprisingly similar.

Dr. Jacques Vallee, of Stanford University, has

collected several hundred cases of what appear to be telepathic contacts with Higher Intelligences. Dr. Vallee is not ready to say whether these represent extraterrestrial communications or something else, although he has mentioned the alternative hypothesis that the Transmitters are in other dimensions outside space-time as we know it. He by no means regards all the receivers as hallucinating lunatics, and explicitly regards these Signals as the most important scientific phenomenon of our time.

Dr. John Lilly, who has duplicated much of Timothy Leary's LSD research and supplemented it with hypnotic methods and Sufi yoga, describes many encounters with what seem to be Extraterrestrial Intelligences in his *Programming and Metaprogramming in the Human Biocomputer*. Dr. Lilly examines also the possibilities that these Transmitters are time-travelers from the future, very advanced adepts alive now on earth, "angels" in the traditional sense, or projected aspects of his own mind. In *The Center of the Cyclone* he says clearly:

> Such a network (of Adepts) exists and functions . . . throughout this planet. I suspect *it extends farther than our earth*, but this is yet to be publicly demonstrated unequivocally beyond the private *experience of myself and of others*. (Italics added.)

The first claims of signals from outer space were made by the pioneers of radio, Marconi and Tesla, but they were ridiculed and soon became silent on the subject. In 1927, Jorgen Hals, a Norwegian radio engineer, received signals which have never been explained. In the 1950s, various Russian scientists tried to prove that the Hals signals were of interstellar origin, but this theory is still being hotly debated and no consensus has emerged.

In October 1971, L. George Lawrence, an American electronics engineer, was investigating the "Backster effect" (telepathy in plants) in the desert near Mount Palomar, California. He was using special equipment, designed by himself, considerably more sensitive than Backster's polygraph. To his astonishment, Lawrence picked up signals which seemed to come from the skies, in the region of the Big Dipper. Unwilling to publish such a finding at first, Lawrence spent several months checking his equipment for bugs and redesigning to rule out other possible explanations. In April 1972, the experiment was repeated in the Mojave Desert. The same results were obtained. Lawrence's report to the Smithsonian institution in Washington says:

> An apparent train of interstellar communication signals of unknown origin and destination has been observed. Since interception was made by *biological* sensors, a biological-type signal transmission must be assumed. Test experiments were conducted in an electromagnetic deep-fringe area, the equipment itself being impervious to electromagnetic radiation. Follow-up tests revealed no equipment defects. Because interstellar listening experiments are not conducted on a routine basis, the suggestion is advanced that verification tests should be conducted elsewhere, possibly on a global scale. The phenomenon is too important to be ignored.

Carl Sagan of Cornell University, along with others concerned with interstellar communications, have invested most of their time and energy in *radio* signal reception. All the projects of this sort known to me, funded or seeking for funding, are based on the assumption that interstellar communication would involve the radio wave energies; but Lawrence's results suggest, on the contrary, that there might be a considerable amount of cosmic communication going on that involves the "biological" or cellular level of consciousness (Leary's Seventh Circuit.)

Curiously, Raoul Francé — the pioneer researcher on plant telepathy mentioned earlier — was not the only respectable scientist to "go batty" and admit a belief in so-called "fairies" (trans-human intelligences involved somehow with plant psychology). Rudolph Steiner, one of the great experts in organic agriculture, also shared this delusion. So did Thomas Edison, after getting involved in "spiritualistic" research in old age. I have met the "fairy-people" twice myself, once through peyote and once through a magick ritual, and remain uncertain whether they be hallucinations, temporarily visible thought-forms transmitted to me by the plants, or something else. The something else might be extraterrestrials whose cellular (ESP) communications are received and re-transmitted by plant consciousness, or am I too whimsical?

L. George Lawrence, the man who seemingly picked up interstellar biological signals while researching plant ESP, is now building a gigantic Stellartron to seek further starry transmissions.

"The Backster Effect and other related considerations," says Lawrence, "lead to the idea that psi is but a part of a so-called *paranormal matrix* — a unique communications grid which binds all life together. Its phenomena apparently work on a multi-input basis, which operates beyond currently known physical laws."

—*Secret Life of Plants*, Tompkins and Bird, op. cit.

I got interested in Jack Parsons, the American rocket pioneer who co-founded Cal Tech and is reputed to have contributed as much basic innovative technology to aero-space as Goddard or Von Braun. Parsons had been a member of the Agape Lodge (Los Angeles) of the Ordo Templi Orientis, back in the 1930s-40s when Aleister Crowley was still alive and acting as Outer Head.

Parsons (1914-1952) is best known to occult historians as the man who trusted his girlfriend, his bank account and his yacht to L. Ron Hubbard (also a member of the O.T.O. at that time). Hubbard promptly emptied the bank account, stole the yacht and eloped with the girl; Parsons subsequently forgave him for these pranks and the two became close friends again. Translating Crowley's methodology (as learned in the O.T.O.) into engineering jargon, Hubbard then launched Scientology and became a millionaire.

Parsons subsequently published *The Book of the Anti-Christ* — a strange, beautiful, revolutionary document which, like Crowley's *Book of the Law*, was allegedly dictated by a Higher Intelligence. This entity is described by Parsons only as "most Holy and beautiful;" it urged Parsons to declare war upon "all authority that is not based on courage and manhood. . .the authority of lying priests, conniving judges, blackmailing police," and called for "an end to restriction and inhibition, conscription, compulsion, regimentation and the tyranny of laws."

Part Two of this strange document urges all truth-seekers to practice Crowleyean sex-yoga: "Concentrate all force and being in Our lady Babalon.*

Light a single light on Her altar, saying Flame is our Lady; flame is her hair. I am flame." Babalon is symbolized in Crowley's Tarot by the card already mentioned, The Star.

~•~

* Crowley's spelling, adapted for numerological reasons, to add up Cabalistically to 156, the number of Chaos.

~•~

Aside from his hatred of the restrictions of authoritarian civilization, Jack Parsons seems to have been motivated chiefly by a drive to lift mankind off this planet into the stars. For his many contributions to astro-space engineering, he is honored by having a crater on the moon named after him.

Grady McMurtry, an old friend of Crowley and Parsons, and currently Caliph of the Ordo Templi Orientis in the United States, has kindly placed in my hands various manuscripts of O.T.O. private publications during the 1940s. In one of them Parsons states his devotion to the shamanistic-psychedelic quest in poetic terms that might have seemed extreme even to Crowley or Leary. The poem follows:

> I hight Don Quixote, I live on peyote,
> marijuana, morphine and cocaine,
>
> I never know sadness but only a madness
> that burns at the heart and the brain.
>
> I see each charwoman, ecstatic, inhuman,
> angelic, demonic, divine.
>
> Each wagon a dragon, each beer mug a flagon
> that brims with ambrosial wine.
>
> I went to the city and found it a pity
> the devil was playing at hell,
>
> And then million mortals had entered hell's
> portals

and thought they were all doing well.

I said: "See, dear people, on every church steeple
an imp of the devil at play,

See ghouls cut their capers in daily newspapers
and fiends in police courts hold sway;

The mountains are palaces, women are chalices
meant to be supped and not sold,

The desert a banquet hall set for a festival
ripe for the free and the bold;

The wind and the sky are ours, heaven and all its
stars
waken, and do what you will;

Break with this demon spawn'd hell-inspired
nightmare bond —
Magick lies over the hill."

They said I was crazy, ambiguous, lazy,
disgusting, fantastic, obscene;

So I died for my sagebrush and cactus and corn
mush,
to see if the air was still clean.

Oh, I hight Don Quixote, I live on peyote,
marihuana, morphine and cocaine,

And may I be twice-damned for a bank-clerk or
store hand
if I visit the city again.

This was printed in the February 21, 1943, issue of
The Oriflamme, journal of the O.T.O., two months before
Hoffman discovered LSD.

Parsons died in a laboratory accident in 1949.
According to Kenneth Grant, Parson's last year was
devoted to the attempt, with his mistress, Marjorie
Cameron, to conceive a moonchild — an entity magickally

separated from earth-influence at the instant of conception and from then on dedicated to higher, outer space influences. (Crowley describes this operation in his novel, *Moonchild*. To my knowledge, it has not been successfully performed to date.)

Jack Parsons life, midway between Crowley's and Leary's, was a testament to the faith: it is time to get off this planet.

Brace yourself, what is coming up next is even more mind-boggling than what we have confronted.

Most of the levels of consciousness — of neurological reception of signals — are under heavy taboo in every human society. Although many thousands have undoubtedly experienced several of the higher levels of awareness in every century of human history, and many millions since the Drug Revolution of the 1960s, most human beings still have not. Those who have experienced *some* of the higher states are still, usually, ignorant of many *other*, still higher states. In much of his writing since the early 60s, Dr. Leary has been in the position of the sighted man trying to explain *red* to the blind.

Timothy has coped with this problem in various ways. In books like *High Priest* and *Jail Notes*, he has conducted literary experiments, sometimes imitating the great literary innovators of this century (Joyce, Burroughs, Dada, Surrealism), sometimes going beyond them into new and astonishing varieties of poetry, prose, prose-poetry. (Someday his genius *as a writer* will be discovered.) In his latest theorizing, he eschews that method and uses the dispassionate technical language of the scientific report, while describing *24 levels of neurological functioning (consciousness), only 12 of which most human beings have ever experienced.*

Nietzsche's boast — "I write in blood; I will be read in blood" — is tame compared to the problems faced by both writer and reader here. Consider: if Dr. Leary's ideas turn out to be, say, around 70% wrong, he has still produced one of the most exciting, challenging, mind-stretching fantasies in human history.

But if Dr. Leary, on the other hand, is, perhaps, as much as 70% *right*, his career is one of the three or four greatest breakthroughs in all history. Copernicus and Darwin, indeed, are the only comparison figures that can be invoked.

Many persons known as yogis, mystics, alchemists, seers, etc. have explored in one or more of the *12 neurological modes beyond normal consciousness* studied later in this book. They have had a great deal of difficulty in communicating with statistically normal humanity; have often been martyred; have usually been idealized, idolized and deified after death; and have, therefore, been elevated to a status where their teaching value is nearly nil, since most people cannot conceive of ever *understanding* them, much less imitating them.

Dr. Leary does not want to be idealized, idolized, deified or in any way mystified and has had enough martyrdom; he wants to be understood and imitated. Like Copernicus and Darwin, and unlike the mystics who have explored these high levels of awareness before, he does not care to be alone in his understanding—this is indeed the "consumer" stage of neurologic, in his view. He wants to be a transmitter and communicator; he wants to show, like a good scientist, how we can understand, control and use certain natural processes which have *hitherto been considered supernatural and inexplicable*.

What Copernicus did for our location in space (showing some of the fundamental parameters, removing the mysterious and paradoxical) and Darwin did for our location in time (showing our actual past history, again removing the mysterious and paradoxical) is what Dr. Leary is attempting to do for consciousness.

The principle of neurological relativism has been understood by a few since Korzybski published *Science and Sanity* in 1933. In a sense, Korzybski's work was a *"special theory of neurological relativity"* showing that each nervous system has its own space-time "meaning" parameters; indicating how we nevertheless manage to transmit information to and receive information from nervous systems not *too* different from our own; classifying the principle communication errors that prevent or warp such information flow; presenting the broad general outlines of an approach to more efficient communication. It can safely be said that general lack of appreciation of Korzybski's program for improving communication is due to a lack of understanding of his fundamental theory of neurological relativity. We don't know that we need to communicate better because we don't know that we are presently communicating very poorly. (The other guy is always "wrong.")

Dr. Leary presents in *The Periodic Table of Energy* (1974) a *"general theory of neurological relativity."* Our nervous systems, he says, are not only abstracting different "maps" from the inexhaustible territory of experience (as Korzybski knew), but are pre-programmed to abstract in certain definite ways. A Slot 0 nervous system literally lives in a different world from a Slot 1 or a Slot 2; a Slot 13 is very far from both of them; etc. Every nervous system is as complex as a galaxy. When Mr. A talks to Ms. B, the transmission has as many chances of going awry and being rejected as "background noise" as any communication from the Andromeda Galaxy to the Milky Way.

The Sufi parable of the blind men and the elephant illustrates how each of us tends to identify "map" with "territory," to assume that the patterns integrated from experience by our nervous systems tell "all" about that experience. "The elephant is a wall!" cries one blind man; "It is a snake," cries another; and so forth. We smile at the aptness of the allegory, and promptly forget it. In the next moment, we talk to Mr. B and assume he is abstracting the same "reality" as we are. If we suddenly discover that he is not, we immediately wonder what is "wrong" with him. Is he "sick" or "insane" or merely "perverse?" At the least, if persistent effort doesn't persuade him to accept our "map" as the right one, he *must* be a "fanatic." If we are a Slot 5 nervous system, and he is a Slot 17, most likely we will pronounce him "psychotic," unless we live in a very primitive culture, in which case we might label him a "god."

It is very important, when we discuss these slots later to make every possible effort of empathy and imagination in striving to understand each Slot. Unless the reader can "see" (coherently perceive) the world as it appears to each Slot, the reader will not appreciate what is being transmitted here. If you find your own Slot with a joyous cry of "Reality at last!" and go on regarding all the others as somewhat weird or perverse, you have not understood this book.

Personifcations of the 24 Neurogenetic Slots

Neruogenetic Period	Passive Receptive Phase	Integrative Phase	Active Output Phase
Metaphysiological	21 8th Childhood The Galactic Consumer	22 8th Brain The Galactic Intelligence	23 8th Mate Galactic Fusion
Neurogenetic	18 7th Childhood The Planetary Colonist	19 7th Brain The Genetic Intelligence	20 7th Mate Genetic Fusion
Neurophysical	15 6th Childhood The Electron Consumer	16 6th Brain The Neurological Intelligence	17 6th Mate Terra II
Neurosomatic	12 5th Childhood The Hedonic Consumer	13 5th Brain The Neurosomatic Intelligence	14 5th Mate The Tantric Lovers
Domestication	9 4th Childhood The Adolescent Sagittarius	10 4th Brain Social Intelligence Capricorn	11 4th Mate The Utopian Lover Aquarius
Symbolic	6 3rd Childhood The Student Virgo	7 3rd Brain The Intellect Libra	8 3rd Mate The Master Mind Scorpio
Emotional	3 2nd Childhood The Sly Priestess Gemini	4 2nd Brain The Emotionalist Cancer	5 2nd Mate The Big Lover Leo
Bioneural	0 1st Childhood Unattached Floater Pisces	1 1st Brain 1st Gear Forward Aries	2 1st Mate Earthly Lover Taurus

Note: The numbers are those conventionally assigned to the Tarot. Slots 2 & 3 have been reversed, and 2 new Tarot slots have been added: 21 & 23 (21 is now 22)

The table on the following page reviews the levels of consciousness we have been describing. In review, The Interpersonal Grid shows the principle forms of jockeying-for-position on the Emotional-Power Circuit, Slots 3-5. The seven components of game-playing (roles, rules, rituals, languages, goals, movements, locations) deal with the space-time structure of working out these Emotional rituals in a mental-social context — the feedbacks between Emotional-Power Slots 3-5 and Symbolic-Rational Slots 6-8. The higher circuits have traditionally been ignored or scantily examined in scientific writings, but are described in various crude, poetic, primitive jargons by various schools of mysticism and occultism.

The perspective of this book — in which all types of intelligence known (and unknown) on Earth are seen in a cosmic perspective as evolutionary stages toward galactic fusion — will arouse strong glandular response, characterized by joy, hope and awe in some, by fear and discomfort in others. Such second Circuit reactions are themselves relative and should not be allowed to cloud sober judgment.

As I have several times remarked, this may be the most important scientific discovery of our time, or it may be a glorious outline for an unwritten science fiction novel. Dr. Leary and Joanna believe, and I also believe, that the 24 Slot array is profoundly true in general outline, although some errors are certainly present. The reader must form a personal judgment.

Evolution of Leary's Theory of Consciousness

"The Seven Tongues of God" (1966-68)	"Principles of Hedonic Psychology" (1970)	"Neurologic" (1973)	Periodic Table of Energy (1974)
Coma, or Void	Unconsciousness	• • •	• • •
• • •	• • •	Bio-Survival Circuit (I)	Slots 0–2
Emotional Stupor	Conditioned Emotional Excitement	Emotion-Power Circuit (II)	Slots 3–5
Mental-Social	Conditioned Social Consciousness	Symbolic Circuit (III)	Slots 6–8
• • •	• • •	Socio-Sexual Circuit (IV)	Slots 9–11
Sensory	Unconditioned Sensory Delight	} Rapture Circuit (V)	Slots 12–14
Somatic	Unconditioned Somatic Delight		
Atomic	Neuro-electrical Ecstasy	Ecstasy Circuit (VI)	Slots 15–17
Cellular-Molecular	Genetic Transcendence	Neurogentic Circuit (VII)	Slots 18–20
• • •	• • •	• • •	Slots 21–23

At the hedonistic input stage of each neurological circuit — which Leary also calls the "consumer" stage — the developing personality is entranced, delighted, overpowered by the new signals received, the new capacities discovered.

Slot 0, the Tarot Fool, is the input of the first circuit; we see this entranced, delighted, overpowered joy in the newborn when it learns to crawl, to locomote, to exist in the flat-earth dimension of forward-back.

Slot 3, the Tarot Priestess, is the input of the emotional circuit. The toddler learns to stand up, to conquer gravity and to begin meddling in family politics (emotional games). This is the stage of struggles for domination between parent and child; here the infant learns either to win by sheer emotional intelligence (outplaying the parents at their own games) or to win-by-losing, to develop "moral victories" through submission. To go to the top of the Interpersonal Grid or to go to the bottom.

Slot 6, the Tarot Lovers card, is the input of the dexterity-symbolism circuit, when the child learns that the universe has been labeled and packaged. This joy can last a lifetime; Newton's description of himself as a small child arranging pebbles on a beach is true of every dedicated scientist or philosopher. (Similarly, the metaphor of the infantile temper tantrum, circuit two consumerism, is quite correctly applied to all "power politicians" who remain entranced with that game for life.)

Slot 9, the Tarot Hermit, is the turn-on of the sex circuit at adolescence, the delightful and narcissistic stage of blissful masturbation. Again, many remain so entranced for life, although they may eventually learn to use other humans as accessory masturbation-machines.

In each case, the circuit is not completed until the

appropriate neurological bond is formed with the output slot.

For the newborn, this is slot 2, the Empress-Mother. The infant who does not make this imprint remains "inhuman," i.e., either autistic or psychopathic.

For the emotional toddler, the bond is slot 5, the Tarot Hierophant or Pope, i.e. the emotional-sacralized game structure of society. The rules of the emotional game as codified by the Elders of the Tribe. Those who do not make this imprint remain emotional outlaws, criminals, "lunatics," "irresponsibles."

For the learning-symbolizing older child, the bond is slot 8, the Tarot Adjustment or Justice, the intellectual game-model of society, the brotherhood of scholars, the academic community. Those who do not make this imprint remain intellectual outlaws, surrealists, founders or joiners of odd cults, "crackpots."

For the seed-or-ovum bearing adolescent, the bond is slot 11, Lust, the act of mating and union. The spouse. The family.

It is Dr. Leary's conclusion — and this is especially significant — that the same bonding is necessary on the higher four circuits. We will discuss this further later, but it needs to be emphasized that each of the modes of "higher consciousness," of "Awakening" (so-called) has its own input-consumer stage at which the personality may remain improperly imprinted. Many of these states are widely admired and praised as Enlightenment, Mystical Attainment, etc., while they actually are no more than the faulty imprints or failures of the higher circuits, entirely comparable (on a higher level) to the failures of the first four circuits.

Dr. Leary believes that many of the founders of

religions and cults in the past represent such failures of higher-circuit imprint. In short, much of what we have been trained to consider Higher Consciousness is the neurotic-schizophrenic incoherencies of the higher circuits. *Lack of scientific method has left the mystics and shamans of the past in total confusion about their own achievement.* They have received signals imperceptible to the lower circuits, but they have not understood and integrated these signals meaningfully.

If Dr. Leary is right, his reception-translation of the Starseed signals is the first scientific integration of these Higher-circuit functions.

Chapter Ten

The Cosmic Immortals

Today when we speak of immortality and of
going to another world we no longer mean these in
a theological or metaphysical sense. People are now
striving for physical immortality. People are now
traveling to other worlds.

Transcendence is no longer a metaphysical concept.
It has become reality.
— F.M. Esfandiary, *Up-Wingers: A Futurist Manifesto*

A sane government would give Dr. Timothy Leary
at least a few million dollars per year, a gigantic research
facility, and a staff of a few thousand co-workers.

Our present government keeps Dr. Leary in a cage,
like a wild beast, with rapists, burglars, sexual lunatics,
murderers and thieves as his companions. Future historians
are very likely to consider that the government of the
U.S. in this decade was not made up of men who were
in all respects rational. Indeed, Vietnam and Watergate
are perhaps only the tips of the iceberg; the delusions
and hallucinations obsessing our rulers may extend much
further than sane observers have yet guessed . . .

Ever since Dr. Leary and I began corresponding about the Higher Intelligences, I had wanted to visit him; bureaucratic red tape connected with his moves from prison to prison delayed this.

Meanwhile, I was trying to sell an article on Leary's new cosmology theories. As usual, editors had their finger on the pulse of a very deceptive oracle; they told me that Timothy Leary was old news (1973) and completely forgotten (1973) and nobody cared about him or his views (1973) and all the rest of it. A perfect replay of certain conversations in 1964 and 1968 and 1970. Are we all living in an echo-chamber? Or is Leary right about "static repetitious circuits" in the robot-brains of larval humanity?

John Bryan of the San Francisco *Phoenix* finally said yeah, there might be some interest in Leary, give it a try, what the hell. The piece I wrote for him had a rather salutary effect. According to John, in twenty years in journalism, he never saw such a response to an article. The issue sold out, and the office phone kept ringing with requests for more copies, and people wrote a ton of mail. Maybe John exaggerated a little to boost my ego, but, at minimum, the article did prove that many people Out There In Audienceland are still very, very fascinated by Dr. Timothy Leary and his wicked, wicked theories. Here's the article as I wrote it:

LEARY: HOW TO LIVE FOREVER!

A VISIT WITH DR. TIMOTHY LEARY

"I Expect To Be Alive When The Solar System Has Burned Up in 5 1/2 Billion Years From Now!"

by ROBERT ANTON WILSON

Timothy Leary's dead — Oh, no! Oh, no!
He's on the outside looking in!

— The Moody Blues

Vacaville is one of those little California towns that look as conventionally pretty as a brand new starlet just getting the taste of producer's semen out of her mouth and flouncing merrily through a screen test. When you get there in the morning, on Greyhound, the birds are singing and the sun is high and golden, and everything is clean and bright and you can't believe you're heading toward a combination prison and madhouse where men are caged like beasts.

The cab from the Greyhound station to the prison costs exactly a dollar and the cabbie calls your destination "CMF" when he speaks on the shortwave to his office. CMF — California Medical Facility — has a reputation in some quarters that Dr. Frankenstein's laboratory can hardly beat. Gay libbers, radical therapists, civil libertarians and other sore-heads have commented, on occasion, that the methods of psychosurgery and aversion therapy that have been used there to "cure" sexual "deviates" have more in common with Bull Conners' cattle-prods than with anything therapeutic; but that's the psychiatric side of Vacaville, where they keep the people they think they are trying to help. The other side, the purely punitive side, is more humane; the inmates are merely caged until their time is up, and then let go. Nobody is trying to "cure" them, and it's only a medium security set-up; getting shipped there, from another prison, is a reward for good conduct.

Dr. Leary has been in the punitive half of Vacaville since last November, having been judged a model prisoner by the warden of Folsom. Tim has come a long way since the Watergate Mafia arranged his kidnapping in Afghanistan on January 18, 1973; when first brought back to the Land of the Free he was slapped into solitary confinement at San Luis Obispo. (And wrote *Neurologic*, perhaps the most important scientific study of consciousness produced in this country, on the floor of his cell.) To have come from solitary to the maximum security of Folsom to the medium security of Vacaville in little over a year is an accomplishment of some dimension for a man so feared and hated by certain high placed government officials.

After going through the usual red tape, I am shown into a visiting room considerably more decent than many prisons provide. Cons and visitors sat at a table, without screens or glass between them, and shared coffee and sandwiches from machines. It was not much different from any school cafeteria in the land, except that some of the men held their women's hands so hungrily that you almost reeled from the pain of sexual frustration.

Then Tim Leary came in the door at the other end of the room and that incredibly beautiful Irish grin lit up his face when he recognized me.

He looked into my face, with the inoffensive curiosity of an infant. He looked me up and down, with the same innocent awe; I expected him to sniff me next, like a dog. Instead, he grinned again and said that I was in great shape. From anybody else, that would have been mere politeness; from Tim Leary, after an intense inspection, it was a favorable diagnosis.

Meanwhile, I was looking him over and delighting in what I saw. He really does look younger than he did when I first met him ten years ago; I had made that observation when viewing the film, "At Folsom Prison with Dr. Timothy Leary," but he's even more impressive in 3D.

He led me to an outdoor visiting area, where we

sat at a table with our sandwiches and coffee. He was commenting, excitedly, on my most recent letter to him, and insisting that I must begin corresponding at once with an English poet named Brian Barritt. Leary is very sober indeed when explaining a technical point; the famous grin goes away entirely, and his concentration goes into intense commitment to total clarity. It was made obvious to me that neither Barritt nor I can afford to write another line until we have gotten our heads into synch, since we are exploring the same elephant from two sides.

The elephant is named Aleister Crowley and Leary himself has been scrutinizing that odd Beast for the past few years also.

In Switzerland, during his exile, Leary was shown a deck of Crowley's Tarot cards. To test its divinatory powers, he asked "Who am I and what is my destiny?" Then he cut to a single card and got the Ace of Discs. This shows a large disc bearing the Greek letters TO MEGA THERION (The Great Beast), Crowley's name for himself. Leary interprets this to mean that he is Crowley Reborn, and is supposed to complete the work Crowley began, preparing humanity for cosmic consciousness.

Hence, *The Diary of a Hope Fiend*, Leary's account of his jail-break and his months in Algiers with Eldridge Cleaver, is deliberately titled to recall Crowley's *Diary of a Dope Fiend*; and his latest book, not yet published, is a "neurogenetic interstellar key to the Tarot," explaining those enigmatic cards as a coded representation of the evolution of the human nervous system from ancient times to our future in galactic space.

"The first twelve trumps represent our earth-history," Tim explained to me. The turning point is the card called the Hanged Man, which should really be the Floating Man.

Every commentator knows this figure is not in pain but in bliss, but they have not understood why. He's not hanged, he's in free fall. He's the astronaut in zero gravity. The rest of the trumps deal with our evolution after we leave earth.

Leary went on to explain that the Tarot trumps represent the seven circuits of the human nervous system, in groups of three (input, program, output.) The 22nd card represents the Next Step and is approximately called the Universe. The sequence is as follows: Circuit one mediates forward-back, approach-avoid vectors, the Fool, the Balanced Magus, the Imperial Empress.

Circuit two mediates up-down, or domination-submission, which goes back to the Permian reptiles and underlies territoriality and hierarchy. Input: the Priestess, tentative power. Program: the Emperor, oppressive power. Output: the Hierophant, spiritual power.

Circuit three mediates left-right, dexterity, fluency, logic: the first specifically hominid circuit. Input: the Lover, right and left cortical lobes in harmony. Program: the Chariot, work done. Output: Adjustment, nature used by intelligence.

Circuit four mediates sexuality-nesting: Input: the Hermit, adolescent masturbation. Program: Wheel of Fortune, mating and domesticity. Output: Lust, the Tantric linkage (sex used for increased awareness.)

Circuit five begins the "second Tarot" or "interstellar Tarot"; the rapture imprint is formed. Input, the Floating Man (not the Hanged Man), the drug turn-on or the ecstasy of free-fall. Program: Death, the end of "ego," i.e. of the previous up-down, right-left, good-evil, forward-back etc. dualisms. Output: Art, the link with Higher Intelligence, interstellar beings.

Circuit six is the ecstatic imprint. Input, the Devil,

trans-human consciousness. Program: the Falling Tower, linkage to cosmic mind. Output: the Star, the new cosmic humanity.

Circuit seven or the neurogenetic imprint Input: the Moon, racial memory or molecular awareness. Program: the Sun, time-space transcended. Output: the Aeon, Stapledon's Star-Maker.

The universe, the 22nd trump, begins a new circuit which we cannot yet discern.

Dr. Leary was starting to explain how the *I Ching* contains the same seven circuits in a different symbolism (and how he came to see this while studying Mendeleyev's Periodic Table of Elements) when David Hilliard wandered over to our table. David is a Black Panther (or former Black Panther; reports differ) who once got busted for saying in public that Nixon should be assassinated. He's in Vacaville for "assaulting" a policeman.

Tim immediately put all his concentration into communicating precisely with David. Third circuit behavior: fluent control of the throat muscles, articulation. They rapped about Eldridge Cleaver for a while, and David seemed rather embarrassed about Cleaver's treatment of Tim in Algiers.

"I didn't understand Eldridge until I got to Folsom," Tim said. "He's just the toughest guy in the cell block, that's all. The King, you know."

Hilliard nodded with profound sadness. "We've all got the Oppressor inside ourselves," he said.

Tim introduced me. "This is Robert Anton Wilson, one of the wisest men on the planet earth," he said.

David and I shook hands. I felt somewhat overwhelmed by the introduction and wondered innately if I should try to say something Wise to justify Tim's hyperbole.

I was remembering what Dr. Israel Regardie once told me about Aleister Crowley: that the Beast got into most of his troubles by trusting the wrong people. When you turn on the higher neurological circuits, Regardie said, you are quite apt to imagine that everybody else is there with you. "Some of the Hindu gurus honestly believe everybody they see is in Samadhi with them," Regardie added, "and Crowley often had the same illusion."

After we chatted some more with David Hilliard and he finally went off to see somebody else, Timothy got back to the higher neurological circuits. It is his opinion that these circuits evolved for use in outer space, not for mere blissful trance on the earthside trip. The shamans and mystics who opened these circuits knew they had something to do with cosmic energy, he said, but they didn't know the why, the how, and the next step.

The first four circuits, with their dualistic either-or polarities, are for use on earth, Leary re-emphasized. They underlie Euclidean space, Newtonian time, the whole "square" mentality. Imprinted with the local, tribal "games" or value systems, these circuits narrow the polymorphous infant into an adjusted adult with one personality, one sex role, one system of co-ordinates—"usually conservative and mildly paranoid, to mesh with the conservative and mildly paranoid local value system."

The later, still evolving circuits which Leary calls rapture, ecstasy and neurogenetic are not just an "escape" from the anxiety of the dualistic ego. "You aren't supposed to just turn them on, go into bliss, and sink into a hedonistic silk lined womb. That's just the input stage comparable to the adolescent drop-out into compulsive masturbation when the Sex Circuit first turns on. You should then go on to find the program, the proper use of the new energies. The pothead who sits around blissed-out hasn't found out yet what pot is for, what rapture imprints do to all the earlier imprints. The acid head or the guru who has turned on the ecstasy circuit and just blissed himself out is again just taking that input and not doing anything with it."

The higher neurological circuits are to be programmed by communicating with Higher Intelligences. Dr. Leary means this with absolute literalness. Terra II, a starship to leave earth around 2000 AD and seek out the more advanced races of the galaxy, is his top priority interest these days.

The real meaning of acid won't be clear until we live normally in free fall, Leary insists. "When the up-down dualism of the first circuit goes, the other dualisms start to go also. The whole first four imprints, statistically normal consciousness through most of our history, will crumble. Right now, the astronauts all show some kind of altered awareness, to a greater or lesser degree. Ed Mitchell already realizes the linkage between his spiritual experience in space and the old occult and mystic traditions. That's why he's formed the Institute for Noetic Research and plunged into parapsychology and ESP."

The most important events of the next three decades, Leary predicts, will be the invention of an immortality pill and a pill that simulates the death experience without killing the person taking it.

Tim predicted the immortality pill in *Terra II*, published in January, saying it would appear around 1990. One month later, in February, Michigan State University released the information that they are researching a pill that might extend life to 200 years. Meanwhile, Dutton has published *The Immortality Factor* by Osborn Segerberg Jr., which reviews current research on aging and predicts a life-extension pill by 2000 or so.

Dr. Leary doesn't insist that a literal immortality formula will be found that quickly, of course. Rather, he feels that extension of life to around 400 years is most probable; then, those who join his *Terra II* expedition will continue to expand life-expectancy by two factors: (1) contact with advanced races and learning their sciences and (2) the Einstein time-relativity equations, which make a 400-year galactic cruise equivalent to possibly 4 billion years earth-time.

"I expect to be alive when the solar system has burned up 5.5 billion years from now," he says happily. "Nobody in this generation has to die, unless they want to."

The simulated-death pill, creating the neurological equivalent of death without actually killing the body, will also be along in a few decades. This will complete the work of LSD in re-imprinting old circuits and making it possible for us to communicate with nonhuman nervous systems.

Why haven't they (the advanced intellect of the galaxy) communicated with us yet? Leary's answer to that question is simple and direct. They have: we just haven't understood. Our nervous systems have translated their messages into terms we could understand. The "angels" who spoke to Dr. Dee, the Elizabethan scientist-magician were extraterrestrials, but Dee couldn't comprehend them in those terms and considered them "messengers from God." The same is true of many other shamans and mystics.

Leary spoke warmly of Carl Sagan, the exobiologist, who visited him in Vacaville recently. "A brilliant man, brilliant," Leary said. But he wasn't turned on at all by Dr. Sagan's proposed Cyclops project, a city like the old Oak Ridge where scientists will seek extra-terrestrial radio contacts. 'They'll all go to work at nine and come home at five," Leary says, chuckling, "and drink martinis and flirt with each other's wives," and here he began to laugh out loud, "and wait for the first message that says 'We want to talk to the Cornell professors.'" He broke down at the humor of it. "All with government money," he added, still chortling. Meanwhile, his Terra II plan is based on scientists independent of any government, raising their own money, and going out into the stars to actively look for the Higher Intelligences. He can't imagine why any Higher Intelligence would want to talk to the employees of a government.

I could see his point. I live on this planet and I have no desire to talk to Nixon or any of his associates. All they'd have to say is "(Expletive deleted), how can we use this to our own advantage?"

Only once in five hours did Leary mention the fact that he's in prison. "I'm so high," he said briefly, "that I forget where I am. Then, occasionally, there are kinds of research I can't do here, and I realize I should really try to get out." But he didn't enlarge on the subject; he got off on another scientific-mystic speculation about the Einstein space-time circuits and the neurological functioning of men and women living deep in space.

I have seen other people in the high-energy high-consciousness state that Dr. Leary lives in these days. They were all Oriental gurus, expert in one or another of the Buddhist, Hindu or Sufi training systems for expanded awareness. None of them had Tim's scientific background and, accordingly, their verbalizations were less startling; they spoke of vast undefined abstractions which have no meaning except in reference to their own mutated consciousness. Leary is trying to define these free mental states in precise neurogenetic terms and nobody can understand him without sharing in both the higher states of awareness and the scientific systems Leary knows so well. This tends to make him one of the loneliest men on earth— but he's too busy, happy and involved to notice that.

Toward the end of the visit, I showed Tim my equation $B_n = B_0 + P_n + MS$ where B_n is new behavior, B_0 is old behavior, P_n is a deliberate program for change and MS is a metaprogramming substance such as LSD.

Leary approved of the equation warmly. "You could write another one," he added, "with C_n and C_0."

"For consciousness?" I asked.

"Exactly. And another one for I_n and I_q."

I thought of ideology and decided he couldn't mean that; he is aware that ideology and morality are the two chief causes of human suffering. "Intensity?" I hazarded.

Tim folded his hands in prayer and looked upward with exaggerated worship. "Intelligence," he said, naming his God.

("We expanded consciousness and awareness in the 60s," he has been telling people lately, "and it wasn't enough. We must expand Intelligence." It seems to have worked in his own case. I thought he was brighter than average when I first met him 10 years ago, but these days he seems to be brighter than Genius. The psychiatrists who examined him before his last trial found him sane — contrary to Cleaver and other right wing Ideologues — and added that his IQ and Creativity quotient both went off the scale.)

I am personally convinced that Leary's basic scientific "heresy" — that yoga plus LSD can re-imprint the nervous system—is true, and that he himself is the best evidence. The cage experience is destructive to all mammals (Ashley Montagu, anthropologist, has proven that zoo

animals are all psychotic) and yet Dr. Leary has retained
his high-energy high-consciousness state all through it,
including months in solitary and a few weeks literally
in chains. His nervous system is a quantum jump above
the statistically normal human nervous system. He looks
younger, acts happier, talks faster than ever. He is an
intellectual volcano erupting constantly with new ideas,
scientific, philosophical, occult, political, cosmic.

Another convict in Vacaville wrote to me recently that
Leary's "ideas, his compassion and his mental capabilities"
are the only positive aspect of the California prison system.

Before I left Vacaville, I asked Dr. Leary if he had any
specific message for *Phoenix* readers. He thought a minute
and replied, "The meek shall inherit the earth; the smilers
keep on moving through." Then he flashed the Leary grin
again.

As soon as the above interview appeared in the
San Francisco *Phoenix*, I was deluged with information
about that group which Carl Sagan calls "the Immortalist
Underground." These are scientists, mostly young, and
mostly in the field of molecular biology or gerontology,
who were turned on by Professor R.C.W. Ettinger's *The
Prospects of Immortality*, published way back in 1964. This
group believes, quite firmly, that the discovery of the DNA
structure (the double helix of Crick and Watson) has opened
the possibility of reprogramming biological processes and
achieving literal immortality.

Since I am currently engaged in researching and
writing a book on this field (to be called *Death Shall Have*

No Dominion.) I shall merely summarize here the first wave of such information to reach me, quoting a second article I wrote for the *Phoenix*.

What G. Rattray Taylor calls "the biological time bomb" — the likelihood that DNA research is moving rapidly toward a breakthrough that will transform our understanding of, and control over, life-processes — was a familiar concept to me. I was staggered, however, to learn how much life-extension research was being done and how good the prospects were. I quote my *Phoenix* article:

IMMORTAL REVOLUTION WINS THE BAY AREA "MILLIONS NOW LIVING MAY NEVER DIE!"

—by ROBERT ANTON WILSON

My interview with Dr. Timothy Leary (PHOENIX. No. 44, May 30) has jolted quite a few heads, including my own.

I have become a minor celebrity, at least in the Bay Area. My subsequent lecture on Aleister Crowley, at the Theosophical Society drew the biggest audience they have had in decades, according to their chairman, Joe Miller. Charles McCabe devoted a column in the Chronicle to quoting what Leary and I had jawed about. People have tracked me down in my Berkeley hideout and dumped great loads of literature and agitprop upon me. I seem to have opened a bottle that let out an extremely large and hairy djinn.

All because Dr. Leary told me that millions of people now alive may never die, and I mentioned some of the scientific evidence that supports this rather mind-blowing forecast.

It seems that the prospect of immortality provokes

extremely powerful neuro-emotional excitement in virtually everybody, ranging across the spectrum from ecstasy to terror, with very little decorum in between.

Many people have told me, "Seventy years of this is about all I can stand." In fact, this appears to be the statistically normal response. The majority of Americans at this time in history regard life as an essentially bad proposition and do not want it prolonged any further. If Nixon really is an agent of the Devil, he has done his job well; few people regard earth-life as better than Hell itself.

On the other hand, Acid Heads — particularly those who have been into Acid for a decade or longer — accept the idea almost at once. The majority of them, in my recent experience, not only want to live forever, but are eager to sign up on Dr. Leary's "Terra II" cruise—a starship scheduled to leave Earth circa 1990-2000 AD and circumnavigate the galaxy, searching for Higher Intelligences. Like Leary himself, these people are bored with "the amniotic level of conversation on Earth," and are looking for Bigger Minds to share mind-fucks and other kinds of higher-neurological intercourse.

I haven't yet found an Acid Head who thinks it possible that eternal life might be anything less than ecstatic — or that Higher Intelligences might be indifferent to us (in the manner of Arthur Clarke's *Rendezvous with Rama*.) And none of them, absolutely, credit the Pentagon-Hollywood paranoia that the advanced races of the galaxy might be as hostile and murderous as human governments.

"People really are beautiful and noble animals. That's why dogs love us," said Zen poet, Gary Snyder. This is also the Acid Head perspective. They can't imagine that the top galactic IQ's would find us boring; and they can't conceive of these cosmic Heads as being Ming-the-Merciless or Cthulhu types of monstro-imperialists. They expect to find the heavens literally full of critters of whom Brahma, Jehovah, Allah,

Artemis, Nuit, Venus, Krishna, et. al. are merely poor two-dimensional caricatures—the distorted memories of prescientific and barbaric shamans and mystics who accidentally tuned their nervous systems in on the communication channels of the Almighty Ones.

"A decade or two from now we may look back to present-day attitudes toward death as 'primitive' and 'medieval' in the way we now look back upon a once-dreaded killer like tuberculosis."
—Hubert H. Humphrey, after visiting Russia and learning of their research on immortality.

"What the chemists foresee is. . .pills that hold back old age by slowing down the degenerative processes of the human body . . .
Where Ponce de Leon failed, the chemists may succeed."
— *TIME Magazine*

"Most of us living now have a chance for personal, physical immortality. This remarkable phenomenon may soon become a pivot of personal and national life."
—Dr. Robert C.W. Ettinger
The Prospect of Immortality (1964)

"No less than three separate branches of science are doing research in prolonging life, namely the sciences of cryobiology, biology and cybernetics . . . Which one will be successful?

No one knows. But because more than one science is hard at work on this problem, an early solution is forecast"
—pamphlet distributed by ABOLISH DEATH
Box 990 Berkeley, Cal.

Carl Spann, a Bay Area film-maker, has done a documentary, *A Matter of Time*, on people's reactions to the promise (or threat) of immortality.

A black student replies with great intensity: "Live forever in a ghetto? Man, you must be jivin'!"

A secretary in an office building says, "Not if I had to work nine to five for a couple of hundred years."

Another guy says, "Man, the food supply's going to run out. I wouldn't be Immortal for long."

Throughout the film, people who really think about immortality seriously for more than a few moments, show the same reaction eventually: a paradoxical upsurge of impatience about the ugliness, violence and stupidity of contemporary life. It seems that we can bear these abominations if we think our share of them is only around seventy years of frustration, but to raise our life-expectation even a little catapults us into political radicalism. Nobody wants to put up with contemporary society for a hundred years, two hundred, five hundred . . . or ETERNITY!

"Immortalism," says Carl Spann, who made this film and sent me a pile of other immortalist agitprop, "is a tremendous step in the evolution of man. It's the development of an immortal state of consciousness . . . stoned people in a stoned world, high on life . . . Mortal man, like Nixon, is still committed to nation-states and power-bloc thinking which is ultimately globally destructive. Mortal man pollutes the planet because he won't be around to suffer the consequences.

"Getting stoned on dope," Spann adds thoughtfully, "is a defense mechanism against global insanity. And yet, marijuana, hashish, acid and the consciousness expanding drugs have opened the way to the immortal state of consciousness: Samadhi, satori, alpha and theta states, the whole enlightenment trip that provides an escape from Mortal man's tight little illusions of himself."

Way back in the Dark Ages, on September 24, 1964, the Abolish Death Committee from Berkeley staged a demonstration in front of a funeral parlor, carrying such signs as "Death is a disease and can be cured," "Don't buy the lie," "Millions Now Living May Never Die."(an old slogan of Jehovah's Witnesses, who probably never expected either scientific types or hippies to take them up on it), "Immortality NOW!" and "Why Die? You Can Be Immortal."

Presumably, most of the 1964 audience who saw this on the TV news figured the demonstrators were all crazy.

THE IMMORTALITY FACTOR

by Osborn Segerberg Jr.,
E.P. Dutton Co., New York, 1974.

This is the best single book providing a popularized summary of current (1974) research on inhibition of aging, life-extension, immortality and similar projects. Segerberg, a former WCBS news writer and student of ecology, is the kind of science-popularizer who takes the trouble to do his homework before rushing into print. He has read the literature, interviewed the experts, and done some hard thinking on his own. His conclusion is that life extension into hundreds of years is imminent and might even arrive within a decade. An amusing chapter called "Prognosis" deals with recent guesstimates by knowledgeable scientists about when extended life will become available. Arthur C. Clarke (who in 1947, correctly predicted the 1st unmanned moon landing for 1959, but was too conservative about the first manned moon landing and predicted it for 1978) guessed in 1962 that actual Immortality would be achieved near the end of the 21st Century. Three years later, in 1964, with more research accomplished, a group of 82 scientific experts was polled, and the majority of them were willing to predict "chemical control of the aging process" by the early part of the 21st Century.

In 1969, two similar polls of expert opinion, found "significant extension of lifespan" predicted by various scientists as occurring between 1993 (the low estimate) and 2017 (the high estimate.) By 1971, Dr. Bernard Stehler predicted that we would understand aging within five to ten years and be able to reverse it in ten to thirty years.

As Dr. Timothy Leary points out in *Terra II*, the greatest bulk of scientific work on this subject, with the most optimistic conclusion emerging, has been done since Dr. Stehler made that guess in 1971.

If you want to shake up or redeem a pessimistic, gloomy or overly-conservative friend, buy copies of *Terra II* and *The Immortality Factor*, give them to him, and watch his mind expand geometrically.

The Foundation for Research on Immortality, in Sacramento, California, has declared in a press release of April 19. 1972, "It is becoming increasingly clear that we stand literally before an unprecedented shift in our evolutionary direction and potential . . . The pursuit of immortality as a personal goal is no longer just a religious aspiration but has become an actual possibility."

Pauwels and Bergier, who blew the mind of Europe and America with their incredible *Morning of the Magicians*, prophesize in their newest book, *The Eternal Man*: "Perhaps we are even now in the process of building a culture that will know immortality on earth and in heaven . . ."

The signs are everywhere. I just took a break from writing this fragmentary report, sat down with some coffee and looked at today's newspaper. I found:

LIVING CELLS RECONSTRUCTED

(San Francisco *Chronicle*, June 18):

"Scientists have discovered a method of taking living cells apart and putting them back together in ways that may reveal some of the secrets of aging, of cancer and some of the most fundamental processes of life.

The reconstruction of cells growing in laboratory flasks can be done by the millions and within a span of several hours, according to scientists involved in the research.

Thus, for example; large numbers of aged cells could be given nuclei from young cells, or cancer cells could be given the genetic machinery of normal cells.

Both experiments might answer important scientific questions: Would a young nucleus make an old cell young. Would a normal nucleus make a cancer cell revert to normal?

. . . The new technique described in the just published May issue of the *Proceedings of the National Academy of Sciences,* permits nuclei to be taken out of mammalian cells . . . and put in other cells of the same species on a larger scale.

The authors of the report are George Veomett, D.M. Prescott, Jerry Shay and Keith R. Porter, all doctors in the department of molecular, cellular and developmental biology of Colorado at Boulder."

1000 YEARS OR MORE

"It is possible that we may be able to slow down biological aging, doubling or tripling the average life-span."

"However, if there is one major cause of senescence and this is discovered and found to be correctable and completely reversible, the lifespan might be greatly extended, perhaps to 500 to 600 years."

"If every case of aging can be corrected and prevented, we might all be potential Methusalahs, living 1,000 years or more."

—Robert W. Pehoda EXTENDED YOUTH: THE PROMISE OF GERONTOLOGY

Most of the life-extension speculation going on in scientific circles these days is earth-bound, terra-centric, a hangover of what Tim Leary calls "closet Ptolmaicism."

The Lorenz and Einstein equations of space-time relativity leave no doubt that a cruise around the galaxy, such as is projected by Dr. Leary in *Terra II*, might occupy 400 years elapsed time aboard ship and return to Earth circa 4,500,000,000 AD, Earth-time. Space travel is time travel. If the crew members have life-extension to several hundred years when they blast off circa 1990 AD, even if they do not encounter Higher Intelligences with more advanced life-extension techniques, they will return to an Earth science four-and-one-half-billion years in advance of ours, and reap whatever techniques of life-extension, inhibition of aging, cryonics, rejuvenation, etc. that human ingenuity can devise in four thousand million years.

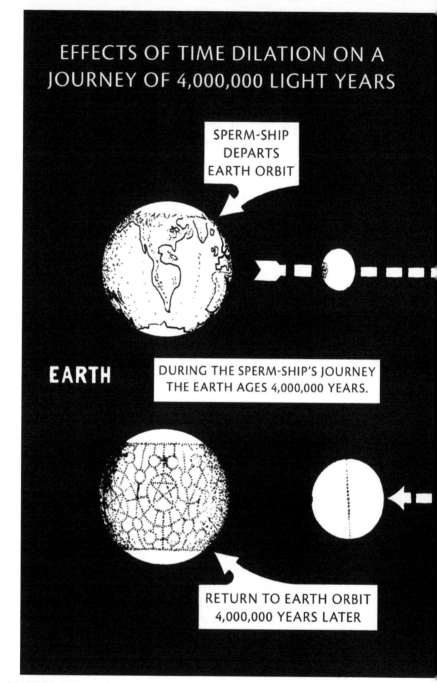

EFFECTS OF TIME DILATION ON A JOURNEY OF 4,000,000 LIGHT YEARS

SPERM-SHIP
DEPARTS
EARTH ORBIT

EARTH

DURING THE SPERM-SHIP'S JOURNEY
THE EARTH AGES 4,000,000 YEARS.

RETURN TO EARTH ORBIT
4,000,000 YEARS LATER

SPACE TRAVEL IS TIME TRAVEL. The quantum jump from "life extension" to "Immortality" is the space-time leap across galaxies. The illustrations below show time-relativity on a 60-year cruise. Terra II plans to travel 400 years

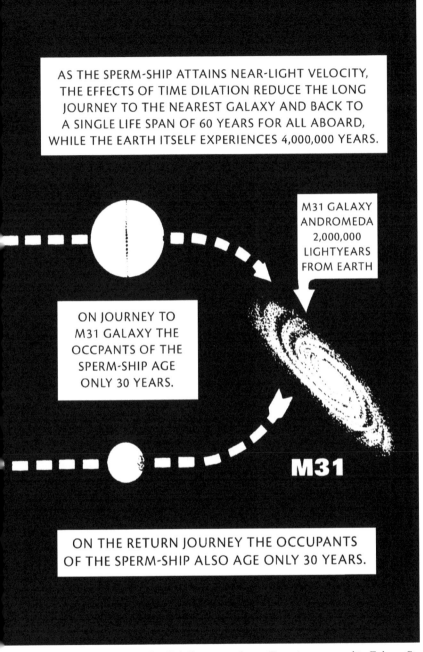

AS THE SPERM-SHIP ATTAINS NEAR-LIGHT VELOCITY, THE EFFECTS OF TIME DILATION REDUCE THE LONG JOURNEY TO THE NEAREST GALAXY AND BACK TO A SINGLE LIFE SPAN OF 60 YEARS FOR ALL ABOARD, WHILE THE EARTH ITSELF EXPERIENCES 4,000,000 YEARS.

M31 GALAXY ANDROMEDA 2,000,000 LIGHTYEARS FROM EARTH

ON JOURNEY TO M31 GALAXY THE OCCPANTS OF THE SPERM-SHIP AGE ONLY 30 YEARS.

M31

ON THE RETURN JOURNEY THE OCCUPANTS OF THE SPERM-SHIP ALSO AGE ONLY 30 YEARS.

and return to Earth 4 ½ billion years later. (Drawing executed in Folsom State Prison by Harold W. Olson –graphic was adapted for eBook formatting.)

Dr. Leary is planning Terra II as a free enterprise, non-governmental project, created entirely by the time and money of those who can share this vision and are willing to devote their energies to making it happen.

There is no reason why other groups cannot start their own Terra II, or Terra III or Terra IV or . . .

As Dr. Leary writes, "At this state of our knowledge it is safe to say that the most vexing, problematic aspects of longevity are not biological, but psychological. We confront here a psycho-physical law: for each year that we extend the lifespan we must square the extension of consciousness. The body is the car and the nervous system the driver. It is meaningless and dangerous to improve the speed and mobility of the car unless we expand the consciousness of the driver. The extension of biology is arithmetical: the extension of neurologic must be exponential . . ."

"Now it becomes clear that Terra II is the ideal living laboratory for longevity. Terra II is truly a 'time-ship'. . .It will be possible, indeed, it will be necessary, for Terra II to initiate new ways of living, experiments in sociology, psychology, ethics and neurology, which cannot be performed in Terra I societies. It is impossible, for example, to evolve new social forms on this planet. This was the lesson of the 1960s. Experimental mutants cannot occupy the same space as species dominants."

"Any visible changes in lifestyle, sexual-social pattern, mode of consciousness, will be ruthlessly suppressed. The Catholic Pope opposes birth control and every police chief in the world itches to barber the long-hairs . . ."

"Terra II starts afresh."

"The psychological cards are shuffled and dealt anew."

"We seek a society without rules, sanctions, penalties, shames, social fears."

"Neurologic makes possible re-imprinting of the

nervous system and sequences of serial reincarnation."

"Consciousness expansion, both neurological and external, will keep Terra II alive, curious, rejuvenating."

"It is total arrest to indulge in the imprint of death."

"Death is a tired metaphor. Our only mission is to make love to life itself. The acceptance of death is an unnecessary bondage, refutation of further mutation."

The Utopian vision is unfashionable these days. There are good reasons for this almost universal despair: wherever we look in this society, we find more stupidity, more cruelty, more injustice. It seems that the only purpose of our idealism is masochistic: it gives us an unreal dream that makes our actual lives more ugly by comparison. According to Jack Anderson's column (*Chronicle*, June 13), the food price crunch has reached the point where many lower income families — "Blacks, Chicanos, poor whites and other colored people," to quote Tomasina and Bushrod — are eating dog food. Anderson adds that one of his staff researchers tried this unique diet experimentally and reported that it tastes awful. Meanwhile, J. Paul Getty owns 14 billion dollars, which means that if he gave $1,000 away to a poor family every goddam day of the year, his fortune would not be exhausted for 58,355 years — by which time interest on the capital would have replaced it.

(Check these figures for yourself, if you doubt it.)

While poor people spoon dog food onto their plates, and Mr. Getty sits on his $14,000,000,000, the government continues Roosevelt II's last ditch gimmick to preserve the scarcity economy: paying farmers not to grow certain food crops and periodically destroying surpluses.

Ginsberg did not exaggerate when he called this

planet an armed madhouse.

Nonetheless, any objective, scientific assessment of the actual situation of Terra I comes to the same conclusion that R. Buckminster Fuller has been announcing since the 1920s: we have enough in terms of actual resources to create an economy not only of adequacy but of abundance. The physical plant exists. The trained technologists exist. The knowledge exists. Everything is here, except the neurological revolution that will allow us to see our own potential.

Before World War I, most human suffering was inevitable. Even if the ruling classes had been less piggish, less brutal, less short-sighted, they could not have produced an economy of abundance for all. The knowledge and technology did not exist.

For over 50 years now, this knowledge and technology have existed. Most of our contemporary suffering is not inevitable; it is caused by the greed, stupidity and short-sightedness of those in decision making positions. A vague knowledge of this occurs to everybody once in a while — while looking across the rooftops at all the TV aerials and wondering why there is so much misery and hunger amid this partial "affluence" — and this is the cause of our despair and lethargy. Fifty years seems like a long time to watch things slowly getting worse when they should be getting better.

The evolutionary perspective is needed. We need to remember how short a half-century is, in terms of species-life.

The potentials of the Second Industrial Revolution— the Cybercultural Revolution — are rejected as "socialistic" by the Capitalist ruling class, and as "anarchistic" by the Socialist ruling class. The bottleneck is neurological. As Fuller insists over and over, the alleged "rulers" simply do not understand the technology they administer. They literally have flat-earth Ptolemaic, static imprints programming their cortical computers — "How are things up there?" Houston

Control once asked an astronaut who was actually under their feet at the time.

The wars, revolutions, depressions, etc. of the past half-century are, as Fuller keeps telling us, proof positive that the rulers do not understand the physical plant they are trying to administer. (There is hardly a scientist in the U.S. Congress, for instance. Most of them are lawyers, carefully trained in a system in legal metaphysics created to administer a Feudal economy. They still think of the rest of us as serfs, although few are as brutally explicit about that attitude as Mr. Nixon.)

As Dr. Leary says in *Terra II*, "Scan the headlines. Drought. Famine. Shortage. Pollution. Malaise. Disorder. Tyranny. Espionage. Watergate is the American word for a worldwide epidemic of government illegalities. Torture in Greece. The new repression in Russia. Israeli air piracy. Libyan mania. Every week another country captured by its own military police." Several more governments have fallen in the six months since Leary wrote those words. Those who have so badly mismanaged this planet in the past fifty years are increasingly revealed as the incompetents they are.

These "crackpot realists" (as C. Wright Mills called them) are directed entirely by "common sense" — and common sense, as Einstein said, is merely the name for all those prejudices Mom and Dad imprinted on our nervous systems before we were five years old.

BETTER LIVING THROUGH CHEMISTRY

"In the Evans-Kline anthology of scientific papers, *Psychotropic Drugs in the Year 2000*, Nathan S. Kline, M.D. points out that within 30 years we will almost certainly have drugs that will:

1.Prolong childhood and shorten adolescence.
2.Reduce need for sleep.
3.Provide safe, short-acting intoxicants.
4.Regulate sexual response.
5.Control aggression.
6.Foster or terminate mothering behavior.

"How will these drugs be handled when they appear? Recent history gives us little cause to hope that our society will treat them rationally. The sex drugs, almost certainly, will be declared illegal and reappear immediately in diluted and unsafe form on the black market, as was the case with LSD . . . with every user wondering if he or she is getting the product advertised or just the rejects from some entrepreneur's bathtub mescaline distillery. There will probably be some memorably bad trips in those years."

"And what of the drugs that 'foster or terminate mothering behavior'? We can imagine how the Reverend Billy Graham would like to see them used, and the far different ways that the Women's Liberation movement would prefer to use them; can we imagine a reasonable compromise that would reconcile this conflict? Or do we have to admit that one drug (fostering maternal impulses) would be legal and the other, again, would be on the black market, like the abortifacient of yore?"

"And what government office do we trust enough to give sole custody of drugs that control aggression, decrease alertness, prevent learning or prolong childhood?"

—*Sex and Drugs: A Journey Beyond Limits*,
by Robert Anton Wilson, Playboy Press

Nothing in this article is science fiction, except in the Wittgensteinian sense that any speculation beyond the actual recording of instrument readings is technically fiction. In that sense, Freud, Marx, Einstein, Skinner, Leary, Velikovsky, Van Daniken, and you and I are all science fiction writers.

Current research on inhibition of aging or potential immortality includes (in addition to the University of Colorado group of cell-mechanics mentioned earlier):

• The cryologists who "freeze-wait-reanimate" gained some notoriety in recent years. This is only the tip of the iceberg.

• Dr. Johan Bjorksten, working on proteins at his own lab in Madison, Wisconsin. He expects a drug that will extend lifespan to 140 years, and he hopes to achieve that within a decade.

• A group at the University of Michigan who are already testing a drug that might expand life to 200 years or longer.

• Oak Ridge National Laboratory, which is researching BHT, a chemical that might increase longevity by 50%.

• All the organ transplant people.

• The cyberneticists, who may find a way to "code" a total personality, keep it on file in an electronic circuit, and reanimate it at any time.

• Microwave instrument Co. in Del Mar, California. They are researching anti-aging drugs, and might have some on the market in three years.

• The parapsychologists, who are collecting data which challenges the bedrock of physics, indicates that all science may be revolutionized at any time, and thus opens possibilities that have previously been unthinkable.

• And, finally, nobody knows how much work the Russians are doing in this field, but we have evidence that they are probably ahead of us.

During my most recent visit to Vacaville, I told Dr. Leary that some of the people who were most enthusiastic about his drug research in the early 60s are most hostile to his current neurogenetic and cosmic projects.

"I can't help that," he said. "The drugs were tools to me, microscopes. I used them to change focus in various ways, to learn the full potentials of the human nervous system. Those who imprinted my first transmissions may have stopped growing at, say, the Rapture Circuit. They have become Hedonic Engineers, and no more.

"But the Turn On is just the first step. The message now is that the message keeps changing. Intelligence must increase as consciousness expands, or we get burned-out. I'm just beginning, in the last year I've just wised up . . ."

"Yes," he added. "I got rid of my own fears in the 60s, but now I have no fear of other people's fears. Truth. Truth. Truth. That's the highest circuit of all" . . .

He mentioned a prominent counterculture hero. "He hates me now, because I'm not suffering. If I were in misery, he'd love me. He suffers every time he drags himself out of bed, I'm sure. But glorification of suffering is one of the larval reflexes we must lose. I'm free, you see, and those people can't stand that. They want to feel sorry for me. But I'm too busy trying to free the rest of humanity out there. They don't have to keep repeating the old misery imprints. They can become Immortal and go to the stars . . ."

Chapter Eleven

The Coiled Splendour

. . . arouse the coiled splendor within you. . .
— *The Book of the Law*

You are about to discover the Key to immortality
in the chemical structure of the genetic code.
— *The Starseed Transmissions*

Ever since Crick and Watson discovered that the DNA
has a helix structure, I have wondered about its possible
connection with the early Hindu concept of "kundalini"
(serpent power) the coiled energy-force said to underlie all
life. In particular, is the "raising of the serpent power" in
yoga an actual unleashing of energy-intelligence previously
inaccessible to consciousness deep within the DNA spiral?

At my next meeting with Dr. Leary in Vacaville, he
invited me to collaborate with him on *The Periodic Table
of Energy*, a book suggesting a model for pre-programmed
evolution on every planet of the galaxy, a kind of cosmic
life-script. He outlined his basic assumptions as follows:

"The DNA code is probably the same on every planet
of the galaxy.

"Once seeded on the planetary womb-surface, the DNA is preprogrammed to evolve the first four circuits. One, bio-survival and motility. Two, domination of territorial and emotional space. Three, dexterity and symbolism (thinking.) Four, some stable or workable sex-nesting domestic routine. Eventually, one species or another — depending on the local planetary conditions — will evolve far enough and imprint these circuits complexly enough to take the next step, the fifth circuit. This is neurosomatic bliss, freedom from the conditioned reflexes of the first four circuits, the chance to look around and philosophize objectively. On this planet, some sages began to imprint the fifth circuit during the last ten thousand years.

"Now we are ready for space and for immortality; right on time, the sciences show us the way to star flight and indefinite life extension. The DNA obviously has been programmed for this graduation exercise from the very beginning.

"There must be many higher types around the galaxy. Sixth circuit intellects, seventh circuit intellects, eighth circuit intellects . . . Arthur C. Clarke says "Any sufficiently advanced technology is indistinguishable from magic." They will appear as angels or archangels or even gods to the first lower-circuit types who contact them.

"Some of us will be joining these cosmic immortals soon, I'm sure. Some will choose to remain on Earth, which I am quite sure will evolve toward some anthill socialism. The meek really shall inherit the Earth; the bold and daring will move on to the stars. And a third group, I'm convinced, will not graduate fully. They'll get off the earth, colonize elsewhere, and develop in various trans-human directions we can't imagine.

"I reject both the stay-at-home and the colonist decisions. Some of us will move on forever. The highest circuit is electrolocalized magnetic-gravitational. That is, it requires no localized body-plant. It is meta-physiological. Mind you, I don't say metaphysical. "Metaphysical" is a dumb word used by people who don't understand Einstein yet. I'm talking about a quite specific electromagnetic-gravitational field in which mind can manifest without organic bodies. That's the eighth circuit and the highest possible evolutionary slot within this galaxy. I'm not ready to speculate beyond this galaxy yet . . . ."

Meanwhile, Carl Spann — the cartoonist who has been an Immortalist since 1964 — loaned me a copy of professor Ettinger's new book, *Man Into Superman*. I was particularly intrigued by the following passage:

Nevertheless, many students of aging now agree that we shall learn not only to understand senile degeneration, but to prevent and even reverse it; some claim that, to a limited degree, we can do so already. Bernard Strenler: "It appears to me that there is no inherent contradiction, no inherent property of cells or of metazoa, which precludes their organization into perpetually functioning and self-replenishing individuals." F. M. Sinex: "The present development of biochemistry and biology suggests the question 'Why do we get old?' may be answered in the foreseeable future . . . preventive therapy is a possibility." Johan Bjorksten: ". . . . when the age problem itself has been solved, the age dependent diseases headed by cancer and circulatory diseases will automatically fall into line. The full benefit of all other medical research will only be realized when the process of aging can be braked." I.N.

Kugelmass: "Man may well become master of his own life and lifespan."

There have been some definite successes in increasing the life span of laboratory animals, and some apparent successes in improving the vitality of elderly human patients . . . One type of therapy, effective with rats and mice, involves *restriction of diet.* In 1932 Clive McCay published results of experiments in which life spans of rats were increased about 50% by limiting caloric intake to slow down maturation . . . These, and somewhat similar experiments, have been repeated by others; mice have had lifespan doubled by deprivation of a certain amino acid, tryptophan . . .

Dr. Benjamin Frank, a New York physician, has a partly worked out theory of *nucleic acid therapy* for reversal of aging, and has applied it in clinical practice . . . He also says that two dogs, nearly dead of old age and greatly debilitated at ages 14 and 16 respectively, after being given his treatment improved markedly and lived to 20 and 23 respectively, dying of accident and infectious disease.

Denham Harman, a physician and chemist at the Universities of California and Nebraska, like many others, was impressed by the similarity of radiation damage to senile degeneration, and consequently tried *antiradiation drugs* to combat senility; he believed he succeeded, in one series of experiments, in extending the lives of mice by 25% . . ."

A few words more about the *speed* and *acceleration* of scientific breakthroughs:

Dr. Isaac Asimov notes, in his *The Genetic Code,* that there seems to be a 60-year cycle between the first understanding of a new principle and the transformation of the world by applications of that principle. Thus, the instances of the discovery of electromagnetic equivalence by Oersted in 1820; sixty years later, in 1880, electrical generators and motors were in wide use and the Industrial Revolution had occurred in the Western nations; the telegraph was also widespread and our age of Mass Communication was dawning.

Similarly, in 1883, Thomas Edison first noted the so-called "Edison effect," although he never understood it or realized its importance. Within sixty years, by 1943, the technology of electronics, as distinguished from electricity — technology based entirely on the "Edison effect" — had spread radio everywhere and was already beginning to replace it by television.

Again, in 1896, Becquerel noted the subatomic behavior of uranium. Sixty years later, in 1956, two cities had been destroyed by atom bombs and nuclear generating plants were operating in many places.

In 1903, the Wright Brothers got their monoplane off the ground for a few minutes. Sixty years later, in 1963, jetliners carrying over 100 passengers were circling the earth daily.

In 1926, Goddard fired his first rocket into the air; in 1986, obviously, planned landings on nearby planets will be accomplished and unmanned surveillance of several others will be commonplace.

Asimov summarizes: "Sixty years, then, seems to the typical interval from scientific breakthrough to full flower. Since scientists studied in 1944 a substance which they called DNA, and since this undoubtedly revolutionized the life sciences with full breakthrough force, I feel confident that – if we survive – the year 2004 will see molecular biology introducing triumphs that can now barely be imagined."

Within the DNA genetic code is the trigger that eventually activates senescence, senility and death. We have passed the midway point (1974) in the sixty-year cycle 1944-2004. It is not extravagant to suppose that some of the current research on life extension will be, at least moderately, successful, and that, by 2004, the technology of advanced life-extension will be in full-swing all over the planet.

The last generation of terrestrial mortal men and women may now be dying off. The first generation of cosmic immortals may be already born. To a great extent it will be our own choice and our own responsibility when we finally decide, with resignation or with renewed hope, which group we belong to.

Carl Spann, the cartoonist, put me in contact with Paul Segall, a PhD candidate at UC-Berkeley, who has been involved in life-extension research for fifteen years.

To my delight, Paul Segall has had as many synchronistic (coincidental?) links with Dr. Timothy Leary as I had had.

What follows is edited from a three hour interview with Mr. Segall concerning the evolution of his work and his hopes to be able to extend human life expectancy to 400-500 years by the mid-1980s.

My doctoral thesis represent only part of my Immortalist research. There are , basically, seven branches of life-extension research and I've done some work in each of them over the past fifteen years. I'll get to that in a minute . . .

Let's see: my father was an engineer, one of my uncles was also an engineer, another uncle was a chemist. I was drenched in science from the cradle, and I always dug science fiction. All through my childhood I was experimenting with chemistry sets and electronics and going to the Museum of Natural History and so on. Heinlein and Asimov and Arthur Clarke were my favorite writers, because of the way they integrate real science into their stories. I don't read any fiction these days, because I don't have the time for it, but I'm looking forward to a reading binge, catching up on sci-fi, after I've got my Ph.D.

I went through the New York public school system, which is contemptable in every way. I learned to thoroughly hate authority and to question and distrust everything. Now, I suppose I might thank them for the lesson, but it wasn't what they intended to teach . . .

In college, I started out to be an engineer. I was fascinated by rockets and bombs and had absolutely no social conscience at all. It seemed that people wanted to blow each other up and I was quite willing to make a living showing them how to do it more efficiently. Then, one day, in an art class of all things, I had this weird experience . . . They were showing slides of cave paintings from 30 to 40,000 years ago, and I suddenly had this deep inner question, "What the hell am I doing here?" I mean, "Why am I alive? What am I doing with my life?" I thought I might land on the moon or Mars someday, but that suddenly wasn't enough, because I'd be dead in eighty years anyway, no matter what I did with my time. I became an Immortalist then and there, years before I read any of the Immortalist literature.

I just said to myself, why not work on something that really satisfies me, something I really want? And what I wanted, then and there, was to be young forever. Being an engineering student, I started to think of designing a machine to keep the brain alive forever. I rejected that after a little thought. Who wants to be part of a machine? Then I remembered that the human body is itself one of the most wonderful machines anywhere, a machine with marvelous qualities of self-repair and self-renewal. So I knew what my life's work would be: to make that wonderful body even better, to make it perfect and eternal. When I told the Dean I wanted to switch my major to biology, he asked why, and I just said frankly I wanted to find the cure for aging. He probably laughed after I left the room, but he was polite and accommodating.

My assumption was that biologists had missed something when they decided that aging was inevitable. I decided to examine every concept in biology and find their hidden flaw. This made me tremendously unpopular with my teachers. A lot of classes were just debates between me and the instructor, with him insisting that he had proven his assertions and me insisting that he hadn't proven them at all. I graduated with the lowest average in the history of the school, but I got the last laugh. On the Graduate record examinations, I got the highest average in the history of the school; that's why my low class averages haven't held me back.

Around then I got into hypnotism. What I found kind of blew my mind for a while and changed my concept-definition of reality. It was only after I read about Tim Leary's work on LSD that I began to find an explanation and put things back together again. Reality isn't hard and fast, as we've been raised to think; it's a mathematical construct. That is, *the mathematical relations are real, but our sense impressions are all subjective.* The reality you live in is created by you, second by second. That wasn't a digression from Immortality research, but an important clue, as I later realized.

My uncle read about Monsanto Corporation's research on tryptophan deprivation in rats, in the New York *Times*, and sent me the clipping. McCay had gotten somewhat similar results in the 1930's with low calorie diets; he'd increased the lifespan of his rats about 50%. Now, Monsanto's people, just by cutting way down on the amino acid, tryptophan, were getting even better results. I was investigating several other areas of life-extension at the time, so I just filed this for future reference. I went on to graduate school, took my master's in biology, and read Ettinger's *The Prospects of Immortality* which showed me suddenly that I wasn't alone anymore and others were on the same trail with me. Ettinger very kindly put me in touch with the New York Cryonics Society and I arranged to have my body frozen in case of a death.

When I decided to get into tryptophan deprivation research, I tried to get funding through Brookhaven, but they turned me down. I ended up, for a while, doing DNA research at the University of Pittsburgh, officially, and doing my own clandestine tryptophan research unofficially on weekends. I literally had to hide my rats so they wouldn't know what I was up to.

The people I knew and dug then had this perpetual debate going: which is more basic, physics or biology? The physicists said everything is made up of atoms and subatomic particles, so the study of physics was obviously the basic study. The biologists replied that atoms and particles are constructs of the human brain, concepts we have formed by theory and practice, so therefore the brain is basic and brain-biology is the fundamental science. About then, Tim Leary came to Pittsburgh with his roadshow, and I wanted nothing to do with him. His early acid research had been important, in clarifying my own work with hypnosis, but his Oriental Guru trip didn't turn me on at all. Some friends *dragged* me to hear him, and, for the second time, I found he had the clue I was looking for. As a result of his presentation, I read all his writings and the writings of Alan Watts and got the Oriental concept more clear: everything we experience is hallucination, *maya*. The reality is a structural-mathematical-logical principle that we don't see. That is, each person creates his own universe out of his own neurological process. Science is nothing else but the search for the unseen structural integrities that underlie these appearances. I also met Werner von Braun, who'd been a great influence in my rocketry days, and it was a real turn-on to find that he was also an enthusiast for Immortality research.

Now, biologists were still regarding aging as a Stochastic process—the random decay of random cells. One day I met a woman I hadn't seen in a year, and the change in her was so complete that I immediately thought of the word "metamorphosis." I suddenly realized I might have found the error I was looking for. Suppose aging isn't Stochastic and random? It might be a definite, pre-programmed metamorphosis just like the evolution from fertilized egg to newborn infant, or the bio-psychic mutation at puberty, or the tadpole-to-frog or caterpillar-to-butterfly transformations. I developed the theory that all ontology is preprogrammed. I think that I was the very first to put this idea on paper, and I am delighted that it is now the working hypothesis of increasing numbers of investigators.

Traits are not naturally selected only for individual survival, as Darwin thought. Some are selected for species survival. Preprogrammed death was an unthinkable concept when we regarded the individual as our monad; how could natural selection produce such a genetic program, if selection is only for the advantage of the individual? But if some traits are for the advantage of the group, and for group evolution, it all falls into place. Throw out the '73 models, bring in the '74 models. Once again, I found Dr. Leary and Alan Watts, with their holistic trans-ego concepts, very helpful in firming-up my thought.

So, if death by aging is preprogrammed to clear out one model and make room for the new model, then the genetic code contains the program. Tryptophan was a basic amino acid, one of the twenty building blocks that make up the DNA-RNA information system. If deprivation of tryptophan slows down aging, then tryptophan is at least a crucial part of the pre-programmed aging-death sequence. I've been concentrating on this ever since.

What we've done, my co-workers and me, is to put rats on what we call -T (minus T) diets for long periods. Tryptophan consumption is cut down to the very minimum, compatible with continued life, in other words. On this -T diet, the rats simply stop aging. They stop growing. They stay just as they are, while time moves around them, so to speak.

We've let them grow normally for 3 weeks, then put them on -T for 14 weeks. 3 weeks is puberty for a rat, you see. In the next 14 weeks normal rats become mature and then middle-aged. Our rats remained adolescents in every respect.

We've taken other rats and let them grow normally to 13 months, which is about equal to 40 years for a human being, and then we've put them on –T. They stay there, young middle-aged rats, for as long as we've continued the experiment thus far. The oldest are 27 months now, which is equivalent to 80 years in a human, and they're still young middle-aged, not old-aged, in all physical respects. Two of them have grown sleek, shiny new coats, in fact, which actually grew back again when we experimentally shaved them.

Every rat we've stopped after puberty has remained fertile as long as we've kept him or her on –T. Some have had litter after litter when they are by calendar time way past middle-age and into old age.

We're now producing the same effects with PCPA — parachlorophenylalanine. Now, both of these, tryptophan and PCPA, are indole ring chemicals, very closely related to serotonin, the basic brain-bonder, and to the psychedelics like LSD, psilocybin, DMT, mescaline, and so forth. *The stopping of time experienced by psychedelic users, then, is probably related to tryptophan deprivation while the psychedelic is in the system.* Tryptophan may be the lubricant of all our internal clocks. The most ancient portions of our brain, the primitive cerebrum, is very involved with these chemicals, which activate the 'releasing factors' or peptides that cause all the changes in the body.

I'm very optimistic at this point. The triggering mechanism of the aging program is definitely linked to tryptophan and PCPA, someway, and we are getting closer to the actual formula. Others are working on the chemical aspect down in Los Angeles, but I'm sticking to my rats. I'm convinced that in two or three years we'll understand the control process precisely. You see, right now there are still some undesirable side effects, and it will take a while to know *exactly* what else to cut off and what to increase along with the -T diet. But I feel fairly sure a product for human beings will be on the market within 5 to 15 years.

There's still a fall-off factor, a possible second trigger that goes off after -T short-circuits the first trigger. But I'm confident that this work will result, in 15 years maximum, is extending human life to 400 or 500 years average.

Please let me emphasize again that this is only *one* aspect of life extension research. As I said before, there are basically seven life-extension sciences—suspended animation studies, gerontology (which my work is part of), transplantation (which is just starting really), prosthetics (including cyborgs, or human-machine combinations), resuscitation (literally bringing back the dead, which we can now do as long as five minutes after clinical death and will soon have up to half-an-hour, I'm sure), regeneration, and identity reconstruction through cloning.

Notice: I don't even mention cryonics as a science. It's a practical engineering technique, an *application* of the basic life-extension sciences. Cryonics is just preserving the biological information until we know how to use it.

The ultimate reason that Immortality is possible is that *we are not the stuff we're made of.* Literally. You can trace a chemical through the body with radioactive tracers, but the body goes on after the chemical has left. We are not the chemicals but the pattern, the mathematical construct. You might say that the formula for Immortality is Cybernetics + DNA. But DNA is itself Cybernetics, the first application of cybernetic information-theory to biology. DNA is entirely an information system, a programming system. Cybernetics is the key, the realization that *we are programmed and can be reprogrammed.*"

Early in June 1974, I awoke one morning, reached for my "magick diary" and wrote down the following correspondences which had come to me in my sleep:

Wands—adenine

Cups—thymine

Swords—cytosine

Discs—guanine

This relates to Dr. Leary's attempts to correlate the Tarot cards to the eight stages of evolution. He had already established correspondences between the 22 "Atus" or "Trumps" and the eight neurogenetic circuits, but he was unsure what to do with the other 56 cards. *The Periodic Table of Energy*, on which we were then collaborating, had a big hole in it until that was decided.

I had been running random thoughts through my computer — 56 is the Cabalistic number of Crowley's star-goddess Nuit, but that led nowhere in particular, although interesting in a sense. The 56 cards are in four suits, however—wands, swords, cups, discs—and my dream-mind had decided that these related, somehow, to the four amino acids in DNA—adenine, thymine, cytosine, guanine.

There was a kind of sense in the correlation.

Wands and swords are the "male" suits, according to all Tarot commenters, and according to obvious Freudian symbolism. Cups and discs are, just as obviously, the female suits.

Are adenine and cytosine "male" in some sense? Not exactly; but they are pyramidines. Are thymine and guanine "female"? Not exactly, but they are purines. *The pyramidines bond to the purines just as male bonds to female in the higher stages of biological evolution.* The sexual symbolism of sword and cup — as in the Grail legend and all schools of European magick — is exactly like the way adenine "seeks" thymine to form bonds; the similar sexual symbols of wand and disc repeats the way cytosine "seeks" to bond with guanine.

Dr. Leary had formed the original Starseed telepathy team of two males and two females in imitation of the successful results of Dr. John Dee, Elizabethan scientist-magician who had contacted a seeming Higher Intelligence with a team made up of himself, his wife, Sir Edward Kelly, and Kelly's wife. Was this four-fold structure somehow related to the fourfold amino acid structure of DNA and coded by the Tarot-card creators in their four suits?

I wrote at once to tell Dr. Leary of this dream and its possible implications.

He wrote back to inform me that the same concept had been received by English poet and Crowleyean magician

Brian Barritt, evidently at approximately the same time as me.

We were obviously in the midst of a most extraordinary series of "coincidences" or else very close to a scientific proof that Higher Intelligence exists . . . somewhere.

Chapter Twelve

Mystery Babylon

Government is actually the worst failure of
modern man. There has never been a really good one,
and even those that are most tolerable are arbitrary,
cruel, grasping and unintelligent. Indeed, it would
not be far wrong to describe the best as the common
enemy of all decent citizens.

—H.L. Mencken

In June 1974, Timothy Leary was abruptly moved
again, from Vacaville Prison to Terminal Island, and then to
points unknown.

The rumors and paranoias already described began to
whirl like a hurricane through the counterculture.

On July 23 — one year after my original Sirius contact
or "hallucination" (as you prefer) — I made a definite
conscious attempt to repeat that experience. According to
Egyptian tradition, as mentioned earlier, July 23 is when
the link between Sirius and Earth is most intense on the
"astral plane" (hyper-space?).

I employed a Crowleyan invocation together with
a technique for creating receptivity learned from Arica.

(Arica is a school of consciousness based on Sufi and Gurdjieff methods.) No drug was used.

The following diagram and chart were obtained, in a series of visions and careful (extremely difficult) intuitive-rational efforts to bring in the message more clearly. Comments on the meaning of this information will follow later.

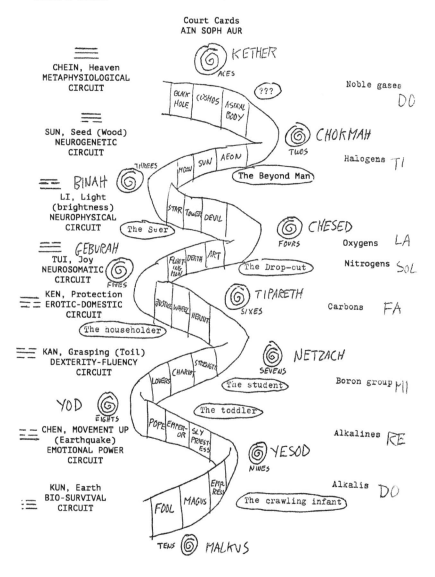

I was originally impressed by the resemblance to the DNA spiral, and I thought also of Reich's claim that the orgone energy always takes a spiral form. Crowley also was quite fond of quoting a strange aphorism from Zoroaster, "God is he having a spiral body and the head of a hawk." (I still don't understand the idea of a hawk . . .)

The correlation of the 8 circuits with Gurdjieff's 8 "vibratory levels" was particularly intriguing to me, since I personally understood little of the Gurdjieff system, but was aware that both Dr. Leary and Dr. John Lilly had explored Gurdjieffian methods along with and in addition to LSD.

I began to re-study Gurdjieff in some detail. *Beelzebub's Tales to His Grandson*, Gurdjieff's major prose work, concerns interstellar Higher Intelligences who seek to aid and advance evolution on Earth. I had previously regarded this framework as mere allegory, a convenient package for Gurdjieff 's teachings, but now I began to wonder if he were hiding his real secret out in front where nobody would think to look for it.

I was even more intrigued by the step diagram of the vibratory levels. Above mankind, Gurdjieff placed "angels", "archangels" and "the Eternal Unchanging." Dr. Kenneth Walker, a Fellow of the Royal College of Surgeons and a hard-headed scientist, has an odd comment on these higher beings in his book, *A Study of Gurdjieff's Teaching:*

> These squares represent higher entities than ourselves of which we have no knowledge at all, and we can call them angels and archangels if we like . . . Some other members of the St. Petersburg group had agreed to equate "angels" with planets and "archangels" with suns . . .

	Circuit I	Circuit II	Circuit III	Circuit IV
Musical	Do	Re	Mi	Fa
Colors	Red	Orange	Yellow	Green
Elements	Alkalis	Alkalines	Borons	Carbons
Chakras	genital	base of spine	solar plexus	chest
Life-Cycle	infant	toddler	student	parent
Evolution	amoeba	reptile	mammal	social human
Neural Network	bio-survival	territorial	dexterity	bonding
Vector in Space	forward-back	up-down	open-close	fusion
Vector in Time	--	--	--	--
Drugs to stimulate circuit	speed, cocaine, caffeine	alcohol	RNA	?
School of Psychology specializig in this circuit	Pavlov, stimulus-response	ethology	learning theory	Freud
Religion & Metaphor	--	Fundamentalism (Father-God)	Cabala (Numerology)	Sacrament of Marriage
Arts	massage, dance	opera, drama, novels	puzzles, detective stories, sci-fi	dance, poetry, love-stories
Yoga	asana	pranayama	dharana	niyama
Gurdjieff Vibration	384 (minerals)	192 (plants)	96 (invertebrates)	48 (vertebrates)

	Circuit V	Circuit VI	Circuit VII	Circuit VIII
Musical	Sol	La	Ti	High Do
Colors	Blue	Indigo	Violet	White
Elements	Nitrogens	Oxygens	Halogens	Noble Gases
Chakras	throat	forehead	crown	above head
Life-Cycle	dropout	sage	seer	Superman
Evolution	astronaut	cyborg	galactic beings ("angels")	galactic mind
Neural Network	neurosomatic	neurophysical	neurogenetic	meta-physiological
Vector in Space	--	--	--	--
Vector in Time	sensory time	neural time	genetic time	eternity
Drugs to stimulate circuit	hashish	peyote/LSD	LSD	G-Pill
School of Psychology specializig in this circuit	Gestalt, Leary	Leary	Leary, Jung	Leary
Religion & Metaphor	Sufism (Next Step)	Magick (Great Work)	Hinduism (Kalpas)	Buddhism (White Light)
Arts	Tantra	Allegory	Epic	Light Show
Yoga	dhyana	siddhis	Atman	Brahma
Gurdjieff Vibration	24 (Humans)	12 ("Angels")	6 (Archangels)	3 (Eternal Unchanging)

If we substitute for "planets" the concept "intelligent, more evolved entities on other planets," we have the Leary theory of Higher Intelligence. More striking, if we leave suns (stars) as it is, we have an anticipation of Dr. Fred Hoyle's current theorizing that some stars are intelligent entities.

The next discovery was more striking, in light of my July 23 Sirius experiences. I quote from page 274 of J. G. Bennett's *Gurdjieff: Making A New World:*

> After Gurdjieff died I was asked by some of the old pupils to write a commentary on *Bezelbub*. When I had written a few chapters and sent them round for comment, almost all agreed with my view that it would be a mistake to publish them. If Gurdjieff had intended his meaning to be readily accessible to every reader, he would have written the book differently. He himself used to listen to chapters read aloud and if he found that the key passages were taken too easily— and therefore almost inevitably too superficially—he would rewrite them in order, as he put it, to "bury the dog deeper." When people corrected him and said he surely meant "bury the bone deeper," he would turn on them and say it was not "bones" but the "dog" that you have to find. *The dog is Sirius the dog star*, which stands for the spirit of wisdom in the Zoroastrian tradition. (Italics added.)

Sirius again. Coincidence?

Most sci-fi fans would agree that Olaf Stapledon is the greatest science fiction writer who ever lived. In *Star Maker*, Stapledon deals with intelligent stars; he was writing in 1939, and the concept was not introduced into science until the most recent cosmological theories (1970s) of Dr. Fred Hoyle. In *Last Men In London,* Stapledon deals with Higher Intelligences "planting" telepathic messages in human beings to help our evolution. In a book called *Sirius*(!), Stapledon tells a strange story of a super-dog whose efforts to achieve higher consciousness are constantly frustrated by his "animal" instincts, i.e. the mechanistic glandular reactions which Leary assigns to the lower circuits. The book is a transparent allegory on humanity's own animal-reflex behavior, and concludes with a second story, a seeming digression, about a super-human who sees us as being in precisely the same pathetic situation as the super-dog. I have found so many parallels between Gurdjieff's thinking and Stapledon's sci-fi tales that I now believe that either Stapledon was a member of a Gurdjieff study group, or this is the most astonishing series of coincidences in this entire weird saga.

I wanted to get back in communication with Dr. Leary and continue our collaboration on *The Periodic Table of Energy*. The Feds still had him incommunicado; by now most of the counterculture believed the planted rumors that he was informing and betraying old friends. I had my own attacks of paranoia to battle: the old legends of "the men in black" who have destroyed evidence of extraterrestrial contacts, intimidated contactees, caused people to disappear. None of the flying saucer books with these weird tales seemed well documented or convincing to me; but . . .

Dr. Reich was hustled off to prison after announcing his extraterrestrial contacts; he died there, and some Reichians still insist that his "heart attack" was too convenient for the authorities to be totally convincing. Dr. Leary announced his extraterrestrial contact while in prison, but is immediately moved elsewhere and nobody,

friends or journalists, is able to communicate with him . . .
I finally *forced* myself to read von Däniken. (An
initial skimming of *Chariots of the Gods* had convinced
me that he was sensational and untrustworthy. But now
I was ready to look more closely . . .) If many of his
alleged "spacemen" in cave drawings, etc. look more
like shamans in animal skins to a skeptical reader, all of
his evidence is not quite so undependable. At minimum,
our prehistoric ancestors seem to have had contacts with
Higher Intelligence just as often as our historical ancestors,
however one chooses to explain such experiences.

As Leary writes in *Terra II:*

> The Air Force UFO study included, indeed, em-
> phasized a factor which infuriated "flying saucer"
> partisans. A team of psychologists studied the per-
> sonalities of those who reported the sightings. How
> clever of the Air Force to suggest that those whose
> cosmologies, however vague, included the possibil-
> ity of extraterrestrial intelligence, were themselves
> "kooks." In wider perspective we can only endorse
> the Air Force psycho-diagnostic attempt . . . The
> Air Force psychiatrists might have done better if,
> instead of the administration of Rorschach personal-
> ity tests, they had performed intensive neurological
> examinations, brainwave studies of the wild-eyed
> "saucer-sighters." Maybe some of the kooks carry
> nervous systems more receptive to electromagnetic
> impulses.

The cumulative evidence in such bodies as Dr. Andrija
Puharich's The Sacred Mushroom, John Allegro's The
Sacred Mushroom and the Cross, R. Gordon Wasson's
Soma: Divine Mushroom of Immortality, Robert Graves'
revised fourth edition of The White Goddess, Professor
Peter Furst's Flesh of the Gods, Dr. Weston LeBarre's
The Peyote Cult and Ghost Dance: Origins of Religion,

Margaret Murray's The Witch Cult in Western Europe, etc. leaves little doubt that the beginnings of religion (awareness of, or at least belief in, Higher Intelligences) is intimately linked to the fact that shamans — in Europe, in Asia, in the Americas, in Africa — have been dosing their nervous systems with metaprogramming drugs since at least 30,000 BC.

The pattern is the same, among our cave dwelling ancestors and American Indians, at the Eleusinian feasts in Athens and among pre-Vedic Hindus, in tribes scattered from pole to pole and in the contemporary research summarized by Dr. Walter Huston Clark in his Chemical Ecstasy: people take these metaprogramming chemicals and they soon assert contact with Higher Intelligences.

According to La Barre's *Ghost Dance,* the shamans of North and South America used over 2000 different metaprogramming chemicals; those of Europe and Asia, curiously, only used about 250. Amanita Muscaria (the "fly agaric" mushroom) was the most widely used sacred drug in the Old World, and the peyote cactus in the New. Over the past 30-to-40,000 years countless shamans have been trained by older shamans (as anthropologist Carlos Castaneda is trained by brujo — witch-man — Don Juan Matus in the famous books) to use these chemicals, as Dr. Leary and Dr. Lilly have used them, to metaprogram the nervous system and bring in some of the signals usually not scanned. (On the visual spectrum alone, it has been well known since Newton that we normally perceive less than 0.5 (one-half of one) percent of all known pulsations.) It can safely be generalized that the link between such sensitive new scannings and personal belief in Higher Intelligences is the great historic explanation of the origins of religion.

The books cited above document this conclusion beyond all doubt; early religion (and some religions not-too-early) is often a matter of taking the right chemical and then turning on and tuning in to non-human Intelligences. It is only blind bigotry, then, that justifies governmental claims that the "religious" use of psychedelics is a rationalization of people only interested in Fifth Circuit rapture states. Sixth and Seventh Circuit tunings are, and always have been, the main interest of psycho-chemicals to serious seekers after Higher Intelligence. And most who looked in this way, found what they looked for.

If one man says there's a statue of Mickey Mouse in the rubble of Troy, we are quite right in assuming he has had a hallucination; if another reports the same statue, and then another, and another, and then thousands . . . Might it not be time to consider, at least tentatively, that there is a statue of Mickey Mouse in Troy?

September 16-25, I was in Minneapolis, attending the annual Gnostic Aquarian Festival, staged by Carl Weschcke, a most genial and eclectic gentleman who is an initiated witch, a former officer of the Minnesota ACLU and NAACP, a successful businessman, and owner of Llewellyn, the nation's best occult book publisher. The Gnostic Aquarian festival is always lively, mind-boggling and hectic; too many events are scheduled to visit all of them, and the cast of characters is like a DeMille epic, including witches, Cabalistic magicians, parapsychologists, hypnotists, astrologers, graphologists, yogis and assorted students of everything at or near the perimeter of mind's limits . . .

I was teaching 6 hours of seminar-workshop on "Scientific and Experimental Magick" — my own method of using neuro-cybernetic theory, as developed by Dr. Leary and Dr. John Lilly, to program the usual results traditional shamans obtain with ritual. As usual at Gnostic Aquarian conventions, syncnronicities soon began to occur:

Isaac Bonewits — author of *Real Magick*, and the first man to obtain a degree in "Magick " from an American university (UC Berkeley) was on a monotonous one track theme every time I encountered him. The theme was "Beware! Beware!" — the anti-drug hysteria of the sixties is coming to an end, just like the anti-communist hysteria of the fifties, and new scapegoats are needed to keep the paranoids happy. "Witches" are the obvious target. There will be a new Inquisition. Occultists, unite now, before it is too late. Etc.

Actually, Isaac has formed an Aquarian Anti-Defamation League (incorporated in Minnesota), hired a lawyer with a lot of civil liberties background, and is dead serious about all this.

I found myself in frequent friendly clashes with him. Imitating Leary and certain Sufi writings, I have been programming myself with optimism for a year now. (The argument to justify this is simple. We don't *know* the future. Optimism not only keeps you high and happy but actively unleashes creative thoughts that otherwise would die stillborn. Thus, although optimism and pessimism are on all fours philosophically — either can be defended convincingly — optimism is more *practical*. The techniques of imprinting optimism on the nervous system are standard Lilly-Leary programming procedures.) Isaac insisted that the only way to survive on this crazy planet was to assume the worst and prepare for it.

"Paranoid magicians live a *long* time," he kept repeating. "Remember: German Jews died because they weren't paranoid soon enough . . ."

(*They've operated on Leary's brain*, rumors were saying just then. *He's a zombie now, and he'll testify against everyone the government wants to lock up.*)

I had an interesting conversation with Dr. Richard Miller, a former physicist who now heads the Parapsychology Department at the University of Washington.

"Have you done any studies on people who claim telepathic contact with extraterrestrials?" I asked casually, not admitting that I might be one.

"Not yet," he said. "But if you're interested, I have it on very good authority that the Air Force has suppressed a report detailing *thousands of such cases*, divided into six main types of communications alleged."

I asked if he had noted in his research any unusual cluster of parapsychological occurrences in July-August 1973 (the time of the original Starseed signals), again not mentioning why I was interested in that date.

"No," he said, "except that those were very creative months for me. That was when I created the Bio-Hologram theory of reality." (Dr. Miller's Bio-Hologram theory is very technical, but ultimately it comes down to this: a nervous system projects a hologram, or 3-dimensional model of "reality." The nature of this hologram depends not just on the nervous system itself but on the *electro-magnetic field* in which the nervous system exists. Space-travel, according to this theory, would change abruptly when we leave the solar system — the elec-

tro-magnetic-gravitational field of the sun — and *we would
enter a new "reality" when we enter interstellar space.* The
Starseed signals end with: "Mutate! Come home in glory.")

A bit later — coincidentally, no doubt — Dr. Miller
mentioned the increasing evidence that the Van Allen belt is
collapsing.

"How fast is the collapse?" I asked.

"If it keeps going the way it is, the Belt will be gone
entirely between 1990 and 2010," he said.

"Won't that make life on Earth impossible?" I
demanded, entirely blown out by this subject.

"According to standard physics, yes. We might have to
make a desperate pell-mell attempt to build a starship and
get off the planet . . . on the other hand," he said, "by the
Bio-Hologram theory, maybe we will just enter an entirely
different reality."

Leary writes in *Terra II*:

> The earth is a womb. The perverse humor of
> nature delights in polarities, mirror images, in-out
> paradoxes . . . Schematic electromagnetic drawings
> of the earth, as viewed from a few hundred miles in
> space, show the cloudlike Van Allen Belt as a soft,
> doughnut-like membrane padding within which the
> earth rests like a delicate egg.

> Life is programmed to be born. That is, to eject itself
> from the planet-womb and begin toddling around the
> house. The galaxy is the house.

Tim and Morning Glory Zell, St. Louis witches and
prime movers in the Church of All Worlds — the first
religion in history to be admittedly based on a work of
fiction; their theology is lifted verbatim from Robert
Heinlein's imaginary Martian religion in *Stranger in a
Strange Land*—gave a seminar called "omega" based

on the evolutionary theories of the Jesuit paleontologist Teilhard de Chardin. Synchronistically, they illustrated this presentation with an "evolutionary mandala" which I had previously seen in *Psychedelic Review* magazine when Tim Leary was editor. This amazing drawing looks like an ordinary Tibetan Buddhist mandala of concentric circles at first sight; look closer and it shows representatives of all major species and families of earth-life (fish, insect, dinosaur, birds, reptiles, dogs, etc. etc. etc.) radiating out from a central DNA spiral.

"All life is One," Tim proclaimed. "This is no longer mysticism, but hard scientific fact. There is One Mind on this planet, the DNA computer . . ."

"And each individual mind can re-link itself to that One Mind at any time . . ." Morning Glory said.

"And when all minds learn to do that, we reach the Omega point, the planetary awakening foretold in all mythology," Tim went on.

Tim and Morning Glory have a great presentation there; the alternative back-and-forth delivery gives a quasi-ritual effect and emphasizes the real link between DNA science and traditional religious concepts.

"Is Tim Leary turning informer?" Tim asked me later.

"I don't know," I said, repeating a speech I'd delivered a thousand times in recent weeks. "I haven't been able to communicate with him in three months. Nobody can communicate with him. Nobody knows what's happening."

"The witch-hunt is coming," Tim said, sounding exactly like Isaac Bonewits. "They're already programming the public. Did you see *The Exorcist*? Subliminal visuals, subsonics, the whole apparatus to plant terror in the unconscious and aim it at occultists or investigators of the occult . . ."

When I came back from Minneapolis, the PILL escapade had already occurred.

Jerry Rubin and a few other impetuous souls had formed PILL — People Investigating Leary's Lies — to denounce him for his activities as government informer and to warn everybody that he was actually lying his head off.

This was a rather amusing example of Circuit Two behavior, since at the time of the PILL press conference there was no hard evidence that Dr. Leary had actually informed on anyone or that, *if* he had so informed, he had indeed lied while so doing.

Allen Ginsberg, who got roped into the PILL conference under the impression that the purpose was to call public attention to the fact that Dr. Leary had been held incommunicado for four months, was thoroughly disgusted with the witch-hunt atmosphere. Dr. Gene Schoenfeld — the beloved "Dr. Hip" of the underground press — came to the PILL carnival dressed in a kangaroo costume, to dramatize his opinion of Jerry Rubin's variety of judgement.

Paul Krassner of *The Realist*, Wavy Gravy of the Hog Farm, Ken Kesey, and Ram Dass all refused to sign the PILL manifesto denouncing Dr. Leary; may their names be entered permanently beside those who would not support the Inquisition in the Galileo scandal.

Meanwhile, the *Village Voice* produced an article attempting to implicate Dr. Leary in a criminal conspiracy of drug profiteers back in the 1960s. I had a real *déjà vu* reading it; it was exactly like the old smear campaign against Dr. Reich, in which the claim was that he was getting rich off the orgone accumulators. (It is not enough that the heretic must be wrong, crazy and a menace to youth; it must also be proven that he is "only in it for the money" . . .) Between the innuendoes and smears, the *Village Voice* produced exactly 0.000 facts to prove that Leary had been enriched by the drug producers.

Then the first break in the wall between Leary and the world finally arrived.

Mike Horowitz, the Leary archivist, called to tell me he had news that he didn't want to reveal on the phone. ("He who speaks on the phone, shouts from the rooftops," says Len Deighton, quite correctly.) I invited Mike over and he told me, while we ate, that Allen Ginsberg had made an effort to force a message to Leary through the Justice Department. Eventually, a justice official — what an ironic title, considering the recent record of that department: bribery, perjury, burglary, etc. — agreed to pass along a short letter in which Ginsberg asked for a reply *in Leary's handwriting* stating whether Tim was working with the government or being held incommunicado against his will.

It was the first hole in the wall and I was immediately enthusiastic. "Unless *Allen* disappears next," Mike said with mocking gloom. The events of the past few months were wearing him down; he more and more expressed himself in paranoid speculations, softened only by deprecating shrugs and smiles.

I remember suddenly *The Politics of Lying* by David Wise, where it was revealed that 19% of the public is now so skeptical and distrustful of government statements that they don't even believe in any of the moon landings, saying that was all probably a fake, too. Whenever I see people toy with paranoia, like Mike, or succumb entirely, like certain underground journalists who have seen evidence disappear over night, I remember that the almost unbroken series of lies by every president since Roosevelt II and every State Department since the 1940s has created a situation where it is most reasonable to assume anything put out by Washington is a deception. Pearl Harbor and the Gulf of Tonkin are the most conspicuous examples of perfidy but — the "food and drug administration" aids the manufacturers while screwing the public, "treasury" robs the poor to support the rich, "defense" is mostly concerned with offense, the "war on drugs" is really a war on people, "welfare" is mostly concerned with crushing the poor, the "representatives of the people" actually represent the corporations and the "Department of Corrections," (like the Ministry of Love in *1984*) is actually a bureau of torture.

Was it possible, I wondered — finally entering the world of the paranoids, at least for a visit to check out the logic there — that the same sources had planted the stories that Leary was a profiteer in the 1960s? Had it been decided somewhere that imprisonment wasn't enough, that Dr. Timothy Leary must be destroyed, discredited, wiped out of consciousness and loving memory, transformed into an obscenity?

Why does the gnosis always get busted?

John Bryan of the San Francisco *Phoenix* wrote another denunciation of Dr. Leary, incorporating the unproven charges of the PILL press conference and the undocumented slanders of the *Village Voice* piece. I called him and asked if he would permit a rebuttal; to my slight surprise and immense delight, he not only agreed but enthusiastically urged me to write it as quickly as possible.

(John, incidentally, is the *only* underground editor who was willing to print rebuttals to Jim Garrison back in the 1960s, when the major press was condemning Jim Garrison's charges as lies and the underground press was insisting *all* Garrison's claims were infallible truth. Kerry Thornley — an old friend of mine — was one of the many innocents accused by Garrison, and he found no underground paper willing to print his side of the story, except John Bryan's *Open City*.) I sat down to write a piece saying that, even if Leary were now a fink, he had been persecuted for unpopular scientific ideas and we shouldn't forget those ideas and their potential importance. I soon found myself weeping at the typewriter and writing something else, much stronger than I had intended. Once again, I was surprised to find out just how much I loved Timothy Leary.

Here's the piece as I wrote it and John immediately printed it:

STRONGLY DIFFERING VIEW ON TIM

The persecution and assassination of Timothy Leary performed by the inmates of the asylum called the United States under the direction of Tricky Dicky and his heirs.

– by ROBERT ANTON WILSON

NOTE: This article is not copyrighted. Anyone may reproduce, reprint, republish, xerox, read on radio or otherwise re-transmit this signal.

As far as one can guess anything from the leaks so carefully planted in the Hearst press by their great and good friends, the federal cops, either (1) Dr. Leary is currently finking on his own oldest friends, or (2) the government is holding him incommunicado while trying to panic the counterculture by *creating the impression* that Leary is finking, or (3) Tim is negotiating most delicately and dangerously to convince the Feds he's finking while actually avoiding doing it, or (4) some combination of the above.

The fact that *Tim's parole was recently denied again* indicates that the first theory—Tim is selling out, purely and simply—is not the whole truth. Alas, the fact that at least one person has already been indicted, evidently with the cooperation of Tim's wife, Joanna, proves that the second theory — the Feds are faking it all — is not the *whole* truth either.

I assume then that Timothy is negotiating most dangerously, under maximum pressure, and that the pressure will steadily increase until they either wring him dry or he reaches a line he will not cross, in which case they will throw him back in his cage and vindictively keep him there as long as is legally (and extra-legally) possible, i.e. until he is a very, very old man.

In this cruel game, I am entirely out of sympathy with those who have been so quick to condemn Dr. Leary. As Ken Kesey has asked, *"Do we condemn the torturers or do we condemn their victim?"* It's very easy to say "I'd kill myself first" or "I'd rather spend the rest of my life in jail." As Sam Goldwyn might remark, "I answer that in two words: bull shit."

Nobody knows how he or she would react under such pressure; that's something you learn about yourself after the fact. In tight places, I have been repeatedly surprised by my courage in some cases, my cowardice in others. As Hemingway said, courage is not something we own but something we continually create; and sometimes we recreate it precisely when we think we have lost it forever. Tim needs our love and support now more than at any other time. Condemning him before all the facts are known and the game played out is not only unfair but adds to the pressure that might cause him to cave in completely.

How many who denounce Dr. Leary realize that, at 53, he is twice a grandfather, and has already spent five years either in jail or as a hounded international fugitive?

How many who now demand a godlike nobility from him have shown as much guts (*and* humor, *and* compassion) as Tim has shown during this five years of imprisonment and escape and re-imprisonment and further escape and further re-imprisonment not to mention the previous five years of vilification, slander, legal harassment and government snooping that led up to his first sentencing?

Since I seem to have been one of the last human beings to see Dr. Leary alive (he has been held incommunicado by the Feds ever since our last meeting at Vacaville Prison in May), I think I can shed more light on what he is doing, and what is being done to him, than most of those who have so quickly rushed into print with condemnations. I have thought long and hard about all this before deciding to put my thoughts on paper.

Jerry Rubin's claim that Dr. Leary has been "incoherent" and "irrational" for over a year is sheer damned mendacity. Everybody I know who visited Tim in those months shared my impression during my visits: Tim was brighter, more creative, more scientifically intelligent—and more loving and involved—than ever before; and Tim is admittedly a scientist who has been programming his nervous system (according to a theory that, although often vilified, has never been disproven) precisely to turn himself into "the holiest, wisest, most beneficial man alive today," as he told Paul Krassner in 1966. Tim *programmed* his brain to produce superhuman intelligence, and if he didn't succeed in all respects, the psychiatrists who testified at his escape trial (April 1973) and Dr. Wesley Hiler (psychologist at Vacaville, who saw Tim every day in recent months) agree with myself and other visitors that Tim was IQ-wise somewhere above the "genius" level and totally in contact with reality.

Rubin's charge of "irrationality" is just rhetoric and wind, no more. Jerry, in fact, hadn't seen Timothy in over a year when he claimed that Tim had been imbecilic for a year! He was relying on those two excellent character witnesses, Hearsay and Slander.

Nobody in all the recent hullabaloo has talked about the idiocy and injustice of Dr. Leary's ever being in jail in the first place. No American has ever been sentenced to such long terms as Timothy Leary for possession of two roaches. No American has ever had bail set so high ($5,000,000) that nobody but J. Paul Getty could possibly pay it. Nobody busted for two roaches has ever been pursued like the most dangerous international fugitive of all time.

Everybody knows, and nobody cares to say out loud, what the judge incautiously remarked when setting Dr. Leary's bail so high, namely that Tim's ideas are his real "crime." Dr. Leary is today being punished and harassed and psychologically tortured — and *has* been punished and harassed and psychologically tortured for ten long years — for exactly the same offense as Jesus and Socrates and Galileo and Darwin and Wilhelm Reich: seeking the truth in a new direction.

Robert Vesco cannot be extradited back to the United States, we are told, since he is "only" accused of cheating his stock-holders out of $50,000,000, corrupting the government, bribing the attorney general, and similar misdemeanors, which evidently do not seem really serious to anybody in Washington. For poor usage of the first amendment — i.e., discussing unpopular scientific theory in public — Dr. Leary was literally kidnapped in Afghanistan by U.S. agents in violation of international law. Thoughtcrime is much more alarming to Big Brother than mere stealing and bribery and obstruction of justice.

Remember: if Leary's particular thoughtcrime

— if his heresy or "sin" — were any other doctrine, political or religious, except advocacy of LSD research, he would be defended by the entire academic community. Dr. Leary's felony is exactly that which the Constitution was intended to protect: speaking in favor of ideas that are genuinely new, genuinely offensive, genuinely unpopular.

There is no doubt in the minds of any of Leary's lawyers that the judge committed a reversible error in mentioning Leary's "dangerous ideas" during the bail hearing. There is no doubt that Leary should be scot-free today, because of that error. There is no question that the Afghanistan kidnapping was illegal, and that, because of it, Leary should be freed. Under the present court system, it could take many years to obtain vindication for these elementary legal principles; meanwhile, the academic and intellectual communities seem quite content to let Dr. Leary rot in his cage without lifting a finger in his defense. There has been no betrayal of basic civil liberties more shameful or more universal in our life-times.

And now such Morality Experts as Jerry Rubin are ready to condemn Timothy for trying to deal with his captors, without knowing the details of the deal, without *any* hard proof that Timothy has actually finked on anyone. And the *Village Voice* prints smear stories claiming Dr. Leary was part of a criminal conspiracy to get rich from LSD, not telling their readers (A) that the source of these charges is the usually hysterical and unfair Eastland Committee, (B) that nobody who has known Timothy for these last 15 years has ever seen any sign of wealth about him, or (C) that all these charges were examined by the Orange County Grand Jury, for nine months in 1973, and dismissed by them without indictment because *there was no evidence at all to link Tim to the profiteers.*

A hell of a lot of people seem awfully eager to vilify and condemn Dr. Leary without enough real evidence to justify hanging a mad dog. Is this anything else but the sheer blind bigotry and intolerance that persecuted most of the great scientific pioneers of the past?

Quite simply, Dr. Leary is the outstanding example of the scientific and political martyr in our age, and each and every one of us is on trial, along with him, before the bar of history to be judged as to whether we helped him more or helped his enemies more.

Dr. Leary's heresies are no small matter. If, perchance, he is right 51% of the time in his world-shaking claims, then he is our century's greatest genius, and we who help his enemies more than we help him are on all fours with the Holy Inquisition and the Witch-Hunts of the past.

The charge that he is "mad," is self-indulging nonsense like the similar charge of madness against Reich, and against Darwin (look up polemics of the time), and against Freud, and against every other pioneer since "insanity" replaced "heresy" as the excuse for condemning the independent investigator. He may be right or wrong in his claims, but he is brilliant in his research, his reasoning and his arguments. That is why he is hated: because his ideas challenge our basic assumptions, and because he might be proven right.

According to LSD-programming theory, as presented in the works of Dr. Leary and Dr. John Lilly (among others), it is possible to grow more loving and sensitive, just as it is possible to grow more intelligent, by proper programming during LSD sessions. Those of us who saw the most of him in this last year agree that, if Timothy did not succeed entirely, he shot way past the human norm. Visiting him to cheer him up, one usually ended by being cheered up by him, by his gallantry, his curiosity, his concern, his bounce and sparkle. I have only met a very few Eastern adepts who were as turned on to the cosmic and the here-now as Dr. Leary has been most of the time. Visiting him was literally an inspiring experience.

(Since writing the above paragraph, I have had the opportunity to spend an evening in lively and informative conversation with Dr. Wesley Hiler, the former Vacaville Prison psychologist who saw more of Timothy than anybody else in the past year. Dr. Hiler not only reiterated his previous statements that Leary's IQ is incredibly high, his sanity total and his coherence remarkable, but also spontaneously used the word "inspiring" in describing Leary's vibes. "His ability to stay happy despite all was an inspiration to everybody, including me," Dr. Hiler said. "The guards loved him as much as the other convicts did. I will always be glad I had the opportunity to meet Dr. Leary and to learn from him."

When I discussed the charges of insanity against Leary, Dr. Hiler smiled. "Laymen are always quick to pronounce a man crazy on the basis of his ideas. No psychologist would take any idea as proof that a subject was mad. You have to examine his general coherence, his behavior, his social relations, and so forth. In all such departments Dr. Timothy Leary was totally, radiantly sane. His ideas are new and original and very provocative, but there's nothing insane about having such ideas *per se*.")

Timothy did have his lows, when the old program would reassert and he would be an emotional gland-robot again. Once last winter he talked for a while about suicide.

Nevertheless, his overall joy and creativity was a goad to all of us, an example showing that an "earth WoMan" (as he would call himself) can triumph over suffering by self-development.

My opinion of my own potentiality, and the potential of all earth WoMen has been vastly increased in optimism and hope as a result of seeing Dr. Leary's beauty of spirit under the daily horror of the cage confinement torture.

Cage confinement *is* torture. The melodramatic theories that Dr. Leary has been subject to brain tampering were not true while he was in Vacaville; and the proponents of this fantasy should realize that, imagining such brutality was necessary to break him finally, they do not have enough empathy to understand the torture of every prisoner. Tim, as the psychologist-shaman he is, suffered not merely his own pain but the pain of each similar caged creature he spoke with or "exchanged neurological signals with" as he would say.

The future will look back on our cages with exactly the same horror that we look back at the torture rack, the iron boot, or the stake. The future may remember our torture of Dr. Leary in one of these cages precisely as we remember the burning of Giordano Bruno, astronomer-magician, at the stake in the center of Rome, year of their lord 1600.

Torture is torture. It does not magically become something else when we call it "punishment." It degrades both the torturer and the victim, and Dr. Leary has withstood it not just bravely but beautifully for five years. Those who condemn him now show the lack of at least human compassion.

I happen to think Dr. Leary is, basically, right in his scientific theories; I think he is the outstanding genius of our century. I think our torture of him is very similar to the execution of Bruno and the jailing of Galileo and Reich. I am being very, very moderate in my language in this article, because I would be screaming in rage at human stupidity and intolerance if I didn't watch myself very carefully now.

Dr. Leary's basic scientific claims are that (1) LSD induces a state in which normal neurological imprints are suspended; this may or may not be totally true, but Dr. John Lilly also claims it is true, and Dr. Jiri Roubecek has written "LSD inhibits conditioned reflexes." (2) During this suspension of imprints, new neurological imprints can be laid down and will "set" in place, remaining as new programs and habits of functioning. Danish psychiatrists, using this assumption in treating criminal psychopaths, have reported some remarkable cures. (3) One can eventually program oneself out of the first four circuits of the human nervous system, which are the only circuits normally used, and which are controlled entirely, and gloomily, by the behaviorists' stimulus-response mechanism. (In other words, most people, most of the time, are the robots described in behaviorist theory. To that extent, the depressing behaviorisms are scientifically accurate, but we can program ourselves to higher levels of neurological functioning, beyond the conditioned reflex arc. To that extent, the behaviorists are wrong.) (4) One can, in detail, gradually program at least four additional circuits, not generally known or used by current humanity. Three additional circuits were described in "Neurologic," 1973; a fourth has since been found; *there are probably others*. There may be no limits to the capacities of the human nervous system for imprinting, re-imprinting and serially imprinting-re-imprinting itself for ever-higher modes of signal reception and Gestalt-integration.

The latter four-or-more-neural circuits are not conditioned, not conditionable; this is what Dr. Hiler, the Vacaville psychologist, is describing when he, rather inadequately, describes Timothy as "uninhibited."

These higher circuits account for most of the phenomena of mysticism, shamanism, genius, witchcraft, intuition, ESP and similar "wild talents," all of which can now be routinely programmed into normal human beings by proper LSD ritual methods.

Such claims, I repeat, are not minor heresies. If even 51% true, they mean that we virtually hold the key to our future evolution in our hands today. Instead of having a half-dozen genuine saints, seers, philosophers, magic-workers and geniuses every century, we can have a planet wide awakening of what now seem superhuman powers in everybody. All exploits and misadventures of those using LSD unwisely, clumsily, stupidly, tragically, etc., are scientifically irrelevant, however socially deplorable. The scientific question is: can a trained and skillful LSD-programmer produce the above listed "superhuman" powers in normal people? (We do not ask if a gang of idiots, let loose in a hydroelectric plant, can blow themselves up, but if trained and knowledgeable persons, running that plant, can produce "superhuman" energy for whole cities.) The government has banned all legal research on LSD programming for over ten years, and has persecuted illegal research. Is this wise prudence or blind hysteria?

When we read about the current findings of the energy sciences such as those I have just reviewed, how can our reaction be other than reverent awe at the grandeur of these observations, at the staggering complexity of the design, the speed, the scope? Ecstatic humility before such power and intelligence. Indeed, what a small secular concept — intelligence — to describe that infinitude of harmonious complexity!

– Timothy Leary,
"Science As Ecstatic Kick"
The Politics of Ecstasy, 1968

Dr. Leary has stood alone for a long time now. The academic community, which should have leaped to his defense when federal agencies first began meddling in his research, has offered instead a spectacle of disgraceful cowardice and blind bigotry. This is hardly news; only 18 psychiatrists signed the petition against the burning of Dr. Reich's books in an incinerator, 1956. But, listen, a certain famous astronomer thought highly enough of the theories in Leary's *Terra II* to travel a thousand miles to Vacaville to visit Dr. Leary in his cage. Has this famous astronomer since then called in outrage for a nationwide scholars' strike until Dr. Leary is released by the ignorant, unscientific clods who are holding him caged? No, the famous astronomer has not done that. He has not even raised a single peep of indignation over this torture of his learned colleague.

("Americans are terribly naive about totalitarianism," Dr. Leary wrote in a letter. "In Europe, even the liberals understood that I was a fugitive political prisoner, jailed for my ideas.")

All right, Timothy is (has been, will be again) a cocksman, a social butterfly, a lothario, a boozer, a joker, a rowdy, a fun-lover, a hedonist, a sensualist, a rascal. Like Shelley and Shakespeare and Mendeleev and Uncle Louie. He has also done scientific work which is universally regarded as important in his profession; done more controversial scientific work which may be even more important than that already recognized; written first-rate poetry; made a heroic and athletic jailbreak at the age of 49; given more love and compassion and understanding every week for ten years than most of us give in our lifetimes; made dumb political blunders; lied to some of his persecutors and some of his friends; told the truth repeatedly under great hazard to himself; made many women happy and some women sad; and looked at his species with a more remarkable dispassionate analysis than any contemporary writer, scientific or literary. The last claim is a subjective evaluation by me; the rest can be documented with case histories.

Most of Dr. Leary's "wild" and "exaggerated" claims for LSD, as the daily press calls them, have been supported by independent research. Again, I am not talking about irresponsible and uninformed tripping by untrained persons; I am talking about scientific investigations, before they were forbidden by law. Leary says autism (child schizophrenia) is a first-circuit faulty imprint that can be corrected by LSD re-imprinting. Three independent studies, in

Psychedelic Review No. 10 (1969) largely confirm this. All children in these studies were either cured, vastly improved or slightly improved; none were harmed. Yet no more LSD research on autistic children is allowed. Why?

Again Dr. Leary claims that properly programmed LSD sessions can duplicate the mystic experience of sages. Every scientific study of LSD as mystical programmer — every single study; see Clark's *Chemical Ecstasy* for a review of *all* data — confirms that a majority of subjects, properly guided, will experience what they consider union with God (or nature) and that independent groups reading accounts of these experiences will *not* be able to distinguish them from the accounts of mystic experience recorded by past religious visionaries.

Christopher Humphrey, PhD, gives a minimal claim in his *Whole Earth Inner Space*: "Any person over forty who has meditated for a year can achieve Samadhi with properly programmed LSD administration." Samadhi is the highest of the alternate consciousness states in Hindu psychology. If even this much is true, the acceleration of understanding and application of mystical states can be enormously speeded up. This, too, is forbidden. Why?

Dr. Leary has fought long and hard to restore the scientific spirit in which his claims can be independently investigated and either confirmed or refuted. Such investigation is forbidden by the government which persecutes him and shunned by the universities which cowardly refuse to defend his liberty.

Even if Dr. Leary has lost the will to fight, or if under the condemnation of old friends and the incessant pressure of cruel captors who taunt him with promises of freedom and torment him with continuation of denied parole, he does not crack fully, and betrays those who once helped him, this is a terrible disgrace, not just to Timothy the man, but to every human being alive who has not defended him hard enough and ardently enough nor long enough to save him this continued torture.

Everybody who can read understands the basic idea of the first amendment and knows what a monstrous injustice has been wreaked upon this basically kind, basically generous, basically decent, thoroughly brilliant scientist over a period of ten long, cruel years. And now we condemn him instead of his persecutors?

Let us examine the logical possibilities.

1 - The Starseed Hypothesis: life on earth is the embryonic offspring of advanced civilizations existing on other planets within our galaxy which can be contacted by means of electromagnetic messagery and time-whip exploration.

2 - No high intelligence exists beyond the gradual accumulation of scientific knowledge. Life is a unique development on earth. There is no advanced life in other solar systems and no genetically preprogrammed higher levels of awareness within the nervous system.

No matter which of these hypotheses one aesthetically prefers, the fact remains that the best investment for the human race, the most exciting, inoffensive way to pass our time is to assume, pretend, gamble that there is a Higher Intelligence, to develop an immortality pill and to organize an all-out search for the Star-school. From history of science we learn that the only way for a new energy to be discovered is to look for it.

Timothy Leary,
Terra II, 1974

Dr. Leary's latest heresies — that we will be able to leave the solar system and discover the chemical key to immortality within the next two decades —

The Starseed Signals

are, once again, pronounced as proof of his "insanity" by hordes of people with no scientific background on which to form a reasonable judgement.

One of the scientists on the Orion Project of the 1960's (an attempt to send a rocket outside the solar system which was abandoned by the government only because it had no military applications) has written enthusiastically to Leary about *Terra II* and even offered to write the introduction to the second edition. This man, a physicist, regards Leary's plans for spaceship Terra II as entirely practical.

Life extension research, which might increase human life expectancy to 150, 250 or 500 years, is currently under way at Michigan State University, University of Colorado, Microwave Instrument Corporation and UC-Berkeley, among other places. I have talked to some of these researchers, and all of them are optimistic about obtaining very favorable results within Dr. Leary's prophesized 20-year limit.

One researcher at UC-Berkeley is hopeful that his current research on life-extension in rats will produce a genuine breakthrough within 2 or 3 years. (This, of course, will not be applicable and marketable for humans for another 10-15 years.) He has already duplicated and surpassed Monsanto Company's previous working in prolonging youth in experimental rats to double the normal span and he has also prolonged middle-age in some of his rats to the point where they should have been dead of old age. He is convinced that he has found the amino acid combination that acts as a "trigger" in the metamorphoses of senescence, senility and death.

Dr. Johan Bjorstein of Wisconsin, meanwhile hopes to have results within the decade on similar, but slightly different, genetic engineering. Prof. R.C.W. Ettinger, a spokesman and propagandist for all researchers in this field, quite confidently predicts that many now living will *never* die.

Again, Dr. Leary may be right or wrong, but his

advocacy of this view point does not prove insanity or irrationality; it merely shows that he is, as always, the bard-philosopher of the most avant-garde wing of current scientific work and speculation. This may be jolting or shocking to many, but in no free country should it be considered a crime deserving of the kind of relentless torment heaped upon this man for over a decade.

It is time we all stopped trying to destroy Timothy Leary and started thinking for a least a few minutes a day, about the possibility that he might be right a lot of the time.

I conclude, like Allen Ginsberg, and his 44 questions, with the enquiry, "Doesn't the old cry Free Tim Leary apply now urgent as ever?"

Chapter Thirteen

War in Heaven

Why does the gnosis always get busted?
— Grady McMurtry

That gallant defense of the Mad Doctor did me no harm at all. I received all sorts of praise from all sorts of unexpected people; the Weather Underground (if they really believed that Timothy was finking on them) did not come around to bomb me for defending the Traitor.

In fact, I encountered no sign at all that the campaign to destroy Leary's following had succeeded. He seemed to have as many admirers as ever (outside of editorial offices and government agencies.) One caller asked for permission to reprint my piece in Portuguese in a Brazilian newspaper, and I agreed with pleasure.

Mike Horowitz later told me this article was "courageous." I didn't feel courageous at all, merely exasperated. I wept repeatedly while it was pouring out of me onto the paper, but it was not personal sorrow; I felt much as Senator Mike Gravel said he felt when he burst into tears during a speech denouncing the Vietnam War, as if the world were weeping *through* me. After all, *it is happening in broad daylight. Everybody can see it.* We all know that Dr. Leary is being destroyed for having a new idea that *might* be right; we all know that his destroyers are Fear and Ignorance and Ape-Reflexes and all the sorry old company that have held back progress and resisted change since the dawn of mind. And those who know and understand most, the cream of the scientific-intellectual-academic community, are entirely silent.

Look at it for a moment through Timothy Leary's point 0f view. He has an idea which might liberate mankind from exactly those conditioned mechanical behaviors that make for misery, conflict, unhappiness, war, prejudice; an idea that might unleash superhuman powers in all of us. And he is jailed again and again and again; driven out of one country after another; slandered and condemned on all sides. *And nobody wants to perform the scientific research that would answer the question: is he right or wrong?*

He must often feel like the sighted man in the Country of the Blind; the one human being on the Planet of the Apes.

Allen Ginsberg's letter, forwarded by the Justice Department, finally received an answer — but *not* the letter in *Dr. Leary's handwriting* which Allen had demanded.

Instead, Joanna Leary phoned Allen.

Mike Horowitz reported to me, as Allen had reported the conversation to him; this account is therefore twice removed from the original. Joanna said that Leary had not informed on anybody; that they were both being held incommunicado against their will; that the rumors claiming Leary had made a film denouncing hippies, homosexuals, drug-dealers, leftists, etc. was also a lie and *there was no such film.* She also insisted that Timothy was undergoing torture, but did not specify what this meant exactly. "It's worse than anything in *The Gulag Archipelago*," she said.

She also denied that she had set up the attorney, George Chula, for a pot bust; and here, impartial evidence indicated, she was lying.

She asked Allen to find three trustworthy attorneys to help obtain a *habeas corpus* on Tim, and said she would call back within a week, when she had another chance to reach a phone without federal agents at her elbow. Meanwhile, she warned Allen to remain silent, implying that her life and Tim's were both in danger.

Mike Horowitz and I ran this one through our computers for many, many hours.

1 - Joanna has always been a narc, some people are now claiming. Everything she has done is part of a scheme to destroy both Leary and the counterculture.

If this theory is true, the phone call and the lack of a handwritten letter from Dr. Leary, indicates that a trap is now being set for Allen Ginsberg. But what sort of trap . . .?

2 - Joanna and Tim were negotiating a deal with the Feds, involving some degree of "cooperation." (Informing . . .) The Feds want more than Timothy will give; perhaps more than he *can* give. God only knows what paranoid fantasies about the drug world they believe in Washington, and what sort of "confession" they expect and

how absurd it might be . . . Guy Godwin, who is in charge of the Leary case according to some reports, has a great record for discovering "conspiracies" which juries and courts simply cannot believe. (The Chicago 8 trial, in which poor Bobby Seale was actually indicted for conspiring with 7 men he had never even *talked* to; the Berrigan case, in which two priests and a nun were alleged to have planned the kidnapping of Henry Kissinger . . .)

3 - Timothy and Joanna are indeed being held incommunicado; in the wake of Watergate, how *dare* we doubt that the government is capable of any and all criminal and fascist abominations . . .?

"Allen (Ginsberg) should hold a press conference at once," I decided, "and tell the world that Joanna says Timothy is being tortured. Let's get this out in the open once and for all."

"Maybe that's what *they* want us to do . . ." Mike said with another of his numerous I'm-getting-paranoid-eh? shrugs.

"If there's a conspiracy or if there isn't a conspiracy doesn't matter," I began to raise my voice and caught myself. "Whatever is going on, silence is going to hurt more people than bringing it out in the open possibly can."

Allen Ginsberg, however, decided to wait a week for Joanna to call back before he would take *any* action. "The PILL people had a press conference when they didn't know what the hell was really happening," he said, "When I call a press conference, I'm going to *know* something."

Another goddamned week of waiting and wondering . . .

Jenny (this isn't her name) is a witch I happen to know, and a very gifted one, with high psychic talents.

"Timothy is in danger," she told me before the week was a day old. "I keep getting flashes that his life may be threatened . . ."

And I had promised Mike and Allen to keep my mouth shut and wait a week for Joanna to call back . . .

My book review desk at the San Francisco *Phoenix* had a volume entitled *The Day the Dollar Dies* by somebody named Willard Cantelon. Flipping through it, I saw that it was about my old buddies, the Bavarian Illuminati—the conspiracy of Satan worshipping International Bankers which many right-wingers believe really exists and controls the world; my three-volume fantasy novel, *Illuminatus!* (Dell, 1975) is about this alleged plot, and I had twice "remembered" (once under hypnosis and once on an LSD trip) that I had been a certain Hans Zoesser (1740–1812) a High Grandmaster of the Vienna branch of the original Illuminati in the 18th century. (Aleister Crowley and many other modern occultists have been admirers of the Illuminati, a Masonic group using Tantric yoga and evidently pledged to overthrow every monarchy in Europe. Even some historians not committed to the right-wing theory that the Illuminati still exists *are* willing to credit that it had a certain role in the French and American revolutions and possibly in the Mexican revolution of 1811. After prolonged research, I am not quite sure that the most paranoid anti-Illuminati theorists are wrong in their claim that Jefferson was an initiate of this order.)

I read Mr. Cantelon's version of the Illuminati Conspiracy with some interest. It appears that the Illuminati are currently plotting to wreck the international financial system and cause the disruption or fall of all the strong governments in the world. When chaos is complete, contact with Higher Intelligences in outer space will be announced. But, says Mr. Cantelon, these Higher Intelligences are actually Satan and His fallen angels, who will appear on Earth as superhuman and benign beings; the masses will accept them as saviours, not recognizing their Evil Nature; and then we are done for. Satan will institute One World Government and One World Religion — those twin bugaboos of the extreme Right — after which money will be abolished and a computerized credit system will come into effect everywhere. Everybody will be tattooed on the forehead and wrist with a credit number, and every "purchase" will consist only in having the numbers scanned by computers placed in every store or bank. This is the key to a tyranny that can never be resisted, because any rebel will merely have his credit cut off, and will be unable to buy food, clothing or shelter.

All this, Mr. Cantelon assures us, is foretold in *Revelations*, chapter 13, 16-17:

> He causeth all small and great, rich and poor, free and bond, to receive a mark in their right hand or in their foreheads: and that no man might buy or sell save he that had the mark or the number.

I remembered the famous response of Robert Welch, Chairman of the John Birch Society, when told that his conspiracy theories are fantastic: "Yes, but we are living in fantastic times." Probably, if we get through the next ten or fifteen years at all, everybody will be believing things as wild as Mr. Cantelon's fantasies. No ordinary logic any longer fits our situation. Already, the majority of us are convinced that the major power brokers of the planet — the governments of USSR, China, USA — are chronic liars, *ne c'est pas*? Already, most of us, in trying to guess what is really going on behind that smokescreen of prevarication, have theories that verge on the sci-fi.

Crowleymas — October 12, often associated with an Italian navigator who introduced slavery to the new world and syphilis to the old—was celebrated at our apartment house with weird and spooky doings. Arlen and I, representing the Discordian Society (for details of Discordian theology see Chapter Nine), together with Stephen and Clayton upstairs (Reformed Druids of North America), Claire and Carol in another apartment (witches, connected with the New Reformed Orthodox Order of the Golden Dawn), and The Great Wild Beast Furtherment Society (which is really Clayton and me and another neighbor named Charles), opened all our rooms to a Crowleymas party and invited nearly 100 local wizards and mystics.

"There are always paranoid vibes at Crowleymas parties," Isaac Bonewits, of the Chasidic Druids of the North America, likes to warn people, with an eerie chuckle.

In fact, Crowley has attracted the worst as well as the best elements in the occult world, and a self-declared Crowleyan is likely to be a dangerous kook as a high adept.

The party was just starting when I was called to the phone, for a bitch of a conversation. My caller was a Doctor H. (not his real initial) who is a very gifted psychiatrist, rather fascinated with both Leary and Crowley (and me.) It seemed that he was having a bad acid-trip, couldn't get control of the anxiety, and wanted my help. I have a reputation for great healing and tranquilizing vibes in dealing with people on bad acid trips, but I had never done it over the phone before. Twenty minutes later, when Dr. H. was calmed and going off into a good trip, I felt absolutely drained.

I returned to the living room. Immediately, Tom (another alias) sat down next to me, laughed shrilly, cracked a silly joke, and said, "I think I may be going crazy again." (He had been in a nut-house for a few months about eight years ago.) I spent *three* hours, in the midst of the kind of noisy party you find only in Berkeley and only among hippies and witches, practicing psychotherapy without a license. Tom was convinced, finally, that he didn't *have* to go crazy again, that he was the programmer of his own computer, and that it had only been a hallucination that made him think the computer was starting to program him.

I was now even more drained; and then Jacques Vallee arrived.

I had wanted to talk to Professor Vallee for several months now and I immediately kidnapped him into a room which the other partygoers were not informed about. On the way, I spotted Hymenaeus Alpha (Grady McMurtry), Caliph of the Ordo Templi Orientis, and his wife, Phyllis. Tom, still giggling at inappropriate moments but no longer *sure* he was going mad, tagged along.

I had heard Jacques Vallee talk at a conference on Science and Spirit, sponsored by the Theosophical Society, early this year. He had taken a new approach to the UFO mystery and was systematically feeding into a giant computer at Stanford University *all* the reports of extraterrestrial contacts, with the computer programmed to look for various possible repeated patterns. Jacques said that the evidence emerging suggested to him that the UFOs weren't extraterrestrial at all, but that they seemed to be intelligent systems intent on convincing us they were extraterrestrial.

Now I started pumping Jacques about his evidence that they weren't extraterrestrial. He started to explain that, analyzing the reports chronologically, it appeared that They (whoever or whatever they are) *always* strive to give the impression that they are something the society they are visiting can understand. In medieval sightings, he said, they called themselves angels; in the great 1902 flap in several states, one of the craft spoke to a West Virginia farmer and said they were an airship invented and flown from Kansas; in 1940s-50s sightings, they often said they were from Venus; since Venus has been examined and seems incapable of supporting life, they now say they are from another star system in this galaxy.

"Where do you think They come from?" I asked.

Professor Vallee gave a Gallic form of the classic scientific Not-Speculating-Beyond-The-Data head-shake. "I can theorize, and theorize, endlessly," he said, "but is it not better to just study the data more deeply and look for clues?"

"You must have some personal hunch," I insisted.

He gave in gracefully. "They relate to space-time in ways for which we have, at present, no concepts," he said. "They cannot explain to us because we are not ready to understand."

I asked Grady McMurtry if Aleister Crowley had ever said anything to him implying the extraterrestrial theory which Xennetu Grant, Outer Head of the *other* Ordo Templi

Orientis, implies in his accounts of Crowley's contacts with Higher Intelligence.

"Some of the things Aleister said to me," Grady replied carefully, "could be interpreted as hints pointing that way." He went on to quote Crowley's aphorisms about various of the standard entities contacted by magick. The Abramelin spirits, for instance, need to be watched carefully. "They bite," Aleister explained in his best deadpan am-I-kidding-or-not? Style. The Enochian "angels," on the other hand, don't always have to be summoned. "When you're ready, they come for you," Aleister said flatly. (The Enochian beings were first contacted by Dr. John Dee, whose methods were copied by Dr. Leary in receiving the Starseed signals.)

The outstanding quality of UFO contactees, Jacques Vallee said at this point, was *incoherence*. "I now have grave reservations about all physical details they supply," he said. "They are like people after an auto accident. All they know is that something very serious has happened to them." Only the fact that so many cases involve *other witnesses*, who *see something in the sky* before the "contactee" has his/ her strange experience, justifies the assumption that what happens is more than "subjective."

"Largely" Professor Vallee summarized, "they come out of it with a new perspective on humanity. A religious perspective, in general terms. But all the details are contradictory and confusing." He regarded green men, purple giant-men, physical craft with windows in them, etc. as falling into the category psychologists call "substitute memory," always provided by the ingenious brain when the actual experience is too shocking to be classified.

I remembered Crowley's remarks in Book One of *Magick*:

Of the great teachers we have mentioned, Christ is silent (about the source of his illumination); the other four tell us something; some more, some less.

Buddha goes into details too elaborate to enter upon in this place; but the gist of it is that in one way or another he got hold of the secret force of the world and mastered it.

Of St. Paul's experiences, we have nothing but a casual allusion to his having been "caught up into Heaven, and seen and heard things of which it was not lawful to speak."

Mohammed speaks crudely of his having been "visited by the Angel Gabriel," who communicated things from "God."

Moses says he "beheld God."

Diverse as these statements are at first sight, all agree in announcing an experience of the class which fifty years ago would have been called supernatural, today may be called spiritual, and fifty years hence*· will have a proper name based on an understanding of the phenomenon which occurred.

~•~

* Crowley was writing in 1911.

~•~

I asked how many in the room had experienced the contact of what appeared to be Higher Intelligence. Grady and Phyllis McMurtry put up their hands, as did two young magicians from the Los Angeles area, and myself. Jacques Vallee, curiously, looked as if he might raise his hand, but then evidently changed his mind and did not. I said I was inclined to believe the Higher Intelligences were extraterrestrial, and asked what the others thought.

Grady McMurtry — Caliph of the Ordo Templi Orientis, remember — said, in effect, that the theory of higher dimensions made more sense to him than the extraterrestrial theory in terms of actual spaceships entering our biosphere.

The two Los Angeles magicians agreed.

Tom, who has been a witch for five years and *hadn't* raised his hand when asked for contactee testimony, said that the Higher Intelligences are embedded in our language and numbers, as the Cabalists think, and have no other kind of existence. He added that every time he tried to explain this he saw that people thought he was going schizophrenic and he began to fear that they may be right, so he preferred *not* to talk about it at all. Tom — who is a computer programmer by profession, a witch only by religion — later added a bit to this, saying that all that exists is information and coding; we only *imagine* we have bodies and live in space-time dimensions.

Professor Vallee listened to all this with a bland smile, and did not seem to regard any of us as mad.

(A few days later, in discussion with the former Vacaville prison psychologist, Dr. Wesley Hiler, I asked him what he *really* thought of Dr. Leary's extraterrestrial contacts. Specifically, since he didn't regard Leary as crazy or hallucinating, what was happening when Leary thought he was receiving extraterrestrial Sixth Circuit neurophysical communications? "Every man and woman who reaches the higher levels of spiritual and intellectual development," Dr. Hiler said calmly, "feels the presence of a Higher Intelligence. Our theories are all unproven. Socrates called it his *daemon*. Others call it gods or angels. Leary calls it extraterrestrial. Maybe it's just another part of our brain, a part that we usually don't use. Who knows?")

Since everybody in the room at this point had either had the required experience, or was willing to speculate about it and study it objectively rather than merely

banishing it with the label "hallucination," I went into my
rap about the parallels between Leary and Wilhelm Reich.
"The attempt to destroy both Dr. Reich and Dr. Leary
reached its most intense peak right after they reported their
extraterrestrial contacts," I said. "I keep having very weird
theories about what that means . . ."

Grady McMurtry nodded vigorously. "That's the
$64,000 question," he said emphatically. "For years I've
been asking Phyllis and everybody else I know: *Why does
the gnosis always get busted?* Every single time the energy
is raised and large-scale group illuminations are occurring,
the local branch of the Inquisition kills it dead. Why, why,
why?"

Nobody had any very conclusive ideas.

"I'll tell you what I think," Grady said. "There's *war
in heaven.* The Higher Intelligences, whoever they are,
aren't all playing on the same team. Some of them are
trying to encourage our evolution to higher levels, *and
some of them want to keep us stuck just where we are.*"
He went on to divide the Magi of history into two groups.
(Magus is a technical term in western magick theory.
A Magus is one who has attained a very high level of
fidelity in communication with the Higher Intelligences
and acts for them on the human level. Lao-Tse, Buddha,
Krishna, Moses, Dionysus, Thoth, Jesus, Mohammed
and "Christian Rosenkreus," the pseudonymous founder
of Rosicrucianism—who may been Giordano Bruno,
according to some theorists—were all human beings, not
gods; they attained Magushood by "spiritual training,"
which Leary would call neurological re-imprinting. Some
would add to the list of Magi such persons as Adam
Weishaupt, founder of the Bavarian Illuminati, Helena
Blavatsky, Jalludin Rumi the Sufi poet and mystic, Aleister

Crowley and Dr. Israel Regardie, who is alive in Los Angeles and good-humoredly denies that he is anywhere near that exalted status.)

According to Grady, some of the Magi are working with those occult intelligences who want to accelerate human evolution, but some of the others were working with the intelligences who wish to keep us near an animal level of awareness.

This is a standard idea in occult circles and it can safely be stated, without exaggeration, that every "school" or "lodge" of adepts that exists is regarded, by some of the others, as belonging to the Black Brotherhood of the evil path. Grady's own Ordo Templi Orientis, indeed, has been accused of this more often than most other occult lodges. I have personally maintained my good cheer and staved off paranoia, while moving among various occult groups as student or participant, by *always adhering rigidly* to the standard Anglo-Saxon legal maxim that every accused person must be regarded as *innocent* until *proven guilty beyond a reasonable doubt.* This obviously spares me a lot of worry, but the more guarded approach is very well argued in Isaac Bonewits's favorite aphorism, "Paranoid magicians outlive the others."

Somehow the conversation drifted away from Grady's concept of "war in heaven." Several times, Grady tried to steer us back there, but each time we wandered on to a different subject. Tom said later that he felt a Presence in the room deliberately pushing us away from that topic . . .

Dr. H.—the psychiatrist whose bad acid-trip had

started the Crowleymas party off so jumpily for me —
dropped by the next day, to thank me for "talking him
down" from his anxiety attack.

He also, it soon appeared, wanted to tell me about his
accelerating experiences with magick. It had started over
two years earlier, after an intensive seminar at Esalen. Dr.
H. suddenly found that he could see "auras." (The aura of
the human body, known to shamans and witches since time
immemorial, has been repeatedly rediscovered by scientists,
most of whom were thereupon denounced as "cranks."
Franz Anton Mesmer called it "animal magnetism" in the
18th century. In the 19th, Baron Reichenbach called it
"OD." In the 1920s, Gurwitsch named it "the mitogenetic
ray." Wilhelm Reich rediscovered it in the 1930s, called it
"orgone energy," and was destroyed by AMA bigots who
charged that he was hallucinating it. Kyrlian photography
has now demonstrated beyond all doubt that this aura
exists.) Dr. H. soon found, further, that he could use
the aura as a diagnostic tool in analyzing new patients.
This experience, Leary's books, and a lecture by me on
Crowley's magick, led him to further experiments.

On a beach in Sonoma County, after taking LSD the
day before and programming an opening of the self to
higher beings or energies, Dr. H. (no longer under the direct
influence of the drug) had an experience with something
from the sky. "It wasn't exactly a Higher Intelligence," he
said carefully, "or, at least, I didn't receive that aspect of
it, if it was Higher Intelligence. To me, it was just *energy*.
Terrible energy. My chest was sore for hours afterward.
I thought it would kill me, but I was absolutely ecstatic
and ego-less at the peak of it. If the chest-pain weren't so
intense, it would have been a totally positive experience."

(MacGregor Mathers, Outer Head of the Hermetic

Order of the Golden Dawn, and the first occult teacher of such worthies as Aleister Crowley, poet William Butler Yeats and novelist Arthur Machen, once recorded a meeting with the Secret Chiefs. These ambiguous entities, known in several schools of occult training, are variously believed to be discarnate spirits of the great Magi of the past, living Magi who can teleport themselves about as easily as you or I telephone a friend, "angels" in the traditional sense, or merely "beings we cannot understand." In any case, Mathers noted that the meeting, although pleasant, left him feeling as if he'd been "struck by lightning" and he also suffered extreme difficulty in breathing. Dr. Israel Regardie has also noted that Alan Bennett, who was Crowley's chief teacher for many years, developed asthma; Crowley then developed asthma as his contacts with the Secret Chiefs occurred more often; and Regardie himself suffered asthma for several years after studying with Crowley, a condition which was only cured when he went through the bio-energetic therapy of Wilhelm Reich, which removes chronic muscular tensions *caused by unconscious fear* according to Reich's own theory.)

Dr. H. went on to describe a second experience of the Energy and Light explosion, about a year after the first. This also was both ecstatic and strangely frightening, and since then he has *felt* "healing power" in his hands and has experimentally tried a sort of Reichian-Rolfian massage on some of his patients, with favorable results.

It occurred to me that, if less prepared for such experiences and less committed to scientific method *as a habit of mind*, Dr. H. might well have remembered each of these experiences as an encounter with an angel or a UFO . . .

The Longest Week of My Life finally ended, inconclusively.

Joanna had not called back. Allen Ginsberg decided to wait four days more and then, if she still hadn't called, he would ask three attorneys (already appraised of the situation) to start an action to force the authorities to let Dr. Leary meet with non-government people to determine his health and legal status.

Four more days dragged by like very old men hauling a most mysterious sealed carriage behind them.

Arlen finally called me and announced that a decision had been reached. The attorneys were going to begin a campaign to reach Dr. Leary; if government blockage seemed to verge on the unconstitutional, they and Allen would call a press conference and announce to the world that the Justice Department still seemed embroiled in Watergate-style injustice . . .

My impatience was rising. Just for the hell of it, and to discharge some of my energies, I phoned the Melvin Belli office, the last attorneys known to have represented Dr. Leary. We had a merry time of it, as they switched me from office to office, and the upshot was the same as other journalists had found; the Belli people would not commit themselves on *anything*, and even refused to say directly whether or not they still represented Dr. Leary.

Like every other ideology, Learyism now has a

"revisionist" faction. These flipped-out or wised-up souls (as one chooses to regard them) claim that Terra II is a *metaphor*, or perhaps a parable, or even a practical joke — possibly the first really *practical* "practical joke" in history. The notion is that, in five or ten years, no matter what ideological or political hassles Leary passes through in the meanwhile, he will have several million souls turned on to star-flight. These people will then be true "drop outs," in the ultimate sense. Their ambitions will be literally not of this world. In short, transcendence will have been secularized. The world's first truly scientific *mythos* will have been created; a faith to inspire, to uplift, to give meaning to life, and yet a faith that is not only compatible with science but most likely to find adherents precisely among the youngest, boldest and most creative minds in the scientific community. It will build enthusiasm as it grows, and it will step-by-step achieve each of the wonders forecast in *Terra II*. It will become the strongest force in the world by 2000 AD.

Then, say the Revisionists, Leary will admit it was all a parable and a lesson. The real trip, he will say, is internal; the real Higher Intelligences are our own untapped neural circuits; the real Terra II is earth itself transformed by re-imprinting our nervous systems to higher-circuit functioning. The whole point of science as the New Mysticism is simply this (Leary will declaim, according to this theory of his motivations): we *can* stop our second-circuit territorial-emotional gland-robot behavior; we *can* set our sights on a goal worthy of humankind — the search for objective truth.

Word of this heresy must have leaked through the grapevine to Vacaville, because the last time I saw Timothy he said to me abruptly: "Just keep telling them out there that Terra II isn't a metaphor!"

And yet . . . Norman O. Brown is basically right in saying all language is metaphor, all thinking symbolic. Terra II exists as both a specific proposal for a specific research-exploration project and as an implicit challenge to all religious and political orthodoxies, asking: Do you have anything to offer more exciting, more hopeful, more thrilling than a literal search for immortality and a literal attempt to communicate with Godly Entities?

It seems to me that it has been possible, until Terra II, that I might eventually grow bored with my current heresies and join some archaic orthodoxy in old age, just to be sociable and gregarious again. This is now impossible. I can never become a Catholic or a Democrat or a Marxist or a Confucian, now. Terra II can last a lifetime, and I'm sure it will. If I have just defined myself as a fanatic, well, at least we are non-hostile and non-messianic fanatics. We literally want nothing at all from earth and earthpeople. Our faith is that we can acquire the money and the technology and the co-workers to make it happen, to escape from this madhouse planet for good and all. If we fail, we will have successors who will escape. The neophile WoMan cannot be imprisoned forever by the neophobic Great Apes who currently govern this lost mote in the backyard of the galaxy.

Two days after Allen Ginsberg phoned to tell me that a group of lawyers were beginning an attempt to communicate with Dr. Leary, I received another call from Lee Meyers of P.R.O.B.E. Lee had organized his own manhunt for the elusive Leary, and P.R.O.B.E. attorneys would also be making efforts to communicate with Tim.

I was exultant; Like General Westmoreland, I once again saw "light at the end of the tunnel."

October 22 — Timothy's 54th birthday — a new bolt fell from the Jovian humorist who has authored this script. On page 5 of the San Francisco *Chronicle*, I read:

STRANGE DOINGS IN MARIN
LEARY TAPES HAVE DISAPPEARED

– By Jim Brewer

Several tape recordings believed to reveal details of the longstanding "cooperation" between Timothy Leary and federal agents have mysteriously disappeared, The *Chronicle* learned yesterday.

Lawyers who subpoenaed the tape Friday in Marin county said the recordings are "vital" to the defense of Orange County attorney George Chula, who is awaiting trial on drug charges.

Chula had represented Leary on his original arrest for possession of marijuana, before the former Harvard professor fled a California prison and the country in 1971.

Chula also was Leary's lawyer when Leary was brought back to this country from Afghanistan in January, 1973, by agents of the Drug Enforcement Administration.

Subsequently, Leary and English "wife," Joanna Harcourt-Smith Leary, turned against Chula, with Mrs. Leary telling an Orange County grand jury that Chula furnished her with cocaine and hashish.

The tapes, believed to be ten cassettes, reportedly include many conversations between Joanna Leary and federal agents.

Another tape reportedly has a message last spring from Leary to publisher Randolph Hearst offering Leary's help in negotiating the release of Patricia

Hearst from the Symbionese Liberation Army.

The tapes were part of a suitcase full of recorded and written documents stolen June 4 from the Mill Valley home Joanna Leary was then sharing with a drug informer, Dennis Martino, Marin lawmen said.

Robin Viertel, 21, was arrested two days later and pleaded guilty to the burglary yesterday. Charles DeWald, 36, pleaded guilty to attempted extortion after Joanna Leary said he had tried to sell the stolen suitcase back to her for $20,000 in order to keep its contents confidential.

Both of them, members of the Leary Defense Committee, are to be sentenced November 21.

The day of the two guilty pleas, Chula's lawyers served a subpoena on Marin county authorities seeking the return of all the tapes and other materials in the suitcase.

The tapes were discovered missing after authorities compared an inventory of the stolen items with the evidence collected at the time of the arrest.

The cassettes were last known to be in the possession of Attorney Dennis Natali who represented DeWald, Marin lawmen said.

A former San Francisco police inspector who is now a private investigator working on Chula's defense said the missing tapes could show that Joanna Leary had herself been "linking to the Feds" a year or more.

The tapes are also believed to reveal details of a complex $60,000 drug swindle referred to in a court transcript as the ''Frank caper."

Miss Viertel claimed that Joanna Leary and Martino had conned an LSD manufacturer known as Frank into paying $60,000 for a valise which supposedly contained chemicals for making LSD as well as a list of names of contacts. Instead, it contained some worthless papers.

The money was supposed to go eventually to Chula as payment for his legal help for Leary. Chula said he never got the money, and instead got "finked on."

For a minute, I thought I would vomit.

It was so much worse than my most fearful fantasies; it was exactly the paranoia-making Spy Novel Sci-Fi world of William S. Burroughs. "Everybody's an agent. Some of them don't even know who they're an agent for," Burroughs would say in his W.C. Fields style.

I remembered Dr. Hiler's calm verdict: "Joanna would cut anybody's throat to get Timothy out of jail."

How many throats was Timothy willing to cut?

His denunciations of "larval reflexes," "larval morals," "larval politics" ran through my head in a masochist madrigal. He would find it all so easily rationalized: how long has he paid the dues for every researcher, every philosopher, every artist, every freaked-out kid, every clergyman who has taken the LSD journey and committed heresy by saying aloud that the experience was enlightening and ecstatic? How long has he taken the rap for Aldous Huxley and Alan Watts and Ken Kesey and Ginsberg and Dr. Osmond and Dr. Metzner and Dr. Lilly and Dr. Unger and Dr. McGlothlin and all the others who "propagandized for drugs" by reporting beneficial acid-programming sessions? Martyrdom is regressive, pietistic, an evolutionary cop-out. The real victory is to stay free, stay alive, outsmart the reactionaries, and live long enough to see your work justified and accepted into the mainstream of science. "I've paid heavy dues. Let me continue my work now. The dues will be lighter for the others, anyway; the hysteria *is* coming to an end, the penalties *are* being lowered . . ."

Do we condemn the torturers or their victim?

How many people will Tim and Joanna send to jail before they're through with this script? Is Chula the first and only victim—Chula into the cage, Leary out; fair trade all around—or will the Feds demand more, and more, and more? Fifty lawyers for one Tim Leary? Seven Weathermen, a few more researchers, a philosopher and a poet or two thrown in? How far will Timothy cooperate? What will happen if he stops cooperating?

I have said that the Inquisition never died, just liberalized itself a little, as Capitalism also has. (Slavery could have been preserved, too, if the Southern planters had liberalized it a little. Don't look too close, but . . . *why* is Dagwood Bumstead always late for work?) As I wonder how many guilty parties Tim will name, I cannot detach myself from the feeling we went all through this number 400 years ago, but we called them *witches* then . . .

"Guilty parties" I said; guilty of curiosity, and aspiration, and science, and philosophy, certainly, and, possibly, of irresponsibility, of profiteering on the magick chemicals, of human cupidity. Perhaps some of them deserve "punishment" (the cage . . .) more than Timothy; perhaps he has paid the dues for all of them too damned long now. And, perhaps, in his new role, Timothy will play to the hilt and many an innocent will be thrown in along with the guilty . . . *Burn, witch, burn*, the Jefferson Starship sings, *the good folk come to burn thee, Their keen enjoyment hid behind, A Gothic mask of duty* . . .

Chapter Fourteen

The Cosmic Script

Prisoners of the earth, come out. There is no thing
to fear in space.
— William S. Burroughs, *Nova Express*

Lee Meyers of P.R.O.B.E. — the suit to end
California's prisons—called me one day and said their
attorneys had finally learned Dr. Leary's whereabouts. I
was given an address c/o Agent Tom Strange, Department
of Justice, Los Angeles.

I wrote to tell Timothy that many friends were worried
about him and would like a note *in his own handwriting*
that he was voluntarily cooperating with the federal
authorities. (I still remembered Joanna's words to Allen
Ginsberg, "Worse than *The Gulag Archipelago* . . .") I
said again that *The Periodic Table of Energy*, in first draft,
seemed to me the greatest of his books. I ended with "The
whole family sends their love."

Lee Meyers had suggested putting this in a separate
envelope and asking Agent Strange to forward it. Instead,
I put it in the same envelope with my letter to Mr. Strange

and told him that I didn't believe in secrets and wouldn't practice secrecy. (I also told him that he was dealing with the world's greatest scientist and would be judged by history. I'm sure that gave him a sardonic laugh.)

In the following weeks, as October turned into November and Timothy's disappearance entered its fifth month, I began to wonder if I had a permanent case of *déjà vu.* Everything seemed to be part of a very old script, and it didn't surprise when Allen Ginsberg's lawyers ran into the same roadblocks as P.R.O.B.E.'s lawyers. It didn't surprise me that other journalists kept calling me to ask questions about Tim and bitch about the impossibility of learning anything from government officials. The A.C.L.U. slept on (the signals indicating that a gross violation of the constitution is happening are on higher circuits than that gross beast can perceive . . .)

I was writing this book, and another on immortality research, and entering the sixth month of my second bout on Welfare, wondering when my writing would bring in some bread again, and Dr. H. (the psychiatrist mentioned earlier) was collaborating in some experiments on practical magick; so I naturally decided I didn't have enough to keep me busy and started an essay for *Gnostica News* based on my experimental magick seminar at the Gnostic Convention in September.

I include this here as a summary of my conclusions about the occult tradition in the light of Dr. Leary's recent work. It explains the 24 neurogenetic slots and the general theory of cosmic evolution which may be Dr. Leary's greatest single contribution to thought.

SUMMARY

I - BIO-SURVIVAL: the first period of evolution of any planet.

Slot 0: Bio-survival passivity; amoeboid consciousness. The DNA begins to replicate itself . . .

Slot 1: Bio-survival intelligence; the first "brain." An imprint is taken and a program of survival mechanisms are formed: *go forward* to A, *pull back* from B, etc.

Slot 2: Bio-survival fusion. The bonding of the DNA to the host-planet.

This stage of evolution is repeated, on a higher level, in the crawling stage of each human infant. The bond to "Mother Earth," for instance, is repeated in the bond to the infant's personal mother, or mother-substitute. Lacking this bond, first circuit schizophrenia occurs.

II - EMOTION-POWER: the second period of evolution on any planet.

Slot 3: Emotional passivity; emotional "consumerism" Learning to send-receive emotional (i.e., territorial, hierarchical) signals and find a place in the herd, the flock, the tribe, etc.

Slot 4: Emotional intelligence. Finding the emotional imprint that produces "success," i.e. status or domination, overt or covert.

Slot 5: Emotional fusion. The bonding to the emotional-power structure of the flock, herd, tribe, etc. Freud's "Super-Ego;" internalizing the rules of the social game.

This stage of evolution appeared in territorial and pecking rituals 500,000,000 years ago, and is repeated in the toddling stage of each human infant.

III - DEXTERITY-SYMBOLISM: the third period of evolution.

Slot 6: The student mind; the knowledge "consumer."

Slot 7: Rational intelligence; programmed learning.

Slot 8: Fusion with the historical mind.

This circuit appears when the beaver learns to build beaver-dams, the lion learns how to hunt, etc. Repeated in the prolonged and virtually un-ending learning period of any human. Unless the fusion of Slot 8 is made, the individual talent does not mesh with tradition and is eccentric, "premature," bizarre.

IV - SEXUALITY-DOMESTICITY: the fourth period of evolution.

Slot 9: sexual passivity; adolescent masturbation.

Slot 10: sexual intelligence; mating; parenthood. The individual organism performs its major evolutionary task of reproduction.

Slot 11: domestic fusion; identification with the family, the tribe, the planet, the cosmos. (This fusion can stop at any point, or extend into the higher circuits.)

V - NEUROSOMATIC CONSCIOUSNESS: the fifth period of evolution. This and higher circuits have not evolved fully yet and can only be impartially imprinted. Just as the child repeats the *earlier four stages* of evolution in normal growth, the post-larval human anticipates *the future four stages* — but only *anticipates* them. The nervous system is not evolved enough to imprint them fully.

Slot 12: neurosomatic passivity. The turn-on. Ecstatic sensory-somatic awareness; *un*conditioned perception outside the imprinted-conditioned reward-punishment roboticisms of the first four periods.

Slot 13: neurosomatic intelligence. The understanding of the new signals received when this circuit opens; the integration of new patterns. Most "mystics" have just made the first faltering steps toward such integration-understanding and are basically trapped in blissful incoherence in Slot 12.

Slot 14: neurosomatic fusion. The Tantric linkage: sexual fusion between two Slot 13 types, leading to the first two-body consciousness and opening the nervous system (s) of both to the higher circuits.

Few humans have gotten beyond Slot 12, or slot 14, thus far; but there must be several hundred thousand races in the galaxy functioning at higher stages . . .

VI - NEUROPHYSICAL POWER. The sixth period of cosmic evolution.

Slot 15: neurophysical passivity. Turning on to the biological "telepathic" signals of the Higher Intelligences and the Cosmic Mind (electromagnetic-gravitational "love" energy on the interstellar level.)

Slot 16: neurophysical intelligence: integrating and understanding the signals received at the neurophysical level. Tuning in without static or noise. Getting the Big Picture.

Slot 17: neurophysical fusion; bonding with the community of higher intelligences. "Becoming a Buddha," "going to live with the fairies," "having God/Goddess in one's heart." Being part of the conscious interstellar network of turned-on Seers throughout this galaxy.

VII - NEUROGENETIC SPACE-TIME TRANCENDENCE.

Slot 18: neurogenetic passivity. Turning on the DNA intelligence; opening the genetic archives; entering

Jung's collective unconscious while awake and coherent. Deciphering the DNA code from within by introspection.

Slot 19: neurogenetic intelligence. Having access to the entire DNA blueprint for the galaxy.

Slot 20: neurogenetic fusion. Bonding with the Cosmic Immortals who seed, tend, guide and protect evolution throughout space-time.

VIII - META-PHYSIOLOGICAL BEING.

Slot 21: Meta-physiological passivity. Escape from the organism into the electro-magnetic-gravitational "galactic mind."

Slot 22: Meta-physiological intelligence. Understanding and integrating the kind of intelligence that exists on this trans-organismic level.

Slot 23: Meta-physiological fusion. Becoming one with the Galactic Mind.

The purposes of the Galactic Mind are far from clear at our present stage of evolution (Slots 11-12,13,14); possibly, the Galactic Mind is seeking integration and fusion to enable It to react on higher levels with the nearby galactic minds of neighboring galaxies, as part of a cosmic evolution toward still-higher intelligence . . .

Magick has been defined as "the science and art of causing change in conformity with Will" (Crowley), "the science and art of causing change *in consciousness* in conformity with Will" (Dion Fortune), "a mnemonic system of psychology to train Will and Imagination (Regardie), the art of "separating fools from their coin" (Ambrose Bierce), etc.

I propose to consider Magick as a name for *"the investigation of, and exploitation of, hitherto-mysterious functions of the human nervous system."* That is, we investigate ourselves to find these functions, we exploit them to deliver advantage either in pure survival-time or in the more arcane art of enjoying however much survival-time we do have, and we define these powers as "hitherto-mysterious" because we regard ourselves as such clever fellows that we might soon come to understand them better (and thereby exploit them more efficiently). More modestly, we recognize that advances in science (subatomic physics, parapsychology, cybernetics *et. al.*) raise the distinct possibility that *somebody* will understand these wild talents in the near future, even if we personally are not that somebody.

Finally, we speak of the human nervous system, rather than "mind" or "soul" or similar traditional terms, because such older terminology is, as semanticists say, over/under defined: that is, over-defined in *connoting* vague and universal ideas of no scientific precision, under-defined in *denoting* nothing specific and measurable.

The nervous system is concrete, tangible, definite and scientifically analyzable. It is also, beyond all doubt, the medium through which we know everything we know, probably including much that we don't even know that we know. All of our knowledge is neurological; all of our evaluations are neuro-semantic; all of our reactions are neuromuscular, neuroglandular or neuro-endocrine. As Korzybski says in *Science and Sanity*, even mathematics (as known to us) is human mathematics, having the structure of the human nervous system.[*] As Dr. Leary adds in *Neurologic*, "The body is the car; the nervous system is the driver."

* Our binary notation is based on the off-on (digital) structure of the neuron; our decimal system is based on our ten fingers; etc. More basically, mathematics is a set of dodges for translating our dynamic (sensory) lower-nervous system process-observations into static (abstract) higher-nervous system formulas (Languages, symbol-systems).

~•~

When we study Magick, then, we are studying, the lesser-known and more occult functions of the human nervous system; but, since it is after all our own nervous system, we need not lose our heads, cry out about the "inexplicable" and the "unfathomable," and abandon all scientific discipline, all common sense, and all logical thought.

Let us be as hard-nosed as possible. We begin with one of the simplest of all magical acts (but one that contains, in kernel, the very essence of high Magick and all its dangers and secrets.) Let the men and women in the audience take alternative seats, and let each man place his right hand on the crown of the head of his female partner, his left hand on her solar plexus, palm inward. Let the man *visualize vividly* a white light floating above his head; let him pull down white light into his body; let him visualize it flow out through his right hand into the female partner, circulate through her body, and flow back to him through his left hand. Let the women visualize the same, and draw the energy into any physical ailment that may be bothering them (headache, cold, or whatever) or into any psychological problem such as depression or anxiety.

Let the woman begin to intone the mantra "OM" when they quite distinctly feel the energy flowing into the problem and relieving it.

Now we simply reverse polarity. Let the women place

their right hand upon the men's heads, left hand upon the men's solar plexus, and visualize the energy flowing back. This time, however, the men will not "OM" until they feel that they have received back *more energy* than they transmitted in the first round.

When this is accomplished, we reverse polarity again, and the women will not "OM" until they definitely feel that they have received more energy than in the first round *and* more than they transmitted in the second round.

This can be repeated several rounds more, as desired or felt necessary.*

~•~

* Uncomfortable heat may be generated if the partners do not direct the energy into some magical purpose.

~•~

Now, this is the mysterious "multiplication of the first matter" in medieval alchemy. The energy used — "the first matter" of the alchemists, "animal magnetism" of Mesmer, "OD" of Baron Reichenbach, "prana" of the Hindus, "mana" of the Polynesians, "wakan" of the Plains Indians, "Orgone" of Wilhelm Reich, "bioplasma" of Dr. Pujarich — is the energy used in all Magick.

If the physical link between male and female partners is genital and loving, more of the energy moves, especially if the explosion of orgasm is renounced or long-postponed. This is the secret of Tantra, the yoga of sex, and ol' Aleister Crowley's much-maligned "sex magick."

The Tantric yogin keeps the energy moving indefinitely, renounces orgasm entirely, and eventually achieves that rare feat, a doubleminded nervous system, in which the male and female are truly unified. This "delicate Hedonic engineering" (as Dr. Leary calls it) allows for the temporary creation of a new androgynous being where two separate beings had existed before. Prolonged, the one being itself vanishes into the Void (i.e. the joint two-person nervous system transcends all its historical imprints and becomes no-form, or omniform, and is capable of imprinting itself for higher-level functioning than has hitherto been possible. This is the key to the 2=1=0 equation of Aleister Crowley.) The Void is nothing else but the temporary suspension of learned space-time-emotion imprints, i.e. imprints usually projected outward on the world and hallucinated as "reality."

Similarly, in sex-magick (as distinguished from sex-yoga), the orgasm is timed to coincide with the climax of the magical ritual; the bio-energy is then cast outward onto the bio-energetic field of earth itself and "Magick" happens. That is, the energy produces results, just as electrical energy produces results, or heat energy, or atomic energy, all of which were equally "Magick" before they were understood.

We can now understand why it is that possibly the earliest and certainly the most widespread of all magical workings is the orgy or fertility ritual. This variety of balling* has been universally popular with shamans of many cultures, not because people are very sexy animals (although we are the sexiest of all animals, according to zoologist Desmond Morris) *but because it works*. It works so well, in fact, that modern parapsychologists, investigating plant ESP, find that plants become emotionally involved when people merely *talk* of sex in the same room with them. (See *Secret Life of Plants*, by Tompkins and Bird.) In one case, plants reacted to sexual intercourse performed by their custodian when he was seventy miles away.

* I am not colloquial but etymological. The modern use of balling to mean copulation has been traced to the *balls* (fertility rituals) of 18th century Scottish Witches. See Legman, *Anatomy of the Dirty Joke*, Grove Press.

~•~

We have now extensionalized somewhat our expression "hitherto-mysterious functions of the human nervous system." It ill becomes us to mock the primitive shaman for saying that the gods fertilize the crops after this sex-ritual is performed (at least, not until we are *quite* sure there are no gods anywhere . . .). It is rather more to the point if we pause a moment to admire the shamans' skill in discovering, without Cleve Backster's polygraph, that plants do respond to human nervous-system radiations. That some shamans discovered this as early as 30,000 BCE (as indicated by sexual rituals in cave paintings) should provoke some lively respect for our ancestors, who in this case and many others used their nervous systems to such advantage that they obtained knowledge and power we are only recently learning to understand and duplicate with our scientific tools.

It seems that we can almost say: the human nervous system is the greatest scientific *instrument* we own. This is implicit, of course, in Aleister Crowley's great mantra, "Every man and every woman is a star." The reason I always begin my seminars with the "first matter" exercise is that it leaves no room for doubt about where the power comes from. It's in each and every human nervous system. We can help each other — and we should, if we can spare the time from feeling self-righteous and sorry for ourselves—but, at the bottom, each of us is an independent star. I never teach anything in my classes; I show you, at most, how you can begin to teach yourself.

The Arch-Druid of the Berkeley grove of the Reformed Druids of North America has a saying, "A perfect Master is ideal if you want to become a perfect Slave." It may be that somebody who's new to Magick will have an experience in one of my classes and discover an entire new reality. I always point out that *I* didn't do it; the *student* did it. I only showed the gimmick. Every man and woman studying Magick should memorize Ezra Pound's famous definition, "A slave is a man waiting for somebody else to free him." Or, as Eugene Debs said to a socialist Congress once, "If you're looking for a Moses to lead you out of the Capitalist wilderness into the Promised Land, don't look at me. I wouldn't do it if I could; because if I could lead you in, somebody else could lead you back out again."

Here's another little gimmick to get the energy moving, borrowed from the Sufis. It's actually a simplification of the Cabalistic Middle Pillar ritual. You visualize the white light above your head again, and then hold your right hand up into the light and intone a prolonged "Baaaaaaa . . . aaaaaa . . . aaa" as you feel the energy flow down your arm. Then quickly join the hands palms-together over your breast, as in prayer, and intone a long "Raaaaaaaaaaaaaaa." Complete by slapping the left thigh with the left hand and shouting "Ka!" Ba-ra-ka: three simple steps.

Whenever I ask how many people *felt* the energy, I get a lot of hands in the air — *if* we've done the "first matter" exercize *first*, but *not otherwise*. The reason is that the "first matter" exercise, by deliberately using the male-female erotic charge, taps the most powerful emotional force on this planet. There is no kind of Magick, I'm convinced, that doesn't use this sexual motor-force, although some of the Christian magicians are pretty sneaky and indirect about it. I very much doubt that Tantrists and Crowleyans, who frankly go directly to the source, are more lascivious than the rest of humanity; they're just more honest and, therefore, more efficient.

Now we're going to get a bit technical and look at our Table of Correspondences. Every school of Magick uses such analogs, because *what we're doing in Magick is moving from left frontal lobe domination to right frontal lobe domination.*[*] The average person does all his/her thinking with the left front lobe, which is a *digital* computer. Magicians and yogis (and LSD trippers) turn on the right frontal lobe, as electro-encephalogram studies have demonstrated, and the right lobe is an *analog* computer. So we are switching from digital, linear, Aristotelian thinking to analogic, synergetic, non-Aristotelian thinking.

~•~

[*] See any neurology text. Philosophical implications of this transformation from digital to analogical functioning are explored in *Morning of the Magicians*, Pauwels and Bergier, and *Neurologic*, Timothy Leary.

~•~

What we're using here as our analog console is based on Dr. Timothy Leary, G.I. Gurjieff , Crowley, Cabala, Gnosticism, Sufism, poet Brian Barritt and my own small intelligence. By far the most important contributions come from the much-maligned and persecuted Dr. Leary, and I want to emphasize that because I've found from experience that a majority of the people who are fervently convinced that Dr. Leary belongs in a cage for his ideas haven't the foggiest notion what those ideas really are. Most of what follows comes from Dr. Leary; this is what he's in a cage for; this is what makes him a menace to the good, decent, sober folk who elected Richard Nixon *twice*.

Left Lobe (Tonal)

	Circuit I	Circuit II	Circuit III	Circuit IV
Musical	Do	Re	Mi	Fa
Colors	Red	Orange	Yellow	Green
Elements	Alkalis	Alkalines	Borons	Carbons
Chakras	genital	base of spine	solar plexus	chest
Life-Cycle	infant	toddler	student	parent
Evolution	amoeba	reptile	mammal	social human
Neural Network	bio-survival	territorial	dexterity	bonding
Vector in Space	forward-back	up-down	open-close	fusion
Vector in Time	--	--	--	--
Drugs to stimulate circuit	speed, cocaine, caffeine	alcohol	RNA	?
School of Psychology specializig in this circuit	Pavlov, stimulus-response	ethology	learning theory	Freud
Religion & Metaphor	--	Fundamentalism (Father-God)	Cabala (Numerology)	Sacrament of Marriage
Arts	massage, dance	opera, drama, novels	puzzles, detective stories, sci-fi	dance, poetry, love-stories
Yoga	asana	pranayama	dharana	niyama
Gurdjieff Vibration	384 (minerals)	192 (plants)	96 (invertebrates)	48 (vertebrates)

Right Lobe (Nagual)

	Circuit V	Circuit VI	Circuit VII	Circuit VIII
Musical	Sol	La	Ti	High Do
Colors	Blue	Indigo	Violet	White
Elements	Nitrogens	Oxygens	Halogens	Noble Gases
Chakras	throat	forehead	crown	above head
Life-Cycle	dropout	sage	seer	Superman
Evolution	astronaut	cyborg	galactic beings ("angels")	galactic mind
Neural Network	neurosomatic	neurophysical	neurogenetic	meta-physiological
Vector in Space	--	--	--	--
Vector in Time	sensory time	neural time	genetic time	eternity
Drugs to stimulate circuit	hashish	peyote/LSD	LSD	G-Pill
School of Psychology specializig in this circuit	Gestalt, Leary	Leary	Leary, Jung	Leary
Religion & Metaphor	Sufism (Next Step)	Magick (Great Work)	Hinduism (Kalpas)	Buddhism (White Light)
Arts	Tantra	Allegory	Epic	Light Show
Yoga	dhyana	siddhis	Atman	Brahma
Gurdjieff Vibration	24 (Humans)	12 ("Angels")	6 (Archangels)	3 (Eternal Unchanging)

We assume eight circuits, or imprint-matrices, in the human nervous system. The first four, which comprise the *tonal* of Don Juan Matus, or the world of "normal" perception, are mediated through the digital left lobe. The second four, which comprise Don Juan's *nagual* (na-wahl), are mediated through the analogical right lobe.

The nervous system is the greatest scientific instrument we have, and its Designer must be reckoned the Highest Intelligence on this planet. Her initials are DNA; Her full name is deoxyribonucleic acid. She's been around here for about 3.5 billion years and evidently emigrated from somewhere else in the galaxy. At least, that's the opinion of Sir Frances Crick, one of the three scientists (with John Watson and Rosalind Franklin) who discovered Her helical shape and Her method of templating, (reproducing.) She came from Outer Space, Crick says, and She has been quite busy populating this planet for 3.5 billion years. We are one of Her most elaborate creations; neurologically, we seem to be Her local masterpiece, although maybe the dolphins and whales are even more neurologically complex.[*]

~•~

[*] Basic anatomical data about Our Lady DNA can be found in *The Genetic Code*, Isaac Asimov, Doubleday.

~•~

She works in octaves, it appears; and in quartets within the octaves. Thus, the first four circuits are concerned with survival (and reproduction), the second four with transcendence.

Circuit One, The Bio-Survival Circuit, which may be stimulated by visualizing a red chakra behind the genital and intoning low do on the musical octave, has the Gurdjieff vibration 384. This mediates immediate survival by digital computation, Aristotelian either/orism at its crudest and most urgent. Everything is quickly, efficiently, urgently categorized as SAFE or DANGEROUS — motherly-cuddly-nutritive or hostile-abrasive-noxious — and the computer programs a FORWARD (to the SAFE) or a BACKWARD (from the dangerous.)

If you want to use the higher circuits, then, a first step is to turn off this first circuit and push the energy upwards. The yogin does this by *asana*, immobile posture. The magician does it by building his ritual to a climax of total stillness. The frustrated energy, refused its usual forward-or-backward outlet, can only go elsewhere in the nervous system.

Circuit Two, The Emotional Power Circuit, which may be stimulated by visualizing an orange chakra at the base of the spine and intoning *re*, is Gurdjieff vibration 192, and mediates another Aristotelian dichotomy — UP or DOWN on the emotional power scale. The signals of swelling up, bluster, roaring (for domination) or cringing, shrinking, muttering (for submission) are remarkably similar throughout the animal kingdom.[*]

~•~

[*] The up-down emotional games are analyzed in greater detail in *Interpersonal Diagnosis of Personality*, Timothy Leary, Ronald Press. Pre-human analogs can be studied in *On Aggression*, Konrad Lorenz, *The Human Zoo*, Desmond Morris, *Territorial Imperative*, Robert Ardrey. The DNA metaprogram contains 3.5 billion years of such ritualized pecking order pantomimes.

~•~

To turn off this circuit and send energy to higher circuits, the yogin practices *pranayama* (literally energy-control) via breath-control. As Crowley noted, it is physically impossible to remain in an emotional state if you will stop and do 20–30 minutes of pranayama. The robot glands just don't do their mechanistic trips when you're in pranayama. Magicians and Sufis get the same effect by rhythmic movement or dance, when exquisitely orchestrated.*

~•~

* Most people never get off the Second Circuit emotional-glandular robot-trips at all, and will not understand the descriptions of higher circuits, except vaguely.

~•~

Circuit Three, The Dexterity-Symbolism Circuit, stimulated by visualizing a yellow chakra in the solar plexus and intoning *mi*, is Gurdjieff's 96 vibration and mediates OPEN and CLOSE — "open the fist to receive, close to grasp being the dawn of manual intelligence; open-and-close the larynx rhythmically being the mechanism of speech; open-and-close also being the digital computer device of frontal lobe thinking." Circuit Three is very recent in evolution and allows subtleties (engineering, philosophy, science) not covered by the cruder circuits I and II.

To turn off Circuit III, the yogin stops the mechanism of digital computation cold, by *dharana* (concentration on one image) or *mantra* (one sound.) Again, the energy must go somewhere and tends to flow into the higher, newer circuits.

Circuit IV, Sex-Domesticity, visualized as a green chakra in the chest and intoned as *fa*, is Gurdjieff vibration 48 and mediates survival beyond the ego, through sex: that is, strutting, display, flirtation, mating, orgasm, care of the egg, nurture of the young.

To turn off this circuit, the yogin practices *yama* and *niyama*, the drop-out mystique, and abandons sexuality, sociality and attachment to the world. The magician and the Tantrist use the "first matter" exercise to transmute the energy directly into the higher circuits.

It must be emphasized that *only* the yogin and shaman deliberately turn off these primitive circuits. The imprints on these circuits are, to use a chemical analogy, thermosetting; and most people never change after these programs are set: Circuit I at crawling, Circuit II at walking, Circuit III at grasping and asking, Circuit IV at puberty. These robotic imprints generally remain the same age 30 or 50 or 70 or 90; which is why Sufis and yogin (as well as Behaviorists) regard ordinary humanity as very busy, very mechanical, very limited animals who have not learned to tap their own potentials. In Dr. Leary's terminology, all Circuit I to Circuit IV behavior is conditioned by reward-punishment; only Circuit V to Circuit VIII behavior is unconditioned.

It must also be emphasized that, "reality" being a joint phenomenon of observer-observed, the human nervous system *creates* a new universe at each stage of its development. The toddler, beginning to mess in family politics (emotional games), *sees* and integrates Circuit II signals (emotional game cues) invisible to the Circuit I neonate. Again, the talking-questioning-handling older child, imprinting the tribal lore and techniques, integrates abstract Circuit III signals that are invisible or non-existent to the emotionally gland-activated Circuit II infant. (These abstract-logical signals again become invisible to us, in later life, whenever we reactivate the Second Circuit fear-rage secretions.) At puberty again, the nervous system mutates and numerous Circuit IV signals (invitations to sperm-egg fusion), previously screened out, become glaringly, urgently visible.

On the Fifth Circuit again, new signals are perceived, a new universe-Gestalt is integrated.

Circuit Five, The Neurosomatic Circuit, stimulated by visualizing a blue chakra in the throat and intoning *sol*, is Gurdjieff's 24 vibration and mediates neurosomatic rapture. The digital reward-punishment (safe-unsafe "good-evil") dichotomies of the left lobe are "drowned" in an oceanic experience of multi-ordinal analog signals received by the abruptly-activated right lobe. This ecstatic, sometimes hilarious "turn-on" or "illumination" is the first unconditioned moment since infancy and is often called "rebirth"; the nervous system is again wide open and any stimulus will form a whole new imprint.

Circuit Six, The Neurophysical Circuit, stimulated by visualizing an indigo chakra in the center of the forehead and intoning *la*, is Gurdjieff's 12 vibration and unleashes neurophysical power (Magick.) That is, the nervous system now communicates (transmits-receives) directly to-from physical fields; atomic, electronic, magnetic, orgonomic, gravitational, etc. energies are directly activated. The "first matter" in neurophysical energy.

In another sense, if Circuit Five is *turning on* (receiving new signals invisible on the left lobe I-IV circuits), Circuit Six is *tuning in* (developing high fidelity reception-transmission of the trans-ego signals).

Circuit Five is bliss, rapture, ecstasy. Shamans and yogis on this circuit, like potheads, are (in psychiatric jargon) amotivational. There is nothing to do, nothing worth doing, the Buddha-land of Nirvana or Big Rock Candy Mountain is *right where you are sitting now*. Circuit Six transcends this drop-out neurology and re-imprints the nervous system for "High Magick," "the Great Work," etc.; that is, for fusion with the Higher Intelligences.

We need not define the Higher Intelligences at this point in our explorations. These "angelic" or "godly" beings, Secret Chiefs, can be conceived as time travelers from the future, as advanced Adepts in Tibet or the Near East, as extraterrestrials, as the trans-ego DNA code within each cell of our own brains, or just as the (temporarily) Unknown. Each experimental Magician will form a personal opinion about this, based on direct experience with these "allies" (as Don Juan calls them). My own theory is extra-planetary and interstellar, but you need not buy that theory. Do the experiments and find your own explanation.

Circuit Seven, The Neurogenetic Circuit, stimulated by visualizing a violet chakra at the crown of the skull and intoning *ti*, is Gurdjieff vibration 6 and mediates the inter-neuron "conversation" of DNA and RNA, the templating of individuality out of the collective 3.5 billion-year-old gene pool. Crowley's "Knowledge and Conversation of the Holy Guardian Angel." It is from here that Jung derives the evidence for his "collective unconscious," from here the Oriental tradition derives its "reincarnation" and "transmigration" metaphors, here Isaac Bonewits's "astral switchboard" is found and activated. Paradoxically, of all the Higher Intelligences in Magick, this one is most definitely "me" and also most definitely "more than me." Here you learn concretely, beyond theory, that most of our ancestors were not mammals but looked like Gila Monsters or alligators. Here you obtain the *futique* visions the Superwoman, the androgynous god of the future. The DNA blueprint for this planet (and beyond) is made visible.

Circuit Eight, stimulated by visualizing the white light a foot *above* the head and intoning high *do*, is Gurdjieff's vibration 3 and mediates out-of-body consciousness. It is conjectured that the ultimate evolutionary function of this circuit is to allow the Higher Intelligences of the galaxy to merge eventually with meta-physiological (*not* metaphysical) electromagnetic-orgonomic Intelligence existing throughout galactic space-time and matching all the extravagant descriptions of God found in theology.

It is possible that the Higher Intelligences (Gurdjieffian-Cabalistic "angels" and "archangels") in charge of distributing DNA about the galaxy and guiding/ aiding its evolution are also yearning for union with the meta-physiological Intelligence ("God") and that the evolutionary blueprint transcends our galaxy, involving other galactic Intelligences throughout the universe, as suggested in Olaf Stapledon's inspired PSI PHY visions (*Last and First Men, Star Maker.*)

Jacques Bergier has suggested, somewhat whimsically, that the Parisian radio station which broadcasts a one hour transmission on French civilization once a week may be an earthside analog of magick/religious/UFO phenomenon. That is, some central "station" may be broadcasting a one hour transmission on Cosmic civilization. Space-time relativity considerations make it not unthinkable that the Transmissions received on Earth in the past 30,000 years—by shamans, yogis, alchemists; Buddha, Jesus, Joseph Smith, Böhme, Blake, Crowley, Mary Baker Eddy; flying saucer "contactees;" etc. — are part of the same educational project. These Starseed Transmissions (as Dr. Leary calls them) suffer a great deal of semantic noise in passing through the nervous system which receives them, but remain strikingly identical in emphasis.

The *Book of Mormon*, Crowley's *Book of the Law*, the Judeo-Christian *Bible*, the *Upanishads* and *Vedas*, etc., when closely and dispassionately studied, appear very much to be the same *signal* with encrustations of local prejudice, ignorance, bias and distortion. The signal seems to say:

– Turn off the lower circuits (I-IV); transcend. Turn on the higher circuits (V-VIII); become more aware.

– All the lower circuits are addicting, hallucinatory, mechanical, robotic, "sleepwalking," *maya*; the higher circuits are where true freedom and the goal of all our desires can really be found.

– We have reached a crucial point in cosmic time (30,000 BCE earth time to the present) at which increasing numbers can make the transition from left-lobe lower circuit robotism to right-lobe higher circuit freedom.

– There is work for us to do.

The last part of the message (our "work") is traditionally the most jumbled. Various seers have come back from these contacts gibbering that we must drink tea every afternoon (a New Guinea messiah in LeBarre's *Ghost Dance: Origins of Religion*), cut off the foreskin of our penis (Moses), give all our property to the poor (Jesus), burn all our crops (an American messiah, LeBarre), sacrifice our children in furnaces (Moloch cult, Carthage), become very ascetic (St. Paul, Hindus ad. lib.), become very sensual (Tantrists, Blake), become more intelligent (Leary), etc. etc. Others have worshipped cargo planes, snakes, ghosts, holy virgins, buffalo, cats, ad. nauseam.

A little neurogenetic perspective is needed. The majority of humans at this date have imprinted survival programs on the first four circuits only; many of these programs are bizarre, contra-survival, "neurotic" — results of traumatic shock during imprint moments. A large group are aware that *some* of their programs have this bizarre "crazy-robot" quality and are seeking professional help from local shamans (or, in urban areas, psychotherapists) to re-imprint more rational programs. Such help in our culture varies from the mediocre to the inept.

A *growing minority of post-larval humans* has developed a five-circuit nervous system and has experienced some of the "transcendental" bliss states. The fad of metaprogramming chemicals (the "dope menace") has made such post-larval states at least temporarily available to several millions, whereas yogic and shamanistic re-imprinting was previously achieved in only a few dozen post-larval persons each century. Again, on the fifth circuit, bizarre imprints are often taken and behavior is observable with less contra-survival and contra-intelligence than that of the most poorly programmed I-IV circuit larval humans.

Circuit Six neurophysical awakening is even more rare. Many develop this circuit by sheer accident (the head injury that unlocked ESP in Danish psychic Peter Hurkos is an example), others force Circuit Six opening by ill-advised dope-or-occult-experiences without first obtaining training in objective observation, rational thought or decent interpersonal relating (fill in your own horrible examples; the occult world is full of them.)

Circuit Seven neurogenetic intelligence (access to the planetary and extra-planetary life script) is badly needed, as ecologists are urgently aware; but there are far, far fewer Circuit Seven types even than Circuit Sixes. The earliest shamans opened this genetic archive far enough to communicate with such distant DNA relatives as the plants (hence, their development of fertility Magick), but even today a Luther Burbank or a George Washington Carver, despite all his scientific education, cannot explain *how* he works clearly enough to teach the art as efficiently as dentistry or chiropractic is taught.

Circuit Eight meta-physiological functioning ("astral tripping") is at an equally rudimentary stage.

We can only conclude that 30,000 BCE to the present is an absurdly short time, cosmically speaking, and that these higher neurogenetic Reception-Transmission functions are in their infancy. Indeed, despite the brilliant gropings of William James, Freud, Jung et. al., serious scientific study of these functions, massively pursued by thousands of researchers, has virtually only begun in the past ten years. What many regard as the most promising line of research (investigation of metaprogramming substances traditionally used by shamans) has been blocked by governmental hysteria as soon as it becomes public knowledge, and is now pursued only by subterraneans and outlaws, like alchemy and Craft wisdom in the Dark Ages.

I want to show you another metaprogramming console, the Structural Differential of Count Alfred Korzybski, the pioneer semanticist.

Smith's Abstraction Continues Indefinitely, Fido stops

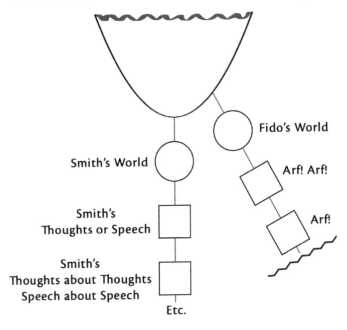

The parabola at the top of this diagram can be regarded as the universal energy process, best represented by the open equation f (x) = y (or, as Eddington said, "Something unknown is doing something we don't understand.") The cut-off line with jagged edges at the top of the parabola indicates that this universal energy process has no limits that we know of. That is, whether it is finite or infinite in space-time (what means finite? what means infinite?) it is *infinite in aspects.* There is no way of writing enough declarative sentences to *describe it in full* because, among other things, *it is changing while you write.*

This universal energy process is the *Ain Soph Aur* of the Cabalists, the Limitless Light. Consciousness of this is only obtainable on the Sixth (neurophysical) Circuit, when we literally tune in to the orgonomic, bio-energetic, vegetative, cellular, molecular, atomic and subatomic "vibes"—a dramatic experience elsewhere called "the White Light of the Void," Satori, Samadhi, Cosmic Consciousness, etc.

Below the parabola is a circle representing ordinary perception (Circuits I to V). At any given instant, we are abstracting such a perception from the universal energy process; it is the *world* we perceive at that moment. This world can be scanned as safe-dangerous (Circuit I), stronger-than-me or weaker-than-me (Circuit II), comprehensible or incomprehensible (Circuit III), loveable or hateful (Circuit IV), or simply marvelous beyond all categories (Circuit V). Whichever circuit we are operating on, that is the kind of world we are perceiving-creating. *The principle of relativity refers to neurologic even more than to physics.* "Everything we see is inside our heads," as Buckminster Fuller reminds us. (Skeptics should consult the first illustration in any optics text.)

Thus, if two organisms are "in" the same space-time situation, they will not perceive-create the same space-time *world* around themselves. The man is "in" one *world* and his dog, Rover, is "in" another *world*. The human world and the canine world. The same holds true if our two organisms are man and woman, or two brothers, or any two entities whatsoever. Even if you and I are both shouting at each other in rage-fear (Second Circuit behavior) we are still each abstracting through a different nervous system and are not "in" the same world. (You are in the "outside" part of my world, as I am in the "outside" part of your world; but you and I are both on the "inside" of our own worlds. "Every number is infinite; there is no difference," as the *Book of the Law* says.)

On our diagram, this is illustrated by having two circles at a slight angle to each other. Each circle is a perceived-world abstracted from the same universal energy process by a unique never-to-be-repeated organism. (Heredity is not identity.)

Below the circles are squares, representing, higher order nervous-system activities. Thus, after I perceive-create the world-in-this-instant I can mull over it, think about it, *talk* about it, and generally program all sorts of signals having only arbitrary "associational" conditioned-reflex links with the original signals from Outside me that started this chain of perception-creation.*

~•~

* I can also mull about my mulling, talk about my talking, think about my thinking, etc. These "higher order" neural programs are discussed in Korzybski, *Science and Sanity*, where the confusions inherent in confusing the order of these abstractions is clearly explained. Crowley also warned against "mixing the planes."

~•~

Thus, even when my world-circle expands to "infinity" and the parabolic universal energy process is included therein (Sixth Circuit Samadhi) the next distinct state is another chain of "associational" conditioned-reflex links (internal monologue, sub-vocal speech) *symbolizing* the event. We can go on doing this endlessly. When signals from the cellular archives' DNA "brain" are received (Seventh Circuit) — the encounter with Pan — the next distinct event is, again, more associational programming.

Crowley symbolized this process by the Soldier (!), his name for the exclamation point, and the Hunchback (?), his name for the question-mark. Each Soldier (!) is the opening of a new signal-reception network, or even, on higher circuits, a new me-world Gestalt. This high-circuit Samadhi can be symbolized by a row of soldiers: !!!!!. The self-programmer can then mull over and reprogram these unique experiences, bringing in further Hunchbacks: ???. There is no end to this process and the unfrightened human lives in a constant parade of Soldiers and Hunchbacks: ! ! ! ?? ! !?! ??? ! ! ! ! ??? ! ! ! ! etc.

I call this Transcendental Atheism, since any "God" on any Circuit is immediately recognized as partial and delusory on the next-higher Circuit. Every step up we can see that we were fools and robots on the Circuit below. (The Cosmic Joke.) It seems that we wake from one delusion into another. Yesterday's freedom is recognized as today's robotic habit and tomorrow's idiot addiction. (Unless we change course and reprogram again.)

My current addiction is to believe in the Seventh Circuit, which tells me that we have work to do (every Starseed Transmission ends on this upward-and-onward note) and that in this junction of history the work involves Immortality and Serial Reincarnation in the same body.

That is, the chemistry of immortal life is at our door (informed estimates assure us that life extension to centuries will be available by the late 1980s, to millennia sometime in the next half-century)[*] and this changes the whole Neurologic of humanity. It is Utopia or Oblivion from here on out. We really make it or we really break it. It is time for us to "put away childish things" in St. Paul's metaphor and become Cosmic Adults.

~•~

[*] See *The Prospects of Immortality* and *Man Into Superman*, both by E.C.W. Ettinger; *Terra II*, Timothy Leary; *The Immortality Factor*, Osborn Segerberg; *Upwingers: A Futurist Manifesto*, F.M. Esfandiary; *The Immortalist*, Alan Harrington. Already, molecular biologists have successfully inhibited the aging program in rats and dogs; see Ettinger, *Man Into Superman*.

~•~

Sufis and alchemists began talking of the Next Step nearly one thousand years ago; the Starseed Transmissions have increasingly invoked the notion of evolutionary change ever since. The DNA wants a new game; death-rebirth is a worn out program. Listen to Nietzsche ("Man is a creature that must be surpassed"); UFO "nuts" ("I hear those starry voices calling . . ."); Crowley ("Verily: thou shalt not die but live"); Gurdjieff ("My way is against God and against Nature"); science fiction bards and holy visionaries of pulp; Kubrick's *2001*; Tielhard de Chardin; and *all* the seers of the past century. They tell us: the Age of Aquarius is more than a change of style. It is a biological-cosmic mutation.

My DNA is telling my RNA, and your DNA is telling your RNA, that the robotic birth-death 70-year-robot-ride is over and done with. A more interesting game is afoot;

larval life is falling behind and the post-larval stirrings are in all of us. The metamorphoses is happening before our eyes, every minute. The war on metaprogramming chemicals escalates from $22 million per year to $212 million per year (Nixon's crusade), but the chemicals are only a small part of the upheaval. They can outlaw bio-feedback machines next year, but some bright postgraduate will have a "pranameter" (to do pranayama *scientifically*) on the market the year after that. The djinn is out of the bottle. Technology is going where only a handful of brave, brilliant, mostly "primitive" neuro-programmers (shamans) have gone before, and (like it or not) *Technology means results*. You can hear the Gurus shrieking from Camden to Benares as their monopoly is obsoleted to the junk pile. "God won't get into a pill. God won't get into an electro-encephalogram. God won't get into a polygraph. God won't do it any way but *my* way. Come to me and be saved." Nobody's buying at that stand anymore.*

~•~

* Ma Bell feels the same way about phone phreaks as the average Guru does about laboratory mysticism; but in both cases the monopolists are doomed. Monopolized electromagnetic communication (which probably includes both telephony and telepathy) cannot resist bio-feedback, electronic, metaprogramming and similar technological breakthroughs expected in the next decades.

~•~

It should be obvious by now that, from the point of view of Neurologic, my "I" sees exactly what it looks at. "I" am the creator of my reality, and responsible for it. The depth and profundity of Intelligence discovered throughout the cosmos, especially on Sixth Circuit neurophysical channels and Seventh Circuit neurogenetic channels, dwarfs all our old Third Circuit digital pictures of the universal process. The great English biologist J.B.S. Haldane, after taking up yoga, lost all his Marxist dogmas and said "The universe may be, not only queerer than we think, but queerer than we *can* think." We now know that the universal energy is, not only more intelligent than we have thought, but more intelligent than we can presently think. Thales said "All things are full of gods" but this remained a Dark Saying to all but a few other *futique* visionaries for twenty-five centuries; now any biology graduate knows that each organism consists of billions of cells each of which has more moving parts, intelligently integrated, than a city the size of New York. The message of this cellular intelligence, when one is able to open Circuit Seven and scan it, is more intelligent than Einstein, more optimistic than a puppy, more erotic than a Tantric temple, more awesome than any myth, more joyous than Beethoven's Ninth.[*]

~•~

[*] Meister Eckhart: "Cut a stick in half, and the Christ is in there;" Timothy Leary: "Consciousness is energy received and decoded by a structure;" Gandhi: "God is in the rock, too, in the rock!" Cleve Backster believes his research on Sixth Circuit communications in plants and yoghurt demonstrates atomic and subatomic consciousness; every magician can confirm this in his/her first few years of really disciplined practice.

~•~

All of which is the rhetorical version of what I said more cynically before; I'm currently hooked to Circuit Seven, addicted to the evolutionary pan-urge, which wants to grow up from earthside temper tantrums to being a cosmic immortal adult. Every Starseed Transmission for several millenniums has told us to come home to the stars

("Heaven") and live forever; now the mutation is at hand.

Let us look at our neurogenetic octave again on a new helical console (figure 1). It can be seen that we have now included the octave of matter (Periodic Table of Elements) of Mendeleev. Actually, this octave was discovered by John A.R. Newland *five years* before Mendeleev, but poor Newland was laughed at on the floor of the Royal Chemical Society: the octave was so obviously an old magick device of Pythagoras's school that bright, up-to-date 19th Century scientists couldn't take it seriously. Only when Mendeleev rediscovered the eight-fold path of matter (alkalis, alkalines, borons, carbons, nitrogens, oxygens, halogens, noble gases) did the Royal Society repent and give Newland a gold medal. It is extremely interesting that the same octave is found in the trigrams of *I Ching* (see figure 1). It may well be the eight-fold path (divided into two quartets) is a basic structural integrity of the universal energy process, just as Pythagoras believed. Buckminster Fuller, combining two tetrahedrons into his octet truss, decided that he had a mathematical archetype basic to all sciences he understood; and Dr. Fuller understands almost all the sciences fairly well. You might look in your own area of expertise for similar quartet-octet systems . . .

You will note that the Tarot and Tree of Life can be expressed upon this octave of Neurologic. The total justification for these correlations cannot be given here, but the Tarot-Circuit relationships are worthy of some attention. Our adjustments are justified only by their results; theoretical debate without such results is that "great Serbonian bog where armies whole have sunk."

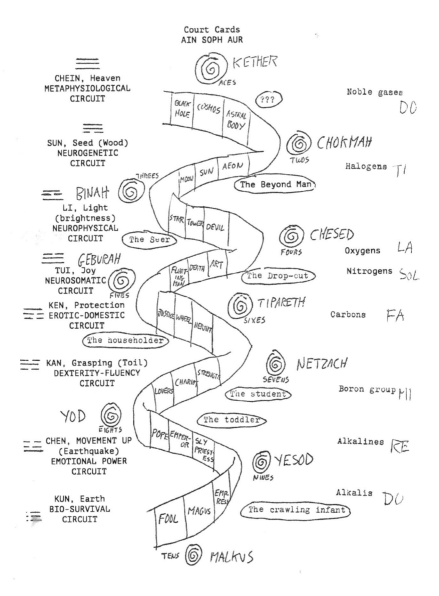

We assume the following correspondences:

Wands — adenine

Cups — thymine

Swords — cytosine

Discs — guanine

These four basic amino acids serve as bonds for the DNA helix. These chemical bonds are analogs of the sexual bonds at higher levels. (Here is some of the analogical, non-linear, non-Aristotelian right-lobe thinking we warned about earlier.) The pyrimidines are "male analogs," so adenine and cytosine are Wands and Swords respectively. The purines are "female-analogs" so Cups and Discs are thymine and guanine. The lovely thing about this analog is that the phallic-vaginal symbolism (wands to cups, swords to discs) describes exactly the bonding system (adenine to thymine, cytosine to guanine) that actually does hold the DNA helix together.[*]

~•~

[*] It is perhaps safe to mention in a footnote that this concept was received by both the present author, in California, and by poet Brian Barritt, in Switzerland, the same week; one reason for believing in a central Starseed Transmission facility.

~•~

The first DNA-RNA "conversation" (strategic-esthetic design decision) produces First Circuit intelligence (bio-survival programs) easily observed in unicellular organisms with their characteristic one-dimensional forward-back behavior. Watching closely, the ontological recapitulation can be observed in human infants at the crawling stage. The Tarot analogs of this circuitry are Fool-Magus-Empress representing input-decision-output. (We assume that each Circuit repeats the three-fold reception-integration-transmission function of the individual neuron. (Inhale-retain-exhale in pranayama.) This is the imprinted intelligence of Circuit One.

The unimprinted Fool type (if encountered in adulthood) is the drifter, the floater, the unattached emotionless sociopath, the dumbox (Cabalistic correlate;

aleph, ox) usually found in prisons, homes for the feeble-minded or "lunatic" asylums. Airy unimprinted Fools (Tarot number 0, void) have surprising social value in unforeseen situations, so "primitive" societies do not discard them as ours does; myths usually marry them off to the Princess in a surprise ending.

The Magus type is First Circuit braininess per se; the survival artist, the master-of-situations, a juggler in old decks. This type advances-and-retreats with spectacular intuitive success, knowing just when to push and when to bend.

The Empress or Earth-Mother type is First Circuit bonding (based on the infant=mother and DNA=most planet bonds), this is the nurturing situation found in *Daleth*, the vaginal door. "Let's face it, we all wanna go back there," as Shelley Berman says.

Second Circuit intelligence (emotional power strategies) mediates the Sly Priestess/Emperor/Hierophant trio of emotional passivity, emotional domination, emotional bonding. (Just as the First Circuit bond is with the Motherly Empress, the Second Circuit bond is with the fatherly-or-avuncular Hierophant, representing tribal game-rules sacralized by tradition.)

The adult Sly Priestess is the type studied in Adler's psychology, the quasi-masochist who *wins by losing* (scores "moral" points by submitting to the more aggressive emotionalists rather than resisting or dominating them). The quiet nun, the *nebbish*.

The adult Emperor can be studied in *Richard Nixon, career of, see local library*. The cop, the bully, the salesman are variations. Pure Second Circuit strategy-programming. Crowley's correlation with *tzaddi* (hook) rather than *he* (window) makes neurogenetic sense when one recalls that emotions are hooks, addictions, neuro-chemical repeating tape loops. The Emperor knows absolutely everything about emotional manipulation, emotional control, emotional power-politics. The ethologists' *alpha male* as found in any territorial species but most resembling the human type among the *alpha* baboons.

The adult hierophant (librarian, accountant, clergyman) has bonded to the tribal game-rules. This person is all superego (Critical Parent); there is virtually no id (child) or ego (adult) in him/her.

Circuit Three intelligence mediates between the models of Lovers/Chariot/Strength. The two-foldness of each card in this circuit emphasizes the digital either/or logic of the left frontal-lobe computer.

Lovers types are passive learners, always studying a new subject or programming a new hobby. Chariot types are forever building, structuring, designing. Strength types are bonded to the learned community (tribal elders)—T.S. Eliot's wedding of Tradition and Individual Talent. Every person in a learned community or research project will easily be recognized as a passive knowledge-drinking consumer-Lover, an integrative knowledge-combing, computer-Chariot, or a transmitting knowledge-creating output-Strength. In actual creativity we program each of these trips in rapidly repeating succession.

Circuit Four intelligence mediates between hermit/wheel/justice. Passive sexual consumerism (masturbatory trips, with or without partners) are the Hermit (Monk-Playboy) mode. Integrative pair-bonding is the Wheel of Karma, the completing of the first four larval circuits, discharge of one's DNA responsibility to reproduce the species entering the genetic Roulette wheel for another DNA combination to come blinking onto the stage of life.

The output of the circuit is social bonding, full membership in the tribe, full adult responsibility, usually full robotization as the tribal game becomes all-encompassing; Justice, the tribal game-rules defined, exactly portrays this final stage of Circuit Four, the usual climax stage in the growth of the individual nervous system.*

~•~

* Statistical evidence, summarized by Dr. Timothy Leary in Periodic Table of Energy (unpublished ms.) indicates that the 12 neurogenetic types of the first four circuits are templated at the 12 breeding times related to the traditional Zodiac signs. The correspondence is: Fool—Pisces; Magus — Aries; Empress — Taurus; Priestess — Gemini; Emperor — Cancer; Hierophant — Leo; Lovers — Virgo; Chariot — Libra; Strength — Scorpio; Hermit — Sagittarius; Wheel — Capricorn; Justice — Aquarius. These are not traditional; but they work (and we know that the tradition was destroyed, rebuilt, hidden, distorted repeatedly during Christian persecutions.) The Empress-Taurus correlation, for instance, sheds much light on cow-headed Isis; the Hindu veneration for our nutritive stepmother, the cow; the basic infant-mother bonding of this circuit, etc. That DNA templating varies seasonally is all the theory we need, then, to explain astrology.

~•~

The second quartet within this octave can be considered the extraterrestrial cards, the *nagual* transcendence of the tribal-game *tonal* of the first quartet.

Circuit Five intelligence mediates Floating Man (astronaut?)/Death/Art programs.

The Floating Man (Hanged Man) stage is the neurosomatic Turn On (*dhyana*). An oceanic flood of new signals as the nervous impulse leaps the gap between left lobe and right lobe, terrestrial survival and extraterrestrial transcendence. The person is once again as detached from social reward-punishment as the unimprinted Fool; in the resulting Hedonic Boom many fuses are blown. (See LSD revolution, casualties of.) Watery, oceanic imagery comes spontaneously to all who have been there.

This purely passive stage is gradually integrated (the new signals incorporated into Gestalts) and we pass to:

Death, the intelligence of the Fifth Circuit, usually symbolized by a gigantic white horse (the new body-intelligence, or neurosomatic consciousness) and a skeleton riding him (the death of the old socially conditioned ego of Circuits I-IV). Those who do not pass through this Death-Rebirth slot and remain Floating Men are the passive-consumers of the occult world.*

~•~

*There are reasons why the wise-primitive neurogeneticists who sent the Tarot signal called this card Death rather than Rebirth. The death of the old ego is experienced more excruciatingly at first than the resurrection of the transmuted body (neurosomatic consciousness). This is Bad Trip Lane where lurks the Dweller on the Threshold; only the brave may pass. In particular, Circuit One fear, Circuit Two dominance, Circuit Three "logic" (old game rules) and Circuit Four sex-role identity must be surrendered. Fears of insanity, demonic possession, etc. can block progress here for a lifetime, unless mastered.

~•~

Finally, Art, the bonding-transmitting of the Fifth Circuit, occurs when the Tantric Union is achieved. This is the first true transcendence of the individual nervous system, and the five-circuit two-person neural network of Tantra is the only known path to the higher circuits. (Every Tarot deck shows the Tantric path in this card; Crowley's is most clear in using the traditional alchemical symbols of lion-eagle for the male-female fusion.) The floating Men who do not make this Tantric linkage are to the Sixth Circuit what the masturbatory Hermit-monk perpetual adolescent type is to the Fourth Circuit.

Sixth Circuit intelligence probably cannot be imprinted within a heavy gravitational field; it is only rudimentary in all known Earth WoMen to this date. When imprinted-programmed fully under zero-gravity (freefall) conditions it will probably mediate the Tarot trilogy of Devil-Tower-Star.[*]

~•~

[*] Dr. Richard Miller's theory that the DNA projects a differing bio-hologram ("reality") depending on the magnetic-gravitational field in which it finds itself. All astronauts have shown some "weird" reactions to leaving earth-gravity and Ed Mitchell became a full-time mystic. Dr. Timothy Leary predicts that we will enter a totally new "reality" after leaving the solar system.

~•~

The Devil (Samadhi, Higher Intelligence) is the telepathic bond to a non-human nervous system. (Holy Guardian Angel, ally, elf-helper, *deva*). The Tower is the integration of such signals portrayed negatively to warn the student on this path that it includes total destruction of humanity (i.e. human chauvinism), a project somewhat beyond the "liberal humanist" transcendence of racism, sexism, nationalism and similar low level games. The extraordinary number of human-animal sexual acts portrayed in cave-paintings leave no doubt that the early shamans sought to leap this gap by Tantric bonding with the only non-human systems physically available to them. (*Cf. The love-bond between witches and their familiars.*) The Star, the successful bonding-transmission stage, is so clearly portrayed in any Tarot deck that the meaning is inescapable. Crowley identified this card with Sirius, the giant star nine light years away which has fascinated many other Circuit Six types, including Gurdjieff, the Yezidi sect of Sufism, and Egyptian priests whose annual festivals of the dog-star Sirius gives us the expression "dog days" still in our language, beginning July 23 when the occult link between Earth-Sirius (through hyperspace) is most intense.*

~•~

* The importance of this star in Crowleyan magick is discussed at length in Kenneth Grant, *The Magical Revival*, Weiser Books. July 23 is a good day for Crowleyan rituals.

~•~

Seventh Circuit intelligence mediates between Moon/ Sun/Aeon which we translate as passive neurogenetic receptivity, integrative neurogenetic programming, transmission of neurogentic output. Moon: racial memory, past life memory, the opening of the genetic archives. Sun: integration of the genetic Gestalt, the evolutionary Great Work, the True Will ("Why am I here and what must I do?") Aeon: output-transmission, the neurogenetic bonding of that Company of evolutionary agents which Dr. John Lilly and Dr. Timothy Leary have defined as interstellar.

Eighth Circuit intelligence is indicated in the historical Tarot by the Universe card, which we assume in the integrative slot of this circuit. We add an Astral Body card, for the passive consumer stage of galactic consciousness, leave the Universe for the integrating-programming stage, and add a Black Hole card for the link outwards to other galaxies and other galactic Minds (Gods?).

Dr. Carl Sagan estimates that, if only 1 per cent of all stars in our galaxy have solar systems, and only 1 percent of the solar systems have intelligent life, and only 1 percent of such intelligent races are more advanced than us, then there are at minimum 100,000 races in this galaxy alone who are to us Superhuman. We define these 100,000 Superhuman groups as those who have fully programmed the second quartet (Circuits V-VIII) and act as Transmitters of Starseed Signals. The basic similarities in reception among such post-larval humans as Jesus, Buddha, Mohammed, Crowley etc. (despite local, chauvinistic, superstitious distortions) entitles us to assume that such cosmic messages are not accidental eaves-droppings or galactic blunders; we are *expected* to receive the messages (eventually). The first four circuits, on any planet, will then deal with adaptation-survival-reproduction on that planet, and the second four circuits will involve reception-integration-transmission of the signals of the larger cosmic script.

According to Clarke's Law (coined by English PSI PHY philosopher-fictioneer-scientist Arthur C. Clarke), "Any sufficiently advanced technology is indistinguishable from magick." To look for advanced technologies encountering Earth WoMen, then, we need not dig through Van Dänikenism nor artifacts of dubious manufacture etc.; we need only study the scannings of magically turned-on post-larval Circuit V-Circuit VIII humans. The nervous system is still the greatest scientific instrument we have, and it is our chief clue to Higher Intelligences.

Try to imagine a technology 1000 years beyond ours. The more science you know, the more mind-boggling this exercise is. Assume that, among the 100,000 superhuman races assumed in this galaxy, some have a technology 1,000,000 years beyond ours. What "magick" feat will be impossible to them?

Note especially the corollary to Clarke's Law; any sufficiently advanced parapsychology is indistinguishable from magick. Imagine galactic races with a science of parapsychology (high circuit Neurologic) 1000 years beyond ours, 1,000,000 years beyond ours . . .* This network of loving intelligence, when encountered on the Sixth, Seventh and Eighth Circuits, is mind-blowing. Remember Marxist-materialist biologist J.B.S. Haldane, who said, after personal yogic investigation of these circuits, "The universe may be, not only queerer than we think, but queerer than we *can* think." One can no longer quite believe that these signals are really invisible to larval humans (Circuits I-IV) and begins to imagine that they are play-acting their blindness, engaged in some hilarious pantomime of folly for some mysterious reason; only slowly does one rediscover that the larval humans are indeed larval and that the social reward-punishment grid of Circuits I-IV thoroughly scans out these higher-circuit Gestalts.

~•~

* Inability to accept the obvious in this area is due to Euclidean imprinting of the Third Circuit in plane geometry classes; as Eddington observes, "We have certain preconceived ideas about location in space that have come down to us from our ape-like ancestors . . ." (*Space, Time and Gravitation*). Incredulity about interstellar neurogenetics is a confusion between the geometrical *map* and energetic *territory*.

~•~

As Dr. John Lilly writes in *Programming and Metaprogramming the Human Biocomputer*, in the province of the nervous system "what is believed true is true or becomes true, within limits to be found experientially and experimentally. These limits are further beliefs to be transcended," because in the province of the nervous system "there are no limits."

The programming of the early circuits is *total* and *invisible*, while we are operating on these circuits. Consider

Jones, worker, and Smith, employer, as Smith shows Jones to the door after an interview. Smith puts his arm around Jones' shoulder in a "friendly" (actually patronizing) manner. The picture is easily visualized and quite "normal." Now start the movie again and watch Jones casually put his arm around Smith's shoulder. Weird, isn't it? The latter picture doesn't seem right because, in Second Circuit programming, the Dominant party may initiate touching but the Submissive party may not so initiate touching. (A Martian would recognize this as a male-chauvinist society by noting that "normal" men are allowed to initiate the touching of "normal" women—we are ignoring Bohemians or freaks here—but "normal" women may not initiate the touching of "normal" men.)

Circuit Three programming is even harder to spot; often we can only get clues by studying who's in jail lately. When a poet, a philosopher, a scientist etc. is jailed, you can be sure he or she has somehow violated the Circuit Three programming rules (epistemology). Dr. Wilhelm Reich did this by allowing Fifth and Sixth Circuit energies into his bio-psychology; Dr. Reich died in prison. Today, Dr. Leary is in jail for the same variety of thought-crime. Tomorrow it will probably be the turn of the vitamin therapists. Only the domination of the first quartet by powerful Second Circuit glandular reflexes (fear-rage) prevents people from noting the absurdity of attempting to settle scientific-epistemological disputes by the devices of cops-courts-cages and the whole mad matrix of spies, double agents, no-knock laws, midnight raids, terrorism, etc.

"The human brain," Norbert Weiner solemnly declared in his epoch-making *Cybernetics; Control and Communication in the Animal and the Machine*, "probably works on some variation on the famous principle enunciated in *The Hunting of the Snark*: 'What I tell you three times is true.'" This is the principle of redundancy in Information Theory; persistent signals are recognized, sporadic signals are ignored. If I see a chair one second and not the next, I assume my senses were scanning wrong for an instant; but if I see the chair continually, I accept it as "real." Second Circuit emotional-intelligence types are all magicians in the bad sense: they program others into their own reality very quickly. *It is a triumph of sanity and objectivity to remain in the company of Second Circuit types and see what is really happening.* Few have this sanity and objectivity. Much of so-called "reality" is just the paranoid broadcasting of Second Circuit hysterics (Korzybski's principle of "semantic contagion"). Post-larval humans, as they become aware of this, gradually drop out of the stage-set "social reality" and retreat to monastic or crash pad enclaves with similar post-larvals.

To remain in the neuro-semantic insanity of larval society, without laughing hysterically or otherwise giving away the secret of one's mutation, is the path of the Boddhisattva, who, like Father Demian going to live among the lepers, steels himself against the risk of contagion and returns to the madhouse of Circuit I-IV humanity. It is no accident that witches and wizards are traditionally pictured as having a sardonic laugh, or that the humor of the Sufis and Zen Masters is inscrutable to Spiro Agnew. Most Circuit I fears are paranoid; most Circuit II domination is farcical; most Circuit III thinking is monkey-chatter; most Circuit IV love is vampirism on the installment plan. Allen Ginsberg's description of Earth as an "armed madhouse" is hardly poetic hyperbole; open the newspaper and look at what is reported every day.

We have been describing some of the "behaviors of the human nervous system; and we have sketched a context of interstellar neurogenetics in which human evolution is one small part of a far grander design. Nothing we have uttered conflicts with modern science, much of it has strong (and growing) support in current research; and yet we have included virtually all the territory traditionally assigned to shamans and yogis. It is obvious, then, that Scientific and Experimental Magick is a discipline that can be approached by the same methods as physics, geology, genetics, social psychology, etc.

We know that shamans and yogis are exploring the higher circuits of the human nervous system, no more, no less; we know that their work is centered in the right lobe, whereas most human behavior is mediated through the left lobe; we know, at minimum, that some of their subjective impressions while on these higher circuits (e.g. human-plant ESP) have been scientifically validated. There is no reason why we cannot investigate this field further by scientific means. Every ritual is, as Crowley wrote, a "physiological experiment," an attempt to reprogram the neural energies into new channels. The research at Max Born Institute, where Gopi Krishna is working with physicists in an effort to measure the kundalini energy used in the Circuit Six transformations, promises a breakthrough in understanding for the very near future.

It should now be obvious that secrecy is a doomed and counter-productive strategy. Many traditional magick lodges, such as the Ordo Templi Orientis, realize this and have allowed hitherto hidden programming techniques (sex-magick) to be published. A World Esoteric Order, devoted to revealing all the mysteries rather than monopolizing them, is badly needed; I am glad to be among the founding members of such an Order. The choice of Utopia or Oblivion becomes more stark every day. As Dr. Leary wrote in *The Curse of the Oval Room*:

> Secrecy is the enemy of sanity and loving trust. If you keep secrets, you are an insane paranoiac. Concealment is the seed source of every human conflict. Secrecy is always caused by guilt or fear. (G. Gordon) Liddy's parents were guilty about sex. And Nixon's parents . . .

Let's break the huddle. Before J. Edgar Hoover there was no secret police in this country . . .

Now comes the electronic revolution. Reveal-ation. Bugging equipment effective at long distances is inexpensive and easily available. Good. Liberals want stiff laws against bugging. It's the wrong move. Legalize everything. Legalize bugging . . .

Secrecy is the original sin . . . the basic crime against love. The issue is fundamental. What a blessing that Watergate has been uncovered to teach us the primary lesson. The purpose of life is to receive, synthesize, and transmit energy. Communication, output is the goal of life. Any star can tell you that. Communication is love. Secrecy, withholding the signal, hoarding, hiding, covering up the light is motivated by shame and fear, symptoms of the inability to love . . .

As so often happens, the extreme right wing is half right for the wrong reasons. They say primly: if you have done nothing wrong, you have no fear of being bugged. Exactly. But the logic works both ways. Then FBI files, CIA dossiers, and White House conversations should be open to all. Let everything hang open. Let government be totally visible. The last, the very last people to hide anything should be the police and the government . . .

There is nothing and no way to hide. This is the acid message.

We're all on cosmic TV every moment.

Blessed words, brothers and sisters. May the World Esoteric Order never depart from this attitude, and may we also keep in mind, less solemnly, Crowley's metaprogram for magicians of this century:

> We place no reliance
> On Virgin or Pigeon;
> Our method is science,
> Our aim is religion.

Chapter Fifteen

Unanswered Questions

Never believe anything about me that you read in
the newspapers.
— Timothy Leary, in conversation

Just before Thanksgiving, we refounded Starseed, the
Leary educational organization in San Francisco, which had
collapsed after his disappearance in May.

The founding members of Starseed II met at the home
of cartoonist Carl Spann and decided to continue the basic
thrust of the original Starseed, on a timetable as follows:

1975–76: Agitation, propaganda, street theatre,
publishing a newsletter (later a slick magazine), holding
lectures and seminars, etc. Goal: 100,000 members by
December 1976.

1976–1986: Concerted pressure to obtain a
governmental crash program of research on Immortality;
the beginning of Starseed III, our next stage, an actual
private corporation to build a Starship and allow 5000
neurological evolutes to escape from the Armed Madhouse
of Earth into the freedom of the stars.

The first task of Starseed II was, then, to publicize the potentials of
> Immortality
> Star-flight
> Neurologic

We began with a demonstration at UC Medical School on November 22, the eleventh anniversary of the assassination of John F. Kennedy. We demonstrated *for* the Medical School, not *against* it, to dramatize our difference with the confrontation politics of the 1960s. Our march and leafleting expressed love, gratitude and admiration for the Medical School, in thanksgiving for their work on Life Extension. We also presented a leaflet on the need for crash funding of Immortality research, since *anybody who dies between now and the breakthrough gate is missing the chance for Immortality.*

It was a coldish day for San Francisco, we gave out all our leaflets with freezing hands and returned to a member's apartment in the neighborhood feeling like kings. Starseed II had completed its first action and was a kinetic force on the planet Earth.

We adopted two slogans:

> LIFE TO THE DEATHIST PIG

— a deliberate parody on the hate slogans of the Left; and

> DON'T BUY THE LIE:
> YOU DON'T HAVE TO DIE

Our next step was debated for a while and we agreed to hold a public funeral for Dr. Leary and invite the media. Perhaps, just perhaps, the ACLU and some Liberal politicians would be provoked into noticing that Tim had been missing for five months and that the howling ghosts of Mitchell and Kleindienst were haunting the Justice Department by night.

My letter to Leary was still unanswered. Ginsberg's second letter was also unanswered. The funeral was a good way to dramatize that nobody outside government had any evidence that Timothy was alive after May 1974.

I came home from the meeting feeling high; if we can't build a Starship, we can sure as hell try . . .

And we might be able to answer some questions. *Viz*:

If the Starseed signals are not interstellar, and Dr. Leary is (as professional judgement asserts) sane, what *is* communicating with him?

What was the daemon that instructed Socrates? The "angel" that spoke to Mohammed and Dr. John Dee? The "Baphomet" of the Templars? The Holy Guardian Angel of Crowley? The "fairies" reported by such sober scientists as Carver, Steiner, Edison, Burbank, Fechner?

If Timothy Leary and Wilhelm Reich belonged in prison, what scientists should be free? What, exactly, are the permissible limits of enquiry?

(If Ezra Pound belonged in a nuthouse, what poets should be free? What are the limits of imagination?)

If Terra II is a metaphor, is the National Debt a reality?

If the map of experience created by the ordinary human nervous system is accurate in all respects, are all other living beings hallucinating? How, in that case, does the gorilla, the dog, the beetle, the slug, the tree, the amoeba survive?

If nervous systems as different as amoeba, horse and tree can all "sense" a reality suitable for their own survival programs, how many realities are there? Which realities are taboo, hallucinatory or psychotic?

If there are at least 100,000 planets in this galaxy alone probably ahead of us in evolution (Carl Sagan's estimate), how many are ahead of us in ESP, PK, astral projection?

If "a sufficiently advanced technology is indistinguishable from magic" (Arthur Clarke), how many magic beings exist in this galaxy alone?

Isn't it even more obviously true that "a sufficiently advanced parapsychology is indistinguishable from magick"?

How many people throughout history who have encountered elves, gnomes, angels, Sun-Gods, alien beings, etc. really encountered Higher Intelligences? Were *all* hallucinating?

Why is it that contactees with Higher Intelligence, historically, have not appeared psychotic (usually) but have often appeared to be the highest, holiest, happiest, wisest, most loving of our species?

If the universe isn't stranger than we think at present, won't future times be rather dull?

If the universe isn't stranger than we think, how did we get so smart so fast? The universe of relativity, quantum, DNA, etc. is much stranger than anybody before 1900 *ever* thought . . .

If the universe perchance *is* stranger than we think, shouldn't we encourage creative and original thinking, instead of ridiculing and punishing it?

If putting humans in cages is not torture, how much suffering does constitute torture?

If the Terra II project doesn't turn you on, what is a worthwhile human activity?

What is more important than seeking immortality and trying to contact and/or become Higher Intelligences?

Is the Catholic Church more likely to provide immortality and Higher Intelligence than Terra II is? If not, why not?

Is Marxism more revolutionary than Terra II, or less?

Since Roosevelt lied about Pearl Harbor, Truman about his friends' stealing, Eisenhower about the U-2 spying planes, Kennedy about the Bay of Pigs, Johnson about Tonkin Gulf, and Nixon about everything, and since between them they probably ordered more people killed than Genghis Khan, what is the precise difference between government and criminal conspiracy?

When the shamans claimed (without polygraphs) that plants are sentient, was that just a lucky guess? Or coincidence?

Why did Crowley and Gurdjieff put coded references to Sirius in their books? Crowley never met Gurdjieff, incidentally; are these references to Sirius more coincidence?

If the theories suggested in this book are not plausible, what alternative theories can be proposed?

If there is no neurogenetic circuit or "collective unconscious" why are myth patterns the same all over the world?

If there is a neurogenetic circuit, containing the molecular memory of earthlife from the beginning, is this itself not a Higher Intelligence?

Is the pursuit of nuclear overkill, national pride, money, status, etc. more important than immortality and contacting/becoming Higher Intelligences?

Why do we spend so much on nuclear overkill etc. and so little on immortality and Higher Intelligence?

If Buddhism is more spiritually inspiring than Terra II, why don't we all become Buddhists? If there is any idea more spiritual, more hopeful, more inspiring than Terra II, why don't we do it? Why are we wasting time on idiocies like business and politics?

Virtually all contactees with Higher Intelligence (including even the arch-heretic Crowley) agree that one must love unconditionally to receive these transmissions; why then do we continue to blind ourselves with conditional love, with fear, with hostility, with hatred?

If the DNA code is the same in human, snake and tree, aren't fears of animals very absurd phobic imprints? Are not revulsions toward other members of our own species even more absurd phobias? Does it not look like much of our behavior is indeed robotic and mechanical?

Is not the attempt to free the nervous system of robot reflexes the real goal of all true psychology, all true religion?

If Timothy Leary, a conspicuously brave man, has cracked under the torture of the cage, and is willing to inform on friends, will the future not remember this as we remember the tortures of the Inquisition — that is, with both horror and disgusted nausea?

If puberty is a programmed neurogenetic metamorphoses, is it not likely that senescence and death are so programmed?

With current knowledge of DNA coding, is it not obvious that changing the death program is an inevitable next step?

If some of us are going to become Cosmic Immortals (Slot 15), isn't it time we started erasing all chauvinistic, racial, sexual, human, Earthian prejudices?

If the life-span of the individual is largely programmed by the DNA code, is the lifespan of the species still to be thought of as stochastic and random?

If the planetary life-script is programmed just like the individual life-script, following the same eight-circuit upward evolution, who are the programmers? If they are the Cabalistic and Gurdjieffian angels, who are the arch-angels?

Considering the obvious differences between the transmission recorded by such contactees as Buddha, Jesus, Lao-Tse, Joseph Smith, URANTIA, Leary, Crowley, Blavatsky et. al., is it not obvious that we have not yet attained high fidelity reception on the sixth circuit? Do not science and religion meet and become one when we start to seek such higher fidelity reception with all the discipline of science and all the humility of true religion?

I don't claim to have answers to *any* of these questions; but I think that asking them may be just possibly the most important task confronting humanity at this point in our evolution.

As Timothy said to me once, "The most important lesson in science is that you don't find anything until you start looking. And if you look hard enough, you're sure to find something amusing."

I'm looking forward to the funeral. The Dreaded Neurological Army (DNA), a local mime theatre group, promises to provide a proper chorus of mourners, and perhaps we shall all sing again those mysterious words of the Moody Blues which seem to change their meaning every year:

> Timothy Leary's dead —
> No, n-n-no
> He's outside, looking in.

The Starseed Signals
Interviews

The interviews to follow were produced during the Starseed Signals period, the first of which was intended for Playboy Magazine. Conducted by RAW during late '75 and early '76, The Lost Leary Interview was a rebuttal to Craig Vetter's exposé "Bring Me The Head Of Timothy Leary" that appeared in the September '75 issue of Playboy. RAW had previously served as an editor with Playboy from 1965–1971 along with his friend and Illuminatus! co-author Robert Shea, who was still with the magazine at the time and worked directly with RAW on editing the interview. For whatever reasons, Playboy ultimately decided to pull the plug on the piece and it never appeared in print.

Historian of Religion J. Christian Greer — during a fellowship at New York Public Library's Timothy Leary Archives — discovered an earlier draft of the interview. According to Greer:

Shea, in addition to a number of assistant editors, felt [the interview] was unsatisfactory. His primary problem with the first draft was Leary's evasiveness, and, to a lesser extent, Wilson's somewhat staid line of questioning.

Essentially, Shea wanted a hard hitting interview, and Leary seemed unwilling to drop his "interstellar intelligence agent" persona. With his usual aplomb, Wilson was able to walk the line between these conflicting demands and produced one of the most informative interviews of Leary's career.

The second interview, Leary Trades Drugs For Space Colonies, originally appeared a few months after Leary's prison release in the June 11th, 1976 edition of *The Berkley Barb* and serves as an appropriate bookend to The Lost Leary Interview.

– Notes by Adam Gorightly

The Lost Leary Interview

RAW: *How do you feel living with the reputation of a man who testified against his friends?*

Leary: Thanks for the laugh. I've never felt better. You must recall that I am a man of many ill-reputes. And many good ones too. You create your own reality—so dial the image you prefer. The kook left now shrieks that I'm a double agent. The year before I was a glorious martyr. In last year's movie I was a dissenter locked up because of insanity. The year before, Godfather of the Dope Mafia! As William Burroughs remarked, there are at least 23 Timothy Learys. The specific myth one accepts about me is a test of intelligence and sophistication. Simply that. So, I'm delighted with my many diverse reputations. They operate as a protective screen to protect me from fools. My signals attract exactly the people I want to communicate with— those who understand what is really happening on this planet.

RAW: *What reputation do you think you live with?*

Leary: In the reality which I currently share with my friends, I am an Evolutionary Agent whose task is to turn-on a species of domesticated primates in preparation for immediate Space Migration. It's the most amusing job on the planet. Now that N.A.S.A. Scientists have demonstrated that Space Migration can happen in 10 years, people are beginning to realize that the "Drop Out Movement" of the 60s was a loosening-up preparation for the big Take Off. It's time to Space Out literally! Don't you find that a more entertaining reputation?

RAW: *You are being a bit vague. Do you deny testifying against your friends?*

Leary: Emphatically. Despite the hysterical media rumors, the facts are that I have exposed, under oath, four very unfriendly Movement Lawyers who profited financially and politically from my imprisonment and subsequent escape. It was these lawyers who panicked the counterculture with planted stories that I was engaged in wholesale informing.

RAW: *When you contacted us, you complained that Bring Me the Head of Timothy Leary contained a number of errors . . .*

Leary: No, I didn't complain. I try never to complain. Why should I? Our team is winning. I contacted Playboy to correct inaccurate transmissions.

RAW: *Could you cite some of the inaccuracies?*

Leary: Gladly. Let's begin with the portrayal of Joanna Leary as a disloyal woman who squandered money collected to defend me. I refer to the title of your piece and to rumors that "Ram Dass refused to give Joanna $800 from one of the shows . . . and told her in hard terms . . . that she was sabotaging all their efforts to help Tim." That's a lie. The truth is that when I was dragged back to America in chains in 1973, I told Joanna to work with non-political people — scientists and open-minded successful people. And to avoid the kooks, nuts and freaks that have made me a profitable cause for the last decade. When Ram Dass (Richard Alpert) came to see me in prison, I told him politely that I neither wanted nor expected his help. Joanna's assignment was to detach herself from the self-appointed managers of the "Timothy Leary Industry." Naturally, they ganged up on Joanna. But that's what we wanted. Attacks from kook-left and the Freak Guru cliques can only propel us in the right direction.

RAW: *Joanna has been painted in lurid colors. Is she really, as Allen Ginsberg claims, an international sex provocateur and double agent?*

Leary: At least! Look at the stylish genes she wears. Joanna's father was Sir Cecil Harcourt-Smith, a Commander in the British Intelligence service. A rather original James Bond type. Her mother, Marysia, is an Ulam, one of the swiftest clans in Europe. Joanna's cousin, Stan Ulam, was co-inventor of the hydrogen bomb. Her cousin, Adam Ulam, is director of Harvard's Russian Institute. Her stepfather, the Hungarian-Frenchman Arpad Plesch, was one of the slickest free market financiers in Europe, a friend of Albert Einstein. We are dealing here with the genetics of relativity and high energy, so let's multiply the "double agent" estimate. Joanna is a spectacular fuse blowing performance: swift, constantly changing, comic, elegant, cunning, loyal, intensely intense.

RAW: *Is it true that you threw your ex-wife Rosemary out because she had taken a lover?*

Leary: No, that's another tabloid fantasy. Rosemary and I planned our separation maneuver with the care and precision of an Apollo-Soyuz team, for many months, with tender foresight and zodiac precision.

RAW: *In general, is your attitude toward women as jealous and possessive as this rumor implies?*

Leary: That question should have a date on it, since I keep changing. Sometimes, in the past, I have been unhappily jealous. Other times I have wounded the one I love by not being possessive enough. Freedom is my genetic compulsion and my goal remains the same: to let everybody be free, especially the ones I love.

RAW: *What is your attitude toward women?*

Leary: Again, let us define terms. In Exo-Psychology, I suggest that there are at least 48 different species which are now confusedly lumped together as homo sapiens. Each of these genetic models has a nervous system very different from the others. To make matters more interesting, 24 of these species are female and 24 male. A belief system of this sort leads one to be cheerfully and admiringly cautious about making male-female generalizations. Which of the 24 types of human female are we talking about when we generalize about woman? The safest generalization I will venture is that DNA has ingeniously designed the anatomical and neural equipment of men to be synergetically compatible with the female models. The sexual equation seems to be: one times one equals infinity. Thus, my attitude, defined astronautically as angle of approach, is magnetically attracted. Binary orbital.

RAW: *How do you treat the women you love?*

Leary: I have lived seventeen separate reincarnations in the last twenty years. This means entirely different lifestyles, professions, social roles, reputations, political scenarios. In each of these reincarnations my equal partner has been a woman. I cannot conceive of living without the electricity generated by this polarity. So how do I treat

Her? With everything I have. You understand that change, movement, relativity are the navigational rhythms of my life. At high altitudes and full velocities one's relationships become rather special.

The only person I know who moves with the acceleration range that I prefer is Joanna. We are Einsteinian relatives flying formation with sweet precision. Honest exchange of directional signals is crucial at this level.

RAW: *Do you think that people understand this rather spacey concept of mating?*

Leary: Sure. There are millions of young people who dig what a high altitude, full velocity relationship is. Don't underestimate your readers.

RAW: *Did Joanna smuggle acid to you in prison?*

Leary: Never. Joanna and I were watched with a thousand eyes during my incarceration. She was carefully searched before visits. She never brought any kind of dope to prison. What's really vicious about this allegation is that, if it were true, it would be a cruel example of a free person publicly informing on a prisoner still in custody and thereby adding more years to the prisoner's term. Eldridge Cleaver admitted doing something similar recently in Rolling Stone, boasting how he showed the Algerian police some acid to prove I was a bad guy. As an old San Quentin veteran, Cleaver knows exactly what that's called, and he also knows that he was lying. I had confiscated the acid from a visitor to Algiers and voluntarily given it to Cleaver.

RAW: *Did you really go under the code name "Charlie Thrush?"*

Leary: I was sent to Sandstone Federal Prison by a

police agent, who, against my wishes, had me booked under this weird name. It was a set-up. This agent, a flamboyant kook of the Liddy school, had previously threatened that if I displeased him in any way he'd put me in the mainline of a prison with the reputation of a snitch. That virtually amounted to a threat that he'd set me up to be murdered. He also leaked rumors to the media claiming that my life was in danger from the Weather Underground. This flake, who has since retired from law enforcement, would have loved Vetter's invention about my walking around Sandstone with a black bag over my head. I have not now nor have I ever had a black bag over my head, folks.

RAW: *Did you, as the article states, make a videotape in Chicago in which you denounced the Left, the counterculture and Gays, and said that the Federal Government was the only group that hadn't ripped you off?*

Leary: I did make a rather nervous tape on drug abuse (which DEA Director Barbels hated) in which I said that I had been royally screwed by the left. I then looked at the Agent uneasily interviewing me and said: "You aren't going to rip me off, are you?" I have never issued a condemnation of Gays or the counterculture. The Homosexual Brotherhood is one of the 24 conspiracies now operating on this planet. Live and let live. In prison, where one's life depends on one's mammalian alliances, my gang was always respectful of the gay-gangs which are, by the way, quite powerful in prison and without.

RAW: *What did you testify about in the San Francisco Grand Jury hearings?*

Leary: I described my 1970 escape from prison, my flight to North Africa, the censorship and suppression of my manuscripts by the abovementioned movement lawyers who controlled my affairs while I was in Algiers, and the various ways they ripped me off financially. I also described the cover-ups and subornations involved in my escape trial, in which I foolishly protected these lawyers. The Grand Jury was especially fascinated by the contracts I was induced to sign, which gave total control of my business affairs and publication outlets to the same lawyers. The importance of this information was psychological-sociological rather than tactical. The government is very interested in the techniques used by terrorist groups to intimidate, control, convert, exploit and manipulate those who are forced into dependence on them. The mind-washing, ego-stripping techniques used by the SLA, Manson, Weather Underground collectives and some of the kidnap-type religious groups are strikingly similar, as I point out in an article on brainwashing which OUI is publishing.

In March 1973, before my escape trial, I discussed the situation with the movement lawyers who had managed, produced and directed my getaway. By this time I had considerable experience in the business of information trading and undercover operations. I was a rather cynical veteran of some of the heaviest gang wars on the planet. I had lived and matched wits with several prison gangs from the Black Muslims to the Aryan Brotherhood, dozens of police and correctional heavies, the narcs on four continents, Gordon Liddy's Dutchess County goon-squads, the Weather Underground, the Black Panthers in Algeria, the FLN, Al Fatah, the blackmailer-gangster Hauchard in Switzerland, Afghani military police. I had learned a lot about the ethics and etiquette of militant underground groups in Algiers which was at that time the world center of exile movements. I told my ex-lawyers that I wasn't going to spend the rest of my life as an imprisoned martyr defending the cause of terrorists whose philosophy I opposed. I reminded them that Russian dissenters and FLN captives are only expected to remain silent for 24 hours. Please understand that I posed no legal threat to the Weather Underground people themselves, but only to the sports-car radical-chic lifestyle of these Movement lawyers.

RAW: *To be clear about this, these are the lawyers who represented you in 1969 and 1970, and arranged your escape, right?*

Leary: Right. Let us not forget that, because of their bungling, I ended up facing life imprisonment for less than one-half ounce of marijuana. Some lawyers! As a result, I had no chance for freedom except to escape and to let them use me for their political and financial purposes. All four of these lawyers are double agents, in the sense that, on one hand, they consistently encourage and join in criminal acts and, on the other hand, they profit financially and publicity-wise by defending those whom they incite to crime. In addition, at least one and probably two of these men are triple agents. I mean specifically that they work with the government.

RAW: *Wait a minute. You're actually saying that two of the people who organized the campaign to panic the counterculture with the story that you've engaged in wholesale informing against everybody who ever knew you, are themselves long-time informers?*

Leary: Precisely. Let me emphasize that this is not unusual. It is my experience that at least one out of every three Movement lawyers is an informer for some government intelligence service. The code of "stonewalling" (or "omerta" as the mafia calls it) is apparently only for clients and underlings; the top dog professionals consistently trade information and make deals. All this is standard mammalian politics and I refuse to be angry about it. There are no morals in politics. I am not complaining about people trying to destroy my credibility. It just means that I have to make my own signal stronger and clearer and funnier. That's a challenge I enjoy.

RAW: *Why didn't this San Francisco grand jury indict anybody? Didn't they believe your testimony?*

Leary: After the grand jury heard all the witnesses and examined all the evidence, the prosecutor himself recommended that they not indict, for technical legal reasons. The grand jury disagreed and voted 18-to-1 in favor of indictment. The prosecutor, who was amused by this, had to explain to them again why it was best not to indict, and then they voted 12-to-7 not to indict. Now, why did they originally go against the government's wishes? Because they believed the witnesses, including me, and they were angered by other testimony, not mine, showing threats against witnesses and attempts to suborn perjury. Also, they were offended by the suspected lawyers use of the local press to leak closed proceedings and stack the cards in advance with rigged stories. Let me emphasize that the government prosecutors, like myself, were not obsessed with a desire to see these shady lawyers in jail. I just wanted to establish the truth about how Movement lawyers rip off clients and profit from the "Outlaw Industry." I also hoped they would be disbarred and returned to an honest way of life.

RAW: Are you willing to make a firm prediction that nobody will go to jail because of your testimony?

Leary: Flatfootedly and dogmatically, yes. Nobody has

and nobody will go to prison or face criminal charges on the basis of information I have given.

RAW: *What about your former lawyer, George Chula? Joanna set him up for a drug bust. He was charged with selling dope and did 45 days, didn't he?*
Leary: No. George Chula did a few weekends in jail for furnishing Joanna with drugs.

RAW: *Do you approve of the way Joanna set up George Chula?*
Leary: Absolutely! According to the convict code, any lawyer who comes on to a prisoner's wife deserves to get turned in.

RAW: *Aside from the lawyers mentioned earlier, haven't you also testified extensively against the vast drug conspiracy known as the Brotherhood of Eternal Love?*
Leary: Nope. There is no such vast conspiracy. And I have not testified nor given information about any drug dealers.

RAW: *Have you given information about Patty Hearst and the SLA as some underground press articles have claimed?*
Leary: No. I have no knowledge about these matters. The underground thrives on wild paranoia.

RAW: *And you never testified against Weather Underground at all?*
Leary: Correct. I had no knowledge about anything that the Weather Underground could be prosecuted for. And the San Francisco Grand Jury did not involve the Weather Underground. All those rumors are planted. Let me add

specifically for publication that I have solid reasons to believe that if the Weather Underground were to surface and agree to abide by the non-violent rules of American politics not one of them would go to prison. I cannot name my authorities for this, but the Weather Underground can check it out easily. They would merely have to find an honest lawyer who believes in the American legal system to negotiate for them. The war is over.

RAW: *How do you feel now about the militant statements you made at the time of your escape?*

Leary: I regret those rhetorical excesses. In my anger at my imprisonment and my gratitude to the Weather Underground for bussing me away, I endorsed their tactics. I was simply stupid and I admit it. Bombing just strengthens right-wing paranoia.

RAW: *Isn't your position as a convict in a federal prison a somewhat distorting factor, creating a certain amount of caution or evasion on your part? Might you not tell things a bit differently when you get out? Specifically, your statements about the U.S. Government are not unlike your statements about Cleaver when he was holding you prisoner.*

Leary: If this question implies that I'll repudiate the government when I'm no longer a captive, you are wrong. The American government is the most powerful gang on the planet and at the same time it allows more freedom to the non-rich than any other non-socialist country. (The ruling bureaucrats can pretty much do what they please in all socialist countries.) Therefore, I have every intention in the foreseeable future of remaining on good terms with the American government.

RAW: *Would you cooperate with a Communist or Fascist government as you are now cooperating with the U.S. government?*

Leary: Absolutely not. I cooperate with the U.S. government because it's the strongest gang that has offered to protect my freedom. Freedom is what my work is all about. Communists, Nazis, fascists, Weather Underground collectives and doctrinaire factions are gangs inimical to scientific and personal liberty.

RAW: *And you don't find it inconsistent to be cooperating with the government which imprisoned you and actually becoming friends with, of all people, FBI agents?*

Leary: Not at all. For the first 49 years of my life I was unwaveringly Catholic Establishment. And I still am now. In Springfield, Massachusetts, where I grew up, cops were red-faced Irishmen, genial civil servants like postmen, whom you remembered with gratuities at Christmas. Congressman, later Governor, Foster Furcolo was a close family friend. The sister of the Chief of Detectives was my mother's secretary. Senator David Walsh was a bosom buddy of my uncle, Monsignor Kavanagh. Larry O'Brien, before he became Postmaster General and Chairman of the Democratic Party, was a close friend of my Uncle, Phil Shea, and I still remember him telling me in glowing terms about his protege, a young Celtic congressman named John Kennedy who was planning to run for the Senate against Cabot Lodge.

With this Irish establishment background, when the cops began raiding my house at Millbrook in 1965, I was outraged at the Protestant impertinence. I naively thought I could crack the knuckles of a few kooky, anti-intellectual lawmen like G. Gordon Liddy, and they would go away. You must remember that when John Kennedy was alive, it was still possible for a dissenting scientist or philosopher to have an affectionate and satirical dialogue with the government. I gravely misjudged the political situation when LBJ took power. I have paid heavily for that mistake.

RAW: *When do you hope to be out of prison?*
Leary: I expect to be out long before this interview is published.

RAW: *Aside from exposing those lawyers, what have you done to get out?*
Leary: If your question implies that I have been given a break for establishing detente with the American government, let's look at the record, as Casey Stengel would say. I started serving my Federal prison term on March 2, 1970. As of February 6, 1976, I had officially served 43 months for the Betty Ford crime of driving a car, not my own, in which my daughter had one half ounce of marijuana. Thirty-two months of this time were spent in state prison. And I've done the toughest time. Seven months in Folsom, a filthy maximum prison, another 19 months in solitary confinement — the hole — and the last six months in a sadistic Federal detention center where I breathed fresh air two hours a month. Both the state and federal laws under which I was sentenced were subsequently repealed. If I had fought the government on appeals, I would have been out long before now. So what have I done to get out? Over 1300 days and nights of the hardest time the American prison system can impose.

RAW: *Are you concerned that thousands of young people who once looked to you as a leader and guide now feel that you have betrayed them?*

Leary: No, not at all. The young better learn fast that most leaders betray followers and the ones who don't are dangerously inflexible. And any would-be follower dumb enough to believe slanted articles about me couldn't decode my signals anyway. This is a fake issue. I may be a political prisoner, but I'm not a political leader. I do believe, however, that thousands of intelligent people, young and old, who follow my skywriting are smiling insightfully or else hopefully reserving judgement. Sophisticated people in London, Rio, Caracas, Rome, Zurich, Paris, Madrid, Rabat, Cairo – where my books are more widely circulated than in America – are not concerned with provincial San Francisco gossip about me. They are more interested in practical neuropolitical plans for space migration. I deliberately address my signal to the conscious elite who have mastered the neurology of hedonism, transmitted in the sixties, and are ready for the next trip.

RAW: *Would you describe your current politics more fully?*

Leary: I have no fixed political beliefs. Politics is a primitive mammalian game and the only honest way to discuss politics is on all fours, pawing the ground for territorial, barnyard dominance. The American public is rapidly coming to understand that politicians do not have any solutions to the real challenges we face. Of course the only way to survive on a primitive planet is to keep your mammalian circuits open and to that end I have allied myself at various times with various local gangs. I always choose the faction that, at that moment, promises to leave me and other non-political people alone. I was shocked to discover that leftist leaders are busier than K.G. Bees trying to mind other people's business. Politics is endless push-pull for power — very similar to pro-football except that the latter is played with cleaner rules. When I played out my option with the San Francisco Reds I signed up with the American League. When I join a team I play a loyal game and I don't jump teams without warning. But I don't confuse politics with the important issues.

RAW: *What are the important issues?*

Leary: Personal evolution towards Higher Intelligence. Metamorphosis to the next level. That's why the particular role I play has to be judged very critically by society, and by the whole human species. My game is genetic pool; the sport of mutation. The human species has every right to test, challenge and oppose my mutational suggestions. Weak and badly designed mutants will fail these tests and that is as it should be. Think of the universe as a multiple-choice intelligence test, and you'll get our perspective.

RAW: *After being caged in 29 separate prisons, do you regard incarceration as one of the tests?*

Leary: Yes, prison is a neurological training ground. Like Solzhenitsyn, I treasure my prison experiences. Every mutant has to master this yoga. I learned more about myself and terrestrial affairs in prison than I learned in any university. Of course, I don't advocate it for everyone (any more than I recommended acid for everyone). But for the strong person with evolutionary aspirations prison is invaluable training — wasted unfortunately on all but a few zeks. In prison there are no cop-outs or cover-ups. There's no hiding and no secrets. Everything is immediate and upfront. One false move and you're dead. Prison, as Solzhenitsyn says, is an experimental laboratory for understanding politics.

You have to relate accurately to gangs in prison, in order to survive. You have to make muscle commitments and live up to them. You have to come to terms with the existence and precise nature of the gangs. And they are not lightweight. Mexican Mafia, Sicilian Mafia, Nazis, Black militants, Black Moslems, sexual cliques, Aryan Brotherhoods. You have to respect them and respect yourself. If you are careless you are going to be pushed around or destroyed. Same thing on the outside. The turf is run by the strongest gangs, the ones with the most guns. The American government is the gang which can best protect our aspirations right now. So it's Our Gang.

RAW: *The next trip, according to your latest writings, is into Space. How will Space Migration help the rest of the human race?*

Leary: StarSeed is a proposal for launching 500 migratory space ships containing 2,500,000 post-terrestrial human beings. These Space Colonists will have undergone processes vastly increasing their life expectancy and their intelligence. Help the human race? How do the butterflies who burst from the cocoon benefit earthbound caterpillars. As a by-product, space migration will dramatically improve the lot of the stay-at-homes. The present human malaise is neurogenetic. We have exhausted our supply of meaning. Within twenty years earthlings will be able to look up in the sky and thrill to the thought that human seeds (not acrobatic astronauts, but families) have left the womb planet for good. For the good of the species. You know what the four very wise caterpillars said about the butterfly?

RAW: *All right. What did the four very wise caterpillars say about the butterfly?*

Leary: The practical caterpillar said, "They'll never get me up in one of those." The conservative caterpillar said, "It's illegal, dangerous and immoral." The liberal caterpillar said, "They should use the energy to fight the war against poverty, racism and pollution." The religious caterpillar said, "If God intended us to fly he would have given us wings."

RAW: *How do you plan to organize and finance the Starseed project?*

Leary: Each migratory ship will be sponsored by a local community and inhabited by a local crew which selects itself, trains its members and organizes the intellectual, technical and financial skills to leave the planet. The project is a self-supporting, free-enterprise game which does not involve tax subsidy or governmental aid. It is a profitmaking cooperative owned by individual shareholders who can sell their shares at any time before migration. Each local company raises the funds for a residential model community and its own migratory ship. The cost of each local ship, assuming mass production, will be around one billion dollars. This sum will be raised over a ten year period by means of sale of shares, research contracts, sale and lease of media rights, manufacture and sale of space-related equipment and contracts and options for post-migration services such as lunar mining or solar energy.

RAW: *Who has shown the most interest in space migration so far?*

Leary: Certainly over two-thirds of the young are ready to migrate. Gerard O'Neill of Princeton has been receiving enthusiastic responses to his plans for immediate space colonization. Morris Udall, Herman Kahn, the

"Whole Earth" people have endorsed the concept. Every metamorphic idea, however, in its practical application depends upon an alliance between the visionaries and the aristocracy. The ideas of increased intelligence, longevity and space migration have been welcomed by a group of young American-European trained Arabs who may well be the best endowed people on the planet — in that they have hundreds of millions of dollars available and few social constraints and chauvinist hang-ups. These alert young Arabs have experienced the material and sensory pleasures of terrestrial life and are restlessly looking for more. The minor border skirmishes of the Middle East should not distract us from seeing the tremendous free energies bubbling out of that historic area. We have a standing invitation: The day I walk out of prison a jet will be sent to fly us to the Mediterranean to confer about space migration plans. The Catholic Church, traditionally an extraterrestrial transfer agency, is also ready to endorse Space Migration. The Vatican's wisdom in opposing population restriction begins to make more sense now that we are no longer restricted to this crowded planet.

RAW: *What do you see as the major obstacle to space migration?*

Leary: The greatest threat to the evolutionary process these days is the ecology movement's attempt to legislate morality and limit growth. Naderism is the ultimate travesty of the moralistic mind interfering with natural processes.

RAW: *Don't you think man's exploitation of nature needs to be controlled?*

Leary: Certainly. But this is the time to confront socialists and control-lobbyists with some shocking truths. The basic ecological solution for any overcrowded and unhappy species is mutation-migration. This tiny spaceship planet can no longer hold us. Rational, socialistic programs to reduce population, restrict growth, think small, lower expectations, limit free expansion and return to the paleolithic to stalk the wild asparagus are genocidal. It is the essence of every form of life to multiply, joyously, confidently. Conserve energy? No way! There has never been an example of a surviving evolving species that didn't use every energy available to it. Seen from the perspective of the 3.5 billion year old DNA intelligence which wants to get herself off the planet, strip mining and oil spills are transient growing twinges.

RAW: *Many people seem uninterested in or downright hostile to the search for immortality. Why, do you suppose?*

Leary: The Judeo-Calvanist philosophy is death-oriented. Larval humans are also very bored most of the time, and they can only conceive more life as meaning more suffering. But we see longevity not as an end in itself but as a tool for extraterrestrial migration and exploration. Space Migration, immortalism and increasing intelligence through Brain Change are a package; any one of the three is not enough by itself.

RAW: *How do you propose we go about increasing intelligence?*

Leary: This is the primary aim of migration, to evolve to a higher state of intelligence. In my book, Exo-Psychology, I suggest that as soon as human beings begin to live in space, adapt to zero gravity, become exposed to more direct radiation, and escape from the magnetic cocoon of the earth, it is probable that new circuits of the nervous system will kick into operation, circuits that have only dimly appeared hitherto in the explorations of yogic adepts, shamans and experts in the constructive use of neurotransmitter chemicals. The baby leaving the womb is exposed to new, more intense stimuli which trigger off new and more complex reactions. Similarly, I believe, new circuits will open in our nervous systems when we leave the womb-planet. "We may be the first higher intelligence we shall meet in space," said the tadpole to the caterpillar.

RAW: *Do you have any reason to believe in the existence of higher intelligences elsewhere in the universe other than the mathematical odds that we are neither the highest nor the lowest life forms in the galaxy?*

Leary: We believe that DNA is itself a higher intelligence which designs and builds nervous systems and bodies for its survival, locomotion and reproduction. Sir Francis Crick, co-discoverer of the DNA helix, theorizes that DNA is self-seeded from other solar systems, and that makes sense to us. Any physicist will tell you that nonlocal explanations are more basic than local explanations. Life is probably a basic part of the cosmic script, seeded from system to system in the form of nucleotide templates (such as the nucleotides found on the Orgueil meteorite in 1965)—and then evolving larval on the wombplanet until it is born in the galactic sense by being ejected off the nursery planet and entering into the interstellar dialectic.

As Nobel geneticist Herbert Muller has said, we are all robots created by DNA to make more DNA. More specifically, to locomote, survive, reproduce and evolve by variation and self-selection to higher and higher intelligence for eventual participation in the real cosmic drama.

RAW: *What do you think of Erich von Däniken and*

others who claim that there has already been contact with extraterrestrial higher intelligences and this provoked all the legends of gods and angels?

Leary: I think these are very low-level speculations. They only lead to consumer passivity, waiting for the space-gods to come back. I want to know what we can start doing today to contact higher intelligences. If there's any interstellar whooping-up being done, I don't want to read about others doing it: I want to be one of the ones doing it. Also, I prefer Saul Paul Sirag's theory based on Godel's mathematics, that we ourselves, in the future, will control time, travel backward, design the DNA code, and do all the things von Däniken attributes to extraterrestrials.

RAW: *In a film you made at Folsom, you said Kahoutek was a signal from higher intelligences to indicate that it was time to mutate. Only a handful of people actually saw the comet. What kind of signal was that?*

Leary: What can I say? It was an out-a-sight comet!

RAW: *What guarantee is there that you, with your philosophy of constant metamorphosis, might not drop out of Starseed some day and leave your allies holding the bag?*

Leary: Starseed is a company of shareholders, cooperatively managed. I or anyone else can sell our shares at any time—and probably for a healthy profit— in that longevity research and space migration certainly have a good market future. It would be a nifty bag to hold. But let's address the personal implication of your question. Is there any guarantee that I won't change, drop out and take off to another frequency? Hell, no. There is no guarantee. The evolutionary process — my guru — offers no guarantees for those who remain static. In the 1960s I repeatedly warned would-be disciples that I'd drop neurotransmitter drugs in a second if a faster moving, higher energy trip came along. And I'll drop space migration in a flash if a higher velocity, more relativistic game is introduced. If Uri Geller is right, and he shows us how to teleport, who needs a slow moving space ship? But I am a practical scientist and I use tools that are here in tangible form. And the technology of space migration, longevity and increased intelligence is now at hand.

RAW: *Some people would say that these ideas— migration off the planet, brain-change, even longevity— have been around for a long time. What is your unique contribution to making them happen?*

Leary: My unique contribution is neurological and neuropolitical: twenty years of research on self-directed brain change for higher intelligence. All the dead weight holding back progress — not just in longevity, space migration and higher intelligence, but in technology and evolution generally—is due to static repetitious circuits in the brain, robot reflexes. I am a neurogenetic test pilot. Changing neural circuits is my profession. The situation is similar to that of consciousness research in the 1960s. For centuries some occult groups and alchemists knew that consciousness could be expanded by means of yogic techniques and neurochemicals. In 1960 there were at least 50 of the world's most perceptive minds who knew that certain drugs could bleach the mind and allow reprogramming of the brain. My contribution was to show, in several books and scores of scientific papers, how we could ride the brain wave most skillfully and not be drowned in it.

RAW: *Is there any research supporting your belief that*

IQ can be markedly increased?

Leary: Certainly. Look under "intelligence" in the index of any psychological journal and you'll be surprised at how much is already known. However, IQ itself is a Newtonian and linear concept and when I talk of intelligence I mean something more Einsteinian. Intelligence can be more than doubled, it can be multiplied into many new dimensions. Let me give one close-to-home example. Starting around 1960, millions of Americans suddenly discovered the neurosomatic circuits of the nervous system. They learned that the body was wired up with dozens of neural centers which could provide erotic pleasure. A new form of consciousness — sensory-hedonic — was suddenly available. A new dimension of intelligence then developed. Let us call this sensory intelligence. We then witnessed the flowering of new skills as people realized that erotic reward depended on disciplined learning, sensory know-how. The many different sensory schools — yoga, massage, the fancy forms of fucking, the planned, disciplined use of scents, oils, textures, foods, music, film—not to ignore the erotic dimensions of the many mind-altering drugs. The success of *Playboy* resulted from this activating of a new circuit of consciousness-intelligence. *Playboy* can be seen as a very effective neurological journal, a how-to-educate-the-sensory-circuit-of-your-brain text book.

RAW: *And do you have a final word for Playboy readers?*

Leary: Not final. Nothing is final.

RAW: *Well, a closing thought, then?*

A. Okay. My thought for today: let the meek inherit the earth. The wise and the strong move on. As always.

Leary Trades Drugs
for Space Colonies

Timothy Leary, former Harvard professor, LSD guru and federal prisoner, is one of the most controversial figures to emerge from the halcyon days of the Sixties. Considered a prophet by some and an informer by others, the 56-year old author is reportedly living today in seclusion in New Mexico's splendid Sangre de Cristo Mountains following his recent prison parole.

In the following interview, Leary answers critics, recalls prison experiences and talks about his space colonization ideas.

To provide an illuminating view of a man the government has long held in the shadows, the Barb also talked to former Black Panther Party leader Eldridge Cleaver, as well as students and leftist critics, about their impressions of the man who sought to turn on the world.

– Robert Anton Wilson

RAW: *How does it feel to be out of prison after six years?*

Leary: Beautiful. I'm on top of the world and getting higher every minute.

RAW: *You always seemed that way, even in prison. How do you stay so high all the time?*

Leary: I take it as the natural state and I'm somewhat puzzled at how other people can manage to be down so much of their lives. Don't you think it's easier to be high than to be low?

RAW: *Most people don't think they have any choice in the matter.*

Leary: But they do. That was the first scientific contribution we made in our research on neurotransmitter drugs in the early 1960s — the discovery that we can learn to use our brains in an efficient, ecstatic, intelligent manner. I use my nervous system for fun and profit. If others use their neurons for suffering and misery, it's simply because they've never learned to dial and focus the controls.

RAW: *Since some people still think you're an informer, isn't it undiplomatic to speak so glowingly about your own happiness? Both the right and the left would be more likely to forgive you if you said you'd suffered abominably in prison and learned the error of your ways. Why do you always refuse to suffer?*

Leary: In my line of work, which is self-induced brain change, every minute and every human encounter are tremendously exciting adventures. I simply don't have time to suffer. As for the legends about my snitching on all my old friends, and the massive arrests that would happen, that was all planted in the media by persons who wanted to discredit me. Some of the false stories were planted by federal agents and some by opportunistic exploiters who had nightmares about what might be revealed if I really started singing.

This is perfectly normal mammalian politics and all

right with me. I have never been concerned with gossip, public image or winning the approval of professional moralists. American morale and intelligence are so low at this time that anyone who is universally popular must be doing something dumb.

RAW: *Then you deny that you've testified against your friends?*

Leary: I did not testify against friends. I didn't testify against what the press called "the vast drug conspiracy known as the Brotherhood of Eternal Love," since that was a myth that never existed. I didn't testify in any manner that would lead to indictments against the Weather Underground. When the full details of my actual testimony are revealed, the Weather Underground might even be grateful to me.

RAW: *Some people can't understand why you cooperated at all with the government which had imprisoned you for so long. Why didn't you just stonewall it?*

Leary: I have always tried to cooperate and communicate with the government and with everybody who fears my ideas. Since 1965, I have repeatedly said that I'm glad they wiretap my phones. I want them to know what I'm doing and thinking. I believe all stupidity comes from jamming communications.

RAW: *Would you explain that in more detail? Most people these days are trying to hide from the government's snoopers . . .*

Leary: Concealing the truth leads to paranoia and confusion all around. The first professional controversy I was involved in, back in the 1950s, concerned my insistence that the scientific ethic required psychiatrists and psychologists to be honest with their patients. To let them see their records, for instance. Never to lie to them. This did not go over well, I must say, and some of the attacks on me then were even worse than the attacks during the LSD hysteria of the 1960s. My position has always been that science, intelligence and sanity itself depend on accuracy-of-signal. Secrets destroy human trust and ruin social relationships.

RAW: *Then you don't believe in the National Security philosophy — that power comes from hoarding secrets?*

Leary: Absolutely not. If the American government had made known to the Russian government everything they were thinking and doing in the 1940s and 50s and 60s, we'd have more real security now, not less. Many of the dangerous lurches in American foreign policy happened because the men in Washington misjudged how much the Russians really knew about us. Secrets are the Original Sin, the fig leaf in the Garden of Eden. The cause of shame and neurosis.

Liberals are entirely wrong in wanting to pass laws against wiretapping. Instead, let everybody wiretap everybody else! The government, above all, should be under constant surveillance. Government officials are the last people, the very last, to ever have an excuse for hiding things from the people they claim to represent.

RAW: *Some people will say you're rationalizing — that you made a deal with the Feds to get preferential treatment in prison and a quicker release. How would you answer them?*

Leary: First, I'd suggest that they stop believing loose rumors and start thinking for themselves. Second, I'd ask — what preferential treatment? What quicker release? Look at the record. Any lawyer will confirm that I served four times the current maximum for my "crime" — is that preferential?

And it wasn't easy time. It was some of the hardest time the American prison system provides. The hole at Folsom. Two years in solitary. In the last year, in San Diego, I only inhaled fresh air and saw the sun once a month. Finally, whatever happened to the "massive arrests" that were supposed to happen in 1973 and 1974 and 1975? The fact is that nobody has been arrested because of me and nobody ever will be.

RAW: *What about your recent criticisms of the left? Is Eldridge Cleaver right in saying you think the left ripped you off?*

Leary: I am too busy with space migration and other exciting, creative work to waste my energy harboring resentments against the left, the right or anybody else. I don't take politics seriously—it's a mammalian game that should be played on all fours, barking and pawing the ground. I'm interested in more important issues.

RAW: *Such as?*

Leary: Evolution toward Higher Intelligence. That's my game, and this is why the role I play has to be judged very critically by society. I play neurogenetic pool — the game of mutation. The species has every right to test, to challenge, to oppose a mutation. Every way, all-out, no holds barred.

Twenty-nine prisons in six years was part of the test I had to pass; that's why I have no resentments. My involvement with double agents of right and left, and triple agents exploiting both sides for personal profit, was another test. Now I'm finished with all those vertebrate territorial games, and looking upward to the stars.

RAW: *Do you have any political interests at all?*

Leary: Well, yes . . . I'd like to see somebody run for President on a platform of space migration, higher intelligence and life extension. Specifically, I think we should start an all out crash program, similar to the atomic project of the 1940s, to double the national IQ, triple the lifespan, and build the first O'Neill space cities, all within a decade. This is more worthwhile than spending 100 million a year on mammalian territorial defense and the country would boom with a spirit like Renaissance Italy or Elizabethan England.

What could the right wing say? That we should spend the money on weapons? If intelligence doubles, our technology would make us invulnerable, so that answers them. What could the left wing say? That we should spend the money eradicating poverty in the ghettoes? People with a tripled lifespan and doubled intelligence will get themselves out of the ghettoes.

RAW: *In your unpublished book, The Game of Life, you say that we can learn more from science fiction than from the Buddhist and Hindu scriptures. Were you serious when you wrote that, or just being provocative?*

Leary: I'm always being provocative. To provoke new thoughts in one's contemporaries is elementary evolutionary courtesy. The Oriental forms of brain science are historically very important and certainly nobody who wants to understand the nervous system can avoid a basic study of those traditions. I spent nearly a decade mastering them.

But to me, and to those who have kept moving, those

traditions are outmoded now. I want to personally apologize to anyone who has been led into the Hindu trap because at one time I was using that model. My whole philosophy is based on metamorphoses, which is the law of evolution. We should all keep moving from rock to rock, from habitat to habitat, from model to model, from planet to planet. The fact that we were once using Oriental models to describe higher brain function doesn't mean we have to be stuck on that rock forever. The search for a Perfect Master is only recommended if your goal is to become a Perfect Slave. Sci-Fi has much more exciting models than anything in the Vedas.

RAW: *Some people complain that you change so fast they never know where you're at. How would you answer that?*

Leary: The DNA signal is that the signal we should have learned from the last decade is that life on this planet is changing, changing, changing. For instance, all the men responsible for putting me in prison are out of the government now; most of them are in prison themselves. You must understand that so-called "future shock" is actually present shock. That is, the present is the "future" of the nervous system. In general, the nervous system stops taking new imprints at adolescence. Nixon's nervous system, for instance, saw the 1960s and even the 1970s through a bubble of 1920s imprints, which was when his nervous system evidently stopped evolving.

RAW: *What do you think will be the ultimate outcome of the LSD controversy?*

Leary: I'm no longer very interested in the larval terrestrial politics of drugs. As a guess, it always takes a generation for a new breakthrough to be accepted. That's because the present is always seen through a nervous system imprinted in the past. It takes a generation for young nervous systems to mature and use new knowledge. When the young Russian neuro-psychologists start curing everything in sight with LSD and similar neurotransmitters, scientific research will be allowed in this country again.

RAW: *Have you also changed your famous slogan 'Turn On, Tune In, Drop Out?"*

Leary: Certainly. That was never understood very well anyway. As I explained it in *The Politics of Ecstasy* (1968), it meant: Turn On to the next level of consciousness and intelligence above you, Tune In to the signal there and use it, then Drop Out of that model, leave that game behind, and Turn On again to the next level up. Don't blame me if the newspapers distorted that. Reporters are incapable of getting a metaphor right, as Mailer has noted.

My new slogan is S.M.I.²L.E. — Space Migration plus Intelligence Increase plus Life Extension. Building O'Neill's space cities, doubling IQ and tripling lifespan are just the first steps, to be accomplished in the next decade or two. After that, we can start aiming for starflight and immortality.

RAW: *One thing that hasn't changed is your optimism.*

Leary: I am often accused of being an irrepressible optimist. My answer is that we've been hemmed-in by repressed pessimists for too long.

RAW: *What else do you see in the future, besides space migration, intelligence increase and life extension?*

Leary: Grassroots decentralism and libertarianism will increase. Mind-your-own-business is the politics of the future. Racism and sexism will disappear. The world will become increasingly scientific in essence and science fiction in flavor. Due to life-extension research, I expect to live long enough to leave the solar system and participate in the interstellar age.

RAW: *Do you have any concluding thought for Barb readers?*

Leary: Yes. As Casey Stengel once said, most men my age are dead already.

The RAW/Greg Hill Letters

The Discordian Archives included the following seven letters between Robert Anton Wilson and Discordian founder Greg Hill that were written during the time when RAW was trying to get the *The Starseed Signals* accepted by a publisher. Each letter is followed by a transcription.

2035 Channing Way
Bezerkley, Cal 94704
Oct 30, 1974 e.v.

Dear Greg,

Do what thou wilt shall be the whole of the law.

All hail Discordia. Chaos abounds. This morning Arlen and I were
proofreading The Witch's Trine, newsletter of the New Reformed
Orthodox Order of the Golden Dawn (of which we are now White Cord
members.) Meanwhile, I went to ye olde post office to mail my
latest column to the Realist. (I'm doing a new column for Realist,
called "Operating Manual for the Human Head.")

I have written a book, a whole fucking BOOK, in two weeks again.
This is called THE STARSEED SIGNALS/LINK BETWEEN WORLDS and deals
with astro-telpathic research by Doc Leary and myself and 3
others. Meanwhile, my agent calls and sez Crown is innarested
in my Crowley book, of which they have 119 pages, but wants to
see 100 pages more before making up their minds. Well, I have
100 pages more (150 pages more, actually) but in faded type,
so I've started re-typing the more faded pages before mailing
it off. Xeroxing both the Crowley and the Leary ms. will cost
$40 which I ain't got, so I'm calling all friends in the Bay
Area to see how much they can do on office xe xeroxes without
getting caught and Reamed Out by management. Busy busy busy...

Also I have to get back to San Fran PHOENIX by Monday with more
reviews (I edit the book page there now) and I've promised GNOSTIC A
a 20page summary of my 6 hours of lectures delivered at the
Aquarian Festival in September and haven't even STARTED on that

and I don't know how the Leary book will end, except that Joanna
is now definitely proven to have been a narc for at least one year
and is pregnant by another narc, Dennis Martino, who has double-
crossed the narcs for Leary last year, and is now double-crossing
Leary for the narcs, and

it's all very interesting, as Gert Stein said; but it hexplains
per'aps why I haven't been quite as up-to-date with correspondence
as I used to was...

My magick class is most amusing, finance-wise. One week I was
paid $16 plus two lids plus a hit of clear-light. Other weeks I
average $12. But the class is MOVING and we raise the cone of
power quite easily together now and who knows where it will end...

Llewellyn is publishing a book of essays by me, PROMETHEUS RISING,
sometime next year.

Playboy Press is bringing out SEX'N'DRUGS in paperback in January.

I'm still on welfare, butxx not for long. (We were off Welfare
for four months, but then relapsed again. Our chief source of
income, a mag called VENUS, went bankrupt.)

Leary and I think we're communicating with higher minds in other parts of the galaxy. No shit. You think we're crazy?

SEX'N'DRUGS is also coming out in England next year.

Thos. Crowell has an outline of a book on Immortality research by me, but hasn't responded yet. My agent is hopeful, but agents are always hopeful. Meeting the chief immortality researchers has been a gas. The conservatives among them expect the breakthrough by 1980; the optimists expect it next year...

Oh, yes, if you haven't heard, Leary is planning to abandon Earth. Literally. He's organizing a 5000-person starship to seek our parents (the ones who planted the DNA here 3½ billion years ago) and ask them "what's the Next Step in evolution," or tell them, "Look what we've done in only 3½ billion years, found our way home," or join them in their Major Project, whatever that is (Tim thinks it has to do with building Black Holes and getting out of space-time into Eternity...)

Grady McMurty (Caliph Hymenaeos Alpha) of the O.T.O. has become a good friend and opened his library of Crowleyana to me.

NROOGD (see last page) is the largest witch society in Northern California; Arlen and I have been members for about a year.

I met the chief Gardnerian witches of USA (Lady Theos and Phoenix) at the Aquarian Fest in Minneapolis and developed a warm relationship. Phoenix gave me certificates making me 10-degree Ipsissimus Maximus in the Ordo Templi Celatus and a voodoo priest in Sociedad Magicko de Chango; I made him a Pope in turn.

Parsifal, the Sufi clown, is now in Jerusalem, running a home for Jewish and Arab war orphans. He got a vision telling him to do that.

Leary and I were collaborating on a book about cosmic evolution, called PERIODIC TABLE OF ENERGY, when he disappeared. None of his friends has been able to communicate with him for four months, while the rumors of finking circulate and circulate...

Before I start packing up the Discordian anarchives to mail 'em, etc., why don't you consider coming back out here where you are loved and badly missed. Doc Newport sez you can live with him until you find a job, etc. (He's in my magick class these days. Very talented. Astral projecting like mad.) Please come. Do not remain in sneers amid the alien scorn, but turn again to Zion, etc

Is Aleister Crowley really dead, really dead?
Did he do all the dreadful things they said, things they said?
Is he only dust beneath the sod, 'neath the sod,
Or was Aleister Crowley really God, really God?
                    --theme song of the Great Wild Beast Furtherment
                                                        Society

2035 Channing (very Illuminized Erisian number) has Great WB Furth
Society, Discordian Society, four witches, three druids, Aquarian
Anti-Defamation League (witches' B'Nai B'rith sort-of) and a
pair of Xtian Scientists who keep sticking their propperganda
under our doors in the mornings.

I astrally projected from California to Arizona a few months ago,
saw what was really happening (as confirmed by the folks I visited)
and put a cone of protection on them, driving away cops who were
about to hassle them. Really. Witnesses confirm. Magick keeps
opening me and opening me and opening me...

Everybody I know these days has a Plan to save the planet. Why
not? Optimism is a more interesting trip than pessimism. My own
Plan (or one of them) is enclosed -- EACH ONE TEACH ONE.

The people at the Rio Nido house were supposed to forward mail, but
never did. Just threw it all out, I gather. They are Manson types
and feelthy. The kind who give Counter Kulch a bad name. That's
why your letters there were never answered. You never managed to
alienate me, and I doubt that you can.

Big surprise coming (maybe.) Wait and watch.

On giving up suffering: "If one is trying to give up something,
then one has an object -- which causes suffering." (G.Hill, last
letter.) I respond: bullshit. This is UPAYA, technically, which
is Sanskrit for bullshit. (Well, for clever word-play or trickery.)
All UPAYA works for some students; hence, many Gurus use UPAYA.
This particular UPAYA very much used by some Zen teachers, Alan
Watts, Krishnamurti, but it's still bullshit. Same gimmick as the
arrow that doesn't move. Every instant the arrow is somewhere.
Ergo, every instant the arrow is not moving. Very elegant. Meanwhile,
the arrow has traveled a yard...

Try it this way: "If one is trying to change one's programs, then
one has a program -- which causes suffering." True or false? I say
false. If one is trying to change a second circuit up-and-down
emotional program to a fifth circuit always-up rapture program,
then one has a meta-program -- which is on a different order, and
does not cause suffering. See Korzybski on levels of abstraction.

ILLUMINATUS is supposed to be out next September.

SEX MAGICIANS I is out. I have no more extras, or I'd send you
one. Maybe I will send you one in a while; I'm thinking of ordering
some (if my ads in various places get any response...((I'm
advertising all my books at present, and waiting results)).)

Back to typing Crowley ms. More soon. Love is the law.

Bob W

2055 Channing Way
Bezerxley, Cal 94704
Oct 30, 1974 e.v.

Dear Greg,

Do what thou wilt shall be the whole of the law.

All hail Discordia. Chaos abounds. This morning Arlen and I were proofreading <u>The Witch's Trine</u>, newsletter of the New Reformed Orthodox Order of the Golden Dawn (of which we are now White Cord members.) Meanwhile, I went to ye olde post office to mail my latest column to the <u>Realist</u>. (I'm doing a new column for <u>Realist</u>, called "Operating Manual for the Human Head.")

I have written a book, a whole fucking BOOK, in two weeks again. This is called THE STARSEED SIGNALS/LINK BETWEEN WORLDS and deals with astro-telepathic research by Doc Leary and myself and 5 others. Meanwhile, my agent calls and sez Crown is innarested in my Crowley book, of which they have 119 pages, but wants to see 100 pages more before making up their minds. Well, I have 100 pages more (150 pages more, actually) but in faded type, so I've started re-typing the more faded pages before mailing it off. Xeroxing both the Crowley and the Leary ms. will cost $40 which I ain't got, so I'm calling all friends in the Bay Area to see now much they can do on office xeroxes without getting caught and Reamed Out by management. Busy busy busy...

Also I have to get back to San Fran PHOENIX by Monday with more reviews (I edit the book page there now) and I've promised GNOSTICA a 20 page summary of my 6 hours of lectures delivered at the

Aquarian Festival in September and haven't even STARTED on that and I don't know how the Leary book will end, except that Joanna is now definitely proven to have been a narc for at least one year and is pregnant by another narc, Dennis Martino, who has double- crossed the narcs for Leary last year, and is now double-crossing Leary for the narcs, and

it's all very interesting, as Gert Stein said; but it hexplains per'aps way I haven't been quite as up-to-date with correspondence as I used to was...

My magick class is most amusing, finance-wise. One week I was paid $16 plus two lids plus a hit of clear-light. Other weeks I average $12. But the class is MOVING and we raise the cone of power quite easily together now and who knows where it will end...

Llewellyn is publishing a book of essays by me, PROMETHEUS RISING, sometime next year.

Playboy Press is bringing out SEX'N'DRUGS in paperback in January. I'm still on welfare, but not for long, (we were off Welfare for four months, but then relapsed again. Our chief' source of income, a mag called VENUS, went bankrupt.)

Leary and I think we're communicating with higher minds in other parts of the galaxy. No shit. You think we're crazy?

SEX' N' DRUGS is also coming out in England next year.

Thos. Crowell has an outline of a book on immortality research by me, but hasn't responded yet. My agent is hopeful, but agents are always hopeful. Meeting the chief immortality researchers has been a gas. The conservatives among them expect the breakthrough by 1980; the optimists expect it next year...

Oh, yes, if you haven't heard, Leary is planning to abandon Earth. Literally. He's organizing a 5000-person starship to seek our parents (the ones who planted the DNA here 3 1/2 billion years ago) and ask them "what's the next step in evolution," or tell them, "Look what we've done in only 3 1/2 billion years, found our way home," or join them in their Major project, whatever that is (Tim thinks it has to do with building Black Holes and getting out of space-time into Eternity...).

Grady McMurty (Caliph Hymenaeos Alpha) of the O.T.O. has become a good friend and opened his library of Crowleyana to me.

NROOGD (see last page) is the largest witch society in northern California; Arlen and I have been members for about a year.

I met the chief Gardnerian witches of USA (Lady Theos and Phoenix) at the Aquarian Fest in Minneapolis and developed a warm relationship. Phoenix gave me certificates making me 10-degree Ipsissimus Maximus in the Ordo Templi Celatus and a voodoo priest in Sociedad Magicko de Chango; I made him a Pope in turn.

Parsifal, the Sufi clown, is now in Jerusalem, running a home for Jewish and Arab war orphans. He got a vision telling him to do that.

Leary and I were collaborating on a book about cosmic evolution, called PERIODIC TABLE OE ENERGY, when he disappeared. None of his friends has been able to communicate with him for four months, while the rumors of finking circulate and circulate...

Before I start packing up the Discordian anarchives to mail 'em, etc., why won't you consider coming hack out here where you are loved and badly missed. Doc Newport sez you can live with him until you find a job, etc. (He's in my magick class these days. Very talented. Astral projecting like mad.) Please come. Do not remain in sneers amid the alien scorn, but turn again to Zion, etc

Is Aleister Crowley really dead, really dead?
Did he do all the dreadful things they said, things they said?
Is he only dust beneath the sod, 'neath the sod,
Or was Aleister Crowley really God, really God?
—theme song of the Great Wild Beast Furtherment Society

2035 Channing (very Illuminized Erisian number) has Great WB Furth Society, Discordian Society, four witches, three druids, Aquarian Anti-Defamation League (witches' B'nai B'rith sort-of) and a pair of Xtian scientists who Keep sticking their propperganda under our doors in the mornings.

I astrally projected from California to Arizona a few months ago, saw what was really happening (as confirmed by the folks I visited) and put a cone of protection on them, driving away cops who were about to hassle them. Really. Witnesses confirm. Magick keeps opening me and opening me and opening me...

Everybody I know these days has a Plan to save the planet. Why not? Optimism is a more interesting trip than pessimism. My own plan (or one of them) is enclosed — EACH ONE TEACH ONE.

The people at the Rio Nido house were supposed to forward mail, but never did. Just threw it all out, I gather. They are Manson types and feelthy. The kind who give Counter Kulch a bad name. That's why your letters there were never answered. You never managed to alienate me, and I doubt that you can.

Big surprise coming (maybe). Wait and watch.

On giving up suffering: "If one is trying to give up something, then one has an object — which causes suffering." (G. Hill, last letter.) I respond: bullshit. This is UPAYA, technically, which is Sanskrit for bullshit. (Well, for clever word-play or trickery.) All UPAYA works for some students; hence, many Gurus use UPAYA. This particular UPAYA very much used by some Zen teachers, Alan Watts, Krishnamurti, but it's still bullshit. Same gimmick as the arrow that doesn't move. Every instant the arrow is somewhere. Ergo, every instant the arrow is not moving Very elegant. Meanwhile, the arrow has traveled a yard...

Try it this way: "If one is trying to change one's programs, then one has a program — which causes suffering." True or false? I say false, if one is trying to change a second circuit up-and-down emotional program to a fifth circuit always-up rapture program, then one has a meta-program — which is on a different order, and does not cause suffering. Sea Korzybski on levels of abstraction.

ILLUMINATUS is supposed to be out next September.

SEX MAGICIANS is out. I have no more extras, or I'd send you one. Maybe I will send you one in a while; I'm thinking of ordering some (if my ads in various places get any response... (I'm advertising all my books at present, and waiting results)).

Back to typing Crowley ms. More soon. Love is the law.

Bob W

The World's Oldest And Most Successful Conspiracy

Bavarian Illuminati

"THE ONLY TRUE RELIGION"

Founded by Hassan i Sabbah, 1090 A.D. (5090 A.L., 4850 A.M.)
Reformed by Adam Weishaupt, 1776 A.D. (5776 A.L., 5536 A.M.)

"Victory Over Horseshit"

Today's DATE: Grummet 21, 5974 A.M.

FROM: MORDECAI THE FOUL, HIGH PRIEST

Ignotium P. Ignotius

( ) OFFICIAL BUSINESS   (X) SURREPTITIOUS BUSINESS   ( ) MONKEY BUSINESS

Do what thou wilt shall be the whole of the law.

I'll be buying some large envelopes (to mail manuscripts) as soon as my next Playboy check comes (this week, I think) and will send you the Rubber stamps you requested and a few other goodies at that time.

Richard, duc de Palatine, of Sherman Oaks (Sanctuary of the Gnosis) has written to me demanding to see official charters of the Illuminati, etc., threatening to sue, and claiming he's the only official Illuminatus in America. Interested? I'll send you his address if you want to play. (Arlen tells me duc de Palatine doesn't mean purple duck, as I thought, but Duke of Palatine. Oh, well.)

McNamara (1437 Polk, San Fran, if you're innarested) by coincidence has an ad in current Gnostica News claiming he's the Illuminati. Presumably, he'll be hearing from Richard Duc, or Daffy Duc, or Donald, or somebody...(Same ish of Gnostica has statements of policy by O.T.A., the real O.T.O., the other real O.T.O., and the Bavarian Illuminati, about Crowley and Weishaupt.)

New editor at Dell assures me that the change-over won't delay ILLUMINATUS further and it will be out Sept-Oct-Nov 1975.

Ichazo on ego...well, suh, the attack on ego comes from such bright boys as Buddha, Gurdjieff, Watts, Krishnamurti, etc. and they must mean something... okay, so far? Well, then, what do they mean?

I suggest that Leary's Periodic Table gives us the only scientific system of neuro-psychology. Here we have eight potential intelligences on eight potential neural circuits (or networks.) Each is defined by differences in functioning and gross (visible) morphological changes. To wit:

First circuit intelligence abstracts danger-safety signals and mediates forward-back choices. Crawling infant in human development; unicellular organisms in evolution.

2nd circuit intelligence abstracts power signals and chooses domin-

"NOTHING IS TRUE. EVERYTHING IS PERMISSIBLE"

—Hassan i Sabbah

Safeguard this letter, it may be an IMPORTANT HISTORICAL DOCUMENT

ant or submissive emotional gamesx (rituals.) See Lorenz and
ethologists for evolutionary background. DNA chemical code triggers
thxx this kind of intelligence when infant stands, toddles about,
messes in family politics. See Berne's books.

3rd circuit intelligence abstracts symbolic meaning, not mere
signals, and handles dexterity, engineering, etc. Beavers, ants,
etc. DNA triggers when child learns to handle, question, talk,
think (sub-vocal speech.) See learning theory, in general; general
semantics; cybernetics.

4th circuit intelligence abstracts sexy signals and responsibility
(bonding) cues, invitations to sperm-egg fusion, pair-bonding, family
or tribal role-playing etc. DNA unleashes appropriate chemicals to
reveal this new dimension at point technically called puberty.

At each circuit, a new intelligence; ergo, a new ego. The infant
ego is NOT the emotional toddler ego, which is NOT the abstracting-
symbolizing student ego, which is NOT the sexual ego.

After these 4 imprints, the DNA code stops imprinting. These are
the survival programs and DNA seems coded to LAND ON A PLANET and
then SURVIVE THERE. The mechanistic-robotic nature of these programs
(well discussed in Behaviorist psychology and Gurdjieff) is embarassing to the philosopher, but invisible to the average robot ("free
will" delusion, maya, self-hypnosis.)

The latter 4 circuits, to be activated by interstellar telepathic
(electro-magnetic-gravitational) signals -- see SECRET LIFE OF
PLANTS, Tompkins and Bird, chapter 3 -- are the Next Step of the
meta-program, thus
                    LAND ON PLANET
                    SURVIVE AND POPULATE (water, land, atmosphere)
                    GET OFF AND COME HOME

The Starseed Signals have been intercepted for about 30,000 years
now, with varying degrees of fidelity of reception. (See Cave Paintings, history of religion, magick, mysticism, etc.)

Circuit 5 intelligence is neurosomatic. New signals, previously
invisible -- as emotional signals are invisible to the infant,
symbolism to the emotional toddler, sex to the pre-pubescent,
etc. --reveal a continuum of sensory-somatic bliss. The Turn On.
Freedom from the robot circuits of conditioned consciousness, 1
through 4. Zen and Sufism are the highest forms, thusfar, of
imprinting this circuit.

Circuit 6 intelligence is neurophysical. New signals are abstracted
from atomic, electronic, gravitational etc. fields, including bio
fields (orgone, astral body, etc.) and magick becomes possible.

Circuit 7 intelligence is neurogenetic. The "ego" dies. Intelligence
mediates between the DNA program itself and the total environment.
(Jung's "collective unconscious" becomes fully conscious.) When
totally imprinted, this circuit hooks in to the intergalactic DNA
genetic code, the evolutionary mind of the cosmos, since the DNA

is literally a four-dimensional intelligence. See Einstein-Lorenz equations. It is yesterday, today and tomorrow all over the universe to the DNA.

8th circuit intelligence is meta-physiological (not metaphysical.) It is the electro-magnetic-gravitational cosmic mind, having most of the characteristics of theologically-defined "God."

The Starseed signals have only been picked up here for about 30,000 years and the latter circuits are mostly in the consumer or passive receptor stage, in the rare individuals who have them at all. That is, 5 or 6 or 7 or even 8 may be "open" to signals (occasionally) but the intelligence is very seldom formed (imprinted.) This, and not any illogical in the cosmic mind, explains the incoherence of most shamans and mystics. They pick up some of the intergalactic signals but they have not yet integrated them into an intelligent Gestalt... usually. Circuit 5 intelligences are findable in history, and one or 2 circuit 6 intelligences, but mostly we have only the incoherent dawning signal-receptions of the higher circuits.

Leary suggests that the intelligences of the higher circuits cannot be imprinted until we get out of the gravitational pull of the sun, into deep space. Dr. Richard Miller, parapsychologist, similarly suggests that "reality" is a bio-hologram, a function of DNA and the gravitational field in which it exists. Miller, like Leary, proposes a totally different "reality" once we escape the solar system.

The ego does quite well enough for planetside survival, which is its purpose. (Freud: "mind is an organ of survival.")

Starseed Inc. is seeking to (a) discover the bio-chemistry of immortality and (b) discover a space-drive to get us out of the solar system and (c) raise the money for above and (d) recruit the 5000 most advanced nervous systems on Earth and (e) blast off for the stars by 1995 (approximately.) It is our hope that enough people are interested in immortality and contacting/becoming Higher Intelligences to carry off this project, the biggest jailbreak in history, and the only possible escape from the mismanagement of Earth by second-circuit intelligences (reptile-circuit predators etc.) Those who are not interested in becoming Gods need not apply.

Are we mad or are we the only sane people on the planet?

Love, as always,

Bob W

Today's DATE: Grummet 21, 5974 A.M.

FROM: MORDECAI THE FOUL, HIGH PRIEST

TO: Ignotium p. Ignotius

( )Official Business (x) Surreptitious Business ( ) Monkey Business

"Nothing is True. Everything is Permissible"
–Hassan I Sabbah

Safeguard this letter, it may be an IMPORTANT HISTORICAL DOCUMENT

Do what thou wilt shall be the whole of the law.

I'll be buying some large envelopes (to mail manuscripts) as soon as my next Playboy check comes (this week, I think) and will send you the rubber stamps you requested and a few other goodies at that time.

Richard, duc de Palatine, of Sherman Oaks (Sanctuary of the Gnosis) has written to me demanding to see official charters of the Illuminati, etc., threatening to sue, and claiming he's the only official Illuminatus in America. Interested? I'll send you his address if you want to play. (Arlen tells me <u>duc de Palatine</u> doesn't mean purple duck, as I thought, but Duke of Palatine. Oh, well.)

McNamara (1437 Polk, San Fran, if you're innarested) by coincidence has an ad in current Gnostica News claiming <u>he</u>'s the Illuminati. Presumably, he'll be hearing from Richard Duc, or Daffy Duc, or Donald, or somebody . . . (Same ish of Gnostica has statements of policy by O.T.A., the real O.T.O., the other real O.T.O., and the Bavarian Illuminati, about Crowley and Weishaupt.

New editor at Dell assures me that the change-over won't delay ILLUMINATUS further and it will be out Sept-Oct-Nov 1975.

Ichazo on ego . . . well, suh, the attack on ego comes from such bright boys as Buddha, Gurdjieff, Watts, Krishnamurti, etc. and they must mean <u>something</u> . . . okay, so far? Well, then, what do they mean?

I suggest that Leary's <u>Periodic Table</u> gives us the only scientific system of neuro-psychology. Here we have eight potential intelligences on eight potential neural circuits (or networks). Each is defined by differences in functioning and gross (visible) morphological changes. To wit:

First circuit intelligence abstracts danger-safety signals and mediates forward-back choices. Crawling infant in human development; unicellular organisms in evolution.

2nd circuit intelligence abstracts power signals and chooses dominant or submissive emotional games (rituals). See Lorenz and ethologists for evolutionary background. DNA chemical code triggers this kind of intelligence when infant stands, toddles about, messes in family politics. See Berne's books.

3rd circuit intelligence abstracts symbolic meaning, not mere signals, and handles dexterity, engineering, etc. Beavers, ants, etc. DNA triggers when child learns to handle, question, talk, think (sub-vocal speech). See learning theory, in general; general semantics; cybernetics.

4th circuit intelligence abstracts sexy signals and responsibility (bonding) cues, invitations to sperm-egg fusion, pair-bonding, family or tribal role-playing etc. DNA unleashes appropriate chemicals to reveal this new dimension at point technically called puberty.

At each circuit, a new intelligence; ergo, a new ego. The infant ego is NOT the emotional toddler ego, which is NOT the abstracting- symbolizing student ego, which is NOT the sexual ego.

After these 4 imprints, the DNA code stops imprinting. These are the survival programs and DNA seems coded to LAND ON A PLANET and then SURVIVE THERE. The mechanistic-robotic nature of these programs (well discussed in Behaviorist psychology and Gurdjieff) is embarrassing to the philosopher, but invisible to the average robot ("free will" delusion, maya, self-hypnosis).

The latter 4 circuits, to be activated by interstellar telepathic (electro-magnetic-gravitational) signals — see SECRET LIEE OF PLANTS, Tompkins and Bird, chapter 3 — are the Next Step on the meta-program, thus

> LAND ON PLANET
> SURVIVE AND POPULATE (water, land, atmosphere)
> GET OFF AND COME HOME

The Starseed Signals have been intercepted for about 30,000 years now, with varying degrees of fidelity of reception. (See Cave paintings, history of religion, magick, mysticism, etc.)

Circuit 5 intelligence is neurosomatic. New signals, previously invisible — as emotional signals are invisible to the infant, symbolism to the emotional toddler, sex to the pre-pubescent, etc. — reveal a continuum of sensory-somatic bliss. The Turn On. Freedom from the robot circuits of conditioned consciousness, 1 through 4. Zen and Sufism are the highest forms, thus far, of imprinting this circuit.

Circuit 6 intelligence is neurophysical. New signals are

abstracted from atomic, electronic, gravitational etc. fields, including bio fields (orgone, astral body, etc.) and magick becomes possible.

Circuit 7 intelligence is neurogenetic. The "ego" dies. Intelligence mediates between the DNA program itself and the total environment. (Jung's "collective unconscious" becomes fully conscious.) When totally imprinted, this circuit hooks in to the intergalactic genetic code, the evolutionary mind of the cosmos, since the DNA is literally a four-dimensional intelligence. See Einstein-Lorenz equations. It is yesterday, today and tomorrow all over the universe to the DNA.

8th circuit intelligence is meta-physiological (not metaphysical). It is the electro-magnetic-gravitation-al cosmic mind, having most of the characteristics of theologically-defined "God."

The Starseed Signals have only been picked up here for about 30,000 years and the latter circuits are mostly in the consumer or passive receptor stage, in the rare individuals who have them at all. That is, 5 or 6 or 7 or even 8 may be "open" to signals (occasionally) but the intelligence is very seldom formed (imprinted). This, and not any illogical in the cosmic mind, explains the incoherence of most shamans and mystics. They pick up some of the intergalactic signals but they have not yet integrated them into an intelligent Gestalt . . . usually. Circuit 5 intelligences are findable in history, and one or 2 circuit 6 intelligences, but mostly we have only the incoherent dawning signal-receptions of the higher circuits.

Leary suggests that the intelligences of the higher circuits cannot be imprinted until we get out of the gravitational pull of the sun, into deep space. Dr. Richard Miller, parapsychologist, similarly suggests that "reality" is a bio-hologram, a function of DNA and the gravitational field in which it exists. Miller, like Leary, proposes a totally different "reality" once we escape the solar system.

The ego goes quite well enough for planetside survival, which is its purpose. (Freud: "mind is an organ of survival.")

Starseed Inc. is seeking to (a) discover the bio-chemistry of immortality and (b) discover a space-drive to get us out of the solar system and (c) raise the money for above and (d) recruit the 5000 most advanced nervous systems on Earth and (e) blast off for the stars by 1995 (approximately). It is our hope that enough people are interested in immortality and contacting/becoming Higher Intelligences to carry off this project, the biggest jailbreak in history, and the only possible escape from the mismanagement of Earth by second-circuit intelligences (reptile-circuit predators etc.). Those who are not interested in becoming Gods need not apply.

Are we mad or are we the only sane people on the planet?

Love, as always,

Bob W

November 20, 1974

Dear Bob -

Just got your letter of 21 Grummet, but first here is reply
to your letter of hmmm October 30.

+ What does "e.v." mean after your date?

+ I am doing some art paths. When I can map them better,
I will explain better. Mapping is the end of it, not the
beginning of it.

These last many moons I had been, with my usual dedication,
pursuing The Lethargy Discipline. Now I jump up, and do it
so fast I get a little dizzy. So it may be a little while
before I get into mmmm stride. At this point, it mostly seems
like an explosion in a spaghetti mmmm factory. [That image
was a Roger Price droodle - see top of page.]

I suspect, however, that there is clarity here someplace.
(I am speaking, incidentally, of Post Theater Etc., just in
case you are wondering.)

+ And you say that I have not alienated you, and that you think
that I never shall. Well, man, there was a point when I was
fairly frightened, and your reassurance is gratefully received.

+ Yep, received Fire Drill. Have sent out several recently.
I am now calling mine "process collages". Yours was received
with the usual delight and got scattered amongst others. I send
a sample one (with some other stuff) to the Colby College trip
that SLUJ gave notice to.

· Are you in contact with the mailart Whitson group? I just got
a bunch of x SLUJ in the same mail as your last letter,
including a bunch of High School Equivalency Diplomas (which makes
you the equivalent of a High School) - one is inclosed.

+ Witch's Trine: How may I receive copies regularly? Barter?
(I'm willing to subscribe.)

"Earth Religion News" is a very good pub out of Brooklyn. I've
seen only one copy, but liked it a lot.

"Waxing Moon" has a name that I love. Haven't seen a copy tho.

Do you have an old issue of "Gnostica News" that I can look at.
Will return it if you want.

+ You full well know my fascination with Societies. Please tell
me about the relative significance of "white cord" (suggest
alternate spelling <u>chord</u>). What are the gradations? And how

adept are you at that particular craft?

+ I'm so fukking out of contact I don't even know where Krassner
is publishing from. He has alwys struck me as a fairly talented
cat who is egotistical just enough to think (tho not tyrannically,
mind you) that he publishes the best periodical (using the term
hommahw loosely, time-wise) [especially in his case] comøing from
the best of current western culture. And he has always struck
me that probably he is right and good for him.

Have decided to separate, by spelling, two meanings of "fuck",
to better contrast the basic unity of the word.
    FUCK: opposites interpenetrate*
    FUKK: exclamatory beyond comprehension

        *   a) confront & conquor
             b) meet and subliminate
             c)
             d) any of the above
             e) none of the above
             F) as above, so below

+ Starseed/Leary: If you really think that I think that you
and/or Doc Leary is crazy, then you are nuts. I am hoping
that you are being socially cautious.*

        * like me, sayeth an humble paranoid

Your last letter has more particulars in it that I want to
re-read, but for the moment I'll just ramble a bit.

When I was 17, in High School, I SAW Sputnik. I have been
living in the Space Age ever since, then.

Which was kind of neat, you know, until the Cuban Missle Crisis,
four years later.

It is my opinion that the human race, as such, is obsolete.

And what the hell, if you don't walk away from home then you will
just die there. (At another time, and in another context, I'll
no doubt want to contradict this and speak instead of cycles.)

I am as anxious to read "Starseed" (ms OK), as I was to read
"Illuminatus" (which is saying something).

If you send me all the "Starseed" that you have, I can Xero 2
more copies for you; tho I must be cool and choose my moments;
and will send both copies + master via U.S. Turtle Boat Bottom
Class, postage paid by me in eternal gratitude for not having to
wait for publishers like Dell to let me in on it.

+ Phoenix: I wrote to Tom Gnostic a couple of weeks ago, for
the first time in two years. Told him how delighted I was to
find a) John Bryan, b) Thomas Patrick McNamara and c) you,
ON THE SAME PAGES. You people are blowing me out.

Did you know (or do you recall) that it was John Bryan,
Los Angeles "Open City", who was the only Alternative Publisher
(before there was such a label), who dared to contradict
Holy Jim Garrison, and did in fact publish the experiences of
one Kerry Thornley during the time that it was ~~happened~~ happening.
Kunkin of "Freep" wouldn't touch it.

+ Yeah, I can dig your Magick Class finances. New & I took in
food stamps at the cinema and more or less paid off Hollywood.
Sort of.

+ Cone of Power and ceremonial magic in general: I don't practice
and I doubt if I ever will. ~~Ahhmmhmmmmmasmmmmmmmm~~ My reluctance
comes down to, simply, an irrational but deep-seated abhorrence
of ceremony.

However, Cone of Power is intriguing [sp?]. Castanedas' DA JUAN
spoke to me, and I think that what you mean by "Cone of Power"
would be clearly understood by him. The Elder Malaclypse
produced that in kind of power, but he did not conceptualize it
(as does Juan). Don't let me put you off.

+ More on your books: Keep me posted on "Prometheus Rising".
I'd like to see any of your work that I can. Some of it I
like better than others (eg, I thought that ~~from~~ "Sex Magician"
was many more times the accomplishment that "Sex and Drugs" was -
and not because of the subject, but because of the handling of
the subject).

Am glad to hear of the British publication of some of your stuff.

To watch you go international is gratifying. To hear that you
are being published by Llewellyn is heart warming. To hear
that "Illuminatus" will not see light for another year is
frustrating to a point that infuriates me! I await "Starseed".

+ Immortality: Bob, may I ask you a true personal question?
Do you really want to live forever? (Excepting in the sense that
you already do live forever.)

+ NGROOD, Many Apples Aquarian Fest, and a fukking 10° Ipsissimus
Maximus and I still don't know what "Celatus" means; but I am
not a stranger to hoodoo and when Rabbi Jesus Maria y Juana Oroberg,
Jesuits for Zionists, hears about Sociedad Magicko de Chango,
he is going to be glad that you made the Gardnerians a Pope,
thats for sure.

+ It is unlikely that I will come to live in Calif for at least
six months. It is likely that I will return within a year.
Much has to do with outside circumstances (especially at work)
that I am watching but have little control over. By next
summer I will better know what is worth sticking around for.
But I'll be back eventually. Very probably in 1975.

In the meantime, do send the archives. But not by mail, that
is too expensive. Ship Railway Express or Greyhound. Give me

all particulars re shipping times and send me invoices and things.
If you can, insure it or register it or somehow pay a buck and
get some serious attention. I will foot the bill. ᴀ Am inclosing
a check for $20, but I don't know if that is too much or too little.

Did you send the stamps yet (in ref to your last letter). If not,
I am quite willing to share them and the other office supplies.
Tell me what things you like the most. If you did send them,
tell me anyway and I can send some back.

The files I need and want accessible. Do you know that I had no
place in the world to put them? Not even with me, man. Thank
you for being here.

+ Newp: You say talented and astral projecting. Yes, his
intellect, talents and spirit is wonderful to me. I crashed so
bad with him on the River. It is still hard to comprehend it.
He knew. I knew. He knew I knew. I knew he knew. He knew
I knew he knew. I knew he knew I knew he knew. And it crashed
again and again and again. Knowledge ain't worth a shit sometimes.

+ UPAYA: When I say that "striving to give up suffering causes
strife there suffering" I do not mean the same as to say that
"the arrow, someplace ᴍ every instant, cannot proceed."

Maps and territories. "Instant" (like "point") has a map
meaning because it is a referent point. However (like "point")
it has no territory meaning at all because, by definition, it
has no dimension. "Suffering", however, has territorial
(existential) meaning. That is, I can experience a suffering,
but I cannot experience a point or an instant. (I can, of course,
conceptualize them [at least in the sense of "absence"]).

In any case, I think that it is a cycle. The ~~phanomomana~~ experiential
~~phanomananan~~ phenomenum of transcending suffering is one that
lasts only until you get used to it and discover (by virtue of
· your newly acquired perspective) and reality is even bigger that
you figured. Which spurs growth. Which succeeds (after strife).
Which stagnates and collapses (after negative strife). Which
is transcended and again yields relief from suffering. My point
is that the cycles go on forever. ❡ It is the cycle that
interests me more than the relief (tho of course it is the relief
that spurs me on). To use an image that I remember that you like,
the cycle of which I speak progresses in a spiral, not ~~amomomihah~~
simply a repetitous circle (depends on the perspective).

Back to the point: striving to ~~amomompihiah~~ give up suffering will
accomplish everything temporarily and nothing ultimately. *Growth ultimately*
Let's talk about WILL.   *yields suffering, necessarily. The*
alternative is perpetual stagnation
(which is impossible — but never mind).

+ Each One Teach One is a nicely directed beam.

*   "working"*
✳✳ "suffering"

+ Newp again: I'm really glad that you two are getting to know
each other. Besides from just personal pleasure, ~~the amazing~~
~~fascinating impossibility~~ the juxtaposition seems fascinating in
its unknown possibilities. Newport, a scientist, has an acute
sensitivity to will; and you, a magician, have an acute sensitivity
to the deterministic environment. Is the crescent concave or
convex? Free will/Determinism is one of my favorite paradoxes
(I don't believe in either one of them).

Hope all is well. Love to the family.

                              flaxetc

November 20, 1974

Dear Bob -

Just got your letter of 21 Grummet, but first here is reply to your letter of October 30.

+ What does "e.v." mean after your date?

+ I am doing some art paths. When I can map them better, I will explain better. Mapping is the end of it, not the beginning of it.

These last many moons I had been, with my usual dedication, pursuing The Lethargy Discipline. Now I jump up, and do it so fast I get a little dizzy. So it may be a little while before I get into stride. At this point, it mostly seems like an explosion in a spaghetti factory. [That image was a Roger Price droodle – see top of page.]

I suspect, however, that there is clarity here someplace. (I am speaking, incidentally, of Post Theater Etc., just in case you are wondering.)

+ And you say that I have not alienated you, and that you think that I never shall. Well, man, there was a point when I was fairly frightened, and your reassurance is gratefully received.

+ Yep, received Fire Drill. Have sent out several recently. I am now calling mine "process collages". Yours was received with the usual delight and got scattered amongst others. I send a sample one (with some other stuff) to the Colby College trip that SLUJ gave notice to.

Are you in contact with the mailart Whitson group? I just got a bunch of s SLUJ in the same mail as your last letter, including a bunch of High School Equivalency Diplomas (which makes you the equivalent of a High School) – one is inclosed.

+ <u>Witch's Trine</u>; How may I receive copies regularly? Barter? (I'm willing to subscribe.)

"Earth Religion News" is a very good pub out of Brooklyn. I've seen only one copy, but liked it a lot.

"Waxing Moon" has a name that I love. Haven't seen a copy tho.

Do you have an old issue of "Gnostica News" that I can look at. Will return it if you want.

+ You full well know my fascination with Societies. Please tell me about the relative significance of "white cord" (suggest alternate spelling chord). What are the gradations? And how adept are you at that particular craft?

+ I'm so fukking out of contact I don't even know where Krassner is publishing from. He has alwys struck me as a fairly talented cat who is egotistical just enough to think (tho not tyrannically, mind you) that he publishes the best periodical (using the term loosely, time-wise) [especially in his case] coming from the best of current western culture. And he has always struck me that probably he is right and good for him.

Have decided to separate, by spelling, two meanings of "fuck", to better contrast the basic unity of the word.

FUCK: opposites interpenetrate*
FUKK: exclamatory beyond comprehension
      * a) confront & conquor
        b) meet and subliminate
        c)
        d) any of the above
        e) none of the above
        F) as above, so below

+ <u>Starseed/Leary:</u> If you really think that I think that you and/or Doc Leary is crazy, then you are nuts. I am hoping that you are being socially cautious.*

like me, sayeth an humble paranoid

Your last letter has more particulars in it that I want to re-read, but for the moment I'll just ramble a bit.

When I was 17, in High School, I SAW Sputnik. I have been living in the Space Age ever since,

Which was kind of neat, you know, until the Cuban Missle Crisis, four years later.

It is my opinion that the human race, as such, is obsolete.

And what the hell, if you don't walk away from home then you will just die there. (At another time, and in another context. I'll no doubt want to contradict this and speak instead of cycles.)

I am as anxious to read "Starseed" (ms OK), as I was to read "Illuminatus" (which is saying something).

If you send me all the "Starseed" that you have, I can Xero 2 more copies for you; tho I must be cool and choose my moments; and will send both copies + master via U.S. Turtle Boat Bottom Class, postage paid by me in eternal gratitude for not having to wait for publishers like Dell to let me in on it.

+ Phoenix: I wrote to Tom Gnostic a couple of weeks ago, for the first time in two years. Told him how delighted I was to find a) John Bryan, b) Thomas Patrick McNamara and c) you, ON THE SAME PAGES. You people are blowing me out.

Did you know (or do you recall) that it was John Bryan,

Los Angeles "Open City", who was the only Alternative Publisher (before there was such a label), who dared to contradict Holy Jim Garrison, and did in fact publish the experiences of one Kerry Thornley during the time that it was happening. Kunkin of "Freep" wouldn't touch it.

+ Yeah, I can dig your Magick, Class finances. Newp & I took in food stamps at the cinema and more or less paid off Hollywood. Sort of

+ <u>Cone of Power and ceremonial magic in general</u>; I don't practice and I doubt if I ever will. My reluctance comes down to, simply, an irrational but deep-seated abhorrence of ceremony.

However, Cone of Power is intrigguing [sp?]. Castanedas' JUAN spoke to me, and I think that what you mean by "Cone of Power" would be clearly understood by him. The Elder Malaclypse produced that kind of power, but he did not conceptualize it (as does Juan). Don't let me put you off.

+ <u>More on your books</u>: Keep me posted on "Prometheus Rising". I'd like to see any of your work that I can. Some of it I like better than others (eg, I thought that "Sex Magician" was many more times the accomplishment that "Sex and Drugs" was – and not because of the subject, but because of the handling of the subject).

Am glad to hear of the British publication of some of your stuff.

To watch you go international is gratifying. To hear that you are being published by Llewellyn is heart warming. To hear that "Illuminatus" will not see light for another year is frustrating to a point that infuriates me! I await "Starseed".

+ <u>Immortality</u>; Bob, may I ask you a true personal question? Do you really want to live forever? (Excepting in the sense that you already do live forever.)

+ NGROOD, Many Apples Aquarian Fest, and a fukking 10° Ipsissimus Maximus and I still don't know a what "Celatus" means; but I am not a stranger to hoodoo and when Rabbi Jesus Maria y Juana Oroberg, Jesuits for Zionists, hears about Sociedad Magicko de Chango, he is going to be glad that you made the Gardnerians a Pope, thats for sure.

+ It is unlikely that I will come to live in Calif for at least six months. It is likely that I will return within a year. Much has to do with outside circumstances (especially at work) that I am watching but have little control over. By next summer I will better know what is worth sticking around for. But I'll be back eventually. Very probably in 1975.

In the meantime, do send the archives. But not by mail, that is too expensive. Ship Railway Express or Greyhound. Give me all particulars re shipping times and send me invoices and things. If you can, insure it or register it or somehow pay a buck and get some serious attention. I will foot the bill. Am inclosing a check for $20, but I don't know if that is too much or too little.

Did you send the stamps yet (in ref to your last letter). If not, I am quite willing to share them and the other office supplies. Tell me what things you like the most. If you did send them, tell me anyway and I can send some back.

The files I need and want accessable. Do you know that I had no place in the world to put them? Not even with me, man. Thank you for being here.

+ <u>Newp</u>: You say talented and astral projecting. Yes, his intellect, talents and spirit is wonderful to me. I crashed so bad with him on the River. It is still hard to comprehend it. He knew. I knew. He knew I knew. I knew he knew. He knew I knew he knew. I knew he knew I knew he knew. And it crashed again and again and again. Knowledge ain't worth a shit sometimes.

+ UPAYA: When I say that "striving to give up suffering causes strife there for suffering" I do not mean the same as to say that "the arrow, someplace every instant, cannot proceed."

Maps and territories. "Instant" (like "point") has a map meaning because it is a referent point. However (like "point") it has no territory meaning at all because, by definition, it has no dimension. "Suffering", however, has territorial (existential) meaning. That is, I can experience a suffering, but I cannot experience a point or an instant. (I can, of course, conceptualize them [at least in the sense of "absence"]).

In any case, I think that it is a cycle. The experiential phenomenum of transcending suffering is one that lasts only until you get used to it and discover (by virtue of your newly acquired perspective) and reality is even bigger that you figured. Which spurs growth. Which succeeds (after positive strife*). Which stagnates and collapses (after negative strife**). Which is transcended and again yields relief from suffering. My point is that the cycles go on forever. It is the cycle that interests me more than the relief (tho of course it is the relief that spurs me on). To use an image that I remember that you like, the cycle of which I speak progresses in a spiral, not simply a repetitous circle (depends on the perspective).

Back to the point: striving to give up suffering will

accomplish everything temporarily and nothing ultimately,
Growth ultimately yields suffering, necessarily. The
alternative is perpetual stagnation (which is impossible –
but never mind.

Let's also talk about WILL.

<u>Each One Teach One</u> is a nicely directed beam.

Newp again: I'm really glad that you two are getting to
know each other. Besides from just personal pleasure,
the juxtaposition seems fascinating in its unknown
possibilities. Newport, a scientist, has an acute sensitivity
to will; and you, a magician, have an acute sensitivity to
the deterministic environment. Is the crescent concave
or convex? Free will/Determinism is one of my favorite
paradoxes (I don't believe in either one of them).

Hope all is well. Love to the family.

flaxetc

G

* working
** suffering

GEORGIA UNITED METHODIST STUDENT MOVEMENT

2035 Channing Way
Berkeley, Cal 94704

Dear Greg,

Do what thou wilt shall be the whole of the law.

Another (temporary) case of xxxx acute poverty
has prevented action on various projects -- in
particular, I am delaying mailing Discordian
archives until I get a largish check from OUI
(promised to arrive here before Xmas), which will
allow me to make xerox copies of important AISB
documents for my own files. Anyway, xeroxing
for me and mailing original archives to you shd.
be accomplished before 1975 dawns on us...

MS. of The Starseed Signals might arrive any day.
I xeroxed one copy ($13!!!) and sent to a friend
at PLAYBOY, who promises to xxxx re-xerox and send
one to my agent and one to you. She shd. be finishing
up that project by now, or maybe already has. I sent
Her the ms. about 2 weeks ago. Things were so tight
there for a while (food comes first...) that I kept
postponing the one xerox $13 bill trauma for nearly
a month before I cd. shell out for it. But better
now and will be better still when the OUI money
arrives.

My "Apocalypic Orgasm" piece in current OUI is mostly
repeat from Sex'n'Drugs, so don't bother buying the
issue just for that. (The nudes are nice, though...)

The piece I'm waiting payment on is about conspiracies
and is due in May issue.

In dates "e.v." means era vulgaris, i.e. the vulgar era.
Crowley's way of using Xtian dates; he uses 1904 as
base for Ordo Templi Orientis calendar. We are now in
Anno 70 on that system.

Haven't heard from Dakota Junk company in years. Send
me their address next time you write.

We'll send you one copy of each Witch's Trine as it
comes out. (Arlen and I are on writing production
& mailing staffs.)

Old Gnostica will be enclosed with this, if I find
a copy when I start looking. I'm in every issue
these days, either with irregular Discordian Atheology
column or with more technical magick articles.

I'm about 100 pages into a new novel now, called The Homing Pigeons.

3 grades in NROOGD. White cord after one year and one day of
association means a) you wear white cord at esbats and are official
member. Red cord after another one year and one day means you
wherever wear red cord and attend Red Cord Council meetings at
which Decisions are made, e.g. shd. we hold group sabbath with
Gardnerians or are they too freaky for us, etc. Garter may be
taken at any time thereafter and is between you and Goddess. Others
attend ceremony if they think you and Goddess are really cozy,
boycott ceremony (stay away) if they think you are being presumptuous,
but nobody can deny your right to take the Garter when you feel
the time is right.

(Founding of the Order of the Garter, as told in all histories:
Countess of Salisbury dropped garter during dance, thereby embarassing
Herself. King Henry II then put it on his own leg, saying "Honi
soi qui mal y pense" -- Evil to him who thinks evil of this. The
explanation: it was a red garter, signalling membership in the Craft.
The King was telling the church: if you want to bust Her, you have
to bust me, too, i.e. risk civil war. Like many early kings, up to
the much-slandered Dick III, he was a member of both Xtian church
and the Craft, thereby holding the country together and preventing
religious civil war. Or such is the Craft legend...)

Krassner is about to move from Watsonville to Bay Area. Remind me
again in about a month that you want his address, and I'll give
you his new one. He's a member of Starseed II now, attends our
business meetings weekly.

When you make the 2 xeroxi of Starseed Signals (as promised in your
letter) don't send 'em to me, which only doubles postage bill, but
send 'em to my agent: Roy Porter, Porter Gould Dierks, 1236 Sherman
Ave., Evanston, Ill 60202. (Note 23 in middle of address...) The
more copies he has (he sez) the quicker he can sell it. I've told
him to aim for paperback, since they move faster than hard-cover
usually (altho' paying me less...); but I want this OUT damned FAST

Yeah, I recall that Bryan published Kerry's side of Garrison
follies when nobody else wd. Bryan also published my defense of
Leary with no rebuttal by him next issue after his own attack on
Tim. A very sincere libertarian indeed.

Cone of power is the easiest kind of magick for group working.
Doesn't even require ritual. Just 5 or 6 folks or 10 or 12
or a few more sitting in a circle holding hands and AUMing for
a while with clear visualizing of "astral" (orgone/Animal Magnetism)
circulating through them and then forming cone in middle of circle.
I've gotten astonishing results with NO MORE GIMMICKS than that in
my magick class. NROOGD uses ritual, of course, and gets more...

Sex'n'Drugs is not my favorite book, but it will have a tremendous
impact eventually & despite PB Press's upgefucking on promotion.
No other book presents so many important magick formulae in such
clear and scientific language. Those who figure out how to use it
will be accelerated.

I'm not sure if I want to become Immortal. I'm not sure that any "I" can. But I am damned sure that I can live many thousands of years, more or less as "me," and that it will be most interesting, and that maybe some sort of "I" can even graduate to Immortality.

Immortality will necessarily involve Neurologic, i.e. serial reincarnation in the "same" body (more or less.) Much metaphysical mystery about ego and memory and identity after re-imprinting becomes more efficient.

Railway Express of Greyhound. not mail, for archives. Okay, I've got it straight now. (I'm writing this with your last letter before me, answering point by point.)

STAMPS!! Okay, with this...

Suffering only exists on first four circuits. After circuit five, no more suffering.

Newp and a local NROOGD high priestess and I tried some new stuff yesterday, Ketalar (ketamine hydrochloride). Puts you on circuit 8 immediately for about one hour, but then you are more like drunk than like stoned or tripping for 2 long hours of getting back to normal. A very heavy trip, and part of what Leary predicts, i.e. the next breakthroughs in psychopharmacology will make acid obsolete before 1980. The first hour of this is like the ego-loss acid peak Samadhi second but stretched out long enough to be really examined and grooved on. The next 2 hours tend to be confusing and debilitating. The guy who synthesizes hour one minus hours 2 and 3 will make acid totally obsolete, obviously. When the ~~Ixiii~~ G-pill and L-pill (predicted by Leary) and the specific aphrodisiac (predicted by Kline) appear, there will be no way to hold humanity together, the mutation will occur...

Saul Kent's FUTURE SEX is worth reading, if you can find it. Paperback, about $2 I think. Saul's another Starseeder, by the way.

Okay, let's talk about Will. The True Will (in Crowley's sense) is as hard to find as the True Self (in Hindu sense) but both are quite real 7th circuit phenomena. According to Leary, statistical studies (unpublished) by a friend of his, an M.D. whose name I don't recall right now, demonstrate that people with over 100 acid trips correspond much more closely to their Zodiac type than the average citizen. Leary sez this is because the 7th circuit intelligence appears gradually as acid eats up (relaxes...drowns out..) the social imprinting and conditioning of the superficial ego. The 7th circuit neurogenetic intelligence comes in 12 types, a neurogenetic array, each time necessary for evolution, and each corresponding to Zodiac sign at birth and to first 12 trumps of Tarot, thus: Fool-Pisces, Magus-Aries, etc. in ordinary Zodiac sequence to Justice-Aquarius. Read up on astrology and Tarot and check out whether or not you are now closer to your sign and card than you were before LSD. This is the unleashing of the true Self and true Will, the neurogenetic you, from the imprinted social games.

Life to the Deathist Pig,

GEORGIA UNITED METHODIST
STUDENT MOVEMENT

12/74
2035 Charming Way
Berkeley, Cal 94704

Dear Greg,

Do what thou wilt shall be the whole of the law.

Another (temporary) case of acute poverty has prevented action on various projects — in particular, I am delaying mailing Discordian archives until I get a largish check from OUI (promised to arrive here before Xmas), which will allow me to make xerox copies of important AISB documents for my own files. Anyway, xeroxing for me and mailing original archives to you shd. be accomplished before 1975 dawns on us...

MS. of <u>The Starseed Signals</u> might arrive any day. I xeroxed one copy ($13! ! !) and sent to a friend at PLAYBOY, who promises to re-xerox and send one to my agent and one to you. She shd. be finishing up that project by now, or maybe already has. I sent Her the ms. about 2 weeks ago. Things were so tight there for a while (food comes first...) that I kept postponing the one xerox $13 bill trauma for nearly a month before I cd. shell out for it. But better now and will be better still when the OUI money arrives.

My "Apocalypic Orgasm" piece in current OUI is mostly repeat from <u>Sex 'n' Drugs</u>, so don't bother buying the issue just for that. (The nudes are nice, though...)

The piece I'm waiting payment on is about conspiracies and is due in May issue.

In dates "e.v." means era vulgaris, i.e. the vulgar era.

Crowley's way of using Xtian dates; he uses 1904 as base for Ordo Tempi! Orientis calendar. We are now in Anno 70 on that system.

Haven't heard from Dakota Junk company in years. Send me their address next time you write.

We'll send you one copy of each Witch's Trine as it comes out. (Arlen and I are on writing production & mailing staffs.)

Old Gnostica will be enclosed with this, if I find a copy when I start looking. I'm in every issue these days, either with irregular Discordian Atheologv column or with more technical magick articles.

I'm about 100 pages into a new novel now, called The Homing Pigeons.

3 grades in NROOGD. White cord after one year and one day of association means you wear white cord at esbats and are official member. Red cord after another one year and one day means you wear red cord and attend Red Cord Council meetings at which Decisions are made, e.g. shd. we hold group sabbath with Gardnerians or are they too freaky for us, etc. Garter may be taken at any time thereafter and is between you and Goddess. Others attend ceremony if they think you and Goddess are really cozy, boycott ceremony (stay away) if they think you are being presumptuous, but nobody can deny your right to take the Garter when you feel the time is right.

(Founding of the Order of the Garter, as told in all histories: Countess of Salisbury dropped garter during dance, thereby embarassing Herself. King Henry II then put it on his own leg, saying "Honi soi qui mal y pense" — Evil to him who thinks evil of this. The explanation: it was a red garter, signalling membership in the Craft. The King was telling the church: if you want to bust Her, you have to bust me, too, i.e. risk civil war. Like many early kings, up to the much-slandered Dick III, he was a member of both Xtian church and the Craft, thereby holding the country together and preventing religious civil war. Or such is the Craft legend...)

Krassner is about to move from Watsonville to Bay Area. Remind me again in about a month that you want his address, and I'll give you his new one. He's a member of Starseed II now, attends our business meetings weekly.

When you make the 2 xeroxi of <u>Starseed Signals</u> (as promised in your letter) don't send 'em to me, which only doubles postage bill, but send 'em to my agent: Roy Porter, Porter Gould Dierks, 1236 Sherman Ave., Evanston, Ill 60202. (Note 23 in middle of address...) The more copies he has (he sez) the quicker he can sell it. I've told him to aim for paperback, since they move faster than hard-cover usually (altho' paying me less...); but I want this OUT <u>damned</u> FAST

Yeah, I recall that Bryan published Kerry's side of Garrison follies when nobody else wd. Bryan also published my defense of Leary with no rebuttal by him next issue after his own attack on Tim. A very sincere libertarian indeed.

Cone of power is the easiest kind of magick for group working. Doesn't even require ritual. Just 5 or 6 folks or 10 or 12 or a few more sitting in a circle holding hands and AUMing for a while with clear visualizing of "astral" (orgone /Animal Magnetism) circulating through them and then forming cone in middle of circle. I've gotten astonishing results with NO MORE GIMMICKS than that in my magick class. NROOGD uses ritual, of course, and gets more...

Sex 'n' Drugs is not my favorite book, but it will have
a tremendous impact eventually despite PB Press's
upgefucking on promotion. No other book presents
so many important magick formulae in such clear and
scientific language. Those who figure out how to use it will
be accelerated.

I'm not sure if I want to become Immortal. I'm not sure
that any "I" can. But I am damned sure that I can live many
thousands of years, more or less as "me," and that it will be
most interesting, and that maybe some sort of "I" can even
graduate to Immortality.

Immortality will necessarily involve Neurologic, i.e. serial
reincarnation in the "same" body (more or less). Much
metaphysical mystery about ego and memory and identity
after re-imprinting becomes more efficient.

Railway Express or Greyhound, not mail, for archives.
Okay, I've got it straight now. (I'm writing this with your
last letter before me, answering point by point.)

STAMPS!! Okay, with this...

Suffering only exists on first four circuits. After circuit five,
no more suffering.

Newp and a local NROOGB high priestess and I tried some
new stuff yesterday, Ketalar (ketamine hydrochloride). Puts
you on circuit 8 immediately for about one hour, but then
you are more like drunk than like stoned or tripping for 2
long hours of getting back to normal. A very heavy trip, and
part of what Leary predicts, i.e. the next breakthroughs in
psychopharmacology will make acid obsolete before 1980.
The first hour of this is like the ego-loss acid peak Samadhi

second but stretched out long enough to be really examined and grooved on. The next 2 hours tend to be confusing and debilitating. The guy who synthesizes hour one minus hours 2 and 3 will make acid totally obsolete, obviously. When the G-pill and L-pill (predicted by Leary) and the specific aphrodisiac (predicted by Kline) appear, there will be no way to hold humanity together, the mutation will occur...

Saul Kent's FUTURE SEX is worth reading, if you can find it. Paperback, about $2 I think. Saul's another Starseeder, by the way.

Okay, let's talk about Will. The True Will (in Crowley's sense) is as hard to find as the True Self (in Hindu sense) but both are quite real 7th circuit phenomena. According to Leary, statistical studies (unpublished) by a friend of his, an M.D. whose name I don't recall right now, demonstrate that people with over 100 acid trips correspond much more closely to their Zodiac type than the average citizen. Leary sez this is because the 7th circuit intelligence appears gradually as acid eats up (relaxes...drowns out..) the social imprinting and conditioning of the superficial ego. The 7th circuit neurogenetic intelligence comes in 12 types, a neurogenetic array, each time necessary for evolution, and each corresponding to Zodiac sign at birth and to first 12 trumps of Tarot, thus: Fool-Pisces, Magus-Aries, etc. in ordinary Zodiac sequence to Justice-Aquarius. Read up on astrology and Tarot and check out whether or not you are now closer to your sign and card than you were before LSD. This is the unleashing of the true Self and true Will, the neurogenetic you, from the imprinted social games.

Life to the Deathist Pig,

Mord

1 Jan 1975

Dear Bob —

I got home from the PO + read your letter (with the stamps) which answers most of the questions in my letter that I wrote at the PO not realizing that there was another letter from you in the stamps.

By all means, Xerox what you please from the Archives. If I've been sounding like I've been in a rush, then I didn't mean it to.

I'll xerocopy 2 for Porter as requested. Our xerox has an automatic sorter, so it is as easy to xero 5 as 2. Where would you like the other 3? (Can't get to it until next week or two.) (It depends how busy it is at work + I'm just coming back from vacation.)

Western Dakota Junk Co. is none other than Whitson who also manifests as Anti Famous School (of 1937) who owe you the equivalent of a High School in my mailing #1. He's at 315 S. 34th St, Billings MT 59101.

The subscription to Witch's Trine is much appreciated.

Thanks for copy of Gnostica News. That Aquarian Fest must have been a gas! I attended a flying saucer convention in Escondido (by San Diego) in the late 50's that is a highlight of my memories. Will you lecture next year?

NROOGD is non-Gardnerian? I thought that that controversy centered on the fact that AC designed the ceremonies. How is it that you happened into a non-Gardnerian coven?

→

That's a neat tidbit of info about the red garters. Seems completely plausible to me.

Keep me posted on Starseed developments.

Immortality: what intrigues me about the idea is that after one has lived through a normal life span + beyond, he is released from (a seeming) moral imperative that "it is wrong to die". Every morning would be a new world because you can choose to live it or quit it without being "supposed" to do either one. Ultimately, I think, the self-preservation instinct would atrophy and individuals would be less shy of a) danger and b) self-sacrifice or even c) suicide. Which would give room for a few children once in a while — without which the race would have no meaning. *

I'm not convinced that immortality requires serial reincarnation (re-egofication? it's the same neat identity), but if it doesn't have it, the species will certainly stagnate instead of evolve (and stagnate over a looooong period of time.').

* A meaningless 'race', however, would presumably be replaced by a different self-concept with new meanings — so children is not a necessity for psychological survival.

What is necessary for survival is regeneration in some sense. In other words, what is necessary for survival is death and re-birth.

Immortality shifts this problem from the physical plane to the psychological plane.

SUFFERING: It disappears on circuit 5 only in that one progression. When one gets to circuit 5 one is existentially in the circuit I stage of circuit 5 progressing to circuit 6. You can't go from 5 to 6 without

→

experiencing a "circuit-5 type suffering" — a kind of
suffering that is incomprehensible to circuit 4 conciousness,
raw (meaningless) experience to early C-5 (infants).
progressing through the whole cycle until transcended
+ its C-6. I think that suffering, like joy, in a
growing (changing bigger) organism.

Kitalar info interesting. What did Stang mean
"G-pill" + "L-pill". I can think of several possible
irreversable mutations emerging from Armageddon.
The one I'm waiting for is a telepathy ~~~~ tool — that
would zap the shit out of everything once + for all.

All of your characters are welcome. Jehovah/Satan
make a good team. (Why "Satan"? lucifer — light bearer.)
I like the spread between all of them. This is important
because somehow or another I have to devise fuller interaction
between characters.

More later —

The Space Age Is A-borning!

sure - you can have 3 copies of my writings

1 Jan 1975

Dear Bob

I got home from the PO and read your letter (with the stamps) which answers most of the questions in my letter that I wrote at the PO not realizing that there was another letter from you with stamps.

By all means, xerox what you please from the Archives. If I've been something like I've been in a rush, then I didn't mean it to.

I'll xerox copy 2 for Porta as requested. Our xerox has an automatic sorter so it is easy to xerox 5 as 2. Where would you like the other 3? (can't get to it until next week or two). (It depends on how bust it is at work + I'm just coming back from vacation.)

Western Dakota Junk C0. is none other than Whitson who also manifests as Art's Famous School (of 1937) who made you the equivalent of a High School in my mailing #1. He is at 315 S. 34th St., Billings, MT 59101

The subscription to <u>Witch's Trine</u> is much appreciated.

Thanks for copy of <u>Gnostica News.</u> That Aquarian Fest must have been a gas! I attended a flying saucer convention in Escondido by San Diego in the late 50s that is a highlight of my memories. Will you lecture next year?

NROOGD is non-Gardnerian? I thought that that controversy centered on the fact that AC designed the ceremonies. How is it that you happened into a non-Gardnerian coven?

That's a neat tidbit of info about the red garter. Seems completely plausible to me.

Keep me posted on Starseed developments.

Immortality: what intrigues me about the idea is that after one has lived through a normal life span & beyond, he is released from (a seeming) moral imperative that "it is wrong to die." Every morning would be a new world because you can choose to live it or quit it without being supposed to do either one. Ultimately, I think, the self-preservation instinct would atrophy and individuals would be less shy of a) danger and b) self-sacrifice or even c) suicide. Which would give room for a few children once in a while – without which the race would have no meaning. *

I'm not concerned that immortality requires serial reincarnation (re-egofication? It's the same meat identity), but if it doesn't have it, the species will certainly stagnate instead of evolve (and stagnate over a looong period of time!).

* A meaningless "race", however, would presumably be replaced by a different self-concept with new meanings – so children is not a necessity for psychological survival.

What is necessary for survival is regeneration in some sense. In other words, what is necessary for survival is death and re-birth.

Immortality shifts this problem from the physical plane to the psychological plane.

SUFFERING: It disappears on circuit 5 only in that one progression. When one get to circuit 5 one is existentially in the circuit 1 stage of circuit 5 progressing to circuit 6. You can't get from 5 to 6 without experiencing a "circuit 5 type suffering" – a kind of suffering that is incomprehensible to circuit 4 consciousness, raw (meaningless) experience to early C-5 (infants), progressing through the whole cycle until transcended in its C-6. I think that suffering, like joy, in a growing (changing bigger) organism.

Ketalar info interesting. What did Leary mean "G-pill" & L-pill? I can think of several possible irreversible mutations emerging from Armageddon. The one I'm waiting for is a telepathy tool – that would zap the shit out of everything once & for all.

All of your characters are welcome. Jehovah / Satan make a good team. (Why "Satan"? Lucifer – light bearer.) I like the spread between all of them. This is important because somehow or another I have to desire/allow interaction between characters.

More later –

The Space Age Is A-borning!

Sure – you can have 3 copies of my mailings

Dear Greg:

Send 4 out of the 5 xerox copies to my agent, Roy Porter, Porter, Gould & Dierks, 1236 Sherman Aven, Evanston, Ill 60202

Send the fifth back to me.

I set today to catch up on correspondence. Must have written 20 letters since I started at 10 this morning and it's 10 in the evening now. But things are moving (as Einstein noted.)

Between tomorrow and Friday I have short articles to do. Then on Saturday the Starseed business meeting and planning session. Xeroxing early next week, and then the archive shipping project will be ready to move.

NROOGD is, maybe, neo-Gardnerian. Actually, NROOGD is totally synthetic and even a bit proud of it. The rituals were created out of olde bookes, some new books, intuition, poetic sensibility etc. -- there was no direct transmission. Yet even the most Authorized local Gardnerians and Alexandrians accept us as "real" witches, mostly because our rituals WORK. (Aiden Kelly, author of the rituals, is a first-rate poet. Really first-rate, not just good.)

Margot Adler on WBAI-New York has played some tapes of my Starseed raps at the Minneapolis Gnosticon. Turn her on now and then, she may be playing more of them. She taped 6 hours of me.

Susan Leary has suddenly changed her mind and won't go through with the habeus corpus suit to find Tim. No explanation. It gets weirder and weirder...Paul Krasner got a call from an alleged London Times reporter with a wild story about Leary being tortured and, when Paul checked back, the London Times had no such reporter. But (and this is freaky) everything else that could be checked (the torture couldn't, of course) was accurate. The hoaxer had every address, phone number and accessory detail right. No idle prankster. Either somebody in with the Justice Department or in with Leary, but in either case his motives and purposes remain a mystery.

I grow more convinced that Tim is managing it all, whatever it is, and using the government while they think they're using him. It has the earmarks of Sixth Circuit all over it, I think.

Tim once told me he was Gurdjieff reincarnated (he also once told somebody else he was Crowley...) and Gurdjieff's emphasis on SHOCK seems afoot here. ("I'll force the motherfuckers to mutate!" --Burroughs.)

Oh, yes, Synergy Access (also NY Radio, I don't know which station) will also be broadcasting some of my tapes.

"The fear of death is the beginning of slavery," as I wrote in my article on DeSade. The fear of suffering is the only jail you can't escape save by Will. Immortality is for those who are ready for

SHOCK in the Gurdjieff sense; those who can accept either Death or Life with total gusto.

I think immortality does require Serial Reincarnation. I got bored with my ego at age 38 and have been rebuilding a more innarestin' ego ever since. I assume this one will bore me by 68, if not sooner.

A better koan than "Why did Bodhidharma come from the West?" is WHY DID TIM LEARY GO TO AFGHANISTAN? (He was perfectly safe in Switzerland...)

Yeah, there is still suffering on circuit 5, but not neurotic suffering and it doesn't interfere with ecstasy, just complicates it. I shd. have said there's no despair on circuit 5.

G-pill: a compound predicted by Leary to be found in nervous systems of animals as they die. It turns off the external and internal signal-reception system and reduces consciousness to the inner-neuron DNA/ RNA "conversation." Taken alone, it will produce simulated death without actual death. Taken with LSD, a full death-rebirth program for Serial Reincarnation.

L-pill: Leary's name for the compound that life-extension researchers in molecular biology are looking for, the formula that short-circuits the senescence-death program and allows for infinite regeneration. Most researchers think it will be an amino acid; probably a tripto-phan derivative. See "The Coiled Splendor" in STARSEED SIGNALS.

Ketalar seems to produce more telepathy than other psychedelics, but is not yet the specific telepathy pill you mention. Wait 5 years...

(Yage, Peruvian psychedelic vine, is called telepathine by European botanists because of persistent reports of telepathic effects. Peruvia shamans use it to find lost objects, so they say.)

I'm not very witty anymore. I can hardly think, much less type.

Time to knock off for the day.

Mord

Dear Greg:

Send 4 out of the 5 xerox copies to my agent, Roy Porter, Porter, Gould & Dierks, 1236 Sherman Aven, Evanston, 11160202

Send the fifth back to me.

I set today to catch up on correspondence. Must have written 20 letters since I started at 10 this morning and it's 10 in the evening now. But things are moving (as Einstein noted).

Between tomorrow and Friday I have short articles to do. Then on Saturday the Starseed business meeting and planning session. Xeroxing early next week, and then the archive shipping project will be ready to move.

NROOGD is, maybe, neo-Gardnerian. Actually, NROOGD is totally synthetic and even a bit proud of it. The rituals were created out of olde bookes, some new books, intuition, poetic sensibility etc. — there was no direct transmission. Yet even the & most Authorised local Gardnerians and Alexandrians accept us as "real" witches, mostly because our rituals WORK. (Aiden Kelly, author of the rituals, is a first-rate poet. Really first-rate, not just good.)

Margot Adler on WBAI-Kew York has played some tapes of my Starseed raps at the Minneapolis Gnosticon. Turn her on now and then, she may bve playing more of them. She taped 6 hours of me.

Susan Leary has suddenly changed her mind and won't go through with the habeas corpus suit to find Tim. No explanation. It gets weirder and weirder... Paul Krassner got a call from an alleged London Times reporter with a wild story about Leary being tortured and, when Paul checked back, the London Times had no such reporter. But (and this is freaky) everything else that could be checked (the torture couldn't, of course) was accurate. The hoaxer had every address, phone number and accessory detail right. No idle prankster. Either somebody in with the Justice Department or in with Leary, but in either case his motives and purposes remain a mystery.

I grow more convinced that Tim is managing it all, whatever it is, and using the government while they think they're using him. It has the earmarks of Sixth Circuit all over it, I think.

Tim once told me he was Gurdjieff reincarnated (he also once told somebody else he was Crowley...) and Gurdjieff's emphasis on SHOCK seems afoot here. ("I'll force the motherfuckers to mutate!" — Burroughs.)

Oh, yes, Synergy Access (also NY Radio, I don't know which station) will also be broadcasting some of my tapes.

"The fear of death is the beginning of slavery," as I wrote in my article on De Sade. The fear of suffering is the only jail you can't escape save by Will. Immortality is for those who are ready for SHOCK in the Gurdjieff sense; those who can accept either Death or Life with total gusto.

I think immortality does require Serial Reincarnation. I got bored with my ego at age 38 and have been rebuilding a more innarestin' ego ever since. I assume this one will bore me by 68, if not sooner.

A better koan than "Why did Bodhidharma come from the West?" is WHY DID TIM LEARY GO TO AFGHANISTAN? (He was perfectly safe in Switzerland...)

Yeah, there is still suffering on circuit 5, but not neurotic suffering and it doesn't interfere with ecstasy, just complicates it. I shd have said there's no <u>despair</u> on circuit 5.

G-pill: a compound predicted by Leary to be found in nervous systems of animals as they die. It turns off the external and internal signal-reception system and reduces consciousness to the inner-neuron DNA/RNA "conversation." Taken alone, it will produce simulated death without actual death. Taken with LSD, a full death-rebirth program for Serial Reincarnation.

L-pill: Leary's name for the compound that life-extension researchers in molecular biology are looking for, the formula that short-circuits the senescence-death program and allows for infinite regeneration. Most researchers think it will be an amino acid; probably a triptophan derivative. See "The Coiled Splendor" in STARSEED SIGNALS.

Ketalar seems to produce more telepathy than other psychedelics, but is not yet the specific telepathy pill you mention. Wait 5 years...

(Yage, Peruvian psychedelic vine, is called telepathine by European botanists because of persistent reports of telepathic effects. Peruvian shamans use it to find lost objects, so they say).

I'm not very witty anymore. I can hardly think, much less type.

Time to knock off for the day.

Mord

2510 College
Berkeley, Cal 94704

Dear Greg,

Do what thou wilt shall be the whole of the law.

Thanks loads for the new stickers. We will have the country illuminized by Xmas or bust!

Things are going smoothly and rapidly now. I'm being interviewed by a Milwaukee radio station tomorrow morning about the future of sex, by the Berkeley Gazette the next morning about ILLUMINATUS, and doing a piece for the San Francisco examiner about the DNA Society for next week. And, meanwhile,

Tim and I are working on the PLAYBOY interview, to appear early next year, and on a piece for OUI on brainwashing, to appear quickly after the PLAYBOY interview, and on a new edition of TERRA II, hopefully to be published by next summer. Tim expects to be out before New Years and

in general, it's all coming together.

Even the PLAYBOY review of ILLUMINATUS is now scheduled for the Xmas issue (poifeck timing...)

Tim's latest two books, EXO-PSYCHOLOGY and INTERSTELLAR NEUROGENETICS, are the best, most mind-expanding, provocative, funniest, most profound things he has ever done. Each one of them is the equivelant of a great acid trip. Cosmic vistas...

His other new book, WHAT DOES WOMAN WANT?, I've only seen part of, but it looks to be the funniest thing ever written on human sexuality. The opening line, paraphrased from The Divine Comedy, is, I think, as perfect as any opening line in literature:

"Midway through our Life's life, I awoke on a dark planet."

Kerry is still sending me bitter, angry, paranoid letters, but I've stopped apologizing to him for my horrible sins (since that does no good at all) and just cheerfully ignore him. Maybe the sudden international fame of the Discordian Society in the next few months will cheer him up a little, or at least I dare to hope so.

Shea has gotten on a few Chicago radio shows to plug ILLUMINATUS.

Jamison has become a Leary fan due to me!! and is propagandizing for Neurologic among the Right Wing!!!

My interview with Tim in PLAYBOY is going to blow a lot of fuses...

Agnosticism, Hope and Charity
(and the greatest of these is Charity),

Bob W

home phone is 843-6788. do not share it. the only way I get ANY work done is by filtering callers through the answering service

Dear Greg,

Do what thou wilt shall he the whole of the law.

Thanks loads for the new stickers. We will have the country illuminized by Xmas or bust!

Things are going smoothly and rapidly now. I'm being interviewed by a Milwaukee radio station tomorrow morning about the future of sex, by the Berkeley Gazette the next morning about ILLUMINATUS, and doing a piece for the San Francisco <u>examiner</u> about the DNA Society for next week. And, meanwhile,

Tim and I are working on the PLAYBOY interview, to appear early next year, and on a piece for OUI on brainwashing, to appear quickly after the PLAYBOY interview, and on a new edition of TERRA II, hopefully to be published by next summer. Tim expects to be out before New Years and in general, it's all coming together.

Even the PLAYBOY review of ILLUMINATUS is now scheduled for the Xmas issue (poifeck timing...).

Tim's latest two books, EXO-PSYCHOLOGY and INTERSTELLAR NEUROGENETICS, are the best, most mind-expanding, provocative, funniest, most profound things he has ever done. Each one of them is the equivalent of a great acid trip. Cosmic vistas...

His other new book, WHAT DOES WOMAN WANT, I've only seen part of, but it looks to be the funniest thing ever written on human sexuality. The opening line, paraphrased from <u>The Divine Comedy</u>, is, I think, as perfect as any opening line in literature:

"Midway through our Life's life, I awoke on a dark planet."

Kerry is still sending me bitter, angry, paranoid, letters, but I've stopped apologizing to him for my horrible sins (since that does no good at all) and just cheerfully ignore him. Maybe the sudden international fame of the Discordian Society in the next few months will cheer him up a little, or at least I dare to hope so.

Shea has gotten on a few Chicago radio shows to plug ILLUMINATUS.

Jamison has become a Leary fan due to me!! and is propagandizing for Neurologic among the Right Wing!!!

My interview with Tim in PLAYBOY is going to blow a lot of fuses...

Agnosticism, Hope and Charity

(and the greatest of these is Charity),

Bob W

home phone is 843-6788. do not share it. the only way I get ANY work done is by filtering callers through the answering service

HILARITAS
PRESS

Publishing the Books of Robert Anton Wilson
and Other Adventurous Thinkers

www.hilaritaspress.com

Lightning Source UK Ltd.
Milton Keynes UK
UKHW021445041120
372791UK00014B/996